American Nursing

ABOUT THE EDITORS

Vern L. Bullough, PhD, RN, FAAN, is currently a visiting professor at the University of Southern California, a Distinguished Professor Emeritus from the State University of New York, and an Outstanding Professor Emeritus from California State University at Northridge. While at Northridge, he founded the Center for Sex Research, and established the Bonnie and Vern Bullough collection on Sex and Gender at the CSUN Library, one of the largest such collections in the world. Dr. Bullough also served as Dean of Natural and Social Sciences at the SUNY College in Buffalo. His research and numerous publications have been in a number of different fields but increasingly he has concentrated in the area of sex and gender. He has also published books and monographs in medieval history and in the history of medicine, science, and nursing.

Lilli Sentz, MLS, was curator of the Robert L. Brown History of Medicine Collection, University at Buffalo, from 1981 to 1997, and has published on a number of subjects, including librarianship and medical history. She compiled and edited *Medical History in Buffalo 1846-1996: Collected Essays* and served as co-editor of *American Nursing, Volume II.* Currently, she is special projects librarian at the Historical Collections of The New York Academy of Medicine.

ABOUT THE CONTRIBUTING EDITORS

Bonnie Bullough, PhD, RN, FAAN, was Dean Emeritus of the nursing school at the SUNY University at Buffalo and a prolific author on nursing subjects. As an original contributing editor she did much of the work in the early preparation of this volume before her death and her biography is included in it.

Olga Maranjian Church, PhD, RN, FAAN, Professor, University of Connecticut. Dr. Church serves on several editorial boards, including the International Journal of Nursing History, and is Department Editor for History for *Western Journal of Nursing Research.* She is also a member of the Research Review Panel of the American Nurses Foundation. She is a recent recipient of a Radcliffe College (Harvard University) research grant and is continuing her investigation of the emergence of psychiatric nursing and the life and work of Hildegard E. Peplau.

Sharon Richardson, PhD, RN, is currently Associate Professor in the Faculty of Nursing at the University of Alberta, Edmonton, Alberta, Canada. She has published historical articles on the Canadian nursing associations and public health/district nursing in Alberta. Currently, Dr. Richardson is writing a book on the history of nursing education at the University of Alberta. Her past clinical practice includes hospital-based acute care in all departments and experience as a hospital nurse administrator, as well as nurse practitioner in an Inuit settlement in the Canadian high Arctic.

American Nursing

A Biographical Dictionary
Volume 3

Vern L. Bullough, RN, PhD
Lilli Sentz, MLS
Editors

 Springer Publishing Company

Springer Publishing Company, Inc.
536 Broadway
New York, NY 10012-3955

Acquisitions Editor: Sheri W. Sussman
Production Editor: J. Hurkin-Torres
Cover design by James Scotto-Lavino
Cover photo by Alice Marino

00 01 02 03 04 / 5 4 3 2 1

Library of Congress Cataloging-in-Publication Data

American nursing.
    [Garland reference library of social science; vol. 368]
    Includes indexes.
    1. Nurses—United States—Biography—Dictionaries.
    I. Bullough, Vern L.   II. Church, Olga Maranjian   III. Stein,
  Alice P. IV. Series: Garland reference library of social science :
  v. 368.
    [DNLM: 1. History of Nursing—United States.   2. Nurses—United
  States—biography. WZ 112.5.N8 A512]
  RT35.A44   1988   610.73'092'2   [B]   87-29076
  ISBN 0-8240-8540-X (alk. paper)

Volume 3
ISBN 0-8261-1296-X (Hardcover)

Volumes 1 and 2 are out of print. Please refer to your library for your reference search.

Photo Credits

E. M. Auger, Medicine Hat Museum & Art Gallery; M. E. Birtles, Medicine Hat Museum & Art Gallery; R. Bradley, Courtesy of R. Bradley (U.S. Army Photo); M. E. Carnegie, Jeffrey John Fearing (Biomedical Communications, Howard University); R. K. Chang, Wiley & Monaghan; M. I. Clark, Gardy L. March (U.S. Army Central Photo); L. Cobb, U.S. Navy Bureau of Medicine & Surgery Archives; L. Creelman, Studio Neri, Geneve (Canadian Nurses Association); E. Cryderman, Lux Photography, Ottawa (Canadian Nurses Association); M. Davidson, Army Nurse Corps Archives; V. M. Dunbar, New York Hospital-Cornell Medical Center Archives; G. M. Fairley, Lux Photography, Ottawa (Canadian Nurses Association); A. M. Hayes, by SFC John Hawley (U.S. Army Photo); M. Hersey, Lux Photography, Ottawa (Canadian Nurses Association); E. Honeycutt, by Kay Hinton (Emory University Photography); Sister D. LeFebvre, Canadian Nurses Association; H. G. McArthur, Lux Photography, Ottawa (Canadian Nurses Assoc.); A. L. B. McDaniel, Yale University Library (Manuscripts & Archives); J. Nesbit, Courtesy of D. Starbuck; A. Reinders, by VandeVusse & Hanson; G. Rowsell, Canadian Nurses Association; F. M. Shaw, Canadian Nurses Association; M. Sheahan, Foundation of NYSNA Archives; R. M. Simpson, Canadian Nurses Association; E. Smith, by Bradford Bachrach; F. Wald, National Women's Hall of Fame; J. S. Wilson, Canadian Nurses Associaton, M. O. Wolanin, Studio Seven (Tucson, AZ).

Printed in the United States of America

This book is dedicated to Ursula Springer, editor, publisher, friend.

Contents

INDEXES

Contributors

Allen, Catherine B., MBA, LhD
Ardalan, Christine, RN, MA
Bartal, Nira, RN, MA
Baviar, Anne, MN, FASN
Beaudoin, Christina N., MSN, RN, C
Benson, Evelyn R., RN, MPH
Birnbach, Nettie, EdD, RN, FAAN
Bjoring, Eleanor L.M. Crowder, RN, PhD
Brewer, Gwendolyn W., PhD
Brink, Pamela J., RN, PhD, FAAN
Brook, Marian J., RN, PhD
Brooks, Jo A., RN, DNS
Brown, Billye J., RN, EdD, FAAN
Brueggemann, David W., BSN, MA
Bullough, Vern L., RN, PhD, FAAN
Calvin, Rosie L., RN, DNS
Cannon, Rose B., RN, PhD
Clayton, Bonnie C., RN, PhD
Cooper, Signe S., RN, BS, MEd, FAAN
Dale, Marcia L., EdD, FAAN
Dibble, Birney J., MD
Donahue, Patricia M., RN, PhD, FAAN
Dudas, Susan, RN, MSN, FAAN
Dunphy, Lynne M., PhD, FNP, CNS
Ebersole, Priscilla, RN, PhD, FAAN
Eisenhauer, Laurel A., RN, PhD, FAAN
Feigenbaum, Janice C., RN, PhD
Fickeissen, Janet L., RN, MSN
Fielding, Jeanne, BA, MLS
Gaines, Barbara C., RN, EdD
Garand, Linda J., RN, MS, CS, ARNP
Greenhill, E. Dianne, RN, EdD
Halloran, Edward J., RN, PhD, FAAN
Hamilton, Diane B., RN, PhD
Hammer, Marjorie S., RN, MSNC
Hanson, Lisa, CNM, DNSc
Haritos, Dolores, RN, EdD
Harris, Barbara L., RN, PhD
Harris, Nancy A., CRNA, MNA

Haylock, Pamela J., RN, MA
Hiestand, Wanda, RN, EdD
Kilby, Sally, RN, MS
Lagerman, Lois, RN, CS, EdD, A.D.N.
Lohman, Becky
Mathews, Irene, RN
Mayer, Susan, RN-C, EdD
Messmer, Patricia, RN-C, PhD
Mirr, Michaeline, RN, PhD, CS
Monteiro, Lois, RN, PhD
Morton, Margaret, A.D.N., BSN
Murphy, Sharon C., RN, MLS
Nehring, Wendy M., RN, PhD
Nichols, D. Jeanette, RN, MSNC
Norman, Elizabeth M., RN, PhD, FAAN
Oermann, Marilyn
Olson, Tom, RN, PhD, CS
Pavri, Julie M., MSN, MLS
Perry, Paulie M., RN, AD
Perry, Shannon E., RN, PhD, FAAN
Pflaum, Jackie, RN, PhD
Prichard, Mary E., RN, BSN, MEd
Richardson, Sharon, RN, PhD
Robinson, Thelma M., RN, MS
Ross-Kerr, Janet, RN, PhD
Rote, Nelle Fairchild
Ruffing-Rahal, Mary Ann, RN, PhD
Sarnecky, Mary T., MN, DNScC, CS, FNP
Sentz, Lilli, MLS
Smalls, Sadie M., MA, MEd, EdD
Smith, Susan L., MA, PhD
Smokvina, Gloria J., RN, PhD
Strodtman, Linda K., RN, PhD
VandeVusse, Leona, PhD, CNM
Vrabel, Mark, MLS
Wolf, Jaqueline H., PhD
Woolley, Alma S., RN, EdD
Zalumas, Jacqueline C., PhD, RNC, FNP
Zilm, Glennis, BSN, BJ, MA

Acknowledgments

This book could not have been written without the assistance and support of the members of the American Association for the History of Nursing. They suggested names and contributed most of the biographies in this volume and acted as referees over who to include. Special thanks are due to all the authors, whether members of the AAHN or not, who did contribute and hung in there to complete the project. But if the book could not have been written without the dedicated work of our contributors, it could not have been published without the special support of Ursula Springer, to whom the book is dedicated. I have had a long connection with Springer publications and the company has published many of the books that I and my late wife, Bonnie Bullough, wrote or edited. I have, however, never publicly thanked Ursula. Dedicating the book to her is one way of doing this. The whole staff at Springer deserves special commendation but especially Sheri W. Sussman, the nursing editor, and Jean Hurkin-Torres, the production editor for this book.

Last of all my co-editor, Lill Sentz, and my contributing editors, Bonnie Bullough, Olga Maranjan Church, and Sharon Richardson should be thanked. Lilli Sentz, even though she lived on the opposite side of the country, has always been supportive and in a crisis always came through. Sharon

Richardson made it possible to include a contingent of Canadian nurses, and her wise counsel is appreciated.

This project has been in the works for nearly 15 years and it was germinating for several years before that as my late wife Bonnie felt that the contributions of nurses were being ignored by the feminist writers of the late 1960's and early 1970's. This is no longer the case, but it took time for the feminist movement to realize the contribution of nurses to their cause, and it was books like this series that helped. Bonnie was active in the planning stage for this volume as well as the other two, and I continue to list her as a contributing editor. When I originally sought help in getting the original project underway back in the early 1980's, Olga Church proved invaluable, and was co-editor with me of the first volume. Some of the early work we did still shows in this volume and for that she is also listed as a contributing editor. In sum, though I am listed an editor, no work of this kind could have been done without a lot of collaborators and a lot of help from others, so many it is not possible to name all of them. I wish, however, to thank all of them even though I might not formally acknowledge them.

Vern L. Bullough

Introduction

This is the third and final volume of what I have come to regard as a biographical history of American and Canadian nursing. Gathered together in the three volumes are the biographies of some 523 nurses, 391 in the first two volumes and 132 in this one. This volume records the movement of nursing and of women into the American (and Canadian) mainstream and serves as a key to documenting the changes in attitude toward professional women during the last part of the twentieth century. For example, since the 1980's many of the standard biographical dictionaries such as *Who's Who* have begun to include large numbers of women, and particularly nurses in their content. Prior to the 1960's, only a handful of nurses ever appeared in such collections. Then they began to appear in such special collections as *Who's Who in American Women*, although not in large numbers. Still that biographical dictionary encouraged the more traditional biographical collections to pay more attention to women. This is much different from the past when the assumption that a woman should be in the background and only achieve notice in the newspaper on three occasions: her birth, her marriage, and her death. As a result the individual achievements of women in general were ignored.

Even the pioneering attempts to redress this neglect of women's achievement in history such as the compilation of *Notable American Women*, ignored the working nurse. The handful of women identified as associated with nursing were for the most part not nurses but rather society women interested in promoting the development of

nursing, a somewhat different thing. This neglect has now changed and it is the increasing recognition of nurses as significant individuals and nursing as an important profession that makes additional volumes in this series highly unlikely and not so necessary. Those interested in biographies of important nurses of today can easily find information on them as compared to the past.

The nurses in this volume were nominated by members of the American Association for the History of Nursing and by an exhaustive survey of various nursing publications. Nurses were considered for inclusion if they had written important books and articles, made innovations in clinical care or in nursing theory, were significant leaders in nursing education or in nursing organizations, were barrier breakers or nurse heroines or role models, had major responsibilities in administration in the civilian or military setting, or had in some way achieved fame on either the national or international level. We also contacted individuals in various regions of the United States and Canada, asking them to suggest the names of nurses who had made significant regional contributions and who might not have been in the "inner circle" of the national nursing organizations. To be included in the first volume, all the nurses had to be deceased although one of those believed to have died turned out to be living and over a hundred years old after the volume was published. In the second volume, while most of the individuals were deceased, included also were those born before 1915 and still living. Those still alive, it was believed, had retired and it was easy enough to assess the contributions they had made. Not surprisingly, few of them were listed in standard biographical compilations. In this volume the date has been moved to those born in 1925 or before, or who are now deceased. The 1925 date was arbitrary, but by the publication of this volume they would have been 75 or older and for those still alive, old enough to have their careers assessed objectively. Those nurses who had been elected by their peers to the American Academy of Nursing were also evaluated for inclusion and many of the pioneers of the Academy are included here. Sometimes, however, nurses were included because they were associated with important people. President William Clinton's mother, for example, is included in this volume, as is the nurse who was the model for Ernest Hemingway in *Farewell to Arms*. Three non-nurses are also included because of their contribution to nursing.

The emphasis on the word *women* in this introduction indicates just how dominant women were in nursing. There were, however, always a few men in nursing, and this volume includes two such men, making a total of eleven for the three volumes. Traditionally the woman who made a career of nursing was unmarried and this remains largely true in this volume although there is a growing proportion of women who married, had children, and also continued to be involved in their career. Some 30 of the women in the study could be identified as having had children, mostly two or three, but one had seven and another had five. There might have been others with children but tracing down the numbers of children is a difficult task. Interestingly many of those who married did so comparatively late, some waiting until retirement to do so. Several of the nurses in this study married more than once.

A number of the women in the study were missionaries or in religious orders, but

fewer than in the two previous volumes. Emphasizing the changing nature of the times, one of the nuns later left the order. Many of the unmarried women in this book lived with other women for most of their lives, and some might well have been lesbians, but in only a few of the biographies are the lifelong partners identified, probably indicative of a continuing reluctance of nurses to mention such issues.

This volume, more than the two earlier volumes, emphasizes the changing nature of nursing education, both in the preparation of students coming to nursing, and in the development of collegiate education. All but three in this study were high school or normal school graduates (i.e. teacher training institutes that were two-year schools often equivalent to the last two years of high school) when they entered nursing school. Some 32 had attended college, some graduating before they decided to become a nurse, although several of them attended colleges with five-year degree programs for nurses. Most of the nurses entered nursing school before they were 20, although 49 were 21 or older, 13 of them were between 26 to 30, and two well into their 30s. Most of the nurses in this study had entered nursing school before 1940, and fewer than 30 after 1941. Of those who entered after 1941, ten were in the cadet corps, but if we had been able to include nurses still alive who were born after 1925, the number would have increased tremendously. Many of those who entered nursing after trying other occupations, and by far the largest number had been teachers. Two entered nursing through a master's program without any undergraduate nursing, a new phenomenon in nursing.

The vast majority of nurses went to diploma schools and more than 100 different ones are listed in the biographies, and only one Canadian school, a university affiliated one, had three graduates. Almost all the rest had only a single graduate. Some of the older schools that played important roles in the early volumes do not do so in this volume in which no school appears to be very dominant. Interestingly almost all of the diploma schools which the subjects did attend are either no longer in existence or turned over their programs to a community college or a school with a baccalaureate program. The fact that so many attended diploma schools had a delaying effect on their future education. In order to gain a college degree most had to spend several years getting a bachelor's degree because many of their credits were not recognized by the colleges and universities. In spite of this handicap, over half of the nurses in this volume went on to graduate school. Over 30 of them had an earned doctorate, another 35 acquired a master's degree, and another 14 were given special certificates for their studies. Many of the others went back and got a bachelor's degree if they did not have one. This shift in nursing education emphasizes the change taking place in the educational levels of nurses and changing public perceptions about them.

Going on to graduate school was not easy, and only a handful went directly to graduate school after earning an undergraduate degree. Most went into the market place, or took time off to have children, before returning to graduate school in their 30s, some in their 40s, and one went back at 57 years old. Teachers College at Columbia University, which dominated the graduate education for nursing in an earlier period, continued to do so and gave advanced degrees to some 25 nurses, although many of these nurses were among those born at the turn of the century since its influence also began to decline. Second to Columbia was New York University with seven advanced degree graduates. Some schools which attracted advanced degree students such as Boston University and the University of Chicago no longer have their programs. Several of the Black nurses in this book went to the University of Toronto or McGill University for graduate study first, in part because of the discriminatory policies of many American schools. All told, the nurses attended more than 40 different graduate schools, increasingly those located in the emerging state universities.

To be an achiever in nursing meant that nurses were mobile. Only ten of those included in this volume can be said to have stayed in the same geographic area for all of their lives, and most of these were in large urban areas. The vast majority lived in two to four different geographical areas, and more than a third lived in five or more different areas. Many of the most transient were in the military and more than 25 in this volume served in the military in one way or another. Several made it their career and included in the volume are the biographies of two Brigadier Generals and one Rear Admiral, a breakthrough for women as well as nurses. Several of the nurses received medals for their heroism under fire.

The scholarship level of nurses increased tremendously in this volume over past ones with the majority of nurses publishing either articles or books. Fourteen of them published extensively with more than five books and numerous articles, and at least one published more than 25 books and over 100 refereed articles. While over a third were mainly associated with nursing education, others made their reputation through nursing administration, nursing organization, public health or clinical expertise, research, theory, and as editors. Several who are in this book were pioneers in establishing the growing graduate specialties in nursing such as nurse midwifery, nurse anesthetists, nurse-practitioners, and clinical nurse specialists.

Nurses for the most part, continue to be long lived. More than 40 of the deceased nurses in this volume died after they had reached their 80th birthday, and one died at 100, another at 101. This continues a trend reported in the first two volumes where nearly a quarter lived past 80. Most of those still alive are in their 80s or older.

These, however, are only statistics. Each nurse is an individual achiever and their lives are fascinating. Many who have read the first two volumes have found them valuable in the classroom, have encouraged students to study them, and have collected data on other nurses not included to see how much nurses of different generations are similar to us, yet at the same time different. For only a few of the nurses in this volume was achievement an easy process. Their lives emphasize what it was like to be a nurse, what kinds of difficulties they encountered, and how they overcome them. The reader will certainly find out a great deal about the nursing presence and about what individual nurses have done to make nursing what it is today.

Vern L. Bullough

A

FAYE GLENN ABDELLAH
1919–

In her long career in the United States Public Health Service, Faye Glenn Abdellah has represented nursing in the formation of health policy across such diverse fields as the progressive patient care delivery system, nursing research and education, care for the aging, AIDS, violence, smoking, and alcoholism. Her accomplishments include numerous "firsts," making her truly a pioneer in nursing and health care in this century.

Faye Glenn Abdellah

Abdellah was born in New York City on March 13, 1919 to H. B. and Margaret Glenn Abdellah. She had one brother, Marty, older than herself. The family was living near Lakehurst, New Jersey in May, 1937, when the hydrogen-filled dirigible, the "Hindenburg," exploded and burned, killing or injuring hundreds of people. Abdellah and her brother responded to help the victims, and Abdellah later identified that as the day she decided to go into nursing. She earned a diploma from Fitkin Memorial Hospital School of Nursing (now Ann May School of Nursing), Neptune, New Jersey, in 1942 and continued studying at Rutgers University, taking liberal arts and chemistry. She completed her B.S. at Columbia University in 1945 and her M.A. from there in 1947. She earned her doctorate in education from Columbia in 1955.

While pursuing her undergraduate education at Rutgers and Columbia University, Abdellah worked as Director of Health Services, Child Education Foundation, NYC, in 1942 to 1943, and Staff Nurse/Head Nurse at Columbia-Presbyterian Medical Center, NYC, from 1943 to 1945. In 1945 she joined the faculty of Yale University School of Nursing as instructor of nursing arts, pharmacology, and medical nursing. During this same time she served as a research fellow and teaching assistant at Teachers College, Columbia University. Desiring to continue research activities, Abdellah joined the U.S. Public Health Service (USPHS) in 1949 and served in Korea from 1950 to 1954. She was appointed Chief Nurse Officer in 1970 and served as a member of the Commissioned Corps until her retirement in 1989. She retired from the position of Deputy Surgeon General with a rank of Rear Admiral (Two Stars).

Early work in the USPHS was carried out through the Division of Nursing Resources Bureau of State Services, Department of Health, Education and Welfare and included nursing needs research in 14 states and the beginning development of a patient classification system based on patient characteristics. This formed the basis of Diagnostic Related Groups (DRG). Another early project resulted in a job reclassification for medical occupations which increased the civil service rating of nurses.

Between 1958 and 1961, Abdellah served as Visiting Professor at the University of Washington, the University of Colorado, and the University of Minnesota, publishing during this time on improving nursing education through research and developing the concept of and evaluating models of progressive patient care. From this work the first intensive care, intermediate care, and self-care units were established. Her seminal book, *Patient Centered Approaches to Nursing*, resulted from this work, and introduced a theory of nursing based on the formulation of patient care around patient problems addressed by nursing actions, rather than around medical diagnoses.

During the decade of the 1960s, Abdellah wrote extensively about nursing science and nursing research, contributing to the development of nurse scientist programs. *Better Patient Care Through Nursing Research* (with Eugene Levine) was published in 1965. This book has been produced in three editions and translated into six languages.

One focus of Abdellah's work beginning in the late 1960s and '70s was health promotion, disease prevention, and long-term care for the aging. Under her leadership, the Office of Long Term Care, Department of Health and Human Services, conducted a nationwide evaluation study of patient care in nursing homes. During this time she participated in the development of the Diagnostic Related Group classification system (DRGs) for Medicare reimbursement and of the PACE classification system, a guide for evaluating long-term care. She

supported the extension of the scope of nursing practice to the preparation of nurse practitioners in school health as well as in the care of aged populations.

In 1981, she was appointed Deputy Surgeon General to C. Everett Koop, M.D., Surgeon General. From this position she shared responsibilities for health policy research and development on many problems affecting the elderly, such as elder abuse, self-help, and incontinence. New policies were demanded to meet the onset of the AIDS epidemic.

Upon her retirement from the USPHS in 1989, Abdellah became Chairperson of the Nursing Task Force, charged with establishing a program for preparing advanced practice nurses at the Uniformed Services University of the Health Sciences (USUHS). When the first class entered in August 1993, Abdellah was appointed Founding Dean and Professor of Research.

In addition to her work in health policy in the United States, Abdellah has served as consultant in many other countries and participated in numerous international delegations under the auspices of the U.S. government and the World Health Organization (WHO). In 1985, Abdellah participated in the first meeting of the International Council of Nurses to develop a plan for providing nursing leadership for meeting WHO's goal of health for all by 2000. She has been invited to participate in seminars on long-term care in Australia and New Zealand, to consult with nursing organizations on the subject of setting up graduate nursing and research education in Israel and Japan and to address the AIDS International Conference in Cardiff, Wales.

From the beginning of her nursing career, Abdellah has been the recipient of 11 honorary degrees and more than 70 awards or commendations. She is the recipient of the prestigious Allied Signal award (1989) and has been honored by the USPHS (C.

Everett Koop Distinguished Lecture, 1993), the Institute of Medicine (1990), Columbia University (Second Century Award in Health Care, 1996) and the USUHS (Leadership Award, 1997). She was among 36 charter fellows named to the American Academy of Nursing in 1974 and served that organization as President and Vice-President. In 1994 she received the Academy's Living Legend Award. Sigma Theta Tau (National Honor Society of Nursing) presented her with the Excellence in Nursing Award in 1982 and the first Presidential award in 1987. The American Nurses Association conferred its Honorary Recognition Award in 1986. She has received numerous military honors including two Distinguished Service Medals and the Surgeon General's Medal and Medallion.

Abdellah makes her home in Virginia. Her nonprofessional interests include classical music, gardening, and hiking. Her professional papers (24 volumes), including an oral history, original publications and a photographic history, are on file at the National Library of Medicine, Bethesda, Maryland.

PUBLICATIONS BY FAYE GLENN ABDELLAH

Books (Selected)

Abdellah, F. G. (1961). *Patient centered approaches to nursing.* New York: Macmillan.
Abdellah, F. G. (1991). *Nurses' role in the future: The case for health policy decision making.* Indianapolis, IN: Sigma Theta Tau International.
Abdellah, F. G., & Levine, E. (1965). *Better patient care through nursing research.* New York: Macmillan (Three editions). (Japanese edition: Igaku-Shoin of Tokyo, 1993).
Abdellah, F. G., & Levine, E. (1994). *Preparing nursing research for the 21st century: Evolution, methodologies and challenges.* New York: Springer Publishing.
Meltzer, L. E., Abdellah, F. G., & Kitchell, J. R. (Eds.). (1969). *Concepts and practices of intensive care for nurse specialists.* Philadelphia: Charles Press.

Articles (Selected)

Abdellah, F. G. (1957). Methods of identifying covert aspects of nursing problems as a basis for improved clinical teaching. *Nursing Research, 6*(1), 4–23.
Abdellah, F. G. (1961). Criterion measures in nursing for experimental research. *Nursing Research, 16,* 21–26.
Abdellah, F. G. (1966). Doctoral preparation for nurses. *Nursing Forum, 5,* 44–53.
Abdellah, F. G. (1969). The nature of nursing science. *Nursing Research, 18,* 390–393.
Abdellah, F. G., & Levine, E. (1957). Developing a measure of patient and personnel satisfaction with nursing care. *Nursing Research, 5,* 100–108.
Abdellah, F. G., et al. (1982). *Report of hospice care in the United States.* Washington, DC: U.S. Department of Health and Human Services (HCFA-82-02152).
Abdellah, F. G. (1988). Incontinence: Implications for health care policy. *Nursing Clinics of North America, 23*(1), 291–297.

BIBLIOGRAPHY

Abdellah, F. G. (1977). U.S. Public Health Service's contribution to nursing research: Past, present and future. *Nursing Research, 26*(4), 244–248.
Abdellah, F. G., Dycus, D. K., Schmeiser, D. N., McClure, E. A., Taggert, F. M., & Yancey, R. (1994). Twenty-one nursing problems. In A. Marriner-Tomey (Ed.), *Nursing theorists and their work* (3rd ed.) (pp. 116–137). St. Louis: Mosby.
Abdellah, F. G. (1997, February). *Biography.* Bethesda, MD: Department of Defense, Uniformed Services University of the Health Sciences.
Charter fellows named to Academy of Nursing. (1973). *American Journal of Nursing, 73,* 521–522.
Profile: Faye G. Abdellah. (1980). *American Journal of Nursing, 80,* 1671, 1674.

Marion J. Brook

JO ANN ASHLEY
1939–1980

Jo Ann Ashley is best remembered for her book, *Hospitals, Paternalism, and the Role of the Nurse* (1976), based on her doctoral dissertation, which identified the patriarchal oppression of American nurses through the apprenticeship system of education in physician-dominated hospitals. Likening the American hospital to the patriarchal family, the physician/father dictated to the nurse/ mother who in turn was expected to "care" tirelessly and diffusely for small remuneration (rather than children). According to Ashley, such subordination marked the origins of exploitation of the work of nursing and in turn, the devaluation of the central nursing ethos of caring. From this ensued the escalation of further deception through devalued images of nursing in terms of subservience, powerlessness, and marginality. Ashley shrewdly observed how such deception perpetuated the social and professional fragmentation of nursing and thwarted any momentum within the profession to unify under the common experience of oppression.

Ashley was the fourth of seven children of Ivan and Jewell Duvall Ashley, born October 25, 1939 in Sweeden, a rural community in Edmonson County near Brownsville, Kentucky. Ashley attended Kyrock School, grades one through 12, which at that time consisted of two rooms. There were 15 students in her graduation class, including one of her older sisters (Jane). JoAnn was valedictorian and Jane was salutatorian. Jane and Jo Ann both attended one semester at Western Kentucky University in Bowling Green, KY. They then were introduced to nursing as a career possibility and enrolled at Kentucky Baptist School of Nursing in Louisville, KY, where they roomed together and received diplomas in 1961. Ashley then continued at Kentucky Baptist Hospital as a Staff Nurse. In 1964, she received the Bachelor of Science in Nursing degree at Catherine Spaulding College in Louisville. From 1964 through 1966, she was an Instructor at Norton Memorial Infirmary School of Nursing in Louisville. In 1966, after moving to Ohio, she took a position as Staff Nurse at the V.A. Hospital in Brecksville. She then relocated to New York

City, and held a position as Staff Nurse at the New York VA Hospital, beginning in the Summer of 1967. She began graduate studies at Teachers College, Columbia, where she received a Masters of Education (M.Ed.) in 1969 and a Doctor of Education (Ed.D.) degree in 1972 with a concentration in nursing education.

Ashley's subsequent career as an academic, scholar, and mentor to graduate students in the emerging discipline of nursing science was shadowed by the diagnosis of breast cancer while completing her dissertation. She lived less than a decade longer. These years were marked by both turbulence and her unflagging resolve to produce a cache of scholarship and historic truth. She frequently was a lightning rod for controversy and misunderstanding. No one would characterize her as lacking courage and a passion for the truth. During her brief career, she held faculty appointments at City College of New York, Pennsylvania State University, Northern Illinois University, Texas Women's University, Wright State University, and West Virginia University. She was a member of the editorial board of *Advances in Nursing Science*, and served on the Board of Trustees of the Nurses Coalition for Action in Politics of the American Nurses Association. She was in demand as a speaker at professional meetings. A collection of some of her prolific professional writings has been published (Wolf, 1997). In 1996, the Jo Ann Ashley Collection (10 linear feet) of materials became available at the Center for the Study of the History of Nursing, University of Pennsylvania.

On November 20, 1980, Jo Ann Ashley died in Morgantown, West Virginia. She is buried near Sweeden, Kentucky.

PUBLICATIONS BY JO ANN ASHLEY

Ashley, J. A. (1973). About power in nursing. *Nursing Outlook, 21*(10), 637–641.

Ashley, J. A. (1975). Nursing and early feminism. *American Journal of Nursing, 75*, 1465–1467.

Ashley, J. A. (1976a). *Hospitals, paternalism, and the role of the nurse.* New York, NY: Teachers College Press.

Ashley, J. A. (1976b). Nursing power: Viable, vital, visible. *Texas Nursing, 50*, 611.

Ashley, J. A. (1977). Health care, American style: Helter skelter, par excellence. *Supervisor Nurse, 8*(2), 46–47, 50–54, 57.

Ashley, J. A. (1978). Foundations for scholarship: Historical research in nursing. *Advances in Nursing Science, 1*(1), 25–36.

Ashley, J. A. (1980). Power in structured misogyny: Implications for the politics of care. *Advances in Nursing Science, 2*(3), 3–22.

BIBLIOGRAPHY

Hurwitz, A. (1977). Review of *Hospitals, paternalism, and the role of the nurse. Nursing Outlook, 25*(7), 468–469.

Obituary. (1981). In memoriam. *Advances in Nursing Science. 3*(3), xiii.

Obituary. (1981). Jo Ann Ashley. *Nursing Outlook, 29*, 193–194.

Roberts, J. I., & Group, T. M. (1995). *Feminism and nursing: An historical perspective on power, status, and political activism in the nursing profession.* Westport, CT: Praeger.

Wolf, K. A. (Ed.). (1997). *Jo Ann Ashley: Selected readings.* New York: NLN Press.

Mary Ann Ruffing-Rahal

EDNA MABEL AUGER
1876–1932

Edna Mabel Auger is a representative of the cadre of Canadian nurses who served overseas during the First World War. She was also one of the few trained nurses who lived and practiced in the raw frontier of southern Alberta prior to the First World War. While overseas during the war, Auger won for herself a reputation for efficiency and dedication in her work and for bravery in the face of danger. Auger went overseas in 1915 with the Number One Canadian General Hospital Corps, spending most of the next 3 years in the war zone. Stationed

Edna Mabel Auger

initially at a clearing hospital in Belgium until the station was shelled out, she was transferred to the No. 1 Canadian Hospital at Etaples, France, where she remained until the cessation of hostilities. Choosing to remain with her patients during the bombing of Etaples, Auger was buried in the rubble but subsequently dug out in time to save her life. A number of physicians, nurses, orderlies, and patients were killed during two successive raids. In recognition for "valuable services with the Armies in France and Flanders," she was awarded the Associate Royal Red Cross in 1918. The Royal Red Cross was instituted by Queen Victoria in 1883 and was the first example of a British Military Order solely for women. The decoration was conferred upon members of the nursing services, irrespective of rank, and upon anyone, British or foreign, who was engaged on nursing or hospital duties with the British Navy, Army, or Air Force and who had been recommended for special devotion or competency.

Edna Auger was born in 1876, in Chatham, Ontario, the only daughter of John and Sarah Auger, who had immigrated to Canada from Cornwall, England, about 1840. When Edna was 7 years of age, the family moved to Maple Creek, in what is now the province of Saskatchewan, where she lived for 7 years and received her early schooling. Edna took high school education back East in Ontario. When this was completed, she returned west to Medicine Hat, in what is now the province of Alberta, where she entered nurses training at the Medicine Hat General Hospital in 1903. Prior to 1905, when the prairie provinces of Saskatchewan and Alberta were created, the vast tract of land that stretched west for over 800 miles from the Manitoba border to British Columbia, and south for almost 2,000 miles from the Arctic Ocean to the northern border of the United States, was known as the North-West Territories. The North-West Territories did not attract large numbers of settlers until the end of the 19th century, in comparison to the American frontier, which had been largely settled by the mid-1880s. The prairie provinces of Alberta and Saskatchewan constituted Canada's "last best West," encompassing the only unsettled agricultural land remaining in the Dominion of Canada.

Following graduation from nurses' training in 1906, Auger remained as an operating room nurse at the Medicine Hat General Hospital until 1910, when she travelled to New York for a postgraduate course. She stayed on in New York as a chief operating room nurse in a private hospital, before returning to Medicine Hat in 1913 as Assistant Superintendent of the Medicine Hat General Hospital. She applied for and was appointed Nursing Sister, Canadian Army Medical Corps, in April 1915 and went overseas in September. Early in 1919, Auger was repatriated to England, before returning to Canada in the fall. In summer, 1920, she went to the isolated Peace River district of northwestern Alberta to organize a new municipal hospital at Grande Prairie. Returning to southeastern Alberta in 1921, Auger became Lady Superintendent of Nurses at the Medicine Hat General Hospital, a position she retained until her death on May 2, 1932.

BIBLIOGRAPHY

Edna Mabel Auger biographical file: Medicine Hat Museum & Art Gallery Archives, Medicine Hat, Alberta, Canada.

Sharon Richardson

HAZEL M. AVERY
1906–1995

During her 41-year career at the University of Michigan, Avery focused her energies on family-centered obstetrical nursing. This concept, now fully integrated at health centers throughout the country, was a novel idea when Professor Avery first introduced it at Michigan. The primary thrust of family-centered obstetrical nursing was to provide regular and sustained access between postpartum mothers and their children, and to encourage fathers to remain throughout labor, during delivery, and in the postpartum period. In addition, she envisioned and implemented a sibling visitation program on the maternity ward.

Hazel M. Avery was born January 16, 1906 in Pittsburgh, Kansas, to Mary Ann Meadows Avery and Joseph Henry Avery. She was originally named Flossie Hazel May Avery but she later renamed herself, Hazel M. Avery and went by this name the rest of her life. In her early childhood, her parents and family moved to Washington State to be closer to her maternal grandmother, Mary Malinda Totman Meadows Bangs. Her parents homesteaded high on the mountain that later got the name of Bangs

Hazel M. Avery

Mountain. Avery started school at Kettle Fall, Washington. Her mother died when she was nine and her father took his surviving family to Montana to be closer to his widowed mother, Mary Ann Hopkins Avery. They settled in the area of Utica and lived for a short time in an old log cabin. The children went to Buffalo School and became used to having their sister Goldie, age 15, as their mother.

When Avery was 16, she left home but continued to attend high school, working out her room and board by taking care of small children and doing light housework. Next she enrolled in the Intermountain Union College in Helena, Montana, where she majored in history with minors in sociology and education, supporting herself by taking care of children for several families, by writing a column for the local paper where she was paid by the line (wrote about all "the doings of her neighbors and friends) and working for the post office (typing reports). When she received her

A.B. degree from Intermountain Union College, Helena, Montana, in 1929, it was difficult to locate teaching jobs because of the onset of the Depression. Avery stated "I had always wanted to teach history or sociology, but in those years, it was a futile ambition." A friend of one of her families that she worked for offered assistance for her to attend the nursing school at The University of Michigan and so she moved to Ann Arbor.

In 1932 she received her Diploma in Nursing from the University of Michigan Hospital School of Nursing and joined the staff of the University of Michigan's University Hospital, rising to the position of night superintendent and supervisor. In 1939 she was asked to transfer to maternity as a supervisor and instructor of nursing and she remained in charge of obstetrical nursing until her retirement in 1973. She set about changing maternity care, dedicating herself to creating a family-centered obstetric service.

In the 1930s a main focus of maternity care was separation of mother and baby following delivery and adoption of a rigid newborn-feeding schedule (4-hour bottle feeding regime). There were several groups that were experimenting with family-centered obstetric service, including a group at Yale University. It was not until 1951, however, that she was able to attend a 2-week course at the Yale family-centered institute. She also found a Detroit hospital with a family-centered approach and for a year, Avery, and a colleague, drove to Detroit each week learning the family-oriented techniques. The primary thrust of the program she established was to provide regular and sustained access for the postpartum mother to her child; encouragement of fathers to remain throughout labor—and during the delivery itself; and sibling participation through visitation.

In 1952 Avery was made an Assistant Professor of Nursing while she continued as a

Supervisor of Obstetrics and Gynecology in the hospital. In 1966 she advanced to Associate Professor and Assistant Director of Nursing Service and in 1967 she was made a full Professor. Throughout her teaching of nurses she was aware that she was a "tough, demanding teacher. I want students to be professionals when they leave one of my classes." One result is that for years students often said, "I'm taking Miss Avery" not "I'm taking Obstetrics."

In 1944, she collaborated with Dr. Norman Miller, chairman of the University of Michigan's department of Obstetrics and Gynecology, in the writing of their book on gynecological nursing. The book was published in five editions from 1944 to 1965.

In mid-life Avery developed osteoporosis that in her elder years caused a collapse of some vertebrae. A few years before her death she returned to the state of Washington, to be closer to her family. She died in Bremerton, Washington, on September 9, 1995.

She gave many professional programs and workshops within the State of Michigan and nationally, including a presentation on "Rooming-in and Patient Care" at a meeting of the Obstetrics and Gynecological Organization for Physicians and Nurses in St. Louis, Missouri; and a 2-week in-service program for nurses at Evanston Hospital, Evanston, Illinois, on "Planning and Management of a Rooming-In Unit." She participated in research studies on "Methods of Teaching the Patient" in 1949–1954 sponsored by the Michigan Department of Health, Children's Bureau and two other projects sponsored by the same organization in 1955–1960 on "Relaxation Techniques as Preparation for Labor" and "The Maternity Patient After Discharge" in 1963–1965. With Dr. S. Behrman, she conducted a research project on "Prenatal Manual Expression to Prevent Breast Engorgement"

(1954–1960). Besides the co-authoring of the gynecological nursing textbook with Dr. Miller, Avery also wrote many patient education booklets including "Your Care After Birth of the Baby." She was also one of the authors of the Diamond Jubilee of Nursing Education at the University of Michigan (1966) brochure, which was distributed to the alumni who attended the event.

PUBLICATIONS BY HAZEL M. AVERY

Book

(With Norman F. Miller). *Gynecology and gynecologic nursing.* Philadelphia: W. B. Saunders. (Editions: 1944, 1949, 1954, 1959, 1965.)

Article

(With A. B. Howe, P. McHoskey, & V. M. Moshier). (1969). Nursing at University of Michigan Hospital: Some observations and prediction. *The University of Michigan Medical Center Journal, 35*(2), 77–81.

BIBLIOGRAPHY

Eulogy prepared by members of Hazel Avery's family for her funeral.
Hazel M. Avery personnel file and the biographical vertical file. Bentley Historical Library, The University of Michigan.

Linda K. Strodtman

MYRTLE KITCHELL AYDELOTTE
1917–

Fondly known as "Kitch," Myrtle Aydelotte has been one of the most influential contemporary leaders in nursing. She assisted with the development of strong foundations for a system of education, administration, and clinical practice that have promoted nursing's professional advancement.

Myrtle Elizabeth Kitchell was born May 31, 1917 in Van Meter, Iowa. Both her parents, John J. Kitchell and Lavara Josephine Gutshall, had been previously married.

Myrtle Kitchell Aydelotte

John's first wife died of cancer; the second wife died after contracting measles during a pregnancy. There were three living children by the first union, one by the second, and five, including Myrtle, from the third. With the combined families there were 10 children (Lavara had one child from a previous marriage) with Myrtle being the youngest daughter of the ten. John was a farmer who eventually moved his family to a bigger farm in northern Minnesota and then to an even larger farm near the city of Ada, Minnesota, and it was here that Myrtle attended high school. She was valedictorian of the class of 1933 at Ada High School.

The Great Depression, which financially depleted the Kitchell family, briefly delayed further education for Aydelotte following her high school graduation. Aydelotte confided to a public health nurse who was visiting her half-brother, who suffered from Parkinson's disease, about her desire to be a nurse, but also wanting a college education. The nurse suggested that she go to the University of Minnesota. Aydelotte applied, was accepted, and began her illustrious nursing career with a Bachelor of Science in Nursing Education in 1939. The financial burdens of college were born through a united family effort with financial assistance from two of her sisters, her parents, and also working for room and board during her freshman and sophomore years.

Following graduation, Aydelotte accepted a position as a head nurse at Charles T. Miller Hospital in St. Paul on a general surgical unit. From here she moved to St. Mary's Hospital School of Nursing where she became a surgical teaching supervisor, the first nurse to do clinical teaching at this school. Her personal dissatisfaction with her performance as a clinical instructor as well as the increasing involvement of the United States in World War II led Kitch to enlist in the Army Nurse Corps as a Second Lieutenant.

Aydelotte's first assignment with the Army was as Assistant Chief Nurse of the 26th General Hospital originally set up in Constantine, Algeria, North Africa. She later moved to Bari, Italy. In 1945, Kitch, now a captain, became Chief Nurse at the 52nd Station Hospital in Naples, Italy for the remainder of the war.

Education once again became the driving force once Aydelotte returned to the States. She returned to the University of Minnesota, where she obtained an M.A. in education in 1948 and a Ph.D. in educational psychology and administration in 1955. During this time, she worked full time as a faculty member at the School of Nursing. As a doctoral student, she became the first woman and nurse to take a course in Hospital Administration at the University of Minnesota. Before completing her doctorate she became the founding Dean and Professor of the newly founded College of Nursing at the State University of Iowa in 1949.

Under her leadership, the College initiated new and revised programs, increased numbers of qualified faculty with solid academic credentials, integrated nursing students into the university at large, gradually withdrew nursing students from nursing service, and developed standards for faculty and students. Strong reactions to the changes, particularly those that affected the traditional hospital service provided by students and removed nursing from under the supervision of the College of Medicine, came from some divisions in the College of Medicine and the hospital administration. Aydelotte, the first woman academic dean at Iowa, held her ground and even began campaigning for graduate education for nurses. She firmly believed that academic credentials were crucial to professional status in the health care hierarchy, especially vis à vis physicians.

On June 22, 1956, she married William Aydelotte, Chairman of the Department of History. He was a specialist in modern English and European History and a pioneer in the use of quantification methods of historical analysis. Among his many honors was membership in the National Academy of Sciences (1974), the second historian to receive this honor. (He died on January 17, 1996.) Aydelotte remained as Dean until the end of the 1956–1957 academic year, when she began a brief hiatus from academia in order to raise her two children, Marie and Jeannette.

Following the birth of her first child, Aydelotte served as Professor in the College of Nursing (1957–1962), as well as Associate Chief Nurse and Chief Nurse for Nursing Research at the Veterans Administration hospital in Iowa City (1963–1964; 1964–1965). This time period proved her credibility as a nurse researcher. Aydelotte and Marie Tener, head of nursing service at University Hospitals, were among the initial recipients of USPHS research funds in the amount of $100,000. This was the first major, externally funded research activity by a member of the College of Nursing faculty. It was a 3-year project designed to test the assumption that more intensive nursing care—achieved either through increased staffing levels or through better training—would enhance patient welfare. The final report, *An Investigation of the Relation Between Nursing Activity and Patient Welfare*, was published in 1960 and became a classic in nursing literature. Although the conclusions were disappointing—"No improvements in patient welfare were produced by substantially increasing the size of the ward staff, by conducting inservice educational programs, or by combining staff increases and inservice education"—the research was nonetheless an important milestone for the College of Nursing, nursing, and Myrtle Aydelotte. Additional research followed, including a *Survey of Hospital Nursing Services* (1968) in conjunction with the National League for Nursing, which produced extensive findings describing the current state of nursing services.

Equally important was Aydelotte's acceptance of the Director of Nursing Service at The University of Iowa Hospitals and Clinics in 1968. She held this position for over 7 years and made significant contributions to the Department of Nursing. Particularly impressive was Aydelotte's acquisition of a separate nursing department budget over which she had control. One significant and related outcome of the reorganization was a shift in the educational background of the nursing staff. A new emphasis was placed on the baccalaureate degree as entry level; recruitment of master's level nurses as administrators and as clinical nurse specialists was initiated. When Aydelotte left the Director position in 1976, the Department of Nursing at Iowa met or exceeded the standards and criteria for Hospital Departments of Nursing Service published by the

American Nurses Association and the National League for Nursing.

Aydelotte has held a number of positions since that time. From 1977 to 1981 she was Executive Director of the ANA. As with her other professional endeavors, she continued to be a visionary and effectively led nurses and nursing through particularly difficult times. One of her major accomplishments, was the restructuring and revitalization of the American Nurses Foundation. Following her resignation, Aydelotte spent a large portion of her time consulting professionally as well as working independently as a mentor and colleague to nurses both nationally and internationally. She was a Visiting Professor at the University of Illinois College of Nursing, Acting Director for the Center for Nursing Innovations in New Haven, Connecticut, Clinical Professor at Yale University, and Professor at the University of Iowa College of Nursing. Although Aydelotte officially retired in 1988, as of this writing she continues to be truly a "living leader" in nursing. She now resides in Rochester, New York and spends as much time as possible with family members. Yet, she continues to actively participate in the work of nursing—to write, consult, mentor, and serve on numerous boards and committees.

Throughout her lifetime, Aydelotte has been recognized for her accomplishments. Her honors and awards include the University of Minnesota Outstanding Achievement Award (1959); Distinguished Service Award, The University of Iowa College of Nursing (1971); Election to the Institute of Medicine (1973); Luther Christman Award (1977); Honorary Doctor of Science, University of Nebraska at Omaha (1981); American Nurses Foundation Distinguished Scholar Award (1986); Sigma Theta Tau International Mary Tolle Wright Award (1987); Sigma Theta Tau *First* International Distinguished Research Fellow Award

(1988); Sigma Theta Tau Hall of Fame Award (1994); the American Academy of Nursing "Living Legend" Award (1994); and The University of Iowa Alumni Award for Distinguished Service (1997). As a tribute to her impact on nursing research, the Myrtle Kitchell Aydelotte Endowed Research Professorship for doctoral students at the University of Iowa College of Nursing was established in her honor by Gamma Chapter of Sigma Theta Tau (1993).

PUBLICATIONS BY MYRTLE KITCHELL AYDELOTTE

Book Chapters (Selected)

Nursing education and practice: Putting it all together. (1974). In J. P. Lysaught (Ed.), *Action in nursing: Progress in professional purpose* (pp. 159–164). New York: McGraw-Hill.

Clinical nursing investigation and structure of knowledge. (1977). In M. H. Miller & B. C. Flynn (Eds.), *Current perspectives in nursing* (pp. 46–52). St. Louis: Mosby.

Trends in staffing of hospitals: Implications for nursing resources policy. (1978). In M. L. Millman (Ed.), *Nursing personnel and the changing healthcare system* (pp. 113–141). Cambridge, MA: Ballinger.

The future health care delivery system and the utilization of nurses prepared in formal educational programs. (1982). In N. L. Chaska (Ed.), *The nursing profession: Views through the mist* (pp. 349–358). New York: McGraw-Hill.

The future health care delivery system in the United States. (1983a). In N. L. Chaska (Ed.), *The nursing profession: A time to speak.* New York: McGraw-Hill.

Professional nursing: The drive for governance. (1983b). In N. L. Chaska (Ed.), *The nursing profession: A time to speak* (pp. 830–840). New York: McGraw-Hill.

Conjoining nursing practice and education. (1985). In H. Grace & J. M. McCloskey (Eds.), *Current issues in nursing* (2nd ed., pp. 288–313). Boston: Blackwell.

The nurse executive of 2000 A.D. (1988). In M. Johnson (Ed.), *Series on nursing administration* (pp. 2–13). Menlo Park, CA: Addison-Wesley.

Entrepreneurs: Issues and barriers to independent practice. (1990). In H. Grace & J. C. McCloskey (Eds.), *Current issues in nursing* (pp. 194–198). St. Louis: Mosby.

Nursing education: Shaping the future. (1992). In L. Aiken & C. Fagin (Eds.), *Charting nursing's future: Agenda for the 1990's* (pp. 462–484). Philadelphia: Lippincott.

Articles (Selected)

Nursing education and practice: Putting it all together. (1972). *Journal of Nursing Education, 11*(4), 21–28.

Nursing research in clinical settings. (1976). *Reflections, 2,* 3–6.

The path toward professional autonomy. (1982). *Military Medicine, 147,* 1048–1050.

Nursing's preferred future. (1987). *Nursing Outlook, 35*(3), 114–120.

BIBLIOGRAPHY

Anderson, L., & Penningroth, K. (1998). *Complete in all its parts. Nursing education at the University of Iowa, 1898–1998.* Ann Arbor: The University of Michigan Press.

Aydelotte, M. K. *Papers.* The University of Iowa Women's Archives. University of Iowa, Iowa City.

Myrtle K. Aydelotte. (1988). In T. Schorr & A. Zimmerman (Eds.), *Making choices* (pp. 7–14). St. Louis: Mosby.

Aydelotte, W. O. *Papers.* The University of Iowa Archives. University of Iowa, Iowa City.

Robnett, M. K. (1986). *The growth of a nursing leader: Myrtle Kitchell Aydelotte.* Master's thesis, The University of Iowa.

College of Nursing Papers. University of Iowa Archives, Iowa City, Iowa.

The University of Iowa Hospitals and Clinics. (1964). *Nursing Service Department, July 1963–1964.* The University of Iowa Archives, Iowa City, Iowa.

M. Patricia Donahue

B

ESTHER ELEANOR BACON
1916–1972

Esther Bacon was a missionary nurse to Liberia. The effect of the things she did there was historically unique, and what she accomplished demonstrated a power greater than that of her peers.

Esther was born in a sod hut on a 40-acre homestead near Burlington, Colorado, on March 19, 1916. Her mother, Anna Leander, and her aunt, Nora Leander, had moved from Iowa to Colorado where each homesteaded a 40-acre plot. Shortly after this, Anna met and married a neighboring farmer, Alva Bacon, and Esther was born a year later. The marriage did not last and Anna returned to Sioux City, Iowa, where Esther grew up. She was a bright child, full of mischief, but always a regular attendant in Sunday School and church.

Knowing that she wanted to be a missionary nurse, she took the unusual step—for

Esther Eleanor Bacon

those times—of taking a year of general college first, before entering the Lutheran Hospital School of Nursing in Sioux City, IA, from which she graduated in 1937. She dedicated her life to God in Christian service in October 1940, at the Seventh Congress of the Lutheran Women's Missionary Society in Des Moines, Iowa. In October 1941, she was commissioned as a Lutheran missionary nurse and assigned to Zorzor, Liberia.

In November 1941, a month before the U.S. entered the Second World War, Bacon sailed aboard the *Acadia* for Liberia. Almost immediately she was escorted upcountry from Phebe Hospital at Harrisburg, near Monrovia, to Zorzor, deep in the northern high forests, accessible only by foot.

She found that she was the only fully trained medical person on the station. There was no doctor, and only locally trained nurses and ward helpers. The lives of the local Loma and Kpelle people were completely controlled by their *zoes*, their witch-doctors and medicine-doctors. The *zoes* held the power in the tribes: the power over life and death, the power to kill, the power to know things such as who's guilty, where lost things are, what dreams mean, and, above all, the power to communicate with the ancestral spirits.

When the *zoes* told the people they must not go to the Lutheran hospital to be treated or to have their babies, most did not go. A few, however, defied their *zoes* and came, especially if they were critically ill or injured, or if the *zoes* had given up on them. Bacon and her small corps of African nurses treated TB, cancer, tetanus, snakebite, yellow fever, leprosy, malaria, cholera, and deep muscle abscesses, and had some success with the new antibiotics just coming into use.

When pregnant women failed to come, Bacon began going out to them. She walked through the jungle to a different village each day until she knew them all and began to know the individual villagers. She offered to come any time a woman was in labor and could not deliver. For a year, she had no "takers," until a woman with a retained placenta who was bleeding to death sent for her. Esther walked through the jungle with the husband to the woman's hut, manually extracted the placenta, stopped the bleeding, and saved the woman's life.

This watershed case led to a gradual increase in cases, and Bacon bought a horse to make her travels easier.

Bacon also took into her own home dozens of babies left orphaned by their mother's death in childbirth or from some other illness. She raised them as her own, and then sent them back to their home villages when they were weaned and were able to be cared for by the child's extended family.

Bacon won a place for the Zorzor hospital by using persistence, understanding, skillful medical techniques, and great physical endurance. She weakened the power of the *zoes*, not with ridicule and hostility, but with love and with successful treatment.

Each time Bacon went home on furlough she continued her education. Eventually she obtained, in addition to her R.N., a degree in midwifery, a Bachelor of Science in Nursing, and a master's degree in Public Health, the latter from Johns Hopkins University in Baltimore, where at the age of 47 she took 2 years work in 1 year and still graduated with honors.

Bacon died prematurely on April 4, 1972, at the age of 56, of Lassa Fever, a disease first identified in Lassa, Nigeria. At the time of Esther's illness, there was no preventive vaccine and no cure. She was buried in a specially dug grave behind the new maternity ward at Zorzor. The depth of the people's love for her was never better demonstrated than in the days following her death and at her funeral. Jeanette Isaacson, a fellow nurse at Zorzor, says that the townspeople passed the shovel around, and "no man dug more than one shovel of dirt that day," including the Mandingoes, a Muslim tribe.

Long before she died, Esther Bacon was recognized by her fellow workers—Africans and missionaries alike—as a living legend. But she was neither legend nor myth. She was a real person in blue slacks on a brown horse carrying a kerosene lantern through a green tunnel of jungle to save the lives of a mother and her unborn child. She was, as Bishop Payne, a native-born Bishop, once said, an outlaw—an outlaw for God—who would break any and every rule in the book if it would save a life.

BIBLIOGRAPHY

Dibble, J. B. (1992). *Outlaw for God.* Hanover, MA: Christoper Publishing.

J. Birney Dibble

VIRGINIA BARCKLEY
1911–1993

In the 1940s, Virginia Barckley saw herself as a "young, visiting nurse in Philadelphia, perky in her navy uniform and white pique dicky" when she attended a meeting at the Bellevue Stratford Hotel in Philadelphia sponsored by the American Cancer Society. The discussion was on "terminal cancer"—in the common verbiage of the times. Much later, she would recall that "you couldn't be a visiting nurse without seeing a great deal of cancer, and you couldn't see a great deal of cancer, especially in the 1940's, without being deeply touched and deeply impressed." Her passion for cancer nursing, she said, evolved and became a part of her perhaps without her even knowing it, to the point where "somewhere inside you decide something's got to be done, and I want to be one of the people who do it." Barckley did change the way nurses view cancer and approach cancer care.

Virginia Barckley, a native of Burlington, New Jersey, was born on November 19, 1911. Her mother, Ethel Smith Barckley, was a homemaker; her father, George Force Barckley worked as a foundry inspector in a pipemaking plant in Burlington. Virginia had one sibling, her older brother, James Wilson Barckley. Barckley completed her nurse's training at Flushing Hospital in Long Island, New York, and a received a B.S. in Public Health Nursing from the University of Pennsylvania in 1943. While working towards the B.S., Barckley worked for the Philadelphia Visiting Nurses Association, and started her lengthy service to the American Cancer Society as a volunteer. She received her master's degree in mental health nursing, from Catholic University, Washington, D.C. From there, she filled many and varied roles, including head and supervising nurse, public health coordinator, and mental health nurse in Pennsylvania, Michigan, New York, and New Jersey. In 1957, the Pennsylvania State Department of Health appointed Barckley as its Mental Health Nursing Consultant. In 1962, Barckley joined the staff of the American Cancer Society (ACS) as National Nursing Consultant, a position she held for 18 years, until her retirement in 1981.

The enormous contributions Barckley made to cancer care in general and oncology nursing in particular reflect her personal motto "do more than you have to." She was a member of Sigma Theta Tau, and constantly urged nurses to do research, and to write. Throughout her lifetime, Barckley was a prolific writer, contributing to professional journals, ACS publications, and other texts and publications. In 1959, the League of Nursing published her book *The Play's the Thing*, a collection of skits and original discussions about nursing. Another book, *Cancer Nursing: Information and Concepts*, was distributed to cancer nurses in underdeveloped and developing countries by the International Union Against Cancer.

As a visiting nurse in the 1940s, young Barckley witnessed the suffering of patients and families—suffering caused by ignorance about cancer. Women with uterine cancer were humiliated by the stigma, believing they had done something wrong to get "*that* kind of cancer." Deadly delays in diagnosis were the result of efforts to protect themselves and their families from humiliation.

The only treatment for cancer during these years was surgery, and survival rates were a dismal 25%. Radiation therapy as an accepted treatment modality was not introduced until the early 1950s. When chemotherapy was first used in the mid-1950s, it was unthinkable that a nurse should ever administer it. The word "cancer" was rarely used, and nurses were prohibited from talking about diagnosis, prognosis, or details of the illness, with their patients. Most hospitalized cancer patients were in terminal stages, and successful symptom control was next to impossible. Not surprisingly, providing care to patients with cancer was at the bottom of student nurses' lists of professional aspirations. Cancer care "consisted of nothing but hard, depressing work with failure at the end."

During her tenure with the ACS, Barckley traveled to all 50 states and many foreign countries in her Professional Education and Service roles. In cooperation with the ACS, Memorial Sloan-Kettering, Roswell Park, and M.D. Anderson Cancer Centers, Barckley and Renilda Hilkemeyer, Director of Nursing at Anderson, created the ACS Work Study Program in Cancer Nursing that would eventually be incorporated into clinical experiences for student nurses. By 1966, Barckley had developed a program to improve care of cancer patients in nursing homes. In 1974, she authored a script for a prizewinning film, "The Nursing Management of Children with Cancer," revised the ACS publication *A Cancer Source Book for Nurses*, and authored the chapters on nursing.

In 1973, Barckley and Hilkemeyer planned and produced the first American

Cancer Society National Conference on Cancer Nursing. They had expected a maximum of 100 nurses: there were 2,500 registrants. This meeting provided the catalyst needed by a small group of registrants who would go on to establish the Oncology Nursing Society. Both served as an advisory board member to the Oncology Nursing Society during its formative stages. The World Health Organization invited the two pioneers to organize the First National Nursing Conference in Peru; again, the 400 registrants exceeded expectations. In 1978, Barckley chaired the first nursing workshop to be included in the program, and also presented a paper, at the International Cancer Congress in Buenos Aires.

In 1975, Barckley established an ACS scholarship program that would provide support for continuing education at cancer centers for nursing faculty. She laid the foundation for a curriculum guide for the oncology nursing specialty master's degree in 1979, and in 1981, the ACS approved funding for the nursing scholarship program, which as of this writing funded over 400 nurses at the master's and doctoral levels.

Barckley received several significant awards and citations starting with the 1961 ACS Citation of Merit. In 1981, she became the first honorary member of the Association of Pediatric Oncology Nurses. The Memorial Sloan-Kettering Cancer Center awarded her its Centennial Medal for Lifelong Achievement in 1984, and she was given the Distinguished Merit Award of the International Society of Nurses in Cancer Care in 1986.

Barckley, who never married, was cared for during the last 5 months of her life by her niece, Ann Callahan. She died in her own home on January 15, 1993, and was buried next to her mother and father in Burlington, New Jersey. Virginia Barckley's collection of papers and professional mementos have been donated to the Archives of the Oncology Nursing Society in Pittsburgh, Pennsylvania.

Virginia Barckley dedicated over 40 years of her life to the American Cancer Society and the specialty of oncology nursing. She continues to touch the lives of generations of cancer nurses, and the patient and families in their care, throughout the world.

PUBLICATIONS BY VIRGINIA BARCKLEY (SELECTED)

Barckley, V. (1959). *The play's the thing. Ten skits.* New York: National League for Nursing.

Barckley, V. (1963). *A cancer source book for nurses.* New York: American Cancer Society.

Barckley, V. (1965). New ideas about old problems. *CA: A Cancer Journal for Clinicians, 15,* 232–233.

Barckley, V. (1965). The visiting nurse and the patient with cancer. *CA: A Cancer Journal for Clinicians, 15,* 189–190.

Barckley, V. (1967). The crises in cancer. *American Journal of Nursing, 67,* 278–280.

Barckley, V. (1968). Grief, a part of living. *Ohio's Health, 20,* 34–38.

Barckley, V. (1969). Occupational health and cancer: A pair with potential. *Occupational Health Nursing, 17,* 9–12.

Barckley, V. (1970a). Cancer consultant to nursing homes. *American Journal of Nursing, 70,* 804–806.

Barckley, V. (1970b). A visiting nurse specializes in cancer nursing. *American Journal of Nursing, 70,* 1680–1683.

Barckley, V. (1971). Work study program in cancer nursing. *Nursing Outlook, 19,* 328–330.

Barckley, V. (1974a). Caring for the cancer patient at home. *Journal of Practical Nursing, 24,* 24–27.

Barckley, V. (1974b). Putting it all together with information and counseling. In *Proceedings of the National Conference on Cancer Nursing* (pp. 138–140). New York: American Cancer Society.

Barckley, V. (1975). Childhood leukemia: Its changing aspects. *Journal of Practical Nursing, 25,* 24–27.

Barckley, V. (1979). *The nursing management of children with cancer* [film]. New York: American Cancer Society.

Barckley, V. (1980). *Basic concepts in cancer nursing.* Geneva: International Union Against Cancer.

Barckley, V., Bettinger, A., Guenther, L. A., & Ross, R. M. (1958). Arthritis and a narrow perspective do not mix. *Nursing Outlook, 6,* 638–639

Barckley, V., & Campbell, E. I. (1959). Helping the handicapped child achieve emotional maturity. *American Journal of Nursing, 59,* 376–379

BIBLIOGRAPHY

Barckley, V. (1985). The best of times and the worst of times: Historical reflections from an American Cancer Society National Nursing Consultant. *Oncology Nursing Forum,* Supplement 12(1), 16–18.

Johnson, J. (Ed.). (1985). *Those were hard days* [video recording]. Pittsburgh, PA: Oncology Nursing Society.

Zanca, J. (1993). Virginia Barckley: A lifetime of service, as told by her lifelong friend, Renilda Hilkemeyer. *Cancer Nursing News, 11*(4), 1–2.

Pamela J. Haylock
With the Assistance of
Mark Vrabel

JEAN BARRETT
1903–1993

Jean Barrett served on the faculty of the Yale University School of Nursing, and was the founding director of the nursing program at Syracuse University. Her writing reflects her concern for the role of the nurse in administrative positions.

Born in San Francisco, October 4, 1903, she was the daughter of Eugene Thompson Barrett and Eva Marie Benton Barrett. She was the second of three sisters; the others were Mary Barrett (Clyde) and Harriet Barrett (Finch).

Barrett decided to enter nursing at age 12, when she visited her grandmother who suffered a fractured femur. She never wavered from this intent, and after she enrolled in college, she selected courses with that in mind.

After graduating from the Anoka, Minnesota High School, she entered Upper Iowa University at Fayette. Here she majored in chemistry, and received a B.A. in 1924. She then enrolled in the Iowa Methodist Hospital School of Nursing in Des Moines, Iowa, receiving her diploma in 1926. Upon completion of the nursing program, she did 9 months of private duty nursing, then went to a 35-bed hospital in Washington, Iowa, where she taught nursing arts, obstetric and pediatric nursing, and was operating room supervisor.

Two years later she moved to the Decatur-Macon County (Illinois) Hospital School of Nursing as instructor in nursing arts. She left to attend Teachers College, Columbia University, where she came under the influence of Isabel Stewart and Martha Ruth Smith, both of whom broadened her concept of the role of the nurse in the provision of patient care.

Barrett completed her M.A. in nursing administration in 1931, and then took a position as an administrative supervisor at the New Haven Hospital, with a courtesy faculty appointment at the Yale University School of Nursing. Over the next 12 years, as first an assistant and later an associate professor of nursing, she taught ward management to graduates and senior students in the School of Nursing.

In 1948 she was named professor and chairman, department of nursing education, Syracuse University, where she founded a nursing program and developed a baccalaureate program for registered professional nurses and, in 1950, graduate programs in clinical teaching and nursing service administration leading to a Master of Science (Nursing Education) degree.

Returning to Yale University School of Nursing she was named Annie W. Goodrich Professor in 1963–1964 and was appointed assistant dean in 1968. She retired 3 years later.

Barrett was interested in international aspects of nursing, and in 1952 served as a nursing consultant for nurse teachers in Formosa (Taiwan) under the auspices of the Western Pacific Region of the World Health Organization (WHO). This led to a number of Taiwanese students attending Syracuse University. She served as a member of the Expert Advisory Panel on Nursing, WHO, from 1951 to 1961. In the summer of 1965, she conducted nursing projects in Teheran, Iran and Alexandria,

Egypt. She was also a member of the National Citizen's Committee for the United Nations. While in Syracuse, Barrett was presented the Woman of Achievement in Health Award by the *Syracuse Post Standard.*

Throughout her career Barrett was concerned with the role of the head nurse, and its impact on patient care. This is evident in the textbooks she wrote.

After retirement, she moved to Eugene, Oregon, where her sister lived. She did some traveling, but her activities were limited as her eyesight grew progressively worse. Jean Barrett died in Eugene on November 20, 1993.

PUBLICATIONS BY JEAN BARRETT

Books

Ward management and teaching. (1949). New York: Appeton-Century-Crofts. (2nd ed. published 1954).
with B. A. Gessner & C. Phelps, *The head nurse.* (1975). New York: Appleton-Century-Crofts.

Articles (Selected)

Simplifying nursing procedures. (1943). *American Journal of Nursing, 43,* 713–716.
How to obtain a degree. *American Journal of Nursing, 49,* 598–600.
Administrative factors in development of new practice roles. *Journal of Nursing Administration, 1,* 25–29.
The nurse specialist practitioner: A study. *Nursing Outlook, 20,* 524–527.

BIBLIOGRAPHY

Barrett, J. Curriculum vita, Yale University School of Nursing.
Barrett, J. (1992, March 16). (Telephone interview with author).
Jean Barrett. (1971). *Who's Who of American Women.* Chicago: A. N. Marquis.
News for nurses: Nursing Department at Syracuse. (1947). *Trained Nurse and Hospital Review, 119,* 90.

Signe S. Cooper

MARJORIE BARTHOLF
1899–1986

Marjorie Bartholf was born January 7, 1899 in Chicago, the daughter of Charles Stephen and Grace Corrine (Bullock) Bartholf. Bartholf graduated from the University of Wisconsin in 1920 with a baccalaureate in economics. After this she enrolled in the Evanston (Illinois) Hospital Training School for Nurses and graduated with a diploma in nursing in 1925. She held a variety of positions over the next decade as a head nurse in Evanston Hospital; visiting nurse, Evanston; staff nurse, Infant Welfare, Health Department, Evanston; obstetrics supervisor, St. Luke's Hospital, Kansas City, Missouri; clinical instructor, the Elizabeth McGee Hospital; assistant professor, Yale School of Nursing; and assistant director, The Cook County School of Nursing, Chicago, Illinois. She was awarded a master's degree in nursing education from the University of Chicago in 1937.

Marjorie Bartholf

In 1942, the College of Nursing of the Medical Branch, University of Texas had undergone a great deal of strife resulting in the departure of the head of the School. The president of the University, President Rainey, was looking for another administrator. He communicated with the Dean of the Yale University School of Nursing. She gave him the name of Marjorie Bartholf, who had taught at Yale School of Nursing. Bartholf accepted the position, arriving in Galveston in October 1942 to serve as administrator of the nursing program at the Medical Branch. She found on arriving that the tremendous resources and potential for the program had not been tapped. It was a challenge that she could not resist.

Within 3 years Bartholf was able to achieve the goal of separating the administration of the College from the hospital. In 1945, the Department of Nursing, which had been in the College of Education at the main university in Austin, was administratively transferred to the Galveston campus. The College of Nursing was reorganized, and Bartholf became the Dean.

After the School was reorganized in 1948, it was approved for membership in the Association of Collegiate Schools of Nursing. The basic professional program was accredited by the National League for Nursing Education in January 1949, and the name of the School appeared in the first list published by the National Nursing Accrediting Service in the *American Journal of Nursing*. Bartholf was a member of the committee that, in 1949, established higher standards for graduate education (master's) which would increase the differentiation between the programs leading to a baccalaureate degree, and those leading to a master's degree. Bartholf was consistently in the forefront in increasing standards of education and practice for nurses.

In 1952, six Southern universities joined together to plan master's degree programs in nursing, under the sponsorship of the Southern Regional Education Board. Those universities were: The University of Alabama, Emory University, The University of Maryland, University of North Carolina, the University of Texas, and Vanderbilt University. The Commonwealth Fund and the W.K. Kellogg Foundation funded this project.

In January 1952, Bartholf was appointed by the State Board of Nurse Examiners to a committee formed to study the feasibility of the 2-year program in basic nursing. In March 1952, the faculty approved a recommendation made by the Basic Curriculum Committee to shorten the diploma program to 2 years. Because of policies and legislation regulating licensure in Texas, the 2-year program was not immediately put into effect. The modified program, referred to as a Junior Staff Program, was started with diploma students entering the School in 1954. The program was designed so that the required didactic work was given in the first 2 years.

Bartholf made many changes in the School of Nursing to improve the quality of education for the students there, and to improve the quality of nursing being provided at the Medical Branch. She had visions of the future for nursing, and she was tenacious in her efforts to improve the nursing programs offered by the University. Profound changes were brought about during the 21 years in which she was administrator of the School. She was a pioneer in nursing education. During the time she was administrator of the School of Nursing, she changed many long-held traditions at the University. She led the change of the school from an indistinct degree at the University main campus, to a program of education for nursing students completely on one campus. She brought a vision of creativity, enthusiasm, and expectation of excellence to the program. Her contribution to nursing education during the time she was administrator, first as Director of nursing service, and then Dean of the nursing program, is legend. She broke the barrier for Black nursing students, in Texas, by admit-

ting them to a previously all-White nursing program. She opened the nursing program to minority students, first to nursing affiliates from Prairie View A & M, and then in the generic program at the School of Nursing. She introduced graduate education in nursing in Texas, and was influential in establishing graduate education in Schools of Nursing in the Southern Region. She was open to experimentation in the diploma program, which allowed for some of the first work in Texas, in converting a diploma program from a 3-calendar-year, to a 2–year preparation time. She was a leader in improving standards of nursing education, not only in her own school, and in the state, but also nationally. During the time she was administrator of the School, she was a recognized leader in nursing through out the United States. She was a risk-taker and a person with vision. Her contributions to the advancement of the profession were recognized in undergraduate, graduate, and continuing education. She established a foundation for excellence in curriculum in the University of Texas Medical Branch at Galveston School of Nursing. Bartholf served as President of both the Texas League for Nursing and the Texas Nurses Association.

To honor her for her many contributions to the profession, the American Association of Colleges of Nursing recognized her with Honorary Associate Status, February 19, 1986. She was unable to attend. Marjorie Bartholf died in Annapolis, Maryland on December 10, 1986, where she had moved to be near her sister. She was 87 years old when she died. Her ashes were scattered in the Gulf off the Galveston Coast by her sister and by two of the graduates of the School who had known her during the time she was dean of the School of Nursing.

BIBLIOGRAPHY

University of Texas Board of Regents. (1941). *Minutes,* July 26, 1941 to August 8, 1942, 1 August 1942, p. 487.

Hawkinson, N. X. (1942, July 15). Letter to President Rainey, University of Texas. Presidential-Chancellor's Archives.

Bartholf, M. (1942, 10 August). Letter to President Rainey, University of Texas. Presidential-Chancellor's Archives, University of Texas.

Brown, B. (1974). Personal interviews with Marjorie Bartholf, 6 May and 27 December.

Information was obtained from records of the American Association of Colleges of Nursing, and from Official Publications, Reports, and Documents of The University of Texas.

Additional information was gained in conversation with Virginia Jarratt and Chloe Floyd, who are graduates of the School of Nursing, and who had known Bartholf since she arrived in Galveston to administer the School.

Billye J. Brown

Irene L. Beland

IRENE L. BELAND
1906–

Irene L. Beland was a scholar, scientist, educator, author, and consultant renowned for promoting a problem-oriented and conceptual approach in educating nurses. This approach was revolutionary for the time and continues to be useful as a means of organizing a vast amount of material into a meaningful whole. In addition, she viewed the person who is ill as a total individual, not a sick arm, leg, or heart. Beland emphasized the application of basic principles of normal physiology as well as pathophysiology, including psychological, emotional, and later spiritual relationships in clinical nursing throughout her writings. Her book on clinical nursing incorporated the basic principles of science and explained the rationale for the design and implementation of nursing and medical interventions. This conceptual approach always attempted to answer the question "Why?" In an interview, she placed much importance on generalizations, while "advising us to take from the altar of knowledge the fire, not the ashes."

Beland was born on June 21, 1906, in Loda, Illinois, daughter of William A. and Kathryn Ryran Beland. As the eldest of nine children, Irene's early years on the farm were filled with many responsibilities. Two of her brothers were afflicted with polio, survived, and lived their lives—one as a paraplegic and one as a quadriplegic. Irene also experienced a critical illness, having suffered and survived a ruptured appendix. Perhaps it was these early experiences that contributed to her desire to become a nurse.

In 1913, the Beland family moved from their farm in Illinois to another farm in Osage, Iowa, as Irene was entering the second grade. She completed all of her elementary and secondary education in this farming community. Upon completion of high school, which included normal training to prepare teachers, Beland taught in a country school for 2 years but did not enjoy teaching young children, and very much wanted to become a nurse despite her father's opposition.

Ultimately, she wore down her father's opposition, and at the age of 20, she entered St. Mary's Hospital school of Nursing in Rochester, Minnesota. Three years later she earned a diploma in nursing. As a student, Beland did some teaching and tutoring along the way, and was encouraged by one of the sisters to continue her education at the university.

She served as an instructor at the Eitel Hospital School of Nursing, took a course in how to teach nursing arts, and attended the University of Minnesota part time, developing a strong interest in the sciences. When a change in administration occurred in the department of her interest at the University of Minnesota, Irene applied and was accepted into the department of physiology and biochemistry. Beland received both her B.S. and M.S. degrees from the University of Minnesota, in 1937 and 1938 respectively.

She taught Medical Nursing at the University of Minnesota from 1938 to 1940. From 1940 to 1947, she supervised clinical instruction at St. Mary's Hospital School of Nursing and was a teaching supervisor in Medical Nursing at Minneapolis General Hospital.

In 1947, she joined the faculty of the College of Nursing, Wayne State University, Detroit Michigan. At Wayne State, Beland's networks enlarged as the college of nursing began to develop graduate programs. In 1965, her first edition of *Clinical Nursing* was published. This was one of the first books to use a conceptual, holistic approach in organizing nursing knowledge. Considering her approach to teaching nursing, it is not surprising that one of Beland's former pupils, Myra Levine, went on to develop conservation principles as a means of organizing nursing knowledge.

Beland was always open to new experiences. She traveled to both Chili and Peru as a consultant in nursing education while under the sponsorship of the Kellogg Foundation, the U.S. State Department, and the Rockefeller Foundation. Among other things, she developed one of the country's first graduate programs to prepare medical-surgical nursing specialists. She authored or co-authored four editions of *Clinical Nursing*, contributed articles to many nursing journals, and authored chapters for other textbooks.

Beland served on many cancer programs for the Metropolitan Detroit Cancer Control, was a member of the Detroit Nurses Association, and served as co-chairperson of the Medical Advisory Panel for Rehabilitation and Continuing Care. In 1963, she was the first faculty member in the Department of Medical-Surgical Nursing at Wayne State to be promoted to the rank of Professor. Following her retirement in 1970, Beland was a Visiting Professor of Nursing at the University of Wisconsin, Madison for one semester.

In 1983, Beland was formally admitted as an honorary fellow of the American Academy of Nursing. In 1998, at the age of 92, she continues to reside at Madonna Towers, a retirement home located in Rochester, Minnesota. She will long be remembered for her contributions to establishing a scientific basis of nursing. She possessed a creative mind and was always concerned with the improvement of patient care. Beland had a tremendous impact on nursing practice and education throughout the world; she was a pioneer in the preparation of advanced practice nurses in graduate nursing education. She was indeed a lady ahead of her time!

PUBLICATIONS BY IRENE L. BELAND

Books

Clinical nursing: Pathophysiological and psychosocial approaches. (1965). New York: Macmillan. (1st edition, 1965; 2nd edition, with Passos, J., 1970; 3rd edition, 1975; 4th edition, 1981).

With Abdellah, F., Martin, A., & Matheney, R. (1973). *New directions in patient centered nursing.* New York: Macmillan.

Articles (Selected)

Report of South American Trip. (1952). Prepared for the W. K.Kellogg Foundation and Department of State, Detroit, Michigan.

A Project in Evaluation. (1955). *Nursing Outlook, 3,* 35–37.

BIBLIOGRAPHY

Beland, I. L. (1970). Preface. In I. L. Beland & J. Passos (Eds.), *Clinical nursing: Pathophysiological and psychosocial approaches* (2nd ed.). New York: Macmillan.

Biographical data. (1978). *American Nurses Library.*

News Release. (1983, August 25). *American Nurses Library.*

Beland, I. L. (1998, April). [Telephone interview with the author].

Heimer, M., Beland, R., & Beland, J. W. (1998, April). [Telephone interview with the author].

Monahan, K. (1998, April). [Telephone interview with the author].

Gloria J. Smokvina

MARY ELLEN BIRTLES
1859–1943

Mary Ellen Birtles played a significant role in shaping pioneer nursing in western Canada. She was one of the first generation of Canadian trained nurses and one, moreover, who demonstrated the worth of trained nursing at both of the first two hospitals in what later came to be the province of Alberta. These were the Medicine Hat General Hospital, begun in 1890, and the Calgary General Hospital, begun in 1891.

Prior to 1905, when the prairie provinces of Saskatchewan and Alberta were created, the vast tract of land which stretched west for over 800 miles from the Manitoba border to British Columbia, and almost 2000 miles south from the Arctic Ocean to the northern border of the United States, was known as the North-West Territories. The

Mary Ellen Birtles

North-West Territories did not attract large numbers of settlers until the end of the 19th century, in comparison to the American frontier, which had largely settled by the mid-1890s. The prairie provinces of Alberta and Saskatchewan constituted Canada's "last best West," encompassing the only unsettled agricultural land remaining in the Dominion before the first world war.

Mary Ellen Birtles was born in 1859 at Hepworth, a village near Holmfirth in Yorkshire, England, where she spent her early childhood. Her father, Joseph, was Master of an Endowed School before emigrating to Canada in 1883 to take up farming near Brandon, Manitoba. Mary Ellen taught school for several years as her father's assistant. She and her sister Sarah entered the 72-bed Winnipeg General Hospital in 1886 "to learn nursing," although there was no training school then. Birtles was immediately put on night duty on the women's ward with five patients and remained there for 5 months. Nurses lived in different parts of the hospital, including the basement. Birtles described her training as "altogether practical, sometimes we got a little instruction from the doctor on his rounds. . . . But we were fortunate in finding some books in a second-hand book store, on anatomy and physiology; from these we studied, together with a book on nursing by Florence Nightingale.[1] When a training school was formed on October 1, 1887, Mary Ellen, her sister Sarah, a Miss McDougall, and four new probationers were admitted. Birtles and the two older nurses wrote their first examinations in May 1889, and graduated in September.

After graduation, Birtles went to a small hospital in North Dakota, staying only a few months before accepting the position of "assistant" at the just-completed Medicine Hat General Hospital, North-West Territories, in what later became the province of Alberta. Her supervisor was Grace Reynolds, a former staff nurse from Winnipeg General Hospital, and the two trained nurses comprised the entire hospital staff; their duties included cooking, cleaning, laundry, and stoking the basement furnace, in addition to looking after patients. Medicine Hat was a divisional point in the Canadian Pacific Railway, so that a large number of hospital patients were injured railway men and a large proportion of the work was surgery. When an operation had to be done, Reynolds gave the anaesthetic and Birtles looked after the instruments and waited on the doctor.

In 1892, a new hospital opened in Brandon, Manitoba, and Birtles took the position of head nurse in October. Her next move was to Calgary in 1894, to become Matron of the new 25-bed Calgary General Hospital. Birtles arrived in Calgary in September to find the cornerstone for the new stone hospital just being laid. She assumed responsibility for the old house which had been used as a hospital and where the din-

ing room also served as the operating room, with the extension dining table for operations.

She began a nurse training program in 1894 with probationer Marion Moody, who was soon joined by six other probationers. They became the nucleus of the Calgary General Hospital Training School, which remained in operating for the next 80 years. Domestic help was hard to get, so that Birtles and her nursing staff often did some of the cleaning and cooking, as well as stoking the furnace and attending to the hydraulic pump for raising water to the storage tank in the upper part of the hospital. Birtles also supervised the hospital dispensary, where she made her own solutions and simple prescriptions from raw supplies.

In 1897, Birtles took a few months leave of absence from the Calgary General to attend the Diamond Jubilee celebrations of Queen Victoria in England. She remained 4 years at the Calgary General before returning to take charge of the Brandon General Hospital in 1898. Birtles remained at the Brandon General until her retirement in 1919. When the Manitoba Association of Graduate Nurses formed in 1913, she was appointed a charter member. In recognition of the part she had played in shaping pioneer nursing in western Canada, Birtles was awarded the Order of the British Empire in 1935. She died June 22, 1943 after a lengthy illness.

NOTES

1. Johns, E. (n.d.). *The Winnipeg General Hospital School of Nursing, 1887–1953* (Winnipeg, Man.: The Alumnae Association, The Winnipeg General Hospital School of Nursing, n.d.), 10.

BIBLIOGRAPHY

Biographical file, Mary Ellen Birtles, Medicine Hat Museum and Art Gallary Archives, Medicine Hat, Alberta.

Birtles, W. (1995). A pioneer nurse. *Alberta History,* *43,* 2–6.

Dirk, M. M. C. (1989). *A healthy outlook: The centennial history of the Medicine Hat Regional Hospital* (pp. 7–38). Medicine Hat, Alberta, Canada: Holmes Printing.

Gibbon, J. M., & Mathewson, M. S. (1947). Chapter XXV: Alberta Up to 1914. In *Three centuries of Canadian nursing* (pp. 216–226). Toronto: Macmillan.

Johns, E. (n.d.). *The Winnipeg General Hospital School of Nursing, 1887–1953.* Winnipeg: The Alumnae Association, The Winnipeg General Hospital School of Nursing.

Sharon Richardson

Ruby Grace Bradley

RUBY GRACE BRADLEY
1907–

Ruby Grace Bradley enjoyed a singular career in the Army Nurse Corps. Beginning with her assignment in 1933 as a Civilian Conservation Corps nurse at Walter Reed General Hospital in Washington D.C., through her retirement from the military on 31 March 1963, Colonel Bradley established a remarkable record, including internment as a Japanese Prisoner of War in the Philippine Islands from 1941 to 1945; front-line service in the Korean War from 1950 through 1953; one of three women officers to hold the Regular Army permanent rank of Colonel in 1958; and at her retirement, the distinction of being the most decorated woman in the history of our country.

Ruth Bradley was born December 19, 1907 in Spencer, West Virginia, the fifth of six children, four girls and two boys, to Fred and Bertha Bradley. After high school, she received a teaching certificate from Biddle State College in Glenville, West Virginia, and returned home to a position in a local elementary school. Her long-term interest in nursing was further sparked by her concern over the health care of the rural children in her classroom. After 4 years, she left teaching, and in 1933 graduated from the Philadelphia General Hospital School of Nursing.

Scarce jobs in rural nursing during the Great Depression led Bradley in December 1933 to the government-sponsored Civilian Conservation Corps and a position as a civilian staff nurse at Walter Reed Hospital in Washington, D.C. On October 16, 1934, Bradley joined the Army Nurse Corps (N 702 770) where, after serving at Walter Reed for six years, she received orders for her first overseas tour, arriving in the Philippines on Valentine's Day in 1940.

Her assignment was to Camp John Hay in Baguio, 200 miles north of Manila in Luzon's Cordillera Central Mountains, the unofficial summer capital and retreat for wealthy Americans. When Japanese pilots made their initial attack in the Philippines at 8:19 a.m. on December 8, 1941 (December 7 U.S. time) on the Camp John Hay, Bradley became the first military nurse under fire in the Philippine Islands. On December 23rd, Bradley joined the other besieged Americans attempting an escape into the surrounding mountains. The men in her party felt that they stood a better chance of outmaneuvering the Japanese without women to slow them down, so Bradley and the other Army nurse from John Hay, Beatrice Chambers, returned to Baguio with a group of civilians and surrendered on 29 December 29, 1941.

The two military nurses joined interned civilian doctors and a dentist to set up a camp hospital. After the Japanese moved their prisoners to Camp Holmes in Baguio, Bradley and two physicians were driven back to John Hay by a Japanese soldier to get toilet paper. However, she found surgical instruments and hemostats and tucked this bundle under her dress. The unsuspecting driver ordered Bradley into the front seat where she sat nervously on the bumpy ride back. As soon as the truck pulled in front of the POW barracks, Bradley climbed off the truck and ran into the building, telling people she had to use the bathroom. She hid the bundle under the mattress of a sick internee. When the Japanese began to search the three Americans, Bradley pulled out bare pockets and showed her empty dress hem.

For the next year and a half, Ruby Bradley and Beatrice Chambers remained isolated. They saw no visitors or heard any outside news. In September 1943, she joined 64 Army nurses imprisoned at Santo Tomas Interment Camp in Manila where she remained until liberation in February 1945.

After the war, Bradley was promoted to 1st Lieutenant (February 18, 1945) and Captain (October 27, 1945). Over the next 5 years, she served at several stateside hospitals and on 27 July 1950 she reported to Fort Bragg, North Carolina to assume the Chief Nurse position of the 171st Evacuation Hospital heading to Korea. On September 21, 1950 the unit arrived in Taegu, Korea. The hospital moved around the front lines with Bradley supervising her nursing staff as they worked with fresh battle casualties. In November 1950, while the 171st was set up near Pyongyau, Bradley almost became a POW again as the entry of the Chinese into the war forced an evacuation. Later, she learned that her presence in Pyongyau had caused military leaders great anxiety. They told the evacuating troops to get Bradley out of the danger zone because it would be a public relations disaster for the United States and a propaganda bonanza for the enemy if she were captured again.

Bradley left 171st in the summer of 1951 to the Chief Nurse of the Eight U.S. Army Far East Command. She was responsible for overseeing the work of approximately 500 Army nurses who served at various hospital facilities in Korea and frequently traveled back to the front lines. On July 23, 1952 she was promoted to Lieutenant Colonel and in June 1953, with the truce talks under way in Panmunjon, she prepared to leave Korea. General Maxwell Taylor, Commander of the 8th Army, recognized her 3-year contribution to the allied war efforts with awards, medals, and a large international military review and parade, an unusual honor for a nurse.

For the second time, Bradley returned to West Virginia as a celebrated heroine and received many tributes from the civilian world, including: the 1953 Virginia Distinguished Service Medal, the 1954 West Virginia Society of Washington D.C. Daughter of the Year, and an honorary Doctor of Science degree from West Virginia University. Ralph Edwards, the host of a popular television show, "This is Your Life," devoted his 10 February 1954 show to her. Afterwards the National Broadcasting Company, which aired Edwards' show, set up a scholarship in her name at her alma mater, Philadelphia General Hospital.

On March 4, 1958, Ruby Bradley joined Inez Haynes and Ruby Bryant as the first women officers in the Regular Army to hold the permanent rank of Colonel.

When Colonel Bradley retired from the Army on 31 March 1963 at the age of 55, she had earned more military distinctions than any other woman who ever served her country. This achievement remains unmatched to the present day.

Upon leaving the service, Bradley bought a small ranch home near her West Virginia relatives, and for 17 years worked inconspicuously for a private duty nursing service, assigning nurses to care for patients in hospitals or private homes. To the present time, Army officials and veteran organization leaders call on her to speak at fund raisers, recruitment affairs, and official ceremonies. At the age of 90, Bradley still continues to appear at events.

MILITARY HONORS

From World War II

Bronze Star Medal
World War II Victory Medal
American Defense Service Medal with one Bronze Star and Foreign Service Clasp
Asiatic-Pacific Campaign Medal with two Bronze Battle Stars
Distinguished Unit Badge, Presidential Unit Emblem with two Oak Leaf Clusters on Blue Ribbon
Philippine Defense Ribbon with one Bronze Service Star
Philippine Liberation Ribbon with one Bronze Service Star
American Campaign Medal and American Theater Ribbon
Philippine Independence Ribbon

From the Korean War until Retirement

American of Occupation Medal with Japan Clasp

National Defense Service Medal
Korean Service Medal with one silver service star (in lieu of five Bronze Service Stars). Two Bronze Service Stars for participation in the UN Offensive, Chinese Communist Forces Intervention, UN Summer-Fall Offensive, Second Korean Winter, Korea-Summer-Fall 1952, Third Korean Winter and Korea Summer-Fall 1953.
United Nations Service Medal
Legion of Merit with an Oak Leaf Cluster
Oak Leaf Cluster for Bronze Star Medal
Commendation Ribbon with Metal Pendant

BIBLIOGRAPHY

Bradley, R. (no date). *Prisoners of war in the Far East* [Unpublished]. Washington, DC: Center for Military History, Army Nurse Corps Archives.
Bradley, R. G. (1989, April 13). (Personal communication)
Miller-Moore, C. (n.d.). [Army Nurse Corps Oral History Program Interview] Ruby Bradley. Washington, DC: Center for Military History, Army Nurse Corps Archives.
Piemonte, R., & Gurney, C. (Eds.). (1987). *Highlights in the history of the Army Nurse Corps*. Washington, DC: U.S. Center for Military History.

Elizabeth M. Norman

BILLYE JEAN BROWN
1925–

Billye Jean Brown has exerted her leadership in nursing as Dean of The University of Texas at Austin School of Nursing and as a hardworking member of various nursing and nursing education organizations. She developed her political skills through a network of committees at the local, state, and national levels and utilized them to bring about changes to strengthen nursing by strengthening its organizations and its educational institutions.

Billye Jean Brown was born in Damascus, Arkansas, on October 29, 1925, the youngest of five children of William A. and Dora Megee Brown. She attended high school in Little Rock in the 1940s and recalls meeting some nurses who influenced her to consider nursing as a career choice. She enrolled in the Arkansas Baptist Hospital School of Nursing under the Cadet Nurse Corps. As a senior nursing student she was selected to assist the nursing arts instructor with teaching nursing fundamentals which stimulated her interest in teaching. She received her diploma in nursing in 1947 and worked for a time at Baptist Hospital and then for a surgeon in Pine Bluff, Arkansas. In 1951 Brown moved to Galveston to enroll in the baccalaureate program in nursing education at the University of Texas. Completing this degree in 1953, she joined the faculty of the University of Texas Medical Branch at Galveston, teaching fundamentals of nursing and medical-surgical nursing. She entered the Master of Science in Nursing Education program at St. Louis University in 1957 and received her degree in 1958. She completed her Doctor of Education degree at Baylor University in Education Administration in 1975.

After her return to Galveston as Associate Professor of Nursing, Brown and a colleague, Mitzi Nuhn, were assigned to open a branch of the School of Nursing at Austin in 1960. She served as Associate Professor of Nursing at Austin until 1967 when the campus at Austin became part of the University of Texas System-wide School of Nursing. She was appointed Associate Dean and then, in 1972 when the School's organization once again changed, became Dean of the System-wide School of Nursing at Austin, a position that she held until her retirement in 1989. During her years at Austin, the University of Texas underwent system-wide reorganization, creating many changes within the Schools of Nursing and

requiring her leadership. Also, as dean, she was instrumental in establishing private endowments as sources of private funding for the School of Nursing at Austin.

In addition to serving on numerous committees of the Texas Nurses' Association, Brown served as President of District Six from 1958 to 1959 and President of the Association from 1966 to 1969. Brown served as a Director of the Executive Committee of the Southern Council on Collegiate Education in 1979 to 1981. She was elected to the Board of Directors of the American Journal of Nursing Company, serving from 1987 to 1995. She served as President of the American Association of Colleges of Nursing (AACN) in 1982 to 1984 and was Assistant Editor of the AACN publication, *The Journal of Professional Nursing* from 1985 to 1986. The AACN presented her with the Sister Bernadette Armiger Award and recognized her as an Emeritus Member in 1990.

Brown was appointed to the National Advisory Council on Nurse Training in 1983, serving until 1987; she also served as a Civilian National Consultant to the Surgeon General of the United States Air Force from 1983 to 1987. In Texas, she was a member of the Texas Higher Education Coordinating Board from 1984 until 1992 and has served as Vice-Chair for that body. In 1992 to 1994 Brown served as a core faculty member for Project FACE, a project funded by the Kellogg Foundation to consult with faculty in historically Black colleges and universities. From 1994 to 1997, Brown was a member of the Advisory Council of the Baylor University School of Nursing. She served as President of Sigma Theta Tau from 1989 to 1991.

In addition to her work with organizations and committees, Brown has consulted with numerous colleges and universities across the United States and has been much in demand as a speaker for commencements and nursing conferences. Her publications and presentations pertain to academic administration, leadership and followership, strategic planning, and resource development, and health care trends and history. Her contributions to the wider community include those to the American Red Cross, the YWCA, and Seton Cove, A Center for Spirituality and Living in Austin.

For her work in nursing and education, Brown has been honored by various groups and institutions. She has been given the Distinguished Alumnus Award by The University of Texas at Galveston and the Alumni Merit Award by St. Louis University. In 1990, The Baptist Medical System School of Nursing presented to her the Distinguished Alumna Award. In 1985, Epsilon Theta Chapter of Sigma Theta Tau International awarded her the Chapter's Mentor Award.

Her contributions to the Austin, Texas community were recognized by the Counseling and Pastoral Care Center of Austin and by the Austin "American Statesman" which, in 1985 named her as one of the city's most influential women in education. In 1989, Brown received the "American Spirit Award" of the United States Air Force Recruiting Services, the first nurse to be so honored. The University of Texas System appointed Brown to The Chancellor's Council of The University of Texas System. The Alumni Association of the School of Nursing at Austin presented to her the Founder's Award in 1991; in 1992 she was selected for the Hall of Fame, University of Texas School of Nursing at Galveston. Also in 1992, St. Joseph College, West Hartford Connecticut bestowed upon her an Honorary Doctorate, Doctor of Humane Letters.

After retirement, Brown continued to travel extensively on behalf of Sigma Theta Tau and as an invited speaker or consultant. When she is at home she enjoys working on her computer, tennis, yard work, and visiting with friends.

PUBLICATIONS BY BILLYE JEAN BROWN

Book Chapters

Browne, B. J. (1987). Strategic educational planning: A giant step into our future. In *Patterns in nursing: Strategic planning for nursing education* (pp. 153–160). New York: National League for Nursing.

Browne, B. J. (1989). Race for resources: Who can, does, and who should obtain them? In S. E. Hart (Ed.), *Doctoral education in nursing: History, process, and outcome* (pp. 33–54). New York: National League for Nursing.

Browne, B. J. (1999). Foreword. In G. Twiname & S. Boyd (Eds.), *Standard Nurse Handbook: Nursing highlights: Difficult concepts made easy*. Stanford, CT: Appleton & Lange.

Browne, B. J. (1998). Foreword. In E. K. Hermann (Ed.), *Virginia Henderson: Signature for nursing*. Indianapolis, IN: STTI Publications.

Articles (Selected)

Brown, B. J. (1980). Follow the leader. *Nursing Outlook, 28,* 357–359.

Browne, B. J., Lasher, W. F., & Embrey, C. L. (1979). A costing methodology for schools of nursing. *Nursing Outlook, 27,* 584–589.

BIBLIOGRAPHY

Brown, B. J. (1998, February 6). [Telephone interview].

Brown, B. J. (1998). *Brief biographical sketch of Billye J. Brown.* Unpublished.

Influx of new Virginia Henderson Fellows. (1997). *Reflections, 23*(2), 28.

Sullivan, E. J. (1997). Legacies of our past Presidents. *Reflections, 23*(3), 12–15.

Marian J. Brook

LILLIAN SHOLTIS BRUNNER
1919–

Lillian Sholtis Brunner is best known for her text, Lillian Brunner and Doris Suddarth *Textbook of Medical-Surgical Nursing,* first published by J. B. Lippincott Co., Philadelphia, PA, in 1964. It went through six editions under authors Brunner and Suddarth, the sixth being published in 1988, and has continued to appear under different authors with the title of *Brunner and Suddarth's Textbook of Medical-Surgical Nursing*. This text has been translated into seven languages and is used by students of nursing worldwide.

Lillian Sholtis Brunner

Additionally, Brunner and Suddarth authored the well-known, much utilized *Lippincott Manual of Nursing Practice*, first published in 1974.

Lillian Brunner was born Lillian Sholtis on March 29, 1919 in Freeland, a small community in eastern Pennsylvania. She was the oldest of two children of Anna (Tomasko) and Andrew J. Sholtis, having one younger brother. An early ambition of Brunner's was to be a teacher of mathematics and chemistry, her favorite subjects. A strong student, she completed four years of high school in three. "Never," stated Ms. Brunner recently, "did I want to be a nurse for the thought of it repelled me." How-

ever, when her father was hospitalized for a ruptured appendix, and Brunner spent time visiting him, her curiosity was piqued. Nursing, she reasoned, was a way to learn a marketable skill whereby she could then earn money to go to college to pursue her desire to teach.

In 1937, she entered the School of Nursing, Hospital of the University of Pennsylvania in Philadelphia, PA, receiving her diploma in 1940. Upon receiving her R.N., Brunner became Head Nurse in the Operating Room of the Hospital of the University of Pennsylvania, and by 1942, had become Supervisor of the Operating Room and concurrently Clinical Instructor for the nursing school. In 1944, Brunner became Head of the Fundamentals of Nursing Department of the School of Nursing. Concurrently she had enrolled in the School of Education, University of Pennsylvania, and in 1945 received her Bachelor of Science degree with a Nursing major.

Brunner's next step was to take a master's degree at the Frances Payne Bolton School of Nursing, Case Western Reserve University, Cleveland, Ohio.

In 1947, Brunner accepted a joint appointment as Assistant Professor of Surgical Nursing at the Yale University School of Nursing, and Administrative Surgical Supervisor, Yale-New Haven Hospital, New Haven, CT, a continuation of the close interweaving of administration and education that attracted Brunner. It was during this time that Brunner first became involved in writing when she signed on as third author of the well-known text *Surgical Nursing*.

In July 1951, Brunner resigned from Yale and married Mathias (Mat) Brunner in September, relocating to Swarthmore, PA, and became a full-time nurse author, rewriting *Surgical Nursing* as well as becoming Section Head of the Surgical Nursing section of the *Study Guide for Clinical Nursing*, the first edition of which was published in 1953. In 1951, Brunner published her first journal article, "Nursing the Elderly Surgical Patient," in the June issue of the American Journal of Nursing. Additionally, Brunner coauthored the text, *Teaching Medical and Surgical Nursing*, published in 1955. Brunner had her first child, a daughter in August, 1952, and the family relocated to Bryn Mawr, Pennsylvania in 1953. By 1956, the Brunners had three children, two girls and a boy. Continuing her writing, in 1955 Brunner accepted a part-time faculty and consultant position at the School of Nursing, Bryn Mawr Hospital, maintaining that affiliation until 1968. Brunner also did postmaster's work in the School of Education, University of Pennsylvania between 1960 and 1963.

Up until the 1960s, following the functional approach that structured caregiving in hospitals settings, nursing curricula had been separated into medical and surgical nursing, as were nursing textbooks. The idea for a combined medical-surgical text was one whose time had come. The result was the very successful collaboration of Brunner and Suddarth that took them through eight subsequent editions of *Medical-Surgical Nursing*, as well as the development of the enormously successful *Lippincott Manual of Nursing Practice*.

Always generously giving of her time, organizational talents, and commitment to nursing, Brunner has served on numerous editorial boards, such as *Nursing and Health Care*, edited Newsletters, specifically the Nursing Newsletter, School of Nursing Hospital of the University of Pennsylvania (1968–72), and the News Bulletin of the Pennsylvania League for Nursing (1974–76); judged a variety of writing awards; and has served in a variety of offices on both the local and national level in diverse arenas. For example, Brunner was an invited member of the National League of American Pen Women, an organization dedicated to excellence in writing, music, and art; Brunner served as Secretary of the Philadelphia chapter from 1972–76, and was National Secretary, 1984–86. She notes in a videotape that she often found herself presenting the meaning and scope of nursing to this unusual group.

A longtime devotee of nursing history, which Brunner attributes in part to her exposure to Anne L. Austin during her Case Western days, Brunner was cofounder (1974–76) of the History of Nursing Museum, Pennsylvania Hospital, Philadelphia, and First Director and Member, Executive committee (1974–85). Additionally, Brunner has served as Chairman of the Board of the Center for the Study of the History of Nursing, 1985–1995, as well as Chairing the Fundraising Committee, 1985–95. The *Lillian S. Brunner Nursing Archives* of the Center for the Study of the History of Nursing, School of Nursing, University of Pennsylvania, were dedicated and named in 1986, as well as the founding of an annual Fellowship Award, to support the study of the history of nursing at the Center.

Serving as a Consultant and Part-time Faculty to the School of Nursing, Bryn Mawr Hospital, Bryn Mawr, PA, from 1955–1968, Brunner held the position of Research Project Director, School of Nursing, Bryn Mawr Hospital from 1973–77. She has been a Consultant to the Presbyterian Medical Center, Philadelphia, PA and has served on the Advisory Boards of numerous Schools of Nursing in the Philadelphia area, some until very recently. Brunner has been a Trustee of the Presbyterian Medical Center of Philadelphia from 1976–88, and 1990–95, as well as devoting many years of service to the Presbyterian Medical Center Foundation, as Secretary from 1983–85, and Member from 1985–94. Brunner also served as a Member of the Education Committee, Hospital Trustee Association, Hospital Association of Pennsylvania, 1982–88. A long-time member of the National League for Nursing, Brunner served as President-elect (1974–76) and President (1976–78) of the Pennsylvania League for Nursing.

Throughout her professional career, Brunner has maintained membership in numerous professional organizations including ANA, NLN, The Association of Operating Room Nurses, the American Association of Critical Care Nurses, the Oncology Nursing Society, the American Association for the History of Nursing, and the Society for Nursing History. She has been a Fellow of the American Academy of Nursing since 1979 and was elected Emeritus Member in 1988. Brunner has served on the American Nurses Association Council of Medical Surgical Nursing since 1985.

As befitting her contributions, Brunner has been honored in a variety of ways. An Honorary Doctorate, Doctor of Letters (Litt. D) was bestowed on her in 1985 by the University of Pennsylvania on the occasion of the 50th anniversary of the School of Nursing, and an honorary Doctor of Science (Sc.D) from Cedar Crest College, Allentown, PA, in 1978 on the occasion of the graduation of the first baccalaureate class in nursing. She is the recipient of numerous other awards from nursing and educational groups.

Brunner stated in a videotape, "My greatest 'award' and satisfaction was to meet nurses who came up to me and expressed appreciation for their 'Brunner Bible' to which I usually replied that I was indeed proud to have been a part of their successful career in nursing. Students were always my prime interest, not awards."

Brunner currently resides with her husband Mathias (Mat), in Lancaster, PA, and continues to give unstintingly to nursing, still serving on an assortment of Boards and fund-raising committees.

PUBLICATIONS BY LILLIAN SHOLTIS BRUNNER

Books

[as Lillian Sholtis Brunner]
With D. Suddarth. *Textbook of medical-surgical nursing* (Eds. 1–8). Philadelphia, PA: Lippincott, 1964, 1970, 1975, 1980, 1984, 1988.
With F. Ginsberg and V. L. Cantlin. *Manual of Operating Room Technology.* (1966). Philadelphia, PA: Lippincott.
With D. Suddarth. *Lippincott Manual of Nursing Practice* (Eds. 1–4). Philadelphia, PA: Lippincott, 1974, 1978, 1982, 1986.
Lippincott Manual of Medical-Surgical Nursing. (1989). (2nd ed.). Philadelphia, PA: Lippincott.
[as Lillian Sholtis]
With E. Eliason & L. K. Ferguson. (1950). *Surgical nursing* (9th ed.). Philadelphia, PA: Lippincott.
With E. Eliason & L. K. Ferguson. (1955). *Surgical nursing* (10th ed.). Philadelphia, PA: Lippincott.
Surgical nursing. (1953). With E. Cardew (Ed.), *Study guide for clinical nursing* (1st ed.); 2nd ed., 1961. Philadelphia, PA: Lippincott.
With J. S. Bragdon. (1955). *Teaching medical and surgical nursing.* Philadelphia, PA: Lippincott.
With J. S. Bragdon. (1959). *Art of clinical instruction.* Philadelphia, PA: Lippincott.
With L. K. Ferguson & E. Eliason. (1959). *Surgical nursing.* Philadelphia, PA: Lippincott.

Articles (Selected)

Nursing the elderly surgical patient. *American Journal of Nursing, 51,* 726–728.
The selection of learning experiences in the operating room. (1956). *ORS-Surgical Supervisor.*
Student experiences in the operating room. (1957). *Nursing World, 131,* 8–12.
A guide to writing your policy manual. (1974). *RN Magazine, 37,* 1–6.
Peptic ulcer. (1976). *Nursing '76, 6,* 27–34.
Essay: The Year in Review/Nursing and 1985. (1981). *1986 Update/Nurses' Reference Library.*
Reminiscences of America's First Trained Nurse: Boston, Whitcomb and Barrow 1911. (1988). *Bulletin of the American Association for the History of Nursing.*

Invisible Philadelphia Community through Voluntary Organizations. (1995). *Presbyterian Medical Center.*

Videotape

A trustee's view: Productivity. (1985). Hospital Trustee Association.

Lynne M. Dunphy

RUBY F. BRYANT
1906–

Ruby Ficklin Bryant was the ninth Chief of the Army Nurse Corps. She served in that capacity from October 1, 1951 until September 30, 1955, a period characterized by rapid change and intense challenges, both in the military and civilian worlds of nursing.

Bryant was born on April 24, 1906 in Emmerton, Virginia, to Mr. and Mrs. William L. Bryant. Her father was the Richmond County, Virginia, sheriff. After Bryant graduated from Farnham High School, she attended the Fredericksburg State Teachers College for 2 years. She subsequently taught school in rural Virginia for several years. After several years of teaching, Bryant decided to resign from her teaching position and fulfill an earlier ambition to be a nurse. She entered nurse's training in the Army School of Nursing at Walter Reed Army Hospital, graduating from its last class in 1933, the height of the depression. At that time the Army Nurse Corps admitted few new members and Bryant while waiting to do so, worked as a Civilian Conservation Corps nurse at Walter Reed Army Hospital.

On December 4, 1934, Bryant's application to become an Army nurse finally was accepted but her initial assignment was to continue as a staff nurse at Walter Reed. She was transferred to the Philippine Department in 1937 and worked first at Fort Mills Station Hospital on Corregidor and

Ruby F. Bryant

then at Sternberg General Hospital in Manila. While at Fort Mills, Bryant helped to set up the hospital within the Malinta Tunnel, which later would become a temporary haven for many Americans who were destined to become POWs after the Japanese invasion of the islands in 1941. Bryant returned to the states during the summer of 1940 and assumed the responsibilities first of the assistant chief nurse at the Station Hospital at Fort Benning, Georgia and later as chief nurse at Edgewood Arsenal, Maryland. In 1943, she transferred to the Third Service Command Headquarters in Baltimore, Maryland and in 1944 became the chief nurse of the Fourth Service Command in Atlanta, Georgia. In 1946 after the end of World War II, Bryant became chief nurse of the Philippine-Ryukyu Command in the Pacific and in 1947 the chief nurse of the Far East Command in Tokyo, Japan. In 1948, she again returned to the states and matriculated at the Medical Service Officers' Advanced Course at the Medical

Field Service School at Fort Sam Houston, Texas. She and four other Army nurses were the first such officers to attend this newly launched military educational program. After completing the course, Bryant became the chief nurse of the Sixth Army at the Presidio of San Francisco and remained there until she transferred to Washington, D.C. to become the ninth chief of the corps on October 1, 1951.

A profound shortage of officers in the Army Nurse Corps was the overriding concern during Ruby Bryant's tenure as chief. The first 2 years of her term coincided with the last 2 years of the Korean War. During that conflict, there always were deficits in the numbers of available Army nurses to support both the battlefield and homefront requirements. The problem of low numbers continued on after the hostilities in Korea ended. To rectify matters during the war, Bryant called reserve nurses to active duty. By January 1952, she also had assigned 10 Army Nurse Corps officers in full-time procurement positions and utilized four Army nurses who had returned from Korea to publicize the need for more nurses. In 1954, Bryant began the Registered Nurse Student Program in order to attract more nurses to service in the Army.

To enhance the efficiency of the Army nurses, Bryant reorganized the structure of nursing care delivery into a stronger, more distinct, identifiable nursing service within the hospital system in all Army hospitals. Prior to this time a nursing service existed in Army treatment facilities, but it was not on a par with other sections in the hospital hierarchy. With the implementation of Bryant's directive, chief nurses were on a level with other chiefs of major services and had direct access to the hospital commander. Bryant recalled that the development and accomplishment of this achievement was extremely difficult. Another feature of the directive mandated the integration of the paraprofessional nursing staff into the hospital's nursing service so that professional nurses might more easily delegate selected duties to these care providers. Prior to that time, enlisted nursing staff answered to the authority of a Medical Administrative Corps officer. Bryant also managed the shortage by expanding the system of practical nurse education for enlisted soldiers to a number of other sites beyond the original school located at Walter Reed Army Hospital in Washington, D.C. In addition, she fostered the grouping of patients with similar care needs in the hospital setting to conserve nursing resources. In 1952, Bryant established a career guidance program for Army nurses as well. Another stellar achievement was Bryant's work toward the August 9, 1955 passage of the Bolton Amendment, which authorized the commissioning of male nurses in the reserve of the Army Nurse Corps. After her statutory term as chief of the Corps expired on October 3, 1955, Bryant remained on active duty but reverted to her permanent grade of Lieutenant Colonel. She accepted an assignment as chief of the Nursing Branch and Nursing Consultant in Europe and served there until 1958. In 1958, she again was promoted to colonel after passage of Public Law 85-155 which authorized permanent rank as colonel in the Regular Army for three Army Nurse Corps officers. Bryant's retirement assignment was as Director of Nursing Activities at Brooke Army Medical Center at Fort Sam Houston, Texas. Her retirement after an illustrious 26-year career in the Army became effective on 30 June 1961.

Among her numerous decorations were the Legion of Merit, the Army Commendation Medal, and the American Defense Service Medal. In 1955, Bryant was awarded an honorary Doctor of Laws degree (LL.D.) by the Medical College of Virginia at its commencement exercises held in Richmond, Virginia.

After a relaxing trip to Europe, Bryant settled near her family in Warsaw, Virginia, and in her leisure pursued her interests in photography, stamp collecting, and shopping for antiques. She resides in Virginia near the Rappahannock River at the time of this writing.

PUBLICATIONS BY RUBY F. BRYANT

Bryant, R. F. (1952). D.A.R. founder of the Army Nurse Corps. *Daughters of the American Revolution Magazine, 86,* 435–436.

Bryant, R. F. (1954). Army Nurse Corps begins 54th Year. *Army, Navy, Air Force Journal, 91,* 642, 666.

BIBLIOGRAPHY

Army's chief nurse to receive honorary LL.D. [Press release]. (1955, April 17). [ANC Archives, U.S. Army Center of Military History, Washington, DC.]

Army to recall reserves. (1952). *American Journal of Nursing, 52,* 1262.

Colhoun, R. D. (1952). Advisory Council of the ANA: Recruitment and utilization of ANC personnel. [ANC Archives, U.S. Army Center of Military History, Washington, DC.]

Free, A. C. (1951). Army nurse corps chiefs are two Virginia women. (1951, October 14). *Richmond Times Dispatch,* p. A-3.

Head of Army Nurses pleads for more help. (1952, February 13). *San Francisco Examiner.* n.p. [ANC Archives, U.S. Army Center of Military History, Washington, DC.]

Heffernon, G. A. (1954). More nurses where they are most needed. *Hospitals, 28,* 101–102.

New ANC chief. (1951). *The Bulletin of the California State Nurses' Association, 47,* 308–309.

Nurse utilization policy outlined. (1952). *Hospitals, 26,* 151.

Oblensky, F. (1963). Eleven women—and the Army nurse. *The Retired Officer, 19,* 32–33.

Recall of Army Nurse Corps and Army Women's Medical Specialist Corps officers. (1952, August 1). *Women in the Army Medical Service Newsletter.* [Archives, U.S. Army Military History Institute, Carlisle Barracks, PA.]

Recall of Reserve Officers of Army Nurse Corps. (1952). *American Journal of Nursing, 52,* 1524, 1526.

Walker, B. (1954, April 28). She heads "Angels In Khaki." *Chicago Sun-Times,* p. 35.

Werley, H. H. (1954). The ANC's career guidance program. *American Journal of Nursing, 54,* 60–62.

Mary T. Sarnecky

RUTH HOPE BRYCE
1923–1989

Ruth Hope Bryce was known internationally for her contributions to nursing. She established and directed the first Master's Degree Program in Rehabilitation Nursing in the south at Emory University. Her long career in the Veterans Administration hospital system involved many leadership and consultative positions. She was a strong supporter of several State Nurses Associations and Sigma Theta Tau.

Ruth Hope Bryce

Bryce was born April 14, 1923, in Atlanta, Georgia, to Roland and Madge Bryce. Her father died when she was 13 years old, and there were many adjustments to be made as her mother struggled to care for her five children.

Upon graduation from high school Bryce entered St. Joseph's Infirmary in Atlanta and received her diploma in nursing in 1943. Her academic degrees were a B.S. in Nursing Education from the University of Georgia (1955), a Master's of Nursing from Emory University (1961), and an Education Specialist degree from the University of Tennessee (1973).

She worked at St. Joseph's Infirmary from 1943 to 1951 as a staff nurse, and was deeply involved in professional nurse organizations and in the community. From 1951–52 she served as Secretary and member of the Executive Committee of *The American Journal of Nursing*. From 1951–59 she served in four different Veterans Administration hospitals. When she was offered a full scholarship by Emory University, she accepted it, and upon graduation was offered a faculty position, moving from Instructor to Associate Professor in a short time. In 1968 she accepted a position as Professor, The University of Tennessee College of Nursing, Memphis, as well as Assistant Director and Chief of Restorative Services Branch, Memphis Regional Medical Program. While there, she conducted workshops and did consultation in Tennessee, Arkansas, and Mississippi, all directed toward rehabilitation.

In 1973, she returned to the Veterans Administration as Patient Care Coordinator, Spinal Cord Injury Service, Memphis VA Hospital. In 1974, she was asked to transfer to the VA Central Office in Washington, D.C., to fill the position of Chief, Nursing Practice, Long Term Care. While in Washington, she was a member of the Federal Drug Administration Panel on Review of General Hospital and Personal Use Devices. She was also a consultant to the Department of Health, Education, and Welfare Office of Long Term Care on the Patient Assessment Care Evaluation Instrument.

In 1981 Bryce accepted the position of Chief, Nursing Service, at the VA Medical Center, Asheville, NC, from which she retired in 1985. During this time she continued to be involved in nursing, education, and community activities. She was an adjunct Associate Professor of Nursing at Duke University and at Western Carolina University and on the Nursing Advisory Committee to the Mountain Area Health Education Center. She was a charter member of Eta Psi Chapter, Sigma Theta Tau, and served as its first President.

During her professional career she served in numerous elected offices in the District and State Nurses Associations in the areas where she lived. She conducted hundreds of Continuing Education programs, gave the keynote address at many nursing conventions, was guest speaker at various university programs, and was a panel moderator or participant on dozens of panels. She was involved in consultative activities even after her retirement.

Bryce received many letters of commendation and Honor Awards throughout her career, but probably the ones that had the greatest meaning came to her near the end of her career. In 1984 she was the recipient of the first annual Excellence in Nursing Award from Eta Psi Chapter, Sigma Theta Tau, Western Carolina University. One month before her death she was told that Eta Psi Chapter was establishing the Ruth Hope Bryce Mentorship Award for Nursing Research in honor of her contributions to nursing, with the declaration that "We want to use this as a token of our high regard and appreciation of you—and to say we love you."

Ruth Hope Bryce died on May 27, 1989. She left life as she had lived it, with style and grace. She is buried in Crest Lawn Memorial Park in Atlanta, Georgia. On June 7, 1997, in the new addition to Grace Episcopal Church, Asheville, NC, a large stained-glass window installed in Ruth's memory was blessed by the Bishop.

BIBLIOGRAPHY

Prichard, M. E. Personal interviews with R. H. Bryce.

Mary E. Prichard

BONNIE BULLOUGH
1927–1996

Bonnie Bullough was a major nurse researcher, a pioneer nurse practitioner, an activist in bringing about change in the nurse practice acts, a historian of nursing and of nurse practice acts, an influential researcher into human sexuality, a college administrator, and an expert on alienation and the health professions in general, and the list could go on.

Bonnie Bullough

She was born January 5, 1927, to Ruth Uckerman and Francis E. Larsen in Delta,

Utah. The marriage had been a forced marriage and Larsen abandoned his new wife and infant daughter right after her birth. Originally named Louise Larsen, Bonnie was taken in by her grandmother for the next 2 years, and her elderly Scottish great-grandfather gave her the name with which she identified for the rest of her life. Her mother later married Harry I. Dempsey, and the newly married couple, after reclaiming Bonnie from her grandmother, moved to Fort Wayne, Indiana, where Bonnie was known as Bonnie Dempsey. When she was not quite 4, she was badly burned when a Halloween Jack O'Lantern which she was carrying caught her clothes on fire. She suffered first-, second-, and third-degree burns on her legs and part of her face, and lost much of an ear. She survived, but was badly scarred, and her mouth was twisted out of shape. Fortunately, a heavy coat protected much of her body.

Later, as the full effects of the depression of the 1930s hit, her unemployed parents, Bonnie, and her two younger siblings, a half-brother and a half-sister, moved West to Manti, Utah. It was not until after the passage of the Social Security Act of 1935, with its provisions for crippled children, that Bonnie could enter into a long-term program to repair some of the damages done to her face, mouth, ears, and legs. Since the hospital was in Salt Lake City, nearly a hundred miles away, and her surgery had to be done in stages, she spent much of the summers for the next 4 years in the hospital, alone and away from her family. It was here she became committed to nursing. The surgery continued after the family moved to Salt Lake City late in 1940, but on a more modest level. Early in 1942, her mother abandoned her three children and in the ensuing divorce, her two siblings went with their father while Bonnie was adopted by a bachelor uncle, Clyde Uckerman, then overseas in the army. Her name officially became Bonnie Uckerman.

In the summer of l944, after graduation from West High School, she enlisted in the U. S. Cadet Nurse Corps in a program run under the joint auspices of the University of Utah and Salt Lake General Hospital. Although all nurses took the same program, those who wanted a baccalaureate degree had to go 6 months longer after receiving their diploma. Bonnie opted for the diploma in order to marry Vern L. Bullough in 1947. Her first job was at Santa Rosa Hospital in California where her husband was still in the army. In 1948, the couple moved to Salt Lake City where she became head nurse in the operating room at Salt Lake General Hospital. In 1951 she moved with her husband to Chicago, where she again worked in the operating room of the University of Chicago hospital, this time as a scrub nurse to a Nobel prize winner. She left this position a year later to join the Chicago Public Health Department. She also returned to school and briefly attended Loyola University, but did not stay long enough to get her degree, in part because she gave birth to her first child early in 1954.

In that same year, the family moved to Youngstown, Ohio, where she worked at St. Elizabeth's Hospital part time and attended Youngstown University from where she finally received her bachelor's degree. In 1956 she gave birth to a second son, and after a few months at home, joined the faculty at Youngstown University as a part-time lecturer in the required health class which was taught by nurses. A third child was adopted in 1958 and in 1959, she moved with her husband to Los Angeles where after working part time for a year at Northridge Hospital, she entered UCLA. She received her M.S. in nursing in 1962, and then went on to earn an M.A. in sociology in 1965 and a Ph.D. in 1968. She joined

the faculty of the UCLA School of Nursing as an instructor while in graduate school and was appointed an assistant professor in 1968.

While she was still in graduate school, the Bulloughs adopted a fourth child, and her graduation was further delayed by her appointment as a Fulbright lecturer at the University of Cairo in Egypt. While in Egypt, her eldest son was killed, and after her return to Los Angeles the Bulloughs adopted a fifth child.

Bullough was an unusual graduate student, since she had been doing major research before she went to graduate school and published her first book in 1964, and as a student had a number of articles published in refereed journals. After her return from Egypt, she established the nurse practitioner program at UCLA and in 1972 was promoted to associate professor. In 1975 she moved to California State University, Long Beach as a full professor and coordinator of its graduate program, as well as serving as director of the Orange County Consortium, an alliance of the University of California, Irvine, California State University, Long Beach, and several community college who joined together to facilitate cooperation on nurse education. At the end of 1979, she was appointed dean and professor at State University of New York at Buffalo and held the position until she stepped down in 1991 because of ill health. She spent two years more at the University as a professor before retiring and moving back to California where she became a professor in the department of nursing at the University of Southern California, a position she held until her death.

During all of her career Bullough continued an active research program into a variety of topics. She was the author, co-author, or editor of more than 30 books, more than 80 articles in refereed journals, and hundreds of articles and columns in other publications. She was also very much a political activist and served as member and President of the Board of Registered Nursing in California from 1977–79. She was a board member of Region III, California Nurses Association, and later of Region I in New York. While in New York she served on the Council for Nursing Education, on the Task force on Nursing Personnel, on the Executive Board of the ANA Council of Primary Health Care Nurse Practitioners, and in a variety of other positions in the ANA, NLN, and other nursing organizations at local, state, and national levels. She organized the Coalition of Organized Nurse Practitioners in New York, and served as its president, and also was influential in organizing nurse practitioners nationally. She was also very active in the communities in which she lived, mainly in groups set up to help the poor and those who suffered from discrimination. In Chicago Bullough founded a group to combat discrimination in hospitals which later became the Medical Committee for Human Rights, in Los Angeles she was one of the organizers of the first Fair Housing Council in the country, and in both Los Angeles and Buffalo she served as a consultant to Planned Parenthood. In Buffalo she served as co-chair of the greater Buffalo, United Appeal. She helped set up the first organization of Parents and Friends of Gays in Los Angeles which quickly became a national organization. She was very much in demand as a lecturer at nursing meetings and lectured or gave papers in most of the states in the U.S. as well as overseas in, among other countries, England, Cuba, Mexico, Cyprus, the Soviet Union, China, Egypt, and Ghana. She was a member of the editorial boards of a number of nursing journals, as well as other professional journals. She was one of the founders for the American Association for the History of Nursing and served as founding co-editor of its original publication, the *Bulletin*.

Much of Bullough's research in later years dealt with nursing and the law and with human sexuality. She was particularly concerned with such things as gender discrimination and wrote extensively on it. While at Buffalo, for example, she chaired a university-wide committee to look at the role of women on the Buffalo campus as well as on all the SUNY campuses. She was always interested in encouraging nurses to do research on topics of their own choosing, and wherever she went, she helped set up research study groups which usually resulted in an increase in publications for the group. Among her many honors was being named Nurse Practitioner of the Year by the national nurse practitioner groups, and receiving the Alfred Kinsey award for her research into human sexuality. She also was co-inventor of a perionometer which was patented posthumously. Her favorite recreation was bridge, but she was also a fair golfer and she enjoyed working in her garden.

During Bullough's later years, she suffered from an autoimmune disease which gradually destroyed her lungs and she died in Los Angeles on April 12, 1996, from the consequences of interstitial lung disease. As she had planned, she was cremated and the ashes distributed in the mountains of Los Angeles. She was survived by her husband, three sons, one daughter, and one granddaughter.

PUBLICATIONS BY BONNIE BULLOUGH

Books (Selected) (some co-authored)

The emergence of modern nursing. (1964). New York: Macmillan. (2nd ed., 1969; in 1979 revised and footnoted as *The Care of the Sick*, New York: Neale Watson.)

Issues in nursing. (1966). New York: Springer. [A series of books under varying titles with various topics published at 5-year intervals through to the 1990s.]

The law and the expanding nursing role. (1975). New York: Appleton, Century, Crofts.

Poverty, ethnic identity and health care. (1975). New York: Appleton, Century, Crofts. (Several editions.)

Sin, sickness and sanity: A history of sexual attitudes. (1977). New York: New American Library.

Women and prostitution. (1987). Buffalo, NY: Prometheus.

The management of common human miseries. (1979). New York: Springer.

Florence Nightingale and her era. (1990). New York: Appleton, Century, Crofts.

Nursing in the community. (1990). St. Louis: C. V. Mosby.

Preventive medicine in the United States: 1900–1990. (1992). Canton, MA: Science History.

Cross dressing, sex, and gender. (1993). Philadelphia: University of Pennsylvania Press.

Human sexuality: An encyclopedia. (1994). New York: Garland.

Sexual attitudes: Myths and realities. (1995). New York: John Wiley.

Gender blenders. (1996). New York: Garland.

BIBLIOGRAPHY

Bonnie Bullough: In Memoriam. (1997). *Western Journal of Nursing Research, 18*, 497–502.

Who's Who in America, 1988–89. (Wilmette, 211). Marquis, MacMillan Directory Division and other editions.

Vern L. Bullough

IRENE MORTENSON BURNSIDE
1923–

The roots of gerontological nursing can be traced to Dr. Irene Burnside, the first nurse to advocate for mental health care of older persons.

It was Burnside's dedication to meeting the health care needs of older persons that led to publication of *Nursing and the Aged* (1976), the first textbook to include content on the psychosocial care of older persons. The fact that gerontological nursing (and the subspecialty of geropsychiatric nursing) is now recognized as a legitimate and much-needed area of specialization in nursing can be traced to the insight, sensi-

tivity, and perseverance of Dr. Irene Burnside.

Irene Mortenson Burnside

Burnside was born in Grove City Minnesota, on October 4, 1923, the daughter of Walter Hollyer and Rebecca (Wortz) Mortenson. She lived with relatives in rural Minnesota after the age of 5 due to her mother's poor health and her parents' separation. Irene received elementary education in a one-room country school. It was Irene's aunt who nurtured both her astute awareness of environments and her compassion for the fine arts, while her high school teacher Abigail Quigley McCarthy (former wife of Eugene McCarthy) instilled the importance of writing well, lessons she remembers fondly.

Burnside entered nurses' training at a diploma program at Ancker Hospital School of Nursing in St. Paul, Minnesota at the young age of 17, and while there joined the United States Army Cadet Nursing program soon after its inception. The Army Cadet Corps provided enlisted nursing students with a uniform, covered the cost of nursing textbooks, and offered a monthly stipend.

Burnside graduated in 1944, at the age of 20, but had to wait until she was 21 to take the Minnesota State Nursing Board Examination. She then joined the Army Nurse Corps and served as Second Lieutenant, and then First Lieutenant in Okinawa and Osaka, Japan (1945–1946). She met her husband, Dean Burnside, while serving in the Army and the couple married on December 20, 1946, after they were discharged. She and Dean (employed as a systems analyst) moved to Aurora, Colorado where they had three children; Mark, Tonya, and Clark.

From 1947 to 1953, Burnside worked as a nurse in a physician's office, a staff nurse on a medical unit at Fitzsimmons Army Hospital, and an industrial nurse for the United States Government, Department of the Army in Denver, Colorado. During this time, she became "quite disenchanted" with nursing. Her disenchantment was not caused by the work of nursing, which she "loved," but by the fact that she usually had to work undesirable shifts for only $1.25 an hour and a babysitter for her children cost $0.75 an hour. This led to Burnside's decision to pursue education in the fine arts while raising her children and continuing to work at a variety of nursing positions.

In 1957, she graduated with a Bachelor of Fine Arts degree from Denver University in Denver, Colorado, after which her family moved to Martinez, California. From 1957 to 1964 she continued working part time as a staff nurse at the Contra Costa County Health Department and as a charge nurse at the Veterans' Administration Hospital in Martinez, California.

At the age of 40, Burnside resumed her nursing education, graduating from the University of California, San Francisco (UCSF), in 1966 with a Master of Science

degree in Nursing. Within one year after receiving her master's degree, she received a Post Master's Certificate in Adult Psychiatric Nursing (1967). This was accomplished while working as an evening charge nurse at the Gladman Psychiatric Hospital in Oakland, California and caring for her family. It was during her Post Masters' Certificate education that Burnside became interested in conducting psychotherapeutic group sessions with older persons. Despite numerous obstacles, she led group psychotherapy sessions in a nursing home from 1967 to 1969. This psychotherapeutic group experience later provided the content for the first manual on group work with elderly persons, an area pioneered by Burnside (1978a).

Burnside began her career as a nurse educator at the University of California, San Francisco (UCSF) in 1967. She continued teaching nursing as a lecturer while working as a research assistant at UCSF until her husband died of amyotrophic lateral sclerosis (Lou Gehrig's disease) in 1970. Widowed at the age of 47 with one child remaining at home, Burnside wanted to learn more about the psychosocial care of older persons and the research process, so she continued her education at the Ethel Percy Andrus Gerontology Center Summer Institutes at the University of Southern California in Los Angeles, California from 1970 to 1972.

From 1972 to 1976, she served as Coordinator of Nursing Education at the Ethel Percy Andrus Gerontology Center but also worked as a freelance author, lecturer, and consultant in gerontological nursing in places such as Norway, Sweden, Finland, Malaysia, Canada, and across the United States from 1976 to 1979. From 1979 to 1980, she worked as a research associate for the Gerontological Clinical Nurse Specialist Program at San Jose State University in San Jose, California and became a lecturer in the Department of Nursing from 1980 to 1981. In 1981, she was promoted to Assistant Professor and held that position until promoted to tenured Associate Professor of Gerontological Nursing in 1984 (1984–1987).

The educational experience Irene received at the Ethel Percy Andrus Gerontology Center led to her decision to pursue a Ph.D. in Gerontological Nursing. Approximately halfway through her course work, Irene was diagnosed with cancer and chronic leukemia. She dropped out of school for 2 years to receive surgical and radiation treatments. During her battle with cancer, she revised the third edition of her classic textbook, *Nursing and The Aged: A Self-Care Approach* and completed her dissertation entitled *The effect of reminiscence groups on fatigue, affect, and life satisfaction in older women.* Burnside graduated from the University of Texas School of Nursing, Austin, Texas with a Ph.D. in Nursing in 1990, at the age of 66.

During the years 1981 to 1991, Burnside held a number of positions including being a Visiting Professor at nursing and medical schools at the Medical University of South Carolina, University of North Carolina, Texas Tech, University of Florida, University of Texas, Georgia State University, and Humboldt State University, Western Caroline University. She was invited to be a guest professor in the Florence Cellar Chair in gerontology at Case Western Reserve University but was unable to accept due to illness. In 1990, she was a Visiting Fellow at the Phillip Institute of Technology, School of Nursing, Melbourne, Australia and as of this writing she holds the position of Adjunct Professor at San Diego State University School of Nursing, in California.

A partial list of contributions Dr. Irene Burnside has made to the field of nursing over the past 50 years includes the publication of more than 10 textbooks, 27 book chapters, and over 50 journal articles. The first editions of her pivotal textbooks, *Nursing and the Aged,* and *Psychosocial Nursing Care of the Aged,* have been translated into Portuguese and Japanese, respectively. She presented the Keynote Address at over 12 international and 18 national conferences and conducted more than 150 workshops and continuing education presentations. She also received over 25 honors and awards from such organizations as the U.S. Nurse Cadet Corps, Sigma Theta Tau International, the American Nurses' Association's Council of Gerontological Nursing, Nurses' Book Society, the American Journal of Nursing, and the American Medical Writer's Association. Additionally, she received the First Long-Term Care Award given by the National League for Nursing, the Brookdale Award from the Gerontological Society of America, the Meritorious Service Award by the American Association of Homes for the Aging, the Geronting Award from the Andrus Gerontology Center, and has been listed in consecutive publications of *Who's Who in American Nursing, Who's Who in International Women, Who's Who of American Women,* and *Notable Women* since 1975.

Throughout her career, Irene Burnside directed her efforts at improving the health and well-being of older persons and mentoring students who subsequently contributed to the field of gerontological nursing. As a nurse leader and prolific author, she promoted changes in the field of nursing which led to the recognition that nurses were in key positions to address the physical and mental health needs of the elderly population.

PUBLICATIONS BY IRENE BURNSIDE (SELECTED)

Burnside, I. (Ed.). (1974). *Sexuality and aging* (1st ed.). Los Angeles: Andrus Gerontology Center.
Burnside, I. (Ed.) (1976). *Nursing and the aged* (1st ed.). New York: McGraw-Hill. (2nd ed., 1981).

Burnside, I. (Ed.). (1978b). *Working with the elderly: Group process and techniques* (1st ed.). Boston, MA: Jones & Bartlett. (Second edition 1984, is in its fifth printing.)

Burnside, I. (Ed.) (1978a). *Psychosocial nursing care of the aged* (1st ed.). New York: McGraw-Hill. (2nd. ed., 1980).

Burnside, I. (1988). *Nursing and the aged: A self-care approach* (3rd ed.). St Louis: Mosby-YearBook.

Burnside, I. (1995b). Themes and props: Adjuncts for reminiscence therapy groups. In B. Haight & J.Webster (Eds.), *The art and science of reminiscing: Theory, research, methods, and application* (pp.). Washington, DC: Taylor & Francis.

Burnside, I., Ebersole, P., & Monea, H. (Eds.). (1979). *Psychosocial caring throughout the life span.* New York: McGraw-Hill.

Burnside, I. M., & Haight, B. (1994). Reminiscence and life review: Therapeutic interventions for older people. *Nurse Practitioner: American Journal of Primary Health Care, 19*(4), 55–61.

Burnside, I., Preski, S., & Hertz, J. E. (1998). Research instrumentation and elderly subjects. *Image: Journal of Nursing Scholarship, 30*(2), 185–190.

Burnside, I., & Schmidt, M. G. (1994). *Working with older adults* (3rd ed.). Boston, MA: Jones & Bartlett.

BIBLIOGRAPHY

Burnside, I. M. (1991). From one who is chronologically gifted: Aging well. *Generations, 15*(1), 19–20.

Ebersole, P. (1998). Looking for a few good nurses. *Geriatric Nursing, 19*(1), 49.

Garand, L., & Buckwalter, K. C. (1997). Psychosocial care of older persons: The pioneering work of Dr. Irene Burnside. In E. A. Swanson & T. Tripp-Reimer (Eds.), *Advances in gerontological nursing: Issues for the 21st century* (Vol. 1). New York: Springer Publishing Company.

Who's Who in American Nursing, 1975 to 1994. Reed Publishing. Washington, D.C. Society of Nursing Professionals.

Wolf, L. (1997). *Comparison of a nurse and a non-nurse leader: Irene Burnside and Maya Angelou.* Unpublished manuscript, Fairfield University, School of Nursing.

Linda J. Garand

DOROTHY FORD BUSCHMANN
1895–1953

While legend states that six students founded Sigma Theta Tau in 1922, the historical record suggests that Dorothy Charlotte Ford Buschmann was the key advisor and the author of the constitution and by-laws, as well as the driving force of Sigma Theta Tau from 1922 through 1934. The President's Award, bestowed biannually by Sigma Theta Tau, was renamed the Dorothy Buschmann Award in 1997 after her portrait was hung in the Sigma Theta Tau International Founders' Room in Indianapolis, Indiana.

Dorothy Ford Buschmann

Dorothy Ford was born in Eureka, Illinois, the only daughter of John and Wilda Ford, on September 12, 1895. Raised in Hooperston, Watseka, and Vincennes, Illinois, she admired the work of Jane Addams, and as a child she dreamed of becoming a physician. When World War I threatened in 1916, her father, a grocer, and her mother, an actress, supported her decision to join the ranks of "useful" women by allowing her to enroll at the Indiana University Training School for Nurses. While a student she met C. Severin Buschmann, a university athletic star and aspiring lawyer from a prominent Indiananpolis family. After graduating in 1919, she married and became active in the School of Nursing Alumnae Association. Concerned that steady relocations of graduate nurses were jeopardizing alumnae alliances, the Alumnae Association produced a newsletter, *The Indiana University Nurses' Bulletin*, and selected Dorothy as the editor.

Upon completion of the newsletter, six Indiana University students approached Buschmann for help with a new project. Exposed to college culture through classes, the students envisioned a Greek fraternity that would promote nursing and asked Buschmann to help formalize the charter, the bylaws, and the constitution. Believing nurses to be rightful members of the university community, and hoping to support the professional spirit within college-educated nurses, she agreed to help. According to Sigma Theta Tau legend, on a beautiful autumn day in 1922, six young women took a street car across town and finalized their plans during a picnic lunch. The next day they met with Buschmann, who possessed an abiding belief that nursing's foundation was love, that its tasks required strength, and above all, that its enduring value embodied honorable service to humanity. The Alpha Chapter of Sigma Theta Tau, National Honor Fraternity for Nurses, founded on the values of love, honor, and courage, was established on October 4, 1922.

Although the founding students of Sigma Theta Tau scattered after graduation, the organization not only survived, but flourished. Dorothy Buschmann spent 1923 in New Haven, Connecticut while her husband earned a master's of law (L.L.M.) at Yale University, but upon her return to Indianapolis, she asked Helen Wood, Director of Washington University School of Nursing in St. Louis, to form the second chapter. When Miss Wood agreed, Buschmann began to envision that other chapters could be initiated throughout the country and world. With this vision in mind, she was elected as national President in 1927. For the next 7 years Buschmann served as President, doggedly determined to extend national recognition for Sigma Theta Tau, and by 1934 she had brought six schools (Indiana University, Washington University, University of Iowa, University of Minnesota, University of Kansas, and University of Ohio) into the fold, had produced the first issue of the Sigma Theta Tau Journal, and had initiated almost 300 members into the organization.

Although Buschmann believed nursing to be a moral endeavor from which knowledge and service emerged, other Sigma Theta Tau officers argued that nursing excellence sprung from a superior mind which, in turn, led to moral choices and social service. When the two perspectives created a smoldering and unresolvable dispute, Buschmann decided to relinquish the Sigma Theta Tau Presidency. She turned her attention to humanitarian work with the League of Women Voters, supporting handicapped Girl Scouts, establishing a prenatal room within an Indianapolis hospital, fundraising for the Service Men's Center, and managing the Marion County Cancer Society. In addition she cared for her three children, C. Severin (b. 1921), Joan (b. 1927), and George (b. 1936). She was divorced in 1946, diagnosed with cancer a few years later, and died in Indianapolis on October 3, 1953. Buschmann's funeral service was held at Christ Episcopal Church in Indianapolis; she was cremated and her ashes were interred at Crown Hill Cemetery in Indianapolis. Her portrait, commissioned by servicemen of Indianapolis in appreciation for establishing the servicemen's centers, was done by Donald

Matteson and hung at 111 North Capital Avenue, until her grandson retrieved it. The portrait now hangs in the Founder's Room of Sigma Theta Tau International in Indianapolis, Indiana.

BIBLIOGRAPHY

Akers, M. (1973). Six stars and a dream. *Image: Journal of Nursing Scholarship, 4*, 8–9.

Hamilton, D. (1997b). The seventh star: Dorothy Ford Buschmann and the founding of Sigma Theta Tau. *Image: Journal of Nursing Scholarship, 28*(2), 177–180.

Hamilton, D. (1997a). *The Image editors: Mind, spirit, and voice.* Indianapolis, IN: Center Nursing Press.

Wright, M. (1973). Yesterday's vision and tomorrow's dawn. *Image: Journal of Nursing Scholarship, 4*, 6–9.

Diane Bronkema Hamilton

C

M. ELIZABETH LANCASTER CARNEGIE
1916–

Born, educated, and practicing nursing in a segregated United States, it was incumbent upon M. Elizabeth Carnegie to provide the opportunity for Black and minority nurses to earn undergraduate and graduate degrees to prepare themselves for leadership positions in nursing, and recount the struggles and achievements of Black nurses.

M. Elizabeth Lancaster was the fourth child of John Oliver Lancaster, a musician, and Adeline Beatrice (née Swann) born in Baltimore, Maryland. When she was 2 years old, her parents divorced and she was sent to live with her extended family, her mother's sister in Washington, D.C. Although born and reared a Catholic, she attended public school, therefore was required to attend special classes conducted by the Oblate Sister of Providence, an all-Black order. After graduating from Dunbar High School at 16, and unable to afford a college education, she settled on the Lincoln School of Nursing in New York City, an all-Black school. To do so she claimed she was 18 rather than 16. She graduated in 1934.

M. Elizabeth Lancaster Carnegie

While a student at Lincoln, she met Mabel K. Staupers, Executive Secretary of the National Association of Colored Graduate Nurses (NACGN), an organization founded in 1908 to fight discrimination against Blacks in education, employment, and organized nursing. Shortly after meeting Mrs. Staupers, Carnegie attended the annual NACGN which in that year used Lincoln School for Nurses, as convention headquarters. She made a solemn pledge that when she graduated, to do all within her power to help change the system and break down barriers that were keeping Black nurses out of the mainstream of professional nursing.

After graduation, she took the civil service examination, although there were only two federal hospitals at that time where Black nurses could be assigned—the all Black Veterans Hospital in Tuskegee, Alabama and Freedmen's, a general hospital in Washington, D.C. Since assignment to Freedmen depended on successful completion of a one-year probation period at the VA hospital in Tuskegee, Carnegie spent a year at Tuskegee before transferring to Freedmen's.

In February 1940, conscious of the desirability of having a bachelor's degree, she enrolled at West Virginia State College, a Black school, financing her education by providing nursing service to the students in exchange for tuition, room, and board. She also earned additional money by working summers at Homer G. Phillips Hospital in St. Louis, as well as at a Girl Scouts' camp. In June 1942, after she was awarded the Bachelor of Arts degree from West Virginia State College, with a major in Sociology and a minor in Psychology and History, she joined the faculty of the nursing program at Medical College of Virginia as a clinical instructor and supervisor of obstetrics nursing. World War II put a great demand on nurses and the nurses in NACGN and other Black leaders had successfully demanded that Blacks be admitted to the Army Nurses Corps, although still on a segregated basis and by quota. Carnegie, ever conscious of discrimination, applied to the Navy Nurses Corps but was refused because the Corps did not admit Black nurses.

Denied entry, she sought other challenges and the opportunity to go into college administration came in 1943 when Hampton Institute, a Black college in Virginia, at the encouragement of the National Nursing Council for War Services, agreed to establish a baccalaureate program in nursing. Since she lacked a master's degree, which would qualify for her deanship, she instead joined the facility as assistant dean of the baccalaureate nursing program, and acting dean until someone else could be found. Shortly after the school opened in February 1944, a White dean took her place but she continued as assistant dean, carrying a teaching load, and is regarded as the real founder of the first baccalaureate nursing program in the state of Virginia. In 1977, the college's nursing archives was named in her honor.

Near the end of her first year at Hampton, Carnegie received a fellowship from the General Education Board of the Rockerfeller Foundation. She enrolled at the University of Toronto in Canada with a major in nursing—a one year certificate program. In Toronto, she met and married in December 1944, Eric Carnegie, a brother of one of her former St. Philips student, who secured lodging for her.

Florida A&M College in Tallahassee, a traditionally Black college, was seeking a dean when Carnegie completed the course in Toronto and she, with the backing of the General Education Board, became the first dean of the school of nursing since her Canadian certificate was judged as the equivalent to the American Master's degree. The challenges facing her in Florida were daunting: reorganizing the school of nursing and obtaining national accreditation; making the school an integral part of the college, and facilitating the visibility of Florida's Black nurses in the eyes of the public and among other nurses.

Florida Black nurses were fighting for full-fledged membership in the Florida

State Nurses Association (FSNA), the only avenue to membership in the American Nurses Association. Although the Black nurses had gained admission to FSNA in 1942, they were not allowed any type of participation beyond payment of dues. Although the FSNA and the Florida Association of Colored Nurses (FACGN) met at the same time, they met in separate sections of the same town to conform to Florida separation laws. The president of FACGN was permitted to attend one program session of the FSNA Convention while the president of FSNA was invited to attend a FACGN session. Slowly, the wheels of progress were set in motion. In 1947, M. Elizabeth Carnegie was elected president of FACGN which automatically made her a courtesy member of FSNA. In 1949, she was elected to the board of directors of FSNA, the first Black nurse, in a Southern state nurses' association. By 1952, there was integration in every aspect except housing accommodations and those events that were strictly social.

In 1951, Carnegie returned to school and in 1952 received a master's degree in educational administration from Syracuse University in New York. Her commitment to nursing, and her attempts to better educate herself, were a major factor in the collapse of her marriage since her husband, Eric, had refused to leave Canada to join her in segregated Florida.

In 1953, the *American Journal of Nursing* (AJN) hired her as assistant editor and in 1970 she became senior editor of *Nursing Outlook*, one of the magazines published by the AJN. While in New York, she continued her education, earning a doctoral degree from New York University in 1972. Her dissertation, *Disadvantaged Students in RN Programs*, was published by the National League for Nursing. A year later, she was named chief editor of *Nursing Research*. Her

first editorial was entitled "ANF Directory Identifies Minorities with Doctoral Degrees." This editorial sparked interest in the educational preparation of minority nurses. In 1974, ANA applied for and received a grant from the National Institute of Mental Health to help minority nurses earn PhDs. Carnegie was appointed to the advisory committee for Nurses Educational Fund which she chaired for many years.

Upon retirement in 1978, M. Elizabeth Carnegie started her own business as a consultant on scientific writing. In 1980, Hampton Institute in Virginia invited her to become a Distinguished Visiting Professor to teach research in the Master's program for 3 years. She then served as Visiting Professor at 9 other institutions of higher learning between 1983 and 1996 (University of North Carolina at Greensboro School for Nursing; Pennsylvania State University; University of Michigan School of Nursing; Oakland University School of Nursing; Adelphi University School of Nursing; Memphis State University; Indiana University School of Nursing; Virginia Commonwealth University; and the University of Massachusetts).

M. Elizabeth Carnegie had been conscious since her student days that Black nurses had been left out of American history of nursing. She filled the void with her book, *The Path We Tread: Blacks in Nursing, 1854–1984*, which was published in 1986. This has been one of her major contributions to nursing. For her book, she received the *American Journal of Nursing's* Book of The Year Award. Now in its third edition, her book focuses on Blacks in nursing worldwide.

Carnegie has garnered numerous awards and honors. A selected list consist of 1) seven Honorary doctorates—Doctor of Laws, Hunter College, City University of New York; Doctors of Science, State University of New York, Brooklyn New York; Doctor of Public Service, Marian College, Indianapolis; Doctor of Humane Letters, Thomas Jefferson University, Philadelphia; Doctor of Humane Letters, Virginia Commonwealth University; Doctor of Science, Indiana University; and Doctorate, Humanus Causam, Syracuse University; 2) Several honorary memberships—Chi Eta Phi (nursing sorority); Freedman's Hospital School of Nursing Alumni; Nursing Education Alumni Associations, Teachers College; Association of Black Nursing Faculty in Higher Education; and Florida State Nurses Association; 3) Several prestigious awards such as: Fellow, American Academy of Nursing; American Nurses' Association, Mary Mahoney Award; Lillian Wald Award, New York Visiting Nurses Association; George Arentis Pioneer Medal, University of Syracuse; and Mabel Stauper Award, Chi Eta Phi; 4) M. Elizabeth Carnegie Endowed Chair established at Howard University College of Nursing, and M. Elizabeth Carnegie Award for Academic Excellence and Service to Others, established by Rutgers the State University of New Jersey College of Nursing.

She has edited and/or written chapters in 27 books; published 72 articles, given over 342 speeches, lectures, seminars and/or workshops and has traveled internationally in behalf of the nursing profession to: North and Central America, Europe, Africa, Asia, South America, Caribbean and Australia.

PUBLICATIONS BY M. ELIZABETH LANCASTER CARNEGIE (SELECTED)

Carnegie, M. E. (1986). *The path we tread: Blacks in nursing, 1854–1984.* Philadelphia: J. B. Lippincott.

BIBLIOGRAPHY

Carnegie, M. E. *Curriculum vitae.*

Schorr, T., & Zimmerman, A. (1988). *Making choices, taking chances: Nurse leaders tell their stories.* St. Louis: C. V. Mosby.

Sadie M. Smalls

ROSIE K. CHANG
1918–

Rosie K. Chang embarked on her long career in nursing at a time when nurses born and raised in Hawaii, "island nurses," as they were described, were paid less than nurses who came from the mainland United States and seldom extended their formal education beyond a hospital diploma. Chang eventually became the first island nurse to earn a master's degree in nursing and went on to lead nearly every major nursing organization in Hawaii, often during crucial periods of the organizations' growth, including the Hawaii Nursing Association and the Hawaii League for Nursing. At the same time, she was pioneering improvements in health care at various locales, including The Queen's Medical Center (previously The Queen's Hospital), which remains the largest private medical facility in Hawaii, and the Hawaii State Hospital, the largest public sector psychiatric facility in the state. Most recently, she became the first nurse to endow a chair in the University of Hawaii School of Nursing.

Rosie Chang was born in Honolulu, March 29, 1918, to parents who had both come to the islands 14 years earlier. Her mother, Mary Park, was only 6 years old when she was brought from Seoul, Korea, a move prompted by famine and widespread concerns about Japanese efforts at colonization. Her father, Chung Chip Kim, was a teenager who gained passage on a ship to Honolulu after lying about his age in order to be approved for work, mostly likely in the vast plantation system that dominated the Hawaiian economy at the turn of the century. In a fortunate turn of events, the truth about her father's age was discovered, and he was given the option to attend a school for Chinese boys.

Rosie K. Chang

Despite a lack of material advantages, Chang in an interview described her childhood as providing "all things needed." Individuals of Korean-Chinese heritage were a relatively small group, she added, so "we mixed in with the larger community." It was a diverse community that included major groups of Native Hawaiians, Filipinos, Japanese, Portuguese, Puerto Ricans, Chinese, and "haoles," or persons from the mainland United States. Chang's immediate family, which initially included a sister and brother, expanded after the death of her father, in 1924, and her mother's remarriage, to include three additional siblings.

She went to Roosevelt High School, the only "English standard" school in Hawaii at that time and it was here she met her husband, John Chang. The fact that he was Chinese and she was Korean presented a problem, because marriages outside of one's ethnic group tended to be discouraged. They were married in 1942 and, several years later, had a son who continues to practice as an attorney. Just after their 51st wedding anniversary, her husband, who worked most of his adult life as a dentist, died while traveling in China.

After high school she tried to enter nursing school, but at 4 feet 10 1/2 inches tall and 85 pounds in weight, she did not meet the physical requirements for nurses' training in force in Hawaii schools at the time. Undaunted, she enrolled in the University of Hawaii and began taking the same general science courses that were required of nurses enrolled in local hospital diploma programs. She also took her case to the Dean of Women at the university. The Dean interceded for Chang with the Director of The Queen's Medical Center Hospital School of Nursing and Queen's accepted her, with the stipulation that she would be on probation for the entire length of her training, rather than the usual 1-year probationary period.

At graduation, in 1942, Chang was presented with the "Best Bedside Nurse Award" in her class and almost immediately she stepped into a position as head nurse of the men's medical unit at the hospital, became a clinical instructor in the nursing school, and resumed her studies in general science at the University of Hawaii. Just a year later, she became a general supervisor in the hospital and, in 1947, graduated with a baccalaureate degree in general science from the University of Hawaii.

She and her husband and young son then left Hawaii to continue their education at the University of Pittsburgh. While her husband studied dentistry, Chang pursued graduate work in nursing administration. In 1950, she was awarded a master's degree in nursing, a first for any nurse born and raised in Hawaii. Other firsts quickly followed. When she returned to Hawaii, later that year, she accepted a position as Director of The Queen's Hospital School of Nursing, and found herself in charge of the same school that just over 10 years earlier had initially refused her admission. No sooner had she settled in, then she began a series of reforms that focused on upgrading recruitment practices and strengthening the curriculum. Shortly after assuming leadership of the nursing program, Chang also became assistant director of the hospital. With her expanded influence, she instituted educational programs for staff nurses and supervised a work setting in which higher pay for mainland nurses was no longer a policy. During the same period, she was elected to a second term as president of the Hawaii Nurses Association, Oahu District, and proceeded to lobby, both formally and informally, for funding of a School of Nursing at the University of Hawaii. Chang observed that the subtle, informal efforts may have been the most effective. Indeed, funding in excess of the amount requested followed a carefully planned dinner, in which Chang's close attention to seating arrangements ensured that influential legislators would hear reasons to lend their support to a School of Nursing. Her efforts on behalf of nursing earned her the distinction, in 1954, of being named "One of the Ten Outstanding Nurses in Hawaii," by the Hawaii Nurses Association.

Chang then undertook one of the most formidable challenges of her career namely reorganizing the Hawaii Territorial Hospital for the mentally ill, which after statehood in 1959 became the Hawaii State Hospital. She was determined to bring nurses to the hospital in order to enhance care which, until then, had been solely in the hands of untrained staff. In addition, she vowed that the hospital would become accredited by the Joint Commission on Accreditation of Hospitals, predecessor to the Joint Commission on the Accreditation of Healthcare Organizations. Such a goal had not even been considered in the past.

Part lobbyist and part administration, Chang successfully garnered money from the legislature and rallied support at the hospital for improvements that ranged from providing decent bedding so that patients had more than newspapers to cover themselves on cool nights, to offering salaries that would attract registered nurses, to establishing a continuing education program to upgrade the skills of hospital aides.

Chang's endeavors always extended well beyond the confines of a single institution or agency. In 1957, for example, she helped to found the Hawaii League for Nursing and served two terms as its president. In the 1960s, she was presented with two major awards by the Hawaii Heart Association for her ongoing efforts in the development and provision of coronary care nursing education in the state. Also during this period, she was selected by United States government officials as one of five Korean-American leaders to participate in a Friendship Mission to Korea, served as president of the Korean University Club, and lead state-wide reform efforts through her membership on the Hawaii Health Advisory Committee, the Hawaii Commission on the Status of Women, and the Hawaii Ethics Commission.

In 1969, she became Associate Director of the Regional Medical Program for Hawaii, American Samoa, and the Trust Territory of the Pacific Islands. Her authority extended over a larger geographic area than any other regional program. Her efforts culminated in the establishment of the first coronary care unit in the state, which continues to function today.

Finishing work in one area once again opened the way for other opportunities, this time to pursue a Master's Degree in Public Health at the University of Hawaii, which she completed in 1977. She received her doctorate in 1984, at Columbia Pacific University, with a focus on the health needs of Korean immigrants. Along with her studies, Chang continued to balance numerous other responsibilities, including serving as a planner for the East Honolulu Health Planning Council, becoming a legislative aide to the Hawaii State Legislature, and providing leadership on the Governor's Commission to Commemorate the 200th Anniversary of the Arrival of Chinese in Hawaii.

Chang continues to serve as a board member and advisor on nursing and health care programs to the Center for Asia-Pacific Exchange (CAPE). For her outstanding accomplishments, Rosie was presented with the University of Hawaii Distinguished Alumni Award in 1995 and, in 1998, she became the first nurse to endow a chair in the School of Nursing, University of Hawaii. Clearly, her determination and enlightened leadership have brought immeasurable benefits to nursing and the larger community. Dr. Rosie Chang's enduring legacy confirms that she has truly come a long way from the young woman who was first refused admission to nursing because of her size.

BIBLIOGRAPHY (SELECTED)

Chang, R. K. (1998). Interview by author, February 20, 1998, Honolulu, HI, tape recording, transcript and personal papers, University of Hawaii School of Nursing, Honolulu.

Daws, G. (1974). *Shoal of time: A history of the Hawaiian Islands.* Honolulu: University of Hawaii Press.

Fuchs, L. H. (1961). *Hawaii Pono: A social history.* New York: Harcourt, Brace and World.

Lewis, F. R. (1969). *History of nursing in Hawaii.* Node, WY: Germann-Kilmer.

Nordyke, E. C. (1989). *The peopling of Hawaii* (2nd ed.). Honolulu: University of Hawaii Press.

Tom Olson

ANN LIVEZEY CLARK
1913–

Ann L. Clark made major contributions in maternal and child health through her practice, teaching, writing, consultation, research, and continuing education activities. She was associated with schools of nursing at three major universities: Rutgers, Arizona State, and the University of Hawaii. She coauthored with Dr. Dyanne Affonso the first maternity nursing textbook to incorporate psychosocial aspects of care. She was coinvestigator in a Division of Nursing funded grant studying Nursing Intervention and Maternal Perception. She is a founding nurse member of Edu-Center for Nurses, a nonprofit corporation devoted to offering continuing education programs for nurses, and the major provider of continuing education for nurses in Hawaii.

Ann L. Clark was born in Bel Air, Maryland, on Thanksgiving Day, November 27, 1913, the oldest of two children of Florence Everitt and Jacob Ott Livezey. She married Marshall Clark in 1937; he died in 1985. They had no children.

Ann Clark is a ninth generation American; her paternal great-grandparents (seven times removed) arrived with the Quakers in 1682 and settled in Philadelphia. Her mother died when Ann was 4 years old, and Clark was raised by a particularly loving stepmother, Maude Archer Livezey. She attended Bel Air Elementary and High Schools and went on to the Maryland Hospital School of Nursing from which she graduated in 1935. She received a bachelor's degree in nursing from Seton Hall University, South Orange, NJ, in 1953, an

Ann Livezey Clark

MA in nursing from New York University in 1957, and an honorary doctorate from Hawaii Pacific University in 1992.

Clark was a staff nurse in obstetric nursing in Baltimore City Hospitals from 1935 to 1939. She then moved to Mountainside Hospital, Montclair, NJ, and held positions as assistant head nurse, head nurse, supervisor, and instructor in obstetric nursing from 1939 to 1954. She was floor supervisor at Margaret Hague Maternity Hospital, Jersey City, NJ, from 1954 to 1955. She then moved into academia as an instructor, assistant professor, associate professor and professor at Rutgers University College of Nursing, Newark, NJ, 1955 to 1970. She joined the University of Hawaii School of Nursing as professor, 1970 to 1973. She also served as a visiting professor at Arizona State University College of Nursing, Tempe, AZ, in Spring, 1975. From 1977 to 1982, she served

as Director, Nursing Education, for the Hawaii Nurses Association. She was Director and President, Edu-Center for Nurses, from 1982 to 1997, and has been CEO of Edu-Center for Nurses since 1997.

Much of Clark's professional writing, speaking and volunteer work was related to pregnancy and adolescents. Her first journal publication took place in 1942 and her last book was published in 1981. She considers her article on "Maturational Crisis and the Unwed Adolescent Mother," published in *Nursing Science* in 1964, to be her "best article ever." She gave numerous presentations on the "Unwed Adolescent" and "Parent Infant Relationships." Clark provided a variety of consultation services over her career: from New Jersey to Hawaii, and Arizona to New York. She served on the National League for Nursing Council on Baccalaureate and Higher Degree Programs as a member of the Advisory Committee for Regional Conferences for Teachers in Maternal and Child Nursing, 1960, and Consultant to Baccalaureate Education, 1967. She was also a member of the Editorial Committee of the *Bulletin of the American Association of Maternal and Child Health* in 1968 and member of the Editorial Board of *Nursing Forum*, 1972 to 1980.

Clark also held many offices at the state level including the New Jersey Board of Nursing from 1968 to 1970; the New Jersey State Nurses Association, 1964–1966; and in the New Jersey League for Nursing, 1942–1950; Hawaii Nurses Association, 1972–1985. Her activity in professional nursing organizations was matched by her community service such as Childbirth Education of New Jersey, Operation Head Start, Ringwood, NJ, 1966, Florence Crittenton League of Newark, American Red Cross Hawaii Chapter, and Board of Governors, Hawaii Medical Library.

Clark received numerous honors and her biography appears in a number of collections including *Who's Who in American Women, 1975–1977*. The Hawaii Nurses Association research fund carries her name, the Ann Clark Nursing Research Fund. She published eight books, three of which received American Journal of Nursing Book of the Year Awards: *Childbearing: A Nursing Perspective* in 1977, *Childbearing: A Nursing Perspective* (2nd ed.) in 1978, and *Culture/ Childbearing/Health Professionals* in 1979.

Clark's contributions to the care of mothers and infants has been significant and far-reaching for many years. She influenced numerous staff nurse and nursing students through her writing and presentations.

PUBLICATIONS BY ANN LIVEZEY CLARK

Books (Selected)

Clark, A. L. (1962). *Leadership technique in expectant parent education.* New York: Springer Publishing Company. (2nd ed., 1973).

Clark, A. L. (1981). *Culture and childrearing.* Philadelphia: F. A. Davis.

Clark, A. L., & Affonso, D. (1976). *Childbearing: A nursing perspective.* Philadelphia: F. A. Davis (2nd ed., 1978).

Periodicals (Selected)

Clark, A. L. (1964). Maturational crisis and the unwed adolescent mother. *Nursing Science, 2,* 113–124.

Clark, A. L. (1967). The crisis of adolescent unwed motherhood. *American Journal of Nursing, 67,* 1465–1469.

Clark, A. (1976). Crib death: Some promising leads but no solutions yet: Nursing implications. An addendum. *Nursing Digest, 4,* 14–15.

Clark, A. L., & Affonso, D. (1976). Infant behavior and maternal attachment: Part I. Two sides to the coin. *MCN, American Journal of Maternal Child Nursing, 1,* 93–99.

Clark, A. L., & Hale, R. W. (1974). Sex during and after pregnancy. *American Journal of Nursing, 74,* 1430–1431.

BIBLIOGRAPHY

Clark, A. L. *Curriculum vitae.*

Clark, A. L. (1998). [Interviews]. February and May, 1998.

Shannon E. Perry

MILDRED IRENE CLARK
1915–1994

Mildred Irene Clark was the 12th Chief of the Army Nurse Corps. It was in great part due to her vitality and diligence that the Army Nurse Corps not only survived but thrived during the Vietnam years, a very challenging and difficult era in both the military and civilian nursing worlds.

Mildred Irene Clark

Clark, the youngest daughter of five children, was born on January 30, 1915 in Elkton, North Carolina. Her mother was Martha Darling Clark and her father, William James Clark, was a farmer and Methodist minister. After receiving her diploma from Baker Sanatorium Training School for

Nurses in Lumberton, North Carolina, in 1936, Clark attended two 6-month-long postgraduate courses. The first was a curriculum in pediatrics offered by the Babies Hospital in Wrightsville Sound, North Carolina. The second program at the Jewish Hospital in Philadelphia, Pennsylvania prepared specialists in operating room administration and technique. Elizabeth Pearson, an instructor in Clark's training school, who had served as a nurse in World War I, initially sparked her student's interest in the Army Nurse Corps. Knowing that competition among applicants for the Army Nurse Corps was formidable, the determined Clark submitted her request for active duty one year in advance while still a student in the post-graduate course. Surprisingly, within 14 days, Clark received a request to report to Walter Reed Army Hospital for a physical examination. After completing her course work, Clark was ready to become an Army nurse. She requested an initial assignment at Fort Bragg, North Carolina, hoping the close proximity to her home would allow her parents to visit and thus allay their fears about army nursing. Her ploy was successful. Six months after signing in at Fort Bragg, the chief nurse queried Clark as to her interest in taking part in an anesthesia course offered at Jewish Hospital in Philadelphia, Pennsylvania. Clark seized the opportunity. Two assignments followed as an anesthetist at the station hospital at Fort Leavenworth, Kansas and the general hospital at Schofield Barracks, Hawaii. It was during her stint at Schofield Barracks that the Japanese bombed that installation and adjacent Wheeler Field, and Clark again demonstrated her mettle. In 1943, the petite dynamo began her administrative career, variously assuming responsibilities as assistant chief nurse and principal chief nurse at Ashburn General Hospital, McKinney, Texas; Brooke General Hospital, Fort Sam

Houston, Texas; Cushing General Hospital, Massachusetts; Halloran General Hospital, New York; Station Hospital, Camp Stoneman, California; and the 382nd Station Hospital, in Korea. In 1947, she became the Director of Nurses of the XXIV Corps in Korea and less than a year later, Chief Nurse of the Far East Command in Tokyo, Japan. Late in 1950, Clark was among the five Army nurses who were selected to attend the first Medical Officers' Advanced Course at the Medical Field Service School (MFSS), Fort Sam Houston, Texas. Her follow-on assignment as Assistant Chief Nurse at Fitzsimons General Hospital in Denver, Colorado lasted for only 3 months, after which she matriculated at the University of Minnesota and earned a bachelor's degree in nursing education. While a student there, Clark fell ill with an undiagnosed viral condition that involved some leg paralysis. This ailment lingered and occasionally hampered Clark's activity.

One of her most lengthy and significant assignments was as Procurement Officer in the Surgeon General's Office beginning in September 1955. In this role, Clark faced enormous recruiting difficulties in the midst of an enduring nationwide nursing shortage. Clark conceptualized and developed a myriad of vehicles to enhance the drive to recruit bright young men and women for the Army Nurse Corps including the Army Student Nurse Program. Clark also wrote "The Prayer of an Army Nurse" which enjoyed a wide dissemination and served as an inspirational public relations tool. A musician set the words of the prayer to music and the United States Army Band recorded the composition. Clark served as the de facto author of Mary M. Roberts' book *The Army Nurse Corps: Yesterday and Today* when the 83-year-old Roberts could not complete the project. A brief assignment as chief nurse of the 6th U.S. Army at the Presidio of San Francisco, California, followed in 1961. In September 1963, a board of officers designated Clark as the next chief of the Army Nurse Corps to replace the retiring Colonel Margaret Harper.

Among Clark's numerous military awards were the Distinguished Service Medal and the Army Commendation Medal. Additionally, she was honored by an array of civilian organizations for her contributions. She was recognized by the Zeta Chapter of Sigma Theta Tau with a lifetime membership in 1962. The College of Education at the University of Minnesota designated her as the outstanding alumna in 1963. Additionally, Clark was inducted into the Michigan Women's Hall of Fame in 1993.

Clark's statutory term as Chief of the Army Nurse Corps concluded in 1967, after which she retired. Following her retirement, she married another retired officer, Colonel Ernest Woodman, and settled in Ann Arbor, Michigan. Until her death on November 25, 1994, Clark continued her activism and interest in the Army Nurse Corps, veterans' issues, and organizational concerns of professional nursing. She was buried in the Nurses' Section in Arlington National Cemetery. In 1997, Womack Army Medical Center at Fort Bragg, North Carolina, broke ground for a 57,000 square foot health care facility, the Clark Health Clinic, which was the first building to be named in honor of a woman at that installation.

PUBLICATIONS BY MILDRED IRENE CLARK

Clark, M. I. (1965). Today's new nurses: What do we expect of them in military hospitals? *Military Medicine, 130,* 698–702.

Clark, M. I. (1957). You can be a civilian and a reservist too. *American Journal of Nursing, 57,* 204–205.

BIBLIOGRAPHY

Adams, N. R. (1986). [Colonel Mildren I. Clark, ANC, Retired.] Project 86-2, transcript, U.S. Army Military History Institute, Carlisle Barracks, PA.

Clark, M. I. In quest of survival, historical summary of Army Nurse Corps and Army Medical Specialist Corps Programs (14 September 1955–31 July 1959). Unpublished manuscript, Archives, U.S. Army Military History Institute, Carlisle Barracks, Pennsylvania.

A curriculum vitae of Colonel Mildred Irene Clark, ANC. (1975, April). General Reference and Research Branch, The Historical Unit, USAMEDD, Fort Detrick, MD.

Ground breaking ceremony. (1997). *The Connection: Retired Army Nurse Corps Association, 22,* 12.

Mallory, P. (1967). Enclosure 2. [Remarks by Major General Phillip Mallory at the unveiling of Clark's portrait during her retirement ceremony.] ANC Archives, U.S. Army Center of Military History, Washington, DC.

Woodman, E. A. H. Colonel Mildred Irene Clark, . . . a brief biography. Unpublished manuscript, ANC Archives, U.S. Army Center of Military History, Washington, DC.

Mary T. Sarnecky

VIRGINIA CASSADY CLINTON (KELLEY)
1923–1994

Virginia Clinton Kelley, daughter of a nurse and mother of our 42nd president, Bill Clinton, had a career of over three decades as a nurse anesthetist. An early specialist in anesthesia in Hot Springs, Arkansas, she built up a large, successful practice through perseverance and hard work. Her independence, her ambition, her toughness, and her Southern loyalties ultimately put her at the local center of the ongoing national interprofessional conflict between doctors and nurses over who can administer anesthesia to patients—nurse anesthetists and/ or doctor anesthesiologists. Ultimately, the anesthesiologists won in her town, and Kelley was forced to retire. She was convinced that sexism played a part in [her] career, from start to finish. She thought doctors disregarded any professional aspirations that happened to be held by a woman.

Virginia Cassady Clinton Kelley

A descendent of Irish immigrants and Cherokee Indians, Virginia Dell Cassidy was born June 6, 1923, in the small, poor farming village of Bodcaw, Arkansas. She was the only child of James Eldridge Cassady and Edith Grisham Cassady. The family moved from Bodcaw to the small town of Hope, Arkansas, where Kelley's mother studied by correspondence to become a nurse. Her father held various jobs— factory worker, ice deliverer, and shopkeeper in liquor and grocery stores. The parents were always supportive. During the years that Kelley went to Louisiana for professional training, her parents cared for the young Bill Clinton.

Kelley decided in high school to become a nurse anesthetist. She thought she would be in the "wave of the future." First, she got her R.N. diploma at Tri-State Hospital in Shreveport, Louisiana, 50 miles from Hope. Then she worked in Hope as a private duty nurse for a few years before going for two years (1946–47) to Charity Hospital in New Orleans to get a certificate as a nurse anesthetist. Back in Hope, she had to do some private duty nursing before she was finally hired at Josephine Hospital as an anesthetist. In earlier days, general practitioners and surgeons administered their own anesthesia or used whoever was available—interns, nurses, medical students. In the larger, more sophisticated city of Hot Springs, Arkansas, where she soon moved with her husband and young Bill, nurse anesthetists were already accepted.

In Hot Springs there was plenty of work at St. Joseph's Hospital, and Kelley soon established herself as a competent anesthetist. Kelley was a dedicated nurse anesthetist who loved her work and empathized with her patients. Besides her regular assignments, she was often on call and rushed to the hospital whenever she was needed. All went well until 1956 when the first anesthesiologist, Dr. Walter Klugh, Jr., established a practice in Hot Springs. In 1958 he set up a Department of Anesthesia at St. Joseph's Hospital. Many doctors preferred to use Dr. Klugh's Department because he provided a buffer in the face of the increasing number of malpractice suits. From then until Kelley was forced out of business in 1981, there was an ongoing feud, fed by much gossip in Hot Springs, between Dr. Klugh and his supporters and Kelley and hers. The Sammons Clinic and St. Joseph's Hospital supported Dr. Klugh and the Burton Eisele Clinic and Ouachita Hospital supported Kelley's group. Both Virginia and Dr. Klugh were strong-willed, determined people, and both considered themselves in the right. The growth in the number of patients brought on in the mid-1970s by Medicaid and Medicare brought in many more patients, enabling Kelley, an independent contractor, to set up her own office and hire an office manager. Medicare provisions, however, required that anesthetists be supervised by an M.D., so Kelley had to employ a doctor to supervise her work and the work of the many other anesthetists she employed—a situation with a built-in, unsolvable power struggle, set in a small Southern city. On October 19, 1981, even though many doctors still supported her, Ouachita Hospital cancelled the services of her group. After 33 years as a nurse anesthetist, Kelley's professional career ended. She was 57.

Virginia Kelley was caught in the decades-old struggle for power between anesthesiologists and nurse anesthetists, that is, between medical doctors who were largely male and nurses who were largely female. The nursing group had established their credentials. They had their own professional organization (AANA, the American Association of Nurse Anesthetists), had established a curriculum requiring solid training beyond the R.N., and had accepted the requirement for M.D. supervision. Most surgeons and hospital administrators supported them. But anesthesiologists continued to challenge their role. The anesthesiologists' dogma was that anesthesia was a specialty of medicine, for M.D.s only, not for nurses. Kelley claimed anesthesiologists "were determined to take over anesthesia in Hot Springs the way they had in a jillion other cities."

Kelley was a spirited, loyal, gutsy woman, and, as one might expect, she had a full life beyond nursing. She was loyal to her parents until their death. She was strongly attached to her two sons, Bill Clinton, the son of her first husband (and who formally took the surname of her second husband), and Roger Clinton, Jr., the son of her second husband. She had four husbands, five marriages, and was widowed three times. She met her first husband, Bill Blythe, during the War while he was in the Army and she was in the middle of nursing school. He was killed in an automobile accident in 1946 while she was pregnant with Bill. Her second husband, Roger Clinton, turned out to be an abusive alcoholic whom she divorced but remarried because she felt sorry for him. She was with him for 20 difficult years until he died of cancer in 1967. Her third husband, Jeff Dwire, was a hairdresser who, she said, treated her "like a queen." She married him in 1969, but diabetes led to his death 5 years later. Her fourth husband and fifth marriage in 1982 was to Dick Kelley, who survived her. Virginia Kelley always had many friends who clustered around her in good times and bad. She was a gregarious woman who enlivened many a gathering. She loved dancing, going to clubs with friends, and especially horse racing. When her son Bill ran for political office, she was an ardent campaigner who enthusiastically recruited her many friends to contribute their time.

In 1990, diagnosed with breast cancer, she had a mastectomy. Then she went through chemotherapy and radiation treatments, all the while playing down the seriousness of her condition to friends and relations. Clinton announced his candidacy for President in 1991 and she did not want her condition to interfere with his political responsibilities. She lived long enough to enjoy the fame of being the President's mother. On January 20, 1993, she was in Washington with her husband and her friends for Clinton's inauguration. She was recognized and feted wherever she went, including Los Angeles and Las Vegas. She spent Thanksgiving at Camp David and Christmas at the White House. She died on January 6, 1994, and was buried in a plot with her father, mother, and first husband in Hope, Arkansas, where she grew up.

BIBLIOGRAPHY

Altman, L. K. (1994, January 8). Vigor masked illness of Clinton's mother. *New York Times*, p. 1, vol. 7.

Bullough, V. L., & Bullough, B. (1978). *The care of the sick: The emergence of modern medicine.* New York: Prodist.

Bullough, B., Bullough, V. L., & Soukup, M. C. (1983). *Nursing Issues and Nursing Strategies for the Eighties.* New York: Springer Publishing Company.

Kelley, V. with Morgan, J. (1994). *Leading with my heart: My life.* New York: Simon and Schuster.

Purdum, T. S. (1994, January 7). Virginia Clinton Kelley, 70, President's mother, is dead. *New York Times*, A:22.

Gwendolyn Whitehead Brewer

LAURA M. COBB
1892–1982

Laura Mae (or Maye) Cobb was the chief U.S. Navy nurse in the Philippine Islands during World War II. A military careerist who entered the Navy during World War I, her steady leadership guided 11 nurses through the opening battles in 1941, and after one of her staff escaped the islands, provided the nucleus for the remaining 10 nurses to survive 37 months as Japanese prisoners of war in three different internment sites.

Laura Cobb was born in Atchinson, Kansas on May 11, 1892, and educated in the public schools of Mulvane, Kansas. Cobb taught school for 18 months before stepping down to enter the Wesley Hospital School of Nursing in Wichita, Kansas, and graduating in June 1917. The reason for her career change remains obscure, but on July 5, 1918, she was appointed a nurse in the U.S. Navy Reserve Force and reported for duty at the U.S. Naval hospital in Fort Lyon, Colorado. One year later, she transferred to the U.S. Naval Hospital in Canacao, Philippines Islands, the same hospital where she would be exposed to her first Japanese assault in 1941.

Cobb was a quiet, slender woman with dark hair and wire-rimmed glasses, known for her stylish clothing and gracious manners. She embodied a group of professional women who emerged from the Great

Laura M. Cobb

War—educated, self-supporting, and socially secure. She returned stateside in January 1921 and, for unknown reasons, resigned and received an Honorable Discharge at Mare Island Naval Station in California on July 21, 1921. Her civilian career was short. After 2 years in charge of the urological building at the University Hospital in Iowa City, Iowa, she applied for a reappointment in the Nurse Corps. On 4 April 1924, she reported for duty at the U.S. Naval Hospital in San Diego, California. In March 1929, Cobb enrolled and completed a course in physical therapy program at the Brooklyn Naval Hospital. For a time she served as Chief Nurse on Guam, and it was here she received her first military commendation for leadership during a 1940 typhoon.

From Guam, she traveled to the larger U.S. Naval Hospital on Canacao, next to Cavite Navy Yard and 15 miles across the bay from Manila. She assumed the Chief Nurse position on February 10, 1941. A courteous, formal leader, she believed she had the right to direct her nurses' leisure as well as their work time. No one questioned her intrusions when she attended their cocktails parties, suggested items to ship home, or commented on the style of their clothes.

Less than one year later, on Wednesday, December 10, 1941, Japanese pilots turned their sights on Canacao and Cavite Navy Yard. Four days later, Cobb, her nursing staff, and other survivors abandoned the ruined base for Manila. The U.S. Army was in charge of managing casualties. Cobb submitted to their command. By New Year's Eve, the Army had left Manila for Bataan and Corregidor, taking one Navy nurse as part of a surgical team. With no orders to move, Laura Cobb, the remaining 10 nurses, physicians, and corpsmen stayed at Santa Scholastica School where they had set up a hospital and cared for their military patients.

On January 2, 1942, the entire group surrendered to the victorious Japanese. Enemy officers ordered the staff to remain at work in the makeshift hospital. Cobb was ordered to catalog all medical provisions, and in doing so she and her nurses assuming that all valuable medications would be filched, mislabeled precious antimalarial drugs like quinine as harmless soda bicarbonate and successfully kept these drugs for their patients.

In early March 1942, the Japanese decided to intern the navy women in the civilian Santo Tomas Internment Camp in Manila. The Navy men were to go to Bilobid Prison, a military POW camp, also in the city. Cobb and her staff again help set up a small internee hospital. Until the U.S. Army POW nurses arrived from Corregidor in August 1942 and took over the administration, she was the hospital's designated

superintendent. In May 1943, the 11 Navy women volunteered to transfer to a new civilian camp at Los Banos, 110 miles southeast of the capital. Cobb left Santo Tomas and successfully carried her staff's personnel files hidden under a large white blouse and several floral necklaces. At Los Banos the nurses set up another small hospital which eventually served 2,154 prisoners. They remained in this camp until liberation on February 23, 1945. None of the Navy women succumbed to starvation or disease, while 21 other Los Banos internees died, including two men the Japanese shot for trying to obtain food.

Cobb hoped to continue with her military career after the war, but during her first assignment at the U.S. Naval Hospital on Treasure Island, near San Francisco, the 50-year-old Lt. Commander realized she no longer had the physical stamina even for hospital administrative work. The 35-pound weight loss and beriberi she had contracted in Los Banos had taken its toll. She retired on June 1, 1947 after 26 years of service to her country.

Despite her weakened state, Cobb enjoyed a long retirement, living for many years in Los Angeles. She kept in touch with members of her wartime staff through the exchange of Christmas cards. In the 1970s, she returned to her hometown of Wichita, Kansas where, after entering a nursing home, she turned over her legal and financial affairs to one of her nieces. Laura Cobb died in 1982 at the age of 86.

MILITARY AWARDS

Bronze Star Medal with a gold star in lieu
  of a Second Bronze Star
World War II Victory Medal
American Defense Service Medal
Asiatic-Pacific Campaign Medal
Distinguished Unit Badge
Philippine Defense Ribbon
Philippine Liberation Ribbon

American Campaign Medal and American
Theater Ribbon
Philippine Independence Ribbon

BIBLIOGRAPHY

Lieutenant Commander Laura M. Cobb personnel
file. Obtained from the National Personnel Re-
cords Center, St. Louis, Missouri under the Free-
dom of Information Act.
*Three nurses who served with Laura Cobb in World War
II were interviewed:*
Dorothy Still Danner (personal communication,
March 3, 1992).
Margaret Nash (personal communication, March
3, 1991).
Mary Rose Harrington Nelson (personal communi-
cation, April 13, 1989).

Elizabeth M. Norman

Signe Skott Cooper

SIGNE SKOTT COOPER
1921–

The success of continuing nursing education in Wisconsin is due to the enthusiasm
and efforts of Signe Skott Cooper. Her vision and understanding of the educational
needs of registered nurses led to one of the
most successful nursing extension programs in the United States. In addition to
her dedication for continuing nursing education, her love for history and writing has
provided a treasury of knowledge of early
nursing leaders in Wisconsin.

Signe Dorothea Skott was born in Clinton County, Iowa, to Clara (Steen) and
Hans Skott. She lived her early years on
a farm in Iowa and attended a one-room
country school through 8th grade. She
graduated from Madison East High School
in Madison, Wisconsin, in 1938.

Following graduation from high school
at age 17, Ms. Cooper was too young to
enroll at Methodist Hospital School of
Nursing, so she enrolled the University of
Wisconsin–Madison, receiving her Certifi-
cate of Nursing in 1943. During World War
II, she joined the U.S. Army Nurse Corps
and served as a staff nurse on medical and
psychiatric units in the China-Burma-India
Theater. While stationed in Fort Belvoir,
Virginia, she was married briefly to Clois
Cooper and was divorced in 1946.

Upon her discharge from the army, Cooper was hired as the head nurse of the Obstetric Unit at University Hospitals in Madison, WI in 1946. She continued taking
course work at the University of Wisconsin–
Madison and received her B.S. in 1948. She
joined the nursing faculty, teaching nursing arts and attended summer sessions at
Teacher's College, Columbia University.
She received her master's degree from the
University of Minnesota. Cooper was offered a joint appointment with University
Extension and the School of Nursing at the
University of Wisconsin–Madison in 1955.
She developed the Department of Nursing
in University Extension from a one-person

operation to a nationally and internationally recognized department of continuing education. She was promoted to associate professor of nursing in 1957 and to full professor in 1962. She served as principal investigator for North Central States Planning Project for Continuing Education in Nursing funded by the Division of Nursing in 1971–1972. She was appointed as a Helen Denne Schulte Professor of Nursing at UW–Madison from 1973–76. She retired as Professor Emeritus in 1983. Promoting interdisciplinary education was a goal in Cooper's overall continuing education planning. She often said, "True interdisciplinary education is built on a recognition of each practitioner as a colleague with a definite contribution to make to the others." Cooper served as a consultant to the Clinical Center at the National Institutes of Health (1975–79), the World Health Organization (1976–1980), International Research Development Centre in Ottawa Canada (1977–78), and PLATO Nursing Project (computer assisted instruction) (1978). She provided numerous informal consultations to a variety of university and international visitors.

Cooper has spoken at numerous national and international conferences and programs on continuing education and self-directed learning. She has been recognized through numerous awards and was cited as one of 71 "nursing influentials" in Connie Nicodemus Vance's dissertation, *A Group Profile of Contemporary Influentials in American Nursing* (1976).

In addition to Cooper's contribution to the development of the continuing nursing education in Wisconsin and the nurse as a self-directed learner, her contribution to the preservation of nursing history in Wisconsin is significant. Her interest in nursing history began in 1960 during her tenure as the Wisconsin Nurses Association President. She has worked closely with the Wisconsin State Historical Society in the acqui-

sition, preservation and presentation of nursing memorabilia. She initiated and maintained an active role in developing a historical collection at the UW–Madison School of Nursing. Caps from current and former nursing programs in Wisconsin and elsewhere are included in this valuable collection. Her motivation to actively preserve Wisconsin nursing history, as she often said, is in part due to her belief that "each person has the responsibility to the next generation."

She is the author meditor of five books, contributed chapters to several others, and numerous articles unrefereed journals. It is not surprising that Cooper's hobbies and interests parallel her professional interests. She loves learning about and riding steam trains, traveling, gardening, word games, quilting, needlepoint, stamp collecting (nursing and Christmas seals) and reading history.

Cooper resides in her family home in Middleton, Wisconsin and continues to work on biographical sketches of nursing leaders in Wisconsin. Her model for continuing education and self-directed learning continue to influence continuing educational offerings for nurses in Wisconsin.

Among her many honors and awards is: Linda Richards Award of the National League for Nursing for pioneering efforts in continuing education in nursing, 1967 and the Distinguished Service Award, University Extension, University of Wisconsin, 1970.

PUBLICATIONS BY SIGNE SKOTT COOPER

Books

Contemporary nursing practice: A guide for the returning nurse. (1970). New York: McGraw-Hill.
Continuing nursing education. (1973). New York: McGraw-Hill.
(with Margo Neal) *Perspectives in continuing education in nursing.* (1980a). Pacific Palisades, CA: NURSECO.

(Editor) *Self-directed learning in nursing.* (1980b). Wakefield, MA: Nursing Resources.
The practice of continuing education in nursing. (1983). Rockville, MD: Aspen Systems.

Articles (Selected)

The motivation factor: Handle with care. (1958). *Nursing Outlook, 6,* 558–560.

University extension courses for nurses. (1963). *Nursing Outlook, 11*(1), 36–39.

Activating the inactive nurse: A historical review. (1967). *Nursing Outlook, 15*(10), 62–65.

A yearning for learning. (1970). *Journal of Continuing Education in Nursing, 1*(1), 17–22.

This I believe in about continuing education in nursing. (1972). *Nursing Outlook, 20*(9), 579–583.

A brief history of continuing education in nursing in the United States. (1973). *Journal of Continuing Education in Nursing, 4*(3), 5–14.

Trends in continuing education in the United States. (1975). *International Nursing Review, 22*(4), 117–120.

Continuing education: Yesterday and today. (1978). *Nurse Educator, 3*(1), 25–29.

BIBLIOGRAPHY

Niles, A. G. (1982). Signe Skott Cooper. In A. Bletzinger & A. Short (Eds.), *Wisconsin women: A gifted heritage* (pp. 216–219, 308). Madison, WI: Wisconsin State Division, American Association of University Women.

Popiel, E. (1983). A tribute to Signe Skott Cooper. (Editorial). *Journal of Continuing Education in Nursing, 14,* 3.

Yoder-Wise, P. (1983). Living History Series: Signe S. Cooper. *Journal of Continuing Education in Nursing, 14,* 32–36.

Dissertations

Wilson, J. D. (1976). *The agriculture extension model's applicability to continuing education in nursing.* Doctoral dissertation, Teachers College, Columbia University, New York.

Michaeline Mirr

LYLE MORRISON CREELMAN
1908–

Canada's first nurse to serve with the World Health Organization (WHO) was Lyle Morrison Creelman. She served with WHO from 1954 to 1968 and propelled international nursing to new heights. Her early dedication to "health for all" principles at the international level remains an inspiration to nurses generations later. On her retirement, an editorial in *ICN Calling,* the news journal of the International Council of Nurses, honored her many contributions, stating: "In these fourteen years [with WHO], she has probably achieved more for nursing throughout the world than any other nurse of her time."

Lyle Morrison Creelman

Creelman was born August 14, 1908, in Upper Stewiacke, a farming area in Nova Scotia, Canada. She moved with her family to Richmond, British Columbia, as a child, and eventually attended the Vancouver Normal School to receive her teacher's certificate. Her first career was as an elementary school teacher for 3 years. She then entered the degree nursing program at the University of British Columbia, and graduated in 1936. Her first nursing job was as a public health nurse in Cranbrook, B.C., for a year, then she moved to the Metropolitan Health Committee (later the Vancouver [B.C.] Health Department).

A Rockefeller scholarship in 1938 took her to Teachers College, Columbia University, in New York, and she graduated with a master's degree in 1939. She returned to Metropolitan Health in Vancouver and served as a supervisor of public health nursing, then director of nursing during the early 1940s. During that time, she was also president of the Registered Nurses Association of British Columbia.

Her international role began in 1944, near the end of World War II, when she was invited by the United Nation's Relief and Rehabilitation Administration (UN-RRA) to be the chief nurse in the British zone of Occupied Germany. Her job was to organize nursing services to help care for the millions of people of many nationalities who had been displaced from their homes during the war. After an intense 2-year period in this work, she returned home to Canada and to her work with public health in Vancouver.

She was soon granted a leave, however, to serve as field director of an extensive study of public health services in Canada conducted by the Canadian Public Health Association. She was coauthor, with Dr. J. H. Baillie, of a highly acclaimed report on this project; their study was used for many years as a reference work for public health professionals in Canada and it marked the direction of public health nursing in Canada.

In 1950, she was invited to become nursing consultant in maternal and child health in the newly formed Nursing Unit of the World Health Organization and, in 1954, she succeeded her British colleague Olive Baggallay as WHO's Chief Nursing Officer. During her work with WHO, she visited many countries, collaborated with nurses of many nations, and recruited many well-prepared nurses to initiate international projects that later could be carried on alone by the individual countries. Her visionary efforts ensured that countries achieve self-sufficiency in health care, often through primary nursing care, and she used her superb administrative abilities to put this philosophy into practice.

Throughout her career, her professional association activities were varied, including many elected and appointed positions on the provincial nursing association and with the Canadian Nurses Association and Canadian Public Health Association. At the international level, she was WHO consultant to the International Council of Nurses, official observer to many non-government organizations, and chair of the membership committee of ICN.

Following retirement, she was commissioned by WHO to help study maternal and child health services in South-East Asia. She continued her long international associations through mentorship of many WHO and ICN nurses, and her home on B.C.'s Bowen Island (near Vancouver) was a frequent rest-and-relaxation stop for international visitors.

She has received tributes including recognition from nurses' associations at the provincial, national, and international levels. She has two honorary doctorates, one in 1963 from the University of New Brunswick and one in 1992 from the University of British Columbia. In 1967, she was awarded the Centennial Medal and in 1971, the Medal of Service of the Order of Canada by the Government of Canada. In 1972, she received a lifetime honorary membership from the Canadian Public Health Association. In 1974, she was given the Jeanne Mance award, the highest honor of the Canadian Nurses Association.

Her hobbies throughout her lifetime were walking, cycling, and photography and she continued these until well in her eighties. In 1998, she was living in West Vancouver and maintains an interest in nursing through the B.C. History of Nursing Group.

Of nursing, she wrote in 1943, and reiterated in the 1990s, that the sentiments still held true:

"What of the future? It is to a very large extent in our own hands. We will make many errors but as long as we know our goal and keep it ever in mind our future is bright and secure" (Creelman, 1943; Shore, 1991).

PUBLICATIONS BY LYLE CREELMAN (SELECTED)

Creelman, L. (1941). What is public health nursing? [Public Health Nursing column]. *The Canadian Nurse, 37*(2), 111–112.

Creelman, L. (1943). What of the future? [Public Health Nursing column]. *The Canadian Nurse, 39*(1), 35–37.

Creelman, L. (1945). With UNRRA in Germany [Letter to the editor]. *The Canadian Nurse, 41*(12), 986–987.

Creelman, L. (1946). Mental hygiene in the public health program. *The Canadian Nurse, 36*(10), 679–684.

Creelman, L. M. (1947a). With UNRRA in Germany [Part 1]. *The Canadian Nurse, 43*(7), 532–536.

Creelman, L. M. (1947b). With UNRRA in Germany [Part 2]. *The Canadian Nurse, 43*(8), 605–610.

Creelman, L. M. (1947c). With UNRRA in Germany [Part 3]. *The Canadian Nurse, 43*(9), 710–712.

Creelman, L. (1950). Lyle Creelman writes. . . *The Canadian Nurse, 46*(6), 477–478.

BIBLIOGRAPHY (SELECTED)

Canadian Nurses Association. (n.d.) *Lyle M. Creelman Biographical File.* Available CNA Helen K. Mussallem Library Archival Vertical Files, Ottawa.

Dier, K. (1992). Nursing practice in international areas. In A.J. Baumgart & J. Larsen (Eds.), *Canadian nursing faces the future* (pp. 200–217). Toronto: Mosby Year Book.

Green, M. M. (1984). *Through the years with public health nursing: A history of public health nursing in the provincial jurisdiction British Columbia.* Ottawa: Canadian Public Health Association.

Names [Lyle M. Creelman]. (1972). *The Canadian Nurse, 68*(9), 55.

Nursing profiles [Lyle M. Creelman]. (1948). *The Canadian Nurse, 44*(4), 294–295.

Nursing profiles [Lyle M. Creelman]. (1949). *The Canadian Nurse, 45*(7), 525.

Nursing profiles [Lyle M. Creelman]. (1954). *The Canadian Nurse, 50*(6), 484.

Lyle Creelman: An appreciation. (c1968). *ICN Calling.* (Reprinted *The Canadian Nurse*). Undated clipping available CNA biographical files and RNABC biographical files.

Registered Nurses Association of British Columbia. *Lyle Creelman: Biographical file.* Available RNABC Helen Randal Library, Vancouver, B.C.

Shore, H. L. (1991). Letter to Dr. John Dennison, Tributes Committee, University of British Columbia. (Personal communication.)

Splane, R. B., & Splane, V. H. (1994). *Chief nursing officer positions in national ministries of health: Focal points for nursing leadership.* San Francisco: School of Nursing, University of California San Francisco.

Zilm, G., & Warbinek, E. (1994). *Legacy: History of nursing education at the University of British Columbia 1919–1994.* Vancouver: University of British Columbia School of Nursing/University of British Columbia Press.

Glennis Zilm

ETHEL MILDRED CRYDERMAN
1892–1963

Ethel Cryderman combined astute management as the District Director of the Toronto Branch of the Victorian Order of Nurses (VON) from 1934 to 1958, with professional leadership in nursing associations at the provincial, national, and international levels. Her clinical training in midwifery enabled her to expand the maternity welfare program of the VON. Established in 1897, under the sponsorship of Lady Ishbel Aberdeen, wife of Canada's Governor-General and first President of the International Council of Women, the VON provided visiting nursing services to the poor and isolated in both urban and rural settings. The

VON was particularly active in Ontario, Atlantic Canada, and British Columbia, but less evident in the prairie provinces of Manitoba, Saskatchewan, and Alberta, where district and public health nursing services were established by provincial ministries of health immediately following the First World War. Under Cryderman's direction, the work of the Toronto Branch more than doubled, and it developed a reputation for a high calibre of visiting nursing service. Cryderman was President of the Registered Nurses Association of Ontario, chairman of various provincial nursing committees, including public health, President of the Canadian Nurses Association from 1948 to 1950, head of the Canadian delegation to the 1949 International Council of Nurses (ICN) Congress in Stockholm and Canadian representative to the ICN Board of Directors.

Born in 1892 in Walkerton, a small town in Bruce County, Ontario, Cryderman was descended from United Empire Loyalists who fled the American Revolution. After completing secondary schooling in Walkerton, she enrolled in the Toronto General Hospital Training School and graduated in 1916. After a few months of private duty nursing, Cryderman enlisted with the Canadian Army Medical Corps and served as a nursing sister until discharged in 1919. She enrolled in the first one-year public health nursing course offered in 1920/21 by the University of Toronto, graduating in 1921 with a certificate. From 1921 to 1924, she was a staff nurse with the Toronto Department of Public Health before being granted leave to earn certificates in midwifery, at the Radcliffe Infirmary, Oxford, and mothercraft from the Mothercraft Training Society, in London, England. Cryderman returned to the Toronto Department of Public Health as a district supervisor from 1925 to 1929, before joining the VON as a travelling supervisor from

Ethel Mildred Cryderman

1929 to 1934. During that time, she began the Maternity Institute which she conducted in various centres across Canada. In 1934, Cryderman conducted a survey of the Toronto Branch of the VON, following which she became its District Director.

As Director of the Toronto Branch of the VON, Cryderman was phenomenally successful. In her first 14 years, staff increased from 50 to 97, the number of cases increased from 8,020 to 13,961, the number of visits from 85,258 to 143,404 and the annual grant from the City of Toronto doubled. During the Second World War, when there was a shortage of nurses, Cryderman inaugurated a scholarship plan whereby nurses received financial assistance for public health training and then returned to the Toronto VON Branch for a term. She also introduced industrial nursing into the VON programme, enabling several industries in Toronto to buy nursing service on contract from the VON. Her administrative ability extended into voluntary membership on the Board of Directors of the Canadian Arthritis and Rheumatism Society, which knew her as a financial wizard. She also served on the Board of Directors of the Community Chest, as vice-chairman of the Health Division, Toronto Welfare Council, and as a member of the Nursing Advisory Committee of the Canadian Red Cross.

After serving as chairman of the Public Health Section of the Registered Nurses Association of Ontario (RNAO), Cryderman was President of the R.N.A.O., a member of several committees of the Canadian Nurses Association (CNA), first vice-President of CNA, and finally its President from 1948 to 1950. During her CNA Presidency, Cryderman advocated shortening the length of prelicensure nursing education programs, expanding enrollment in schools for nursing aides, and using paraprofessional aides to relieve graduate nurses of routine and non-nursing tasks which caused so much job dissatisfaction and contributed to an escalating shortage of graduate nurses. She agreed with many graduate nurses employed in hospitals that unnecessary time at work was being spent on clerical, secretarial, and housekeeping duties at the expense of professional nursing service.

In failing health for some time, Cryderman retired from the VON late in 1958. In 1960, the CNA conferred honorary life membership upon her in recognition of a life of professional nursing service. Ethel Cryderman died in Toronto on 17 October 1963.

PUBLICATIONS BY ETHEL M. CRYDERMAN

Several reports and articles in *The Canadian Nurse* journal, especially during her time as CNA President. For example: Cryderman, E. M. (1950). The immediate task. *The Canadian Nurse, 46,* 693–698.

BIBLIOGRAPHY

Ethel Cryderman, President. (1948). *The Canadian Nurse, 44,* 622–623.

Gartshore, E. Ethel Cryderman of Toronto V.O.N. named C.N.A. head. Available from the CNA Library, 50 The Driveway, Ottawa, Ontario, K2P 1E2.

Meilicke, D., & Larsen, J. (1992). Leadership and the leaders of the Canadian Nurses Association. *Canadian Nursing Faces the Future* (2nd ed.). Toronto: Mosby Year Book.

Nursing Profiles: Ethel Cryderman. Available from the CNA Library, 50 The Driveway, Ottawa, Ontario, K2P 1E2.

Obituary. (1963). *The Canadian Nurse, 59,* 1171.

Sharon Richardson

D

RUTH DAVIDOW
1911–1999

Ruth Davidow was a nurse with the Abraham Lincoln Battalion during the Spanish Civil War, and one of its few women members. In 1996 the government of Spain made her an honorary citizen in recognition of her service to the republic from 1936 to 1939.

Born in Russia in 1911, she emigrated to New York City at the age of three. In 1936 she received her nursing diploma from the Brooklyn Jewish Hospital. Shortly after she joined the medical team of the Abraham Lincoln Battalion and went to Spain. On her return she married Fred Keller, a union organizer who had been a commissar in the Abraham Lincoln Battalion. They were the parents of a daughter, Joan.

A public health nurse, Davidow devoted much of her life to liberal and radical causes. From 1960 to 1962, following the Castro revolution, she worked with the Public Health organization in Havana. During the "Freedom Summer" of 1965 she traveled to Mississippi to aid Freedom Rider as a member of the Medical Committee for Human Rights. From 1969 to 1971 she traveled regularly to Alcatraz to provide health services for the Indians who had taken over the island. In 1997, she traveled to the Third International Women's Congress in Beijing as a delegate.

She was the subject or key figure in several documentaries including *The Good Fight, Their Case was Liberty,* and the Academy Award nominee, *Forever Activists.* She also produced 21 films herself on such subjects as health, geriatrics, and political movements, including *Do No Harm, Love Letter to Cuba,* and *My Brother Michael.* This last was a profile of her brother who had been a reporter for the *Daily Worker* and lived in Moscow for many years.

Davidow moved to San Francisco in 1955 and received an advanced degree from the University of California, San Francisco. She remained active as a nurse in radical causes almost up until her death. She died June 28, 1999, in San Francisco, California at the age of 87.

BIBLIOGRAPHY

"Obituary," *San Francisco Chronicle,* July 14, 1999, p. A17.

Vern L. Bullough

MAUDE CAMPBELL DAVISON
1885–1956

Maude Davison was a military officer whose career in the Army Nurse Corps spanned the two world wars. At the outbreak of World War II, she was the Chief Nurse, U.S. Army Forces in the Philippines. Her firm and determined leadership style was responsible, in part, for the survival of 87 Army nurses during the December 1941 siege of Manila, the bloody battles of 1942 in the Bataan jungles and on the island fortress of Corregidor, and more importantly, the survival of the 66 Army nurses who surrendered to the Japanese and who spent thirty-four months as prisoners-of-war.

Born March 27, 1885 in Cannington, Ontario, Canada to Ernest John Campbell and Janet Siddus, Davison began her profes-

Maude Campbell Davidson

sional life as a dietitian after graduating in 1909 with a certificate from the MacDonald School of Home Economics at the Ontario College of Agriculture in Guelph, Ontario. For several years she worked at Baptist College in Brandon, Manitoba, Canada before emigrating to the United States and working as a Dietitian and Domestic Science Instructor at Epworth Hospital in South Bend, Indiana.

Maude Davison attended the Pasadena Hospital Training School for Nurses in California and graduated as a registered nurse in 1917 at the age of 32. During her training, Davison roomed with the Jacksons, a Canadian emigrant family. Three decades later, Reverend Charles Jackson would become her husband.

She became a Reserve Nurse in the Army Nurse Corps and reported for duty on June 3, 1918 as a general staff nurse caring for war casualties at Camp Fremont Base Hospital in Palo Alto and later at Letterman General Hospital in San Francisco. In 1920, while serving at her third duty station, the U.S. Disciplinary Barracks Hospital, Fort Leavenworth, Kansas, Maude Davison became an American citizen and a Regular Army member of the Nurse Corps (ANC 700 404) with the relative rank of Second Lieutenant.

Her dual specialties in dietetics and nursing made her a timely asset to a War Department trying to cope with casualties, flu victims, and legions of war refugees. From May 1921 until June 1922 she worked as a dietitian with the Occupation Forces at Station Hospital in Coblenz, Germany. Her duties with famine victims from Russia and eastern Europe was a foreshadowing of her own future when, as a POW, she would suffer from the devastating physical consequences of starvation.

Davison returned to the United States, and on December 1, 1924, after passing the Army's Chief Nurse Examination she was promoted to 1st Lieutenant, relative rank. From 1926 to 1928, in detached service from the ANC, she completed the requirements for a Bachelor of Science degree in Home Economics from Columbia University. (Less than 10% of American women graduated from college during that time period.) During the next decade, she served and as a nurse and dietitian in stateside Army hospitals. Evaluations from that time period noted her reliability, systematic planning, and thorough knowledge of dietetics.

In March 1939, at the age of 54, Davison sailed for the Philippines and assumed the Chief Nurse position at Fort Mills Station Hospital on Corregidor. By July 1941, Japanese troops were on the offensive in the Pacific. More American troops and nurses arrived in the islands to boost defenses. After 17 years as a lieutenant, Davison was promoted to Captain, relative rank, and became Chief Nurse of the Philippine Army

Nurse Corps Department. Her seniority, experience, and outstanding evaluations supported this promotion.

Davison looked like a grandmother. She was a short, small-framed woman with stark white hair that she tied into a bun. A quiet person, she enjoyed a glass of sherry or whiskey. The younger nurses nicknamed her "Ma Davison," but none looked to her for maternal comfort. Davison was a strict disciplinarian who kept her distance from her staff and demanded that her nurses follow protocol. With no tolerance for nonsense, she used her strong will and determination to keep the expanding department under control.

On December 8, 1941 when the Japanese attacked the islands, Davison hired civilian nurses to help care for the huge numbers of casualties pouring into military facilities. During a bombing raid, she fell, injured her back, and was hospitalized (2nd Lt. Josephine Nesbit took over her duties). Despite her injury, on December 29, Davison left Manila with the last American Army troops going to Corregidor or the jungles of Bataan.

From the underground tunnel complex on Corregidor, she coordinated nursing activities during the fierce jungle and tunnel fighting from January until May 1942. (The top-grossing 1942 movie *So Proudly We Hail* presents a fictional version of Davison on Bataan and Corregidor in the character called Captain "Ma" McGregor, played by actress Mary Servoss.)

When surrender became inevitable in May 1942, Davison had no precedent to follow, so she used common sense and ordered her remaining staff to stick together and wear their homemade khaki uniforms and Red Cross arm bands at all times.

Davison was intimidated neither by the Allied civilian businessmen the Japanese put in charge of the daily details of Santo

Tomas Internment Camp in Manila, nor by the Japanese themselves. From May 1942 until liberation in February 1945, whenever she sensed there was an effort to disband her 66 member ANC staff or to force these women to perform non-nursing tasks, she successfully argued the need to keep her group together. One night, when Japanese guards wanted to search the nurses' sleeping quarters, Davison prevented them from entering until all the women got dressed. For almost 3 years, she was the chief nurse of the Santo Tomas prison hospital. Many of her POW-army nurse staff credit Davison's determination to keep them working and living together as a reason none of the 66 women died in a prison camp that held 3,785 inmates of whom 390 men, women, and children died from starvation and illness.

On Liberation Day, February 3, 1945, the 60-old Davison was gravely ill with an intestinal obstruction. She did leave her hospital bed and came home to receive a heroine's welcome with her staff. Several top Army officers, including General Douglas MacArthur, wanted to honor Davison's leadership in the war with the Distinguished Service Medal, but their effort was denied by the War Decorations Board, who felt that the position of Chief Nurse of a field command lacked the responsibility and independent initiative physicians and combat commanders had. Instead, she received the Legion of Merit.

Davison was medically retired from the Army on January 31, 1946. She married the widower Reverend Jackson in 1947 and stopped communicating with her wartime staff. The two lived a quiet life until June 11, 1956 when Davison died at the Veterans Administration Hospital in Long Beach, California, from a massive stroke. At the age of 71, she was the first of the former POW nurses to die. Davison's husband buried her in their native Canada at an unknown site.

MILITARY AWARDS

Legion of Merit
Bronze Star Medal
World War II Victory Medal
American Defense Service Medal with Foreign Service Clasp
Asiatic-Pacific Campaign Medal with two Bronze Battle Stars
Distinguished Unit Badge, Presidential Unit Emblem with two Oak Leaf Clusters on Blue Ribbon
American Campaign Medal and American Theater Ribbon
Philippine Defense Ribbon with one Bronze Service Star
Philippine Liberation Ribbon with one Bronze Service Star
Philippine Independence Ribbon
World War I Victory medal
Army of Occupation of Germany Medal, World War I

BIBLIOGRAPHY

Comeau, G. K. (1961). *A concise biography of Major Maude C. Davison, ANC.* Historical Unit USAMEDS, Walter Reed Army Medical Center, Washington D.C. Located in Washington D.C.: Center for Military History, Army Nurse Corps Archives, Uncataloged files.

Davison, Maude C. Major ANC N700 404, (1957). Two-page typewritten biography, author unknown. Located in Washington D.C.: Center for Military History, Army Nurse Corps Archives, Uncataloged files.

O'Hare, E. (1945, March 24). [War Department interview by the Judge Advocate Department.] Transcript, Supreme Command for the Allied Forces (SCAP) collection, National Archives, Suitland, MD. RG 153. Case 40-633.

Major Maude Davison personnel file. Obtained from the National Personnel Records Center, St. Louis, Missouri under the Freedom of Information Act.

Wallach, L. (September 8, 1968). Letter to Adjutant General's Office regarding an honor for Major Davison. Located in Washington DC: Center for Military History, Army Nurse Corps Archives, Uncataloged files.

Robert Jackson (Personal communication, November 5, 1993). [Mr. Jackson is Maude Davison's stepson.]

Elizabeth M. Norman

NAOMI DEUTSCH
1890–1983

Diligent, hardworking, disciplined, proud, arrogant, and rigid. These words characterize Naomi Deutsch, the second child born to Rabbi Dr. Gotthard and Hermine (Bacher) Deutsch in Brno, Moravia, of the kingdom of Bohemia on November 5, 1890. In 1891, Deutsch emigrated to Cincinnati, Ohio, with her parents, brother Herman, and sister Edith. Brothers Eberhard and Zola were born in Cincinnati. Gotthard Deutsch, an ordained Reform rabbi and professor, accepted a position as professor of history at Hebrew Union College. Gotthard Deutsch, a prolific author, was fiercely proud that he was able to trace both his and his wife's ancestry back into 15th-century Germany. Through his writings, he was embroiled in the Dreyfus affair, even though it was occurring in France.

A rather tall, striking woman, Deutsch graduated from Walnut Hills High School in 1908. She travelled extensively to England, France, Switzerland, and Italy from 1902 to 1909. She graduated June 11, 1912, from the Jewish Hospital School of Nursing, Cincinnati.

Naomi Deutsch had positions with the Visiting Nurse Association of Cincinnati and then with the Irene Kauffman Settlement House, Pittsburgh, Pennsylvania (1912–1916). In November 1916 Deutsch gave a paper entitled "The Future of Public Health Nursing" to the Graduate Nurses Association of Pennsylvania.

She attended Teachers College, Columbia University (1916–1917 and 1919–1921)

Naomi Deutsch

and received her B.S. degree. She enrolled with the American Red Cross on November 2, 1920, and was given badge number 36,776.

While in New York, she worked for the Henry Street Settlement (1917–1924) as supervisor, field director, and acting director. Naomi was the supervisor at the Morrisania office in the Bronx when she came up with the idea of using abandoned saloons when more spacious quarters for offices were required. She was refused for military service during World War I because of her birth in a nation with which the United States was at war. She was an early member of the National League of Women Voters when that organization was founded in February 1920 as an outgrowth of the National American Woman Suffrage Association.

Deutsch directed the San Francisco Visiting Nurse Association from 1925 to 1934. She became a lecturer in Public Health Nursing at the University of California,

Berkeley in 1933, was appointed assistant professor in 1934, and later assumed full charge of the public health nursing program at Berkeley.

Speeches Deutsch made during this time indicate her concern about organizing in order to avoid duplication of services, the importance of bedside nursing in public health work, and the reorganization of the profession in light of community needs. She also wanted to de-emphasize full-time nursing in the home and replace it with the hourly visiting nurse who could nurse and teach the family at the same time.

Memberships in professional organizations were very important to Deutsch and she was a member of the National League of Women Voters and the National League of Nursing Education, member, and later, on the board of directors of the National Organization of Public Health Nursing, a member of the Professional and Business Women's Clubs, and the California State Conference of Social Work. She was elected president (1933) of the California State Organization for Public Health Nursing and president of the Social Workers' Alliance of San Francisco. She was a member, and later, on the board of directors of the California State Nurses Association.

Naomi Deutsch was included in the 1928 *Women of the West* book of biographical sketches. She was invited to the White House Conference on Child Health and Protection, February 1931, and again, in 1940, to the Conference on Children in a Democracy.

In 1935, Deutsch accepted the position of organizing and directing the Public Health Unit of the Federal Children's Bureau, Department of Labor in Washington, D.C. Membership in professional organizations now included the governing council of the American Public Health Association, the American Nurses Association, the American Association of Social Workers, the National Conference of Social Workers, and Delta Omega. She was listed in *Who's Who in the East* (1943) and *Who's Who of the World* (1948).

Naomi Deutsch assumed position as staff member (1943) of the Pan American Sanitation Bureau. She served as principal nurse consultant, and collaborated in the development of health programs in the Caribbean and Central America, where she travelled extensively.

Deutsch was not hailed for her driving habits. Her nephew remembers that on a family visit to California, Aunt Naomi always "flipped up" the rear-view mirror. Her belief was that the cars in back of her had to be careful of her. It was not her responsibility to check for drivers in her rear-view mirror. Her nephew also called her the "terror of Catholic hospitals." Whenever she saw a statue of a saint standing in sunshine, she immediately moved it and pushed a patient's bed there in its place enabling the patient to benefit from the sunshine.

In the post-World War II years, Deutsch served as an Associate in Research in Nursing Education, Teachers College Columbia University (1945–1946) and part-time instructor (1946 to 1950). Her early retirement years (1950–1973) were spent in New York City. Deutsch never married but did develop a deep friendship with Lillian Wald, and she was close to her sister Edith. Her frail health required Deutsch to move to New Orleans for the last 10 years of her life. She was still active in Planned Parenthood and the League of Women Voters. Deutsch died November 26, 1983, and was cremated.

PUBLICATIONS BY NAOMI DEUTSCH

Deutsch, N. (1935). Generalized public health nursing services in cities. *American Journal of Public Health, 25,* 475–478.

Deutsch, N. (1937a). Public health nursing in programs for crippled children. *Public Health Nursing, 29,* 10–15.

Deutsch, N. (1937b). Role of public health nurse in service for crippled children. *Public Health Nursing, 29,* 350–356.

Deutsch, N. (1938). What every health officer should know: Public health nursing. *American Journal of Public Health, 28,* 1087–1090.

Deutsch, N. (1939). Economic aspects of maternal care. *Public Health Nursing, 31,* 619–624.

Deutsch, N., & Hilbert, H. (1936). Public health nursing under the Social Security Act: Development under the Children's Bureau. *Public Health Reports, 28,* 582–585.

Deutsch, N., & Willeford, M. D. (1941). Promoting maternal and child health: Public health nursing under Social Security Act, Title V, Part I. *American Journal of Nursing, 41,* 894–899.

BIBLIOGRAPHY

Binheim, M. (Ed.). (1928). *Women of the West.* Los Angeles: Publishers Press.

Bullough, V., Church, O. M., & Stein, A. P. (Eds.). (1988). *American nursing: A biographical dictionary.* New York: Garland.

Bullough, V., Sentz, L., & Stein, A. P. (Eds.). (1992). *American nursing: A biographical dictionary.* New York: Garland.

Hawkins, J. (1988). Naomi Deutsch. In M. Kaufman (Ed.), *Dictionary of American nursing biography* (pp. 92–93). Westport, CT: Greenwood Press.

Howes, D. (Ed.). (1941). *American women, 1935–1940: A composite biographical dictionary* (Vol. I). Detroit, MI: Gale Research Co.

Lashman, L. E. (1996, January 3). Telephone interview [Nephew of Naomi Deutsch].

Mayer, S. L. (1996). *The Jewish experience in nursing in America: 1881 to 1955.* Ed.D. dissertation, Teachers College, Columbia University.

Werminghouse, E. (1950). *Annie W. Goodrich: Her journey to Yale.* New York: Macmillan.

Susan Mayer

MARY A. DINEEN
1922–

Mary A. Dineen's leadership in the area of nursing education and administration promoted the integration of nursing education programs into institutions of higher education and provided a firm foundation for further evolution of nursing as an academic discipline.

Mary A. Dineen

Mary Dineen was born on September 13, 1922 in Niagara Falls, New York, where she received her elementary and secondary school education. She received her nursing training at Mt. St. Mary's Hospital located in her home town of Niagara Falls.

After working briefly as a staff nurse at Mt. St. Mary's Hospital, she moved to St. Louis where she received her baccalaureate in nursing at St. Louis University in 1946.

Dineen then began her teaching/administration career at Niagara University College of Nursing where she rose through the ranks of faculty and administrative positions to become Assistant Dean in 1963. At the same time she continued her education earning a M.A. in education from Niagara University in 1950 and an Ed.D. in administration of baccalaureate nursing programs at Teachers College, Columbia University in 1959.

In 1963 Dineen resigned from her position at Niagara University to join the staff at the National League for Nursing (NLN) in New York City. Serving initially as Consultant and subsequently as the Director of the Department of Baccalaureate and Higher Degree Programs, she soon developed a national reputation for leadership in the areas of curriculum and accreditation. Her advice on nursing education, accreditation, and organizational structures, was sought formally and informally both during her service at NLN and throughout her career. Her contributions to the NLN continued after she left her position at the NLN. She served on NLN Board of Directors (1983–1987); the Executive Committee of Baccalaureate and higher degree Programs Council (1979–1983); the Constitution and By-Laws Committee of the NLN (1987–1991); and chaired the Long-Range Planning Committee of the NLN (1985–1987), and the Nominations Committee (1987–1989).

In 1972, Dineen left the NLN to assume the deanship at the Boston College School of nursing. During a deanship which spanned 14 years, she further developed the baccalaureate and master's programs, guided the curriculum and faculty through an era of increasing enrollments, and provided the groundwork for the Ph.D. in nursing program which led to its approval by the trustees of Boston College a year after her retirement.

Dineen served on various committees of the American Association of Colleges of Nursing and on advisory and executive boards for multiple organizations such as the Massachusetts Board of Higher Education, the Catholic Hospital Association, the Western Interstate Commission on Higher Education, Massachusetts Nurses Association, the New England Council of Higher Education in Nursing (NECHEN), New England Organization for Nursing (NEON), and the International Nursing Index.

Mary Dineen's contributions to nursing have been recognized through her induction as a member of the American Academy of Nursing in 1977, by receiving the Achievement Award in Nursing Education of the Columbia University Teachers College Nursing Alumni Association (1984), and the Mary Adelaide Nutting Award by the National League for Nursing (1985). Additionally she was a member of Sigma Theta Tau, Pi Lambda Theta, and Kappa Delta Pi, and Alpha Sigma Nu, the Jesuit honor society. In 1992, she was awarded an honorary degree from Niagara University, where she currently serves on the Board of Trustees.

PUBLICATIONS BY MARY A. DINEEN (SELECTED)

Dineen, M. A. (1965). A nursing major without nursing. *Nursing Outlook, 13*, 66–67.

Dineen, M. A. (1969). Current trends in collegiate education. *Nursing Outlook, 17*, 22–56.

Dineen, M. A. (1972). The open curriculum: Implications for further education. *Nursing Outlook, 20*, 770–774.

Dineen, M. A. (1975). Career mobility and baccalaureate nursing education. In *Open learning and career mobility in nursing* (pp. 98–105). St. Louis: Mosby.

Laurel A. Eisenhauer

VERONICA MARGARET DRISCOLL
1926–1994

A pioneer in the struggle for economic security for nurses, Veronica Driscoll devoted her career to improving nursing's status as an independent profession. She was the driving force behind enactment of the ground breaking 1972 New York State Nurse Practice Act, and a key figure in the development of *A Blueprint for the Education of Nurses in New York State*, a document which provided guidelines for strengthening nursing's educational base.

Veronica Margaret Driscoll

A fourth-generation American, Driscoll was born in Brooklyn on April 24, 1926, one of seven children of Francis Aloysius Bartholomew and Madeline (Daly) Driscoll. As a child, she attended Catholic school, then P.S. 207 in Brooklyn. During her senior year at Midwood High School, she won first prize in a short story contest. Although her first career choice was journalism, her early experiences with personal and family illness influenced her to pursue a career in nursing.

Following graduation from St. Catherine's Hospital School of Nursing in Brooklyn (1948), Driscoll earned a Bachelor of Science degree from St. John's University (1953), a Master of Arts degree from New York University (1958), and a Doctor of Education degree from Teachers College, Columbia University. In 1948, Driscoll accepted a position as a general duty staff nurse at St. Catherine's Hospital earning $45 per week. Two years later, she was appointed supervisor of the student health program at that institution and, in 1953, joined the faculty of the school of nursing as an instructor.

In 1960, Driscoll applied to the New York State Nurses Association (NYSNA) for a position in the counseling and placement service. Instead, she was offered and accepted the position of assistant executive director in the newly formed NYSNA economic security program which was established in response to the growing movement toward collective bargaining as the way to improve working conditions for nurses. Driscoll was named associate director in 1963, a position she held for the ensuing 6 years.

During those years, working conditions for nurses were abysmal. Salaries for a beginning staff nurse in New York were $99 a week—less than the wages of sanitation workers. In 1966, Driscoll led NYSNA's negotiations for nurses employed in the 21 municipal hospitals that comprised the New York City Department of Hospitals. After 8 months of struggle, a precedent-setting contract was signed which increased salaries by 20 percent and provided improved benefits and working conditions.

As deputy executive director, Driscoll staffed the committee that prepared *A Blueprint for the Education of Nurses in New York State*, published in 1966. The blueprint had a single objective, as stated in the introduction: "That the nursing needs of the people of New York State will be met by qualified practitioners of nursing prepared in institutions of higher education." It proposed that there be no further development of hospital diploma programs nor new programs in practical nursing. It enunciated a plan whereby existing nursing education programs would be transferred to schools of higher learning by 1972, and affirmed the 1965 American Nurses Association (ANA) position statement regarding baccalaureate degree preparation for beginning professional nursing practice and associate de-

gree preparation for beginning general nursing practice. The ideas embodied in the blueprint were central to Driscoll's vision of professional nursing, and the document subsequently received attention from other state nurses' associations across the country.

In the summer of 1969, Driscoll was appointed Executive Director of NYSNA, the position she held until her resignation in June 1979. During her tenure, NYSNA's membership more than doubled and NYSNA became the nation's largest collective bargaining agent for registered nurses. Driscoll played a pivotal role in the enactment of the 1972 revision of the New York State Nurse Practice Act. Considered a model practice act by the nursing community, it was the first legislative recognition of nursing's independent role and diagnostic function. The definition of nursing contained in the 1972 practice act survives to this day, was incorporated into ANA's *Social Policy Statement*, and widely copied by other state nurses' associations.

Known as a skilled strategist and charismatic communicator, Driscoll implemented sweeping organizational changes in NYSNA that streamlined operations such as fiscal management, the processing of data, and the role of staff. Under Driscoll's leadership, publication of NYSNA's *Report* and *Journal* was begun, the office of president-elect was introduced, the Foundation of NYSNA was established, and the NYSNA headquarters building was erected in Guilderland, New York. Upon Driscoll's retirement, the building was named the Veronica M. Driscoll Center for Nursing, in her honor.

Driscoll's sphere of influence extended beyond NYSNA. She served as chair of the ANA Commission on Economics and General Welfare, as a member of the ANA board of directors, as secretary of the board of directors of the American Journal of

Nursing Company, and as a member of the New York State Hospital Review and Planning Council. Her extraordinary vision and dedication were acknowledged through conferral of the Teachers College Nursing Education Alumni Association Achievement Award for Professional and Allied Organization Leadership; the NYSNA Honorary Recognition Award; and the ANA Honorary Recognition Award.

Following retirement in 1979, Driscoll remained active as secretary of the Foundation of NYSNA and consultant to the NYSNA Records Management and Archives Project. She was frequently invited to present papers and workshops on such topics as legal, professional, and organizational issues to regulatory agencies, professional societies, voluntary health organizations, and nursing associations.

Throughout her career, Driscoll was uncompromising in her rejection of the status quo. She was critical of and frustrated by nursing's inability to project a unified professional image. She spoke of nurses as the migrant workers of the health care field, who provided an essential service but were oppressed by external forces determined to keep nurses dumb, down, and dispersed. To the last, she was convinced that nursing is illegimate as a profession because nursing is largely perceived to be subsumed under medicine; the intellectual component of nursing practice is undervalued; and hospitals persist in their attempts to control nursing. Irrespective of Driscoll's convictions regarding professionalization, the 1972 New York State Nurse Practice Act stands in testimony to her wisdom, her determination, and her adherence to the mission of NYSNA.

Veronica Driscoll died on January 30, 1994, and is buried in St. Agnes Cemetery in Menands, New York. Remembered by colleagues as a courageous risk-taker, loyal friend, and valued mentor, she left behind an incomparable legacy of leadership.

PUBLICATIONS BY VERONICA MARGARET DRISCOLL

Books

Legitimizing the profession of nursing: The distinct mission of the New York State Nurses Association. (1976). New York: Foundation of NYSNA.

Articles (Selected)

Liberating nursing practice. (1972). *Nursing Outlook, 20,* 24–28.
New York State Nurses Association. (1973). *Journal of Nursing Administration, 3,* 16.
Beware the circling opportunists. (1974a). *Nursing Digest, 2,* 56–57.
The myth of two hats. (1974b). *Supervisor Nurse, 5,* 24–27.
Remedies for a troubled health care system. (1980). *Journal of New York State Nurses Association, 11,* 15–22.

BIBLIOGRAPHY

In memoriam. (1994). *New York State Nurses Association Report, 25,* 16.
New York State Nurses Association. (1966). *A blueprint for the education of nurses in New York State.* New York: Author.
New York State Nurses Association. (1988). *Professionalization of nursing in New York State.* New York: Author.
Stapleton, D. H., & Welch, C. A. (Eds.). (1994). *Critical issues in American nursing.* New York: Foundation of NYSNA.

Nettie Birnbach

VIRGINIA MATHEWS DUNBAR
1897–1986

Virginia M. Dunbar, an early advocate of baccalaureate education for nurses, served as an administrator of nursing services for the American Red Cross, 1939–1946, and as dean of the Cornell University–New York Hospital School of Nursing, 1946–1958. She was one of the founders and incorporators of Nurses Educational Funds, Inc.

Virginia Mathews Dunbar

Dunbar was born in Altoona, PA, on November 29, 1897, the daughter of William Otis Dunbar and Ann Elizabeth Mathews Dunbar. She received her B.A. from Mt. Holyoke College in 1919, and her diploma from the Johns Hopkins Hospital School of Nursing in 1923. She held staff positions at Johns Hopkins and the infirmary of the Lawrenceville School in N.J., and then earned the M.A. at Teachers College, Columbia University, in 1930.

She held management and supervisory positions at Englewood Hospital in N.J., taught in the Teachers College Department of Nursing 1930–1932, and was instructor and assistant director of the University of California School of Nursing at San Francisco from 1933–1938. On leave of absence during 1935, she became the first nurse in the U.S. to receive a scholarship from the American Red Cross for advanced study at Bedford College in London and the Florence Nightingale International Foundation.

She was awarded certificates in public health nursing and in the history of nursing.

In 1938 Dunbar first became assistant director, later director, and then administrator of the American Red Cross Nursing Services, with responsibility for enrolling nurses in the Red Cross Nurses Reserve, directing nurses in disaster, and overseeing the home hygiene and care of the sick courses. The Red Cross Reserve of over 39,000 nurses provided disaster relief for the Red Cross, as well as for the Army and Navy Nurse Corps.

She resigned in 1946 to accept the dual position of dean of the Cornell University–New York Hospital School of Nursing in New York City, and director of nursing services of The New York Hospital, a common arrangement at the time. In 1947, however, the dual positions were separated, and Dean Dunbar was able to devote full time to the school and its development until her retirement in 1957.

The school was in the throes of conversion from a hospital to a university school, and Dean Dunbar's task was to educate students, faculty, and the public about university procedures as well as the role of baccalaureate nurses within a medical center unaccustomed to these concepts. She strove to reduce the students' work week and led curriculum changes that emphasized patient teaching, community and public health, and psychosocial concepts. She encouraged faculty members to write journal articles, carry out clinical studies, and publish textbooks. She began an endowment fund for the school, and was one of the founders and incorporators of Nurses Educational Funds, Inc.

Many of her writing efforts were directed toward helping the Medical Center and the Hospital understand the role of collegiate nursing. As a scholar of nursing history and Florence Nightingale, she collected nursing history memorabilia that are now in the nursing archives at the Mugar Library of Boston University.

In 1952 Dunbar was honored by Mt. Holyoke College at a convocation on Science and Human Values. The citation read, "Administrator and Author; as Director of Nursing during World War II you rendered valuable service to your country; as Author you have added to the dignity of your profession of nursing; as Dean of Nursing at Cornell University, you are carrying forward significant work through the training of young women."

Dunbar died October 23, 1986, at her retirement home, Medford Leas, Medford, N.J., and is buried in Canton Cemetery in Canton, Massachusetts.

PUBLICATIONS BY VIRGINIA MATHEWS DUNBAR (SELECTED)

Internationalists in the making. (1936). *American Journal of Nursing, 36,* 433–437.

Nursing in Northern Europe. (1937). *American Journal of Nursing, 37,* 123–130.

Educational standards in relation to the preparation of nurses in wartime. (1943). National League of Nursing Education: *Annual Report, 1943,* and *Record of Proceedings of the 47th Convention, 1943,* 177–181.

Florence Nightingale's influence on nursing education. (1954). *International Nursing Review, 1,* 17–23.

A look at education for nursing, 1899–1959. (1959). Paper read at the 60th anniversary celebration of the Division of Nursing, Teachers College, Columbia University. In *Education for Nursing: Past, Present, and Future.* New York: League Exchange #43.

(With M. Beard). Wanted—10,000 Nurses! (1939). *American Journal of Nursing, 39,* 227–232.

(With G. Banfield). Red Cross Nursing Service Contemplates Changes in Enrolment Plan. (1946). *American Journal of Nursing, 46,* 82–84.

BIBLIOGRAPHY

Allen, J. C. (1982). *The History of Cornell University–New York Hospital School of Nursing, 1942–1979.* Doctoral Dissertation, Columbia University Teachers College, 1982.

Archives of The New York Hospital–Cornell Medical Center. School of Nursing; New York, NY.

Archives of the American Red Cross. Hazel Brough Records Center, Falls Church, VA.

Hazeltine, L. (1987). Virginia M. Dunbar, 1898–1986. *Newsletter of Nurses' Educational Funds, Inc., 7,* 2.

Nursing Archives. "Virginia M. Dunbar." Mugar Library Special Collections, Boston University, Boston, MA.

Sykes, W. G. (1998, August). Personal communication to the author, Carlisle, MA.

Alma S. Woolley

LILLIAN DUNLAP
1922–

Lillian Dunlap was the 14th Chief of the Army Nurse Corps. She served in this key position from September 1, 1971 until August 31, 1975. Her first year as chief coincided with the closing days of the Vietnam War and her tenure continued into the immediate post-war years, during which time the Army Nurse Corps recovered from the after effects of the cataclysmic war in South East Asia.

Dunlap, the oldest in a family of five girls, was born on January 20, 1922 in Mission, Texas to Ira and Mary Schermerhorn Dunlap. In 1939, when she was 17 years old, Dunlap entered the Santa Rosa Hospital School of Nursing in San Antonio, Texas. In her senior year of nurses' training, the Japanese attack on Pearl Harbor occurred, and that event motivated the young graduate to join the Army Nurse Corps. On November 16, 1942, Dunlap was assigned to Brooke General Hospital at Fort Sam Houston, Texas. In March 1943, Dunlap and 23 other Army nurses from Brooke were sent to the 59th Station Hospital and service in the Southwest Pacific. The sequential settings for Dunlap's World War II service were first in New Guinea, then in the Admiralty Islands, and finally, on the Philippine Islands. While in New Guinea, the young Army nurse met and fell in love with

Lillian Dunlap

a paratrooper, who was killed during the battle for the Philippines. In 1945 she returned to the states, ill with a debilitating bout of malaria. After her recovery, Dunlap returned to duty at Brooke General Hospital and served on the women's ward, the officers' ward, and later the surgical research unit whose mission at that time was the treatment and study of osteomyelitis. In 1949, she transferred to the hospital at Camp Chaffee, Arkansas and served there as assistant chief nurse and later chief nurse, for six months before being ordered to Fort Hood, Texas. From Fort Hood, she was assigned to the U.S. Army in San Antonio, Texas where she assumed recruiting responsibilities for nurses to serve in reserve units during the era of the Korean War. She returned to Fort Hood and served there until September 1953 at which time she entered Incarnate Word College in San Antonio to pursue her undergraduate degree in nursing. After graduation in 1954,

Dunlap was assigned to be head nurse at the 1,000 bed 98th General Hospital in Neubrücke, Germany. Upon her return to the states, after a short 7-month tour at Fort Jackson, South Carolina, she was sent as a student in the Master of Hospital Administration course jointly sponsored by the Army and by Baylor University at the Medical Field Service School (MFSS) in San Antonio, Texas. Dunlap subsequently completed the program's required year-long residency in administration at Fitzsimons General Hospital in Denver, Colorado and returned to MFSS to serve in several key faculty roles. In 1965 Dunlap accepted a transfer to Okinawa where she served as Chief of Nursing Service at the Army hospital there. After 11 months, the Chief of the Army Nurse Corps requested that Dunlap be returned to the states to be Chief of the Army Nurse Corps Assignment Branch in the Office of the Surgeon General in Washington, D.C., an assignment which coincided with the intensive Vietnam War buildup years of 1966 to 1968. Dunlap's next assignment after a brief interval as Special Assistant to the Chief of the Army Nurse Corps was as chief nurse of the First U.S. Army. Three years later, she became chief nurse of Walter Reed General Hospital and director of nursing activities at Walter Reed Army Medical Center. Dunlap had but a few months under her belt at Walter Reed when the Army Chief of Staff, General William C. Westmoreland, notified her that she had been selected to be the next chief of the Army Nurse Corps with the accompanying promotion to brigadier general.

During Dunlap's term as Chief, various senior officers in the Army Nurse Corps helped to implement educational programs to prepare Army nurses for a number of expanded roles which were projected to be nursing's wave of the future. The entire initiative was referred to as the Army Nurse Corps Contemporary Practice Program

(AN-CP). It envisioned the future practice of Army nurses as encompassing the traditional domains of nursing as well as physician-delegated responsibilities with an added emphasis on health education and maintenance. Among the advanced practice nurses were ambulatory care; obstetrical/gynecological and psychiatric nurse clinicians; and pediatric nurse practitioners, all prepared to serve in outpatient settings. The AN-CP program also educated nurses to function as intensive care nurses. Later a program was initiated in cooperation with the University of Kentucky to prepare nurse midwives for service in the Army as well. Dunlap's implementation of the Contemporary Practice Program ushered the Army Nurse Corps into the modern area of nursing practice.

Another facet of Dunlap's advocacy for education was reflected in her efforts to extend the efforts of her predecessors to establish the baccalaureate degree as the entry level for all Army Nurse Corps officers. By 1972, the degree was required for all officers seeking a regular Army commission in the Army Nurse Corps. Although the actual regulations setting the standard did not materialize until 1976, Dunlap made it a practice to accept only those with a bachelor's degree into the Army Nurse Corps during the last 2 years of her tenure. Without question, this quality upgrade in the baseline credentials of Army Nurse Corps officers enhanced the excellence of their total contributions and once again confirmed the stature and leadership of the Army Nurse Corps as the world of professional nursing confronted the complex entry for practice dilemma.

On August 31, 1975, Brigadier General Lillian Dunlap retired from the Army after 33 years of service and returned to live in San Antonio, Texas. She, however, still remained active in an vast array of endeavors, including the development of the Army Medical Department (AMEDD) Museum at Fort Sam Houston, Texas, establishing a master of science curriculum within the nursing program at Incarnate Word College and in the endowment of the Brigadier General Lillian Dunlap Professional Chair in Nursing at the institution. Dunlap served with the United Way, the Texas Governor's Commission for Women, the board of the National Bank of Fort Sam Houston, the Board of Directors for GPM Life Insurance Company, and with the Texas National Guard Armory Board. She is an advisor to the Army Nurse Corps Foundation. The Dunlap lecture, an annual keynote address at the 7th MEDCOM Military Medical Surgical Clinical Congress in Garmisch Germany, was established in her honor in 1988. Dunlap has been accorded the signal honor of being elected as a Fellow of the American Academy of Nursing and was recognized with the 1998 Living Legacy Patriot Award from the Women's International Center.

BIBLIOGRAPHY

Nurse Corps assignment officer chosen. (1966, August 22). News Release No. 238-66; ANC Archives, U.S. Army Center of Military History, Washington, DC.

Beasley, N. (n.d.) BG Dunlap: Nursing's lone star. Newsclipping; ANC Archives, U.S. Army Center of Military History, Washington, DC.

Dedication of the Brigadier General Lillian Dunlap Endowed Professorial Chair in Nursing [printed program]; ANC Archives, U.S. Army Center of Military History, Washington, DC.

Gurney, C. (1987, February). Interview (Lillian Dunlap). ANC Archives, U.S. Army Center of Military History, Washington, DC.

Hammarlund, M., to Dunlap L. [ca. 1961] [Questionnaire]. ANC Archives, U.S. Army Center of Military History, Washington, DC.

HQ 7th Medical Command Public Affairs Office, Dunlap Lecture. (n.d.). ANC Archives, U.S. Army Center of Military History, Washington, DC.

Official Biography, Lillian Dunlap, September 1971. (1971). Typewritten document, ANC Archives, U.S. Army Center of Military History, Washington, DC.

Tibbets, A. (1987, July 2). Female general recalls Army career. *Recorder-Times*, p. 10, ANC Archives, U.S. Army Center of Military History, Washington, DC.

Mary T. Sarnecky

E

KATHLEEN WILHELMINA ELLIS
1888–1968

Kathleen Wilhelmina Ellis was one of the true "characters" of early Canadian nursing, although it is likely that few of her contemporaries perceived her in that persona. She was one of the best educated of the second generation of Canadian nurses and was instrumental in reorganizing the Vancouver General Hospital Nursing Division, when Ethel Johns successfully persuaded the University of British Columbia to permit her to focus on the degree nursing program UBC had instigated in 1919. Ellis was one of the most astute and effective nursing administrators of the first half of this century, in both hospital, university, and professional nursing association milieus. She was also the Emergency Nursing Advisor for the Canadian Nurses Association (CNA) during the Second World War and Canada's best known nursing "propagandist" of that era. Ellis contributed significantly to the development of provincial professional nursing associations in British Columbia and Saskatchewan, as well as nationally to the CNA and what later became the Canadian Association of University Schools of Nursing (CAUSN). She was one of the founders of CAUSN in 1942 and its President from 1942 to 1948.

Kathleen Ellis was born in 1888 near Penticton, British Columbia, where her father

Kathleen Wilhelmina Ellis

was a prosperous rancher, reputed to have been the first man to introduce cattle into the Okanagan Valley. The family became prominent, prosperous and influential as a result of successful ranching. One of nine children, Kathleen early showed determination by having her "finishing education" in Canada, rather than England, as her older sisters had done. According to Saskatchewan nursing historian Lucy Willis, Kathleen and her sisters were brought up to be "ladies" first, with the social graces that went with their position in Penticton's frontier society, including lessons in French and golf. Kathleen declined to spend her adult life in leisurely pursuits in Victoria, on Vancouver Island, B.C., where her family eventually moved. Once her primary education was completed, she insisted, against her father's wishes, on studying nursing. Kathleen graduated from Johns Hopkins School of Nursing in Baltimore, Maryland, in 1915.

Following graduation from hospital nurse training, Ellis returned home to serve for the remainder of the First World War as Matron of the Vancouver Island Military Hospital. After the war, Ellis joined the senior staff of the Henry Ford Hospital in Detroit, Michigan, before proceeding to the Toronto General Hospital, where she was an assistant to Superintendent of Nurses, Jean Gunn. Ellis returned to British Columbia in 1921 as Director of Nursing at the Vancouver General Hospital (VGH) and staunch supporter of the University of British Columbia's degree program in nursing—the first in Canada. During her years at the VGH, which was at the time Canada's second largest hospital, Ellis was active in provincial and national nursing associations. She was President of the Registered Nurses Association of British Columbia (RNABC) from 1927 to 1929 and first Vice-President of the Canadian Nurses Association in 1929. Zilm and Warbinek credit her with being instrumental in ensuring that the 1930 national survey of nursing in Canada, co-sponsored by the CNA and the Canadian Medical Association (CMA), and conducted by Professor George Weir of the University of British Columbia (UBC), went ahead. The subsequent "Survey of Nursing Education in Canada," colloquially named the Weir Report, became a milestone in Canadian nursing history.

Ellis earned a Bachelor of Science degree from Teachers College, Columbia University, New York, prior to assuming administrative responsibility at the VGH in 1922. In the early 1930s, under the auspices of the league of Red Cross Societies, she earned a certificate in public health nursing at Bedford College, London, England. When she returned to Canada, Ellis became Advisor to Schools of Nursing and Secretary/Treasurer of the Saskatchewan Registered Nurses Association (SRNA) in 1937. A year later, she agreed to work half-time for the University of Saskatchewan as head of their new degree nursing program, while continuing half-time as Secretary/Treasurer, Registrar, and Advisor to Schools of Nursing for the SRNA. The two agencies each paid half her salary, and the University provided office and secretarial services. Ellis continued as Director of the new Nursing Department at the University of Saskatchewan in Saskatoon, until her retirement in 1950.

Perhaps Ellis's most significant contribution to Canadian nursing, and one which she was uniquely prepared to fulfill, was her role of "Emergency Nursing Advisor" for the CNA during the Second World War. Early in the Second World War, the CNA Executive Committee approached the federal government for money under the guise of "emergency nursing needs." Their primary goal was to stop the Canadian Hospital Council from convincing the federal government to finance expansion of hospital nurse training programs in institutions with inadequate clinical facilities or nursing instructors. Their secondary goal was to advance recognition of nursing as a profession rather than a vocation. Prior to the Second World War, the CNA was a politically weak amalgam of loosely federated nursing organizations without sufficient membership to significantly influence public policy affecting nursing work and education. Kathleen Ellis' success as nursing propagandist extraordinaire in her formal role of "Emergency Nursing Advisor" was both visionary and unprecedented. Ellis successfully negotiated with the President of the University of Saskatchewan for 18 months' release from her conjoint salaried role at the University and as Registrar of the SRNA. From January to July 1942, Ellis visited each of the nine provinces to meet with representatives of nursing associations, members of hospital boards, members of provincial medical associations, government officials, and interested public. She gave a total of 104 addresses and 49 special conferences on nursing. She also sent information to each province about salary schedules of nurses across the country, refresher courses for graduate nurses, scholarships, in-service education, and the status of general hospital staff nurses and private duty nurses. Continuous "propaganda," as Ellis called it, was carried on during her visits by press and radio. She considered such "propaganda" essential to stimulating thoughtful consideration by all stakeholders of policy issues surrounding nursing work and education. During 1943 and 1944, Ellis attended the meetings of hospital associations in British Columbia, Saskatchewan, Manitoba and Ontario, and met with nurses in these provinces and Alberta. By July 1944, when she relinquished her role as CNA's Emergency Nursing Advisor, Ellis had paid at least two visits to each province. Through her transcontinental travels she emphasized CNA's national role as a clearinghouse for information on nursing and raised the association's national profile. Ellis also acted as CNA Executive Director from 1943 to 1944, while she was Emergency Nursing Advisor.

By the time she came to Saskatchewan, in 1937, Ellis was a woman of independent means and lived in a suite in the newly opened Hotel Bessborough. She often entertained there, in style, in the dining room with hotel staff in constant attendance. Willis reported that a corner of the public dining room would be curtained off after dinner and she and her guests would spend a social evening discussing cultural or nursing events. She was always immaculately dressed, in modish and colorful clothes, with her graying hair in place, and topped by a hat. Ellis had an extensive collection of hats, as befitted a true "lady," and wore them when teaching and to all meetings and public appearances. She possessed an independent and creative intellect, and a pithy wit. For example, in her description of the 1942 national meeting of the Canadian Hospitals Council, Ellis addressed hospital boards' reluctance to implement an 8-hour work day for nurses by commenting that boards " . . . are equally proud of a new and progressive idea, once they been actually convinced they are responsible for its birth, although it is often conceived and delivered only after periods of labour and stress" (Ellis, 1943).

Ellis retired from the University of Saskatchewan in 1950 and moved back to Penticton, B.C. In 1955, the university conferred on her a honorary Doctor of Laws degree, and a year later the new nurses' residence was named in her honor. During retirement, she served Penticton in a number of ways, including as a member of the hospital board. Ellis died in 1968.

PUBLICATIONS BY KATHLEEN WILHELMINA ELLIS

Numerous articles & editorial published in *The Canadian Nurse* journal during the Second World War dealing with her role as CNA's Emergency Nursing Advisor, as well as the founding of the Canadian Association of University Schools of Nursing in 1942.

BIBLIOGRAPHY

Ellis, K. (1943). Breezes blow through the West. *The Canadian Nurse, 39,* pp. 22–25.

Collections in the University of Saskatchewan Archives, Saskatoon, Saskatchewan: Alumni File, Dr. K. W. Ellis; Faculty Biography File, Ellis, K.; Presidential Papers, Series II B-121(1), Nursing, School of, 1938–1941 & B-121(2), Nursing, School of, 1942–1949; S. E. Murray Collection E.VII-I.1.bbbb) E–F.

Willis, L. Chapter One: 1938–1950. (1988). *Fifty Years: Just the Beginning* (pp. 1–5). Saskatoon, SK: College of Nursing, University of Saskatchewan.

Zilm, G., & Warbinek, E. (1994). *Legacy: History of nursing education at the University of British Columbia, 1919–1994* (pp. 55, 64, 85–86, 107). Vancouver, BC: UBC Press.

Sharon Richardson

F

HELEN FAIRCHILD
1884–1918

Helen Fairchild is noted for the 100 pages of letters she wrote about war and the battlefield from May 1917 to December 1917, in World War I. Despite the censorship, she managed to mention names, dates and a description of her circumstances, giving us a first-hand description of war. She died, one of the heroines of World War I.

Helen Fairchild was born November 21, 1885, in Turbut (Northumberland County) to Ambrose and Adda Dunkle Fairchild, a prominent farming and banking family in the Milton area in central Pennsylvania. Helen was the middle child, with 6 brothers and sisters, all of them required to work hard on the family farm.

She graduated in 1913 from Pennsylvania Hospital, Philadelphia, PA, then returned to her home area to work as a nurse. When the U.S. entered the war in April 1917, Fairchild volunteered to go overseas with 63 other nurses from Pennsylvania Hospital in May 1917. In June, according to her letters, the group was welcomed and entertained in England before going on to

Helen Fairchild

France, where in July, the 64 nurses took over a 2,000-bed British Base Hospital, changing the name to American Base Hospital No. 10, in Le Treport, France, on the Belgian border. On July 31, 1917, she was assigned to Casualty Clearing Station No. 4, as a surgical nurse with three doctors. Expecting to stay only a few days, they were unprepared for what they faced, the Third Battle of Ypres-Passchcndaclc. Night aftcr night their tents were bombed, one nurse losing her eye. They operated standing in mud over their ankles, too often by the light of a flashlight. Thousands of men passed through their station who had been gassed with mustard gas, and the effects of the dark, syrupy liquid contaminated the nurses as they removed the soldiers uniforms making casualties of the nurses as well. The faces and hair of the nurses turned yellow, and their eyes were streaming.

Through it all, her letters spoke of others with praise and admiration and encouragement for those at home, never revealing she was ill, in fact, denying it so they would not worry. Unable to eat, she requested exploratory surgery and died three days later on January 18, 1918, of "acute atrophy of the liver," according to General John Pershing of the American Expeditionary forces in France. Although it is believed her condition was caused in part form exposure to the Mustard gas, surgery revealed a massive ulcer.

Helen was buried at Le Treport in a temporary cemetery, her body later removed to Somme American Military Cemetery, Bony, France. She was "given a military funeral, a most solemn and impressive ceremony, and buried in the uniform of an American Army nurse. Her funeral was attended by an entire garrison of English, Canadian, French and American officers, nurses and troops."

In 1920, women veterans organized the Helen Fairchild American Legion Post No. 421 in Philadelphia, PA. An oak tree was planted on the grounds of Pennsylvania Hospital in Fairchild's honor, where a memorial ceremony was held every Memorial Day.

The Women in American Military Service, Memorial and Museum plan to honor her in the World War I exhibit, featuring her portrait, cape and handbook. The Museum and Memorial officially opened August 1987. Helen is one of five nurses buried in Somme American Cemetery, and this writer registered them in the registry of the Museum and Memorial, located in Arlington, Virginia. The Daughters of The American Revolution Magazine published a 6-page story November 1987, using excerpts of Fairchild's letters, compiled by this writer.

> "Helen's story reached across the years and spoke to the very moment I was training in. Her story must be told to serve as timeless monument to her life and her cause, at it vividly illustrates the capabilities of women on the battlefiled."
>
> Capt. Lynne Ann Nicklas-Stepaniak, R.N., USAF
> July 15, 1997

BIBLIOGRAPHY

Fairchild, H. (1917). Letters. Collection of Nelle Fairchild Rote, Lewisburg, PA.

Hoeber, P. B. (1921). *Pennsylvania Hospital Unit In the Great War.* New York: Author

McDonald, L. (1980a). *The roses of no man's land.* London: Michael Joseph.

McDonald, L. (1980b). *They call it Passchendaele.* London: Michael Joseph.

Rote, N. F. (1997). My Aunt, My Hero. *The Daughters of the American Revolution Magazine, 131*(9), pp. 668–673.

Wagner, F. E. *A brief history of the Helen Fairchild Nurses Post No. 412.* American Legion, (1938). Self published.

West, R. M. (1933). *History of nursing in Pennsylvania.* Philadelphia: The Pennsylvania State Nursing Association.

Irene Mattthews
Nelle Fairchild Rote

GRACE MITCHELL FAIRLEY
1881–1969

Grace Fairley was a hospital administrator who successfully used her formal position

and authority to improve working conditions of graduate nurses and pupil nurses during hospital training. An ardent supporter of advanced education for nurses, Fairley was instrumental in persuading McGill University's Faculty of Medicine to consider plans to establish a School For Graduate Nurses at the university while she was Lady Superintendent of the Alexandra Hospital, Montreal, from 1912 to 1919. As Superintendent of Nurses at the Hamilton General Hospital, from 1919 to 1924, Fairley established a student government in the training school, introduced graduate nurses into the hospital, and ended the 24-hour private hospital duty system, whereby nurses were on call 24 hours a day. Through important offices she held in Canadian and international associations, Fairley increased the stature of Canadian nursing. She was active provincially and nationally in Canadian nursing associations, where she provided often innovative and proactive leadership. For example, it was Fairley who spearheaded the Canadian Nurses Association's (CNA) successful campaign to capitalize on the "crisis" of the Second World War to counter plans of the Canadian Hospital Association to increase pupil nurse enrollments beyond hospitals' clinical and supervision capabilities. From 1942 to 1946, the CNA received from the federal government a total of $774,000 to improve teaching in hospital and university schools of nursing, provide bursaries for graduate nurses, recruit qualified applicants to hospital training programs, and pay the salary and expenses of the national Emergency Nursing Advisor, Kathleen Ellis. The government grant also enabled the CNA to establish a permanent secretariat and formalize its corporate structure.

Grace Fairley was born in Edinburgh, Scotland, June 21, 1881, and educated at the Merchant Company School, Edinburgh Ladies College and Edinburgh School of

Grace Mitchell Fairley

Home Economics, before graduating in 1905 from the Swansea General Hospital in Wales and doing postgraduate work at the Swansea District Isolation Hospital. She was head nurse, then night superintendent at the Oldham Royal Infirmary, Lancashire, England and assistant matron at Glasgow City Hospital, before emigrating to Canada in 1912 to become Lady Superintendent of the Alexandra Hospital in Montreal, a communicable disease institution for English-speaking patients. She was subsequently Superintendent of Nurses at the Hamilton General Hospital, from 1919 to 1924 and Superintendent of Nurses at the Victoria Hospital, London, Ontario, from 1924 to 1929. During her sojourn in London, Fairley played a part in the creation of the degree nursing program at the University of Western Ontario in 1924. Fairley was active in American, Canadian and Quebec nursing and hospital associations dur-

ing this period, serving as Vice-President of the American Hospital Association from 1916 to 1917, first President of the Association of Registered Nurses of Quebec, on the executive of the Registered Nurses Association of Ontario (RNAO), and President of the Canadian Association of Nursing Education, which, in 1924, merged with the Canadian National Association of Trained Nurses to become the Canadian Nurses Association.

In 1929, Fairley became Director of Nursing and Principal of the School of Nursing at the Vancouver General Hospital, in British Columbia, a position she retained until retirement in 1943. She hired many more graduate nursing staff to "free up" pupil nurses for learning, and made many improvements in the training school curriculum. Fairley also hired more nursing instructors for the VGH training program, including some with college degrees. She supported the degree nursing program at the University of British Columbia which used VGH clinical facilities. While at VGH, Fairley continued professional association involvement, as a member of the B.C. Hospital Association, chairman of the nursing education section of CNA, from 1930 to 1934, President of the Registered Nurses Association of British Columbia, from 1935 to 1938, President of the CNA, from 1938 to 1942, and third Vice-President of the International Council of Nurses, from 1941 to 1953. With the outbreak of the Second World War, Fairley was appointed Matron-In-Chief of the Royal Canadian Army Medical Corps. Although the position was largely honorary, it involved considerable administration, as well as support for recruitment of nurses for overseas duty.

As CNA President, in fall 1941, Fairley instigated a joint 3-day conference of CNA Executive Committee members with representatives of nursing departments in seven Canadian universities to discuss ways of enhancing the education of nurses during wartime. A number of recommendations offered by the university nurse educators at that meeting to improve learning conditions for pupils in hospital training programs, increase hospital training program enrollments, optimize use of existing university postgraduate courses in nursing, expand nursing inservice programs, recall married and inactive nurses for active service, enhance graduate nurses' status, and improve their salaries, were endorsed by the CNA executive and subsequently implemented. An unanticipated outcome of the 1941 and follow-up 1942 joint meetings of CNA executive with university nurse representatives was creation of an organization separate from CNA which became the Canadian Association of University Schools of Nursing (CAUSN).

In 1942, the CNA awarded Fairley the Mary Agnes Snively Memorial Medal in recognition of her significant contributions to Canadian nursing, both in providing leadership in its professional organizations, and in raising standards of nursing education through her administrative skill. Fairley died in Vancouver on March 15, 1969.

PUBLICATIONS BY GRACE MITCHELL FAIRLEY

Numerous editorials and President's addresses in *The Canadian Nurse* from 1924 to 1942.

BIBLIOGRAPHY

Biographical Information File. Available from the CNA Library, 50 The Driveway, Ottawa, Ontario, K2P 1E2.

Ellis, K. (1942). Grace M. Fairley. *The Canadian Nurse, 38,* 383–384.

Obituary. (1969). *The Canadian Nurse, 65,* 18.

Tunis, B. L. (1966). *In caps and gowns: The story of The School for Graduate Nurses, McGill University, 1920–1964.* Montreal, Quebec: McGill University Press, 3–4, 7–8, 9, 23, 27, 29, 69, 71, 98.

Zilm, G., & Warbinek, E. (1994). *Legacy: History of nursing education at the University of British Columbia,*

1919–1994 (pp. 64, 74-76, 82, 86, 101, 105, 109, 116). Vancouver, BC: UBC Press.

Sharon Richardson

BARBARA FASSBINDER
1953–1994

Barbara Fassbinder's was one of the first recorded cases of a health worker infected with the AIDS virus on the job. But she battled not only the disease, but ignorance and misinformation about it as long as she was able.

Born on September 29, 1953, little is known about her early life. Her original family name was Herring and she lived in Monona, Iowa and was married to David Fassbinder. A graduate of the University of Iowa College of Nursing, she worked in the Memorial Hospital in Prairie du Chien, Wisconsin. She was infected with HIV in 1986, while helping treat a badly injured victim of a car accident in the emergency room. Blood from a wound seeped through the gauze she was using to apply pressure, and into a cut she had received while gardening.

For the rest of her life, Fassbinder traveled extensively, educating others about the disease. She was given special recognition at the 1992 ANA convention for her courage in revealing that she had the virus in order to educate the public and other health care providers on the need for universal precautions.

Fassbinder served on the National Health Care Reform Task force convened by Hilary Rodham Clinton and was a member of the Iowa State Commission on AIDS. In 1992, she received national recognition from the U.S. Surgeon General and the Department of Health and Human Services for her efforts in AIDS education. She also appeared before congressional committees to testify against mandatory testing of health care workers.

Barbara Fassbinder

Fassbinder died at the University of Iowa Hospital, Iowa City, Iowa, on September 20, 1994. Funeral services were at St. Patrick's Church, Monona, Iowa; she was buried in the Monona City Cemetery. She was survived by her husband David, two daughters, Eva and Emily, and a son, Joel.

Barbara Fassbinder was a "model of quiet courage" in her reaction to the diagnosis of AIDS. One of the martyrs of nursing, along with Clara Louise Maass, Edith Cavell, and others, she will be remembered for her courage in the face of insurmountable odds.

BIBLIOGRAPHY

AIDS steals another hero. (1994, September 23). *Capital Times* (Madison, Wisconsin).

Ceremony honors nursing's best, brightest. (1992, June 25). ANA *Convention News.*

Nurse Barbara Fassbinder dies from AIDS disease. (1994, September 21). *Courier Press* (Prairie du Chien, Wisconsin).

Nurse made safety sole aim. (1994, September 21). *LaCrosse* (Wisconsin) *Tribune.*

Obituaries: Barbara Fassbinder. (1994, September 21). *Telegraph Herald* (Dubuque, Iowa).

Profession mourns loss of Barbara Fassbinder. (1994). *The American Nurse.*

Signe S. Cooper

Theodora Floyd

THEODORA FLOYD
1896–1996

Theodora Floyd had a long and productive career in providing community-based nursing care and public health supervision in the Hawaiian islands, and later held administrative positions in public health in the South and in Georgia. She served as the Director of Public Health Nursing in the Division of the Georgia Department of Public Health from 1946 until her retirement in 1963.

Floyd was born July 5, 1896 in rural Miller County in southwest Georgia, but soon afterward her parents moved to Donalsonville, Georgia, a small town with a population of 1500. It was here that Floyd attended elementary and secondary schools. Her father, Joshua William Floyd, was a schoolteacher who later cared for several small farms he had inherited along with a blacksmith shop. Her mother, Alice Reagan Floyd, had been a student in Joshua Floyd's classroom. They were married when Alice was 16, and their eight children were born between 1896 and 1913. Floyd grew up with intellectual riches, in a home there were numerous books to read, an organ on which to practice music lessons, and the encouragement to gain as much education as possible.

Early in life, she decided to be a teacher missionary. Upon her graduation from high school in 1914, she set about to solve the problem of earning enough money to attend a college where she could learn Chinese. For 2 years she remained at home to help her mother with the younger children. At the age of 20, she was able to take a 6-week course at the University of Georgia to earn a teaching certificate.

With money accumulated from 4 years of rural school teaching she chose Pasadena College in California as her next educational stepping stone to China. There she could study Chinese and work to pay her own tuition.

During the four years at Pasadena College Floyd completed her B.A. in English and Education, and studied Chinese. After her graduation she was disappointed to learn there were no teaching positions for her in China. In her usual determined manner, she turned to nursing to give her another entry point to her long-held dream. She enrolled in the Los Angeles General Hospital's 3-year diploma program in nursing, the only one in her class of 100 with a college degree. She graduated in 1927 at the age of 31, having been voted as the ideal nurse of the Class of 1927.

With still no signs of a job in China, she enrolled at the University of California in Los Angeles for a 6-week course on child hygiene, a specialty of great interest to her. It was through the University's placement office that she was offered a position in public health nursing at the Palama Settlement in Honolulu, which seemed to her the first step on her way to China. For 3 years she enjoyed working as a staff nurse in public health. She could also act as interpreter for the Chinese patients, and this was as close as she ever got to China.

Her work in Hawaii led to her being awarded a scholarship by the Hawaii Foundation to study for a master's degree in supervision in public health nursing at Teachers College in New York City. Upon returning to the Palama Settlement in 1932, she was given added responsibilities for teaching and supervision, and then promoted to supervisor on the rural island of Kauai. There she directed the Welfare Program and performed other duties including planning public health nursing in homes and schools, arranging with plantation hospitals' medical and nursing personnel to get care for non-plantation families when needed, and organizing transportation for leprosy patients to the island of Molakai. She also served 1 year as the Territorial Board of Health's advisory nurse on maternity and infancy health work for all eight islands of the Hawaiian group, and designed of the first public health nursing course at the University of Hawaii in Honolulu.

In 1938 Floyd began to inquire into the state of public health work in her home state of Georgia. She became convinced that her knowledge and expertise were much needed back home where maternal and infant death rates were high in comparison to other sections of the country. Her conviction was transformed into action with her 1940 New Year's resolution to return to Georgia. In learning of her desire and qualifications, the State Health Officer in Georgia created a position for Floyd as consultant nurse in maternal and child health.

The needs for maternal and child services escalated with the advent of WWII. Floyd's contribution to the war effort was to take a leave of absence from her position in Georgia to become the maternal-child health consultant for the U.S. Children's Bureau in the southeastern states. She relocated to New Orleans, Louisiana. In this position she assisted in the development of maternal and child services and educational programs for wives and children of service men serving in WWII, and established programs to lower rheumatic fever rates.

In 1946 Floyd returned to Georgia to take the position of Acting Director of the Public Health Nursing Division. She soon was made Director, a position she held until her retirement in 1963. Some of her major accomplishments were development of a family record that included all of the members of the family, not just the designated sick person; the identification, registration, and training of granny midwives; and helping to launch the Visiting Nurse Association of Atlanta.

After her retirement, she and her sister made their home in Atlanta, Georgia where they continued to be active in church and community work. They later moved to Tallahassee, Florida. Approximately 2 months after a festive 100th birthday celebration, Floyd died on September 18, 1996. She is buried in Earley Cemetery in Cedar Springs, Georgia.

Always imaginative, she spent the majority of her career creating better health conditions for mothers, infants, and children through preventive measures. Never married, Floyd capitalized upon her formative years spent in Georgia. Her willingness to take positions in a variety of geographical locations, and to learn from many different cultures, were two important ingredients in her effective leadership.

BIBLIOGRAPHY

Floyd, T. (1987). *Oral history interview.* In Georgia Public Health Oral History, Special Collections, Robert W. Woodruff Library, Emory University, Atlanta, GA.

Yost, E. (1947). *American women of nursing* (pp. 155–175). Philadelphia: Lippincott.

Rose B. Cannon

ADA FORT
1914–1998

The life and contributions of Ada Fort demonstrate remarkable progress in the areas of nursing practice, education, and administration. She was for nearly three decades, Dean of the Nell Hodgson Woodruff School of Nursing at Emory University in Atlanta, Georgia. In 1954, the School launched the Master of Nursing Degree program, the first of its kind in the Southeast, which prepared nurses for positions in teaching and administration. Under her leadership, the first African-American students at Emory University were enrolled in the graduate program of the School of Nursing in 1962. "This event antecedent to the nation's formal Civil Rights movement, endures as evidence of Dean Fort's vision, perseverance, and fearlessness as she negotiated the tight passages enroute to massive cultural upheaval" (Parsons, 1998). Fort's efforts and leadership enabled development of programs in international health and community-based nursing care, both of which exist today in evolved and refined structures.

Ada Fort was born October 5, 1914, in Dallas county, Alabama. She was the youngest of four children; two sisters, Everette

Ada Fort

Fort Green and Josephine Fort Ormond, and a brother, Boykin Fort. When, many years later, Ada spoke in reference to admitting and graduating the first African-American students at Emory, she reflected on her Alabama roots. "We integrated the university." She acknowledged the giant steps that she had taken in her own thinking since her childhood near Selma, Alabama (Smith, 1975).

Ada Fort was educated in the Orville, Alabama elementary and High School and attended Livingston State Teachers College from 1931–33, and received a teaching Certificate. Few teaching jobs were available at that time and she attended the South Highlands Infirmary School of Nursing in Birmingham, Alabama from 1933–36, and received a Diploma. She attended the George Peabody College for Teachers from 1939–40 and received a B.S. in Public Health Nursing. She attended Teacher's College at Columbia University in New York and was awarded the M.A. in Nursing Education (1940–43) and the Ed.D (1955–60).

Fort's nursing career began as a staff nurse in the operating room from 1936–37 at Baptist Hospital in Selma, Alabama and at the Veteran's Hospital in Columbia, South Carolina from 1938–39. She was a public health nurse from 1941–42 at the East Alabama Training Center, in Opelika, Alabama. From 1943–45, during graduate study in New York, she was Instructor in nursing arts at Hardwick College at Oneota, New York. She was Director of the School of Nursing, at the South Highlands School of Nursing in Birmingham, Alabama form 1945–46. She came to the School of Nursing at Emory University in Atlanta in 1946 and for a year was Instructor in Nursing Arts. She was named Associate Dean of the School in 1947 and was appointed Dean in 1950. She retained this position until her retirement in 1975. At the time of her retirement in 1975, Fort was senior nursing school dean in the United States in length of service in the position as dean (Press Release, 1974).

Two innovative programs were established during Fort's tenure in the Nell Hodgson Woodruff School of Nursing, the International Nursing Services Association and the Emory Community Nursing Service. In 1973, the International Nursing Services Association (INSA), was established in collaboration with the Women's Division of the United Methodist Church to prepare nurses from outside the United States with skills and expert knowledge so that they could contribute to the health care needs in their own countries. In 1992, INSA was renamed Global Health Action, which reflected an expanded mission of "leadership training for a healthier world" (Zalumas, 1998). The new title also more accurately reflected the group's activities with a range of health care providers.

The Emory Nursing Service was established in 1974. This was an innovative structure which allowed School of Nursing faculty to deliver health care to the community in nurse managed clinics. "In its first years, this highly innovative venture generated sufficient income to fund several faculty salaries and ensured that hundreds of metropolitan residents had access to quality health care" (Parsons, 1988). This model served as a prototype for a Wellness Center at Williamsburg Apartments, a residential community for seniors, which Fort helped to found in 1990. This is a nurse-managed clinic that provides a range of health care services for older adults.

Fort was the recipient of many honors and awards throughout her professional career. She was selected as Atlanta's Woman of the Year in 1954. She was awarded an honorary degree from Wesleyan College in 1958. Livingston State College in Livingston, Alabama named her to the Society of the Golden Key in 1966. In 1970, she was named Woman of the Year in the Professions for the Atlanta Area. In 1982, she was honored as one of the women who shaped the direction of Emory University at a special exhibit. In 1998, for her significant contributions to health care, she was honored as a "Woman Pioneer in Health Care" by the Georgia Commission on Women and the Georgia Women's History Month Committee in a ceremony at Agnes Scott College (Bass, 1998).

Fort is listed in Who's Who in America, Who's Who in American Education, Who's Who in Methodism, Who's Who in American Women, and the Dictionary of International Biography.

Fort's contributions encompassed a range of practice, education, and administrative priorities. Her influence was felt, not only at Emory University and the South, where she made a contribution for such a long time, but in the international nursing and health care communities. A former student and faculty colleague acknowledged

Fort's many accomplishments in a memorial tribute after her death in 1998. It seems to adequately portray her contributions. "As a leader among her peers in the region, she ensured that the Nell Hodgson Woodruff School of Nursing became synonymous with quality. Most important perhaps, among all of her accomplishments, was her ability to maintain focus for the School of Nursing. Its main purpose, she said in 1966, was to produce *the extraordinary nurse*, extraordinary in her sense of values, in her ability to understand and accept the great overall purpose of life and in her ability to be an investigative, competent, and imaginative clinical nurse practitioner" (Parsons, 1998).

BIBLIOGRAPHY

Bass, C. "Ada Fort," obituary. *Atlanta Journal-Constitution*, Tuesday, April 28, 1998, B6.

Parsons, M. K. (1998). "A Memorial Tribute to Ada Fort, Professor Emeritus and Former Dean of the Nell Hodgson Woodruff School of Nursing," Library, Nell Hodgson Woodruff School of Nursing.

Press Release, September 18, 1974, "Dean Ada Fort resigns at Emory." Ada Fort Private Papers.

Smith, H. "Emory Nursing Dean Plans Retirement," *Atlanta Constitution*, Sunday, August 3, 1975.

Zalumas, J., Interview with Virginia Proctor, October 20, 1998, Atlanta, Georgia.

Jacqueline C. Zalumas

G

RUTH LAVERNE GALLMAN
1924–

Ruth Laverne Gallman is a Texas nurse who distinguished herself in numerous areas of nursing education, including helping to move a highly respected hospital diploma program into an institution of higher learning. Her commitment to maximizing the potential of students, especially graduate students, earned her the reputation as a strong student advocate.

Gallman was born April 22, 1924, to Eva Leota James Gallman and James R. Gallman. She was the second of three children. Her siblings and their birth order are: Billie Gallman (Martin) and James Gallman, Jr.

Gallman received her primary and secondary education in Big Springs and Gladewater, Texas, having graduated from the latter in 1941. Her educational goal was to go to nursing school, however, her young age precluded admission to nurse's training at the time. In deference to her parents' wishes, she enrolled at Kilgore Junior College in Kilgore, Texas, earning an Associate of Arts degree in May 1943. That September, she enrolled in the Scott and White Hospital School of Nursing in Temple, Texas. She graduated 3 years later with the diploma in nursing.

While a nursing student, Gallman's potential for leadership was recognized by Anna Laura Cole, who administered both the nursing school and the nursing service of the hospital. Immediately after graduation Gallman was hired by Cole to work at Scott and White Hospital, serving in several capacities. The first 8 months, she worked as the night supervisor, moving on to serve as a staff nurse for the Intravenous Therapy Department at a time when few nurses had such skills, and indeed, such practice was frowned upon in many circles.

Ruth LaVerne Gallman

Gallman credits Cole for her mentorship. Cole made certain that Gallman's work schedule was flexible enough to facilitate more formal education. She commuted 60 miles to The University of Texas at Austin for classes from September 1947 till January 1948. She completed her baccalaureate degree during full-time study in the spring semester of 1949, at The University of Texas Medical Branch at Galveston, Texas.

After completion of the baccalaureate degree, Gallman accepted a position as an Instructor in Scott and White Hospital School of Nursing. Exposure to the role of teacher led her to recognize the need for an advanced degree. Gallman once again commuted to Austin to earn a master's degree in education in 1957. She went on to become the Educational Coordinator, then the Associate Director, of the Scott and White's School between late 1952 and 1969.

After the publication of the "Position Paper" in 1965, Cole began laying the groundwork for the Scott and White Hospital School of Nursing to phase into a baccalaureate program in nursing at neighboring Mary Hardin-Baylor College. Gallman was included in this planning stage during the latter part of this endeavor. When the move was made in the fall of 1969, Gallman was appointed to the helm of the school at Mary Hardin-Baylor as Professor and Chairman of the Department of Nursing.

The publication of the American Nurses Association's "Position Paper" had created a schism within nursing, threatening the predominant method of training nurses in hospital diploma programs. However, Gallman credits the success of the transition from the hospital-based training of nurses from Scott and White to Mary Hardin-Baylor to Cole's efforts in preparing the faculty, alumni, and people in the community for the change to baccalaureate education in nursing. The major hurdle was recruitment of qualified nursing faculty to a small, rural town in central Texas. While directing this program, Gallman was also appointed an adjunct faculty member at the nursing school at The University of Texas at Austin.

While Gallman was going through the rigors of essentially establishing a new school of nursing, she was also pursuing a doctor of philosophy degree at the University of Texas at Austin (UTA) again undertaking the 60-mile commute for classes. She earned the degree in January, 1970.

After 6 years at the helm of Mary Hardin-Baylor's nursing program, Gallman was tiring of administrative roles and wanted to pursue another area of nursing. Upon hearing Gallman's desire to leave administration Dean Billye Brown offered her a position teaching at UT's School of Nursing. Dean Brown once confided to this author that she considered it a "coup" getting Gallman to join that faculty.

As an Associate Professor at UT, Gallman became one of the most involved faculty members there. She became a full Professor in 1984. In addition to teaching, research, and community involvement she quickly became recognized for being a student advocate. During her tenure at UT she chaired a total of 55 doctoral dissertation committees. However, she did not escape administrative roles totally, filling roles of Assistant Dean for Undergraduate Curriculum, and Interim Associate Dean for Academic Programs 1986–1987 and 1987–1989 respectively.

Myriad honors have been bestowed on Dr. Gallman in recognition of her outstanding contributions to nursing and nursing education. They include membership in the Honor Societies of Sigma Theta Tau, International, Phi Kappa Phi, and Pi Lambda Theta. She was awarded the Distinguished Alumnus Awards of Scott and White Hospital School of Nursing, and The University of Texas Medical Branch at Galveston School of Nursing. The latter also inducted her into its Nursing Alumni Hall of Fame. She received several teaching excellence awards. The quality that Gallman will probably be most remembered for was her ability to mentor students as she had been mentored. In spite of a demanding workload, she always had time for students. It was the graduate students at the University of Texas at Austin who were responsible for suggesting and getting a Lectureship established in her honor at that School.

Gallman retired as a Professor Emeritus in 1992, but continues to hold membership in numerous professional associations. In addition she works as a volunteer in the Southwest Center for Nursing History at The University of Texas School of Nursing and serves in other volunteer capacities at the school. She is also an associate in a recruiting firm.

PUBLICATIONS BY RUTH LAVERNE GALLMAN (SELECTED)

Laura Cole: A leader in Texas nursing. (1992). In V. L. Bullough, L. Sentz, & A. P. Stein (Eds.),

American Nursing: A Biographical Dictionary (Vol. II). New York & London: Garland.

Derivations of the shoulds and oughts in nursing practice. (1988). In B. Heater & B. Aubuchon (Eds.), Controversies in critical care nursing. Rockville, MD: Aspen.

Selections of clinical experiences and teaching strategies for masters students. (1981). Proceedings of Southern Region Education Board Conference on Clinical Practice.

BIBLIOGRAPHY

ANA's First Position Paper on Education for Nurses. (1965). American Journal of Nursing, 65, 106–111.

Kilby, S. (1998). [Interviews with R. L. Gallman].

Sally Kilby

MARY ANN LEONARDA GARRIGAN
1914–

Mary Ann Garrigan was the founder of the Boston University Nursing Archives, a special collection of the Boston University Library. This achievement is important in that the B.U. Archives was the first of the Centers for Nursing History that have since been established at other major universities. Garrigan showed foresight in recognizing the importance of collecting the papers and materials of U.S. nursing organizations and of prominent 20th-century nurse leaders. She also was a nurse educator and administrator in collegiate education for nurses.

Mary Ann Garrigan was born on January 24, 1914, in New York City, the daughter of Wilhelmina Fredericks Garrigan and Thomas Garrigan. Her parents were of German/Hungarian and Irish descent. She had three sisters, Grace, Helen, and Margaret, and one brother, Thomas. She grew up in Westchester County, New York, and graduated from the Westchester School of Nursing in Valhalla, New York in 1934.

Mary Ann Leonarda Garrigan

Garrigan had a special interest in maternity nursing, and in 1936 received a certificate in maternity nursing from the Women's Hospital of New York. She then worked as a staff nurse and head nurse at Grasslands Hospital in Valhalla from 1935 to 1937. From 1937 to 1941, she worked as a supervisor at Westchester Hospital School of Nursing while studying for a bachelor's degree, which she received from Teachers College of Columbia University in 1941, with a major in supervision and public health nursing. After graduating from Columbia in 1941, she took a position as a staff nurse at Henry Street Visiting Nurse Service where she worked until she joined the Army Nurse Corps in 1943. Because of her educational background, she was assigned to be an instructor in the Women's Army Corps and Medical Corps Training Program for medical and surgical technicians at Halloren Hospital in Staten Island, New York. She was assigned to the management and training of Cadet Nurses from the many schools in the region. During her term of enlistment at Halloren, she had

poliomyelitis that left her with a permanent weakness in one leg. She was discharged in 1946.

She then moved to Boston and received a master's degree in Education from Boston University in 1947. She accepted a position as an instructor in the new School of Nursing at Boston University, despite another offer from the U.S. Public Health Service. She was to make Boston University the site of her academic career from 1947 until her retirement as a full Professor in 1981. During that time she taught and was the administrator of the 4-year baccalaureate nursing program at the university. She was known as an innovative leader who befriended students and faculty. She frequently entertained friends and colleagues at her summer home in Cape Neddick, Maine.

What started as a love of history and teaching the basic course in nursing history led Garrigan to be concerned in the 1960s about the preservation of historical materials. Garrigan decided that nursing's history must be protected. She served as Chairman of the Historical Resources Committee of the Massachusetts League for Nursing, and during that time took the first steps toward the development of a nursing history collection at B.U. Under Garrigan's urging, the Massachusetts League for Nursing requested that Gustave Harper, Director of Libraries at Boston University, designate a nursing archive and, in 1966, the Nursing Archives became an official collection of the University Library. Professor Harper asked Mary Ann Garrigan to serve as Curator. Garrigan had done much of the University political activity necessary to make the Archive happen.

The archives became more stable in 1967 when Garrigan was awarded a $150,000 grant from the U.S. Department of Health, Education and Welfare for the archives to improve the teaching of nursing history, to foster historical research, and preserve resource materials in nursing history. The archives became nationally prominent when, in 1971, it was designated as the official repository of the American Journal of Nursing Company and the American Nurses' Association. In 1976, the Massachusetts Nursing Association gave Mary Ann Garrigan a Distinguished Service Award and, in 1977, the Columbia University Teachers College Alumnae gave her a Distinguished Service to Nursing Award. She was elected a Fellow of the American Academy of Nursing in 1977. In 1979 she received honorary doctorate of humane letters degrees from the University of San Diego and from Boston University and, in the same year, was the recipient of the Edith Moore Copeland Founders Award of Sigma Theta Tau. In 1986, the Journal of Nursing History, a publication of the B.U. Nursing Archives, paid tribute to Garrigan as its founder in a special issue.

Mary Ann Garrigan lives in a nursing home in Marblehead, Massachusetts, where she has made her home.

Lois Monteiro

ESTHER ANNE GARRISON
1905–

Esther Anne Garrison pioneered in the field of psychiatric-mental health nurse education. Her exceptional skills and dedicated leadership brought noteworthy advances in this area. Health advocates applauded Miss Garrison's work with honors and awards during her 25 years with the United States Public Health Service.

Garrison was born March 10, 1905 in Middletown, Illinois. Her father, William H. Garrison, had a secondary education, and worked in real estate. Garrison described her mother, Mary Blake Garrison, as "intelligent and pretty" and emphasized

Esther Anne Garrison

that she had attended college. While the family lived in Arkansas a tornado struck the area and demolished their home. Eleven-year-old Garrison suffered a Colles' fracture.

Esther graduated from Mt. Vernon Township High School in Mt. Vernon, IL in 1924. With her mother's moral support and earnings from various jobs Garrison continued her education.

In 1925 Garrison entered the St. Louis City Hospital Training School for Nurses in St. Louis, Missouri. She earned her diploma and became a registered nurse in 1928. Garrison worked at her home hospital from 1928 to 1936, advancing from staff nurse to assistant night supervisor, then operating room head nurse, instructor and assistant to the educational director, and finally to operating room supervisor, a position she held for 5 years.

From 1936 to 1941 Garrison attended the University of Minnesota School of Nursing, receiving her bachelor of science degree in nursing education. From 1938 to 1944 she held the position of teaching supervisor of operating room at Minneapolis General Hospital. Garrison again became a full time student at the University of Minnesota and received her master of arts degree in educational psychology in July, 1944.

Lucile Petry, a recognized nurse leader in the U.S., was Esther's mentor and advisor during her years as a student at the University of Minnesota. After Petry became director of the Cadet Nurse Corps she recruited Garrison to serve as a nurse education consultant.

Esther A. Garrison was sworn into the Commissioned Corps of the United States Public Health Service in December 1944. Looking sharp in her officer's uniform, petite brown-haired, blue-eyed Garrison traveled out of the Richmond, Virginia office to consult with schools of nursing participating in the Cadet Nurse Corps. The deprivation and poverty of many of the schools of nursing she encountered as a nurse education consultant were in sharp contrast to her previous experience. Many of the schools of nursing which Garrison visited were below the standards of the Cadet Nurse Corps, and most hospitals suffered shortages of staff.

On October 1, 1946, Garrison terminated her services with the Cadet Nurse Corps and moved to the National Institute of Mental Health, which recruited her to provide leadership for the new Psychiatric Nursing Training and Standards Branch. At this time advanced nursing education was set up along functional lines. Graduate students prepared for careers in teaching, supervision, or administration. With the possible exception of some programs in pediatric nursing, advanced clinical nurse education, such as psychiatric nursing, did not exist.

In preparation for her future work, Garrison elected to go to Columbia Teachers College where she spent the 1946–1947 school year. Due back without a break the day after Labor Day, Garrison became AWOL due to a transportation strike and received a reprisal from her commanding officers.

The task that laid before Garrison challenged her. More custodial than therapeutic, psychiatric nursing took place mainly in state mental hospitals. Psychiatric content for student nurses was recommended, but not required, in basic nurse training. Graduate work in psychiatric nursing was unavailable. Garrison focused these early programs on developing leadership for the field, including both teachers and expert clinical practitioners. Educational programs moved nursing from functional and custodial to therapeutic and preventive orientation. Over the next 10 years, the essential curriculum elements for specialization in psychiatric nursing were established.

Garrison exercised her leadership firmly but subtly. She introduced new knowledge and viewpoints and encouraged innovative thinking. The decisions on program policy, curriculum content, and certification requirements were hammered out in special committees and in professional organizations such as the National League for Nursing and the American Nurses Association. Garrison conducted a series of special conferences and promoted pilot projects supported by NIMH. As Chief of the Psychiatric Nursing Training Branch she worked to secure recognition of and status for psychiatric-mental health nursing education in universities and colleges. She interpreted the mental health mission and stimulated self-appraisal among program directors and faculty. Psychiatric nurses now practiced in the community as well as in institutions.

Long before the term became popular, Garrison served as a "role model" for students who received mental health nurse trainee awards. Garrison met with trainees and personally encouraged and counselled them concerning careers and employment opportunities.

In 1954 Rutgers University offered the first graduate level program to prepare specialized nurse clinicians. In the following years other programs developed including psychiatric nursing for children and community mental health nursing. Over the next 22 years Garrison's accomplishment became evident. NIMH grants supported 50 graduate programs in six different specialty areas, 134 baccalaureate programs, and a number of research and special projects. More than 50 nurses had completed doctoral programs initiated by the Nursing Training Branch in 1956.

Success was reflected in the honors Garrison earned in both the academic world and USPHS. St. Xavier College in Chicago awarded her a Doctor of Law degree in 1965. This small college took the lead in Illinois in developing graduate psychiatric nursing education. St. Xavier honored Garrison with a degree on the day the college graduated their first students from the new graduate training program. Making use of NIMH training monies Boston University led the way in developing graduate nursing programs leading to the master's and doctoral degrees. This Massachusetts university honored Garrison with a Doctor of Science degree in 1968.

Garrison received the American Theatre Ribbon, the World War II Victory Ribbon for her work with the Cadet Nurse Corps. On October 5th, 1966, the Surgeon General awarded her the Commendation Medal for outstanding service and achievements in the field of Psychiatric Nursing. In 1969 she received the USPHS Meritorious Service Medal for her high level of achievement and outstanding contributions to the mission of Public Health Service.

In 1969 after spending 25 years with USPHS, Esther A. Garrison retired. Thanks to Dr. Garrison's leadership, a new nursing specialty had been created and continues to contribute to the improvement of mental health throughout our country.

BIBLIOGRAPHY

Garrison, E. A. Historical Reference Files, Office of the Public Health Service Historian, Rockville, MD.

Miller, N. R. (1970). The first lady of research retires. *Journal of Psychiatric Nursing and Mental Health Services, 8,* 45–47.

Robinson, T. M., & Perry, P. M. (1998, January 18). [Interview with E. A. Garrison]. San Francisco, CA.

Thelma M. Robinson
Paulie M. Perry

JOSEPHINE GOLDMARK
1877–1950

Josephine Goldmark was not a nurse, but as a pioneer in the field of social research, she was instrumental in enriching the nursing profession. Within the nursing community she is best-known for her contribution to the landmark study, *Nursing and Nursing Education in the United States* (1923), often referred to as the Goldmark or Winslow-Goldmark report. In 1920, Goldmark had also published the results of an extensive health and hospital survey that focused attention on the problems of inadequate housing facilities for nursing students. Goldmark was closely associated with Lavinia Dock, Lillian Wald, and several other extraordinary women, who sought independence and fulfillment in their lives while devoting themselves to humanitarian causes and to social reform in an era that was ripe for change.

Josephine Goldmark was born in Brooklyn, New York, October 13, 1877, the youngest of 10 children. Her parents, Joseph Goldmark and Regina Wehle Goldmark, were Jewish immigrants from the Austro-

Josephine Goldmark

Hungarian Empire in the aftermath of the Continental Revolutions of 1848. In her book, *Pilgrims of '48*, Goldmark wrote about her parents and their extended families. Although Goldmark's father, a research chemist and physician, died when she was only 3 years old, the family was left in comfortable circumstances and she grew up in a culturally and intellectually enriched atmosphere. Her oldest sister was married to the founder of the Ethical Culture Movement, Felix Adler, who was like a father to Josephine. Another sister married Louis Brandeis, who served on the U.S. Supreme Court. Other notable members of the Goldmark family include her uncle, Karl Goldmark, and her cousin, Rubin Goldmark, who were distinguished composers and musicians; her brother, Henry Goldmark, who designed the Panama Canal Locks; and her sister, Pauline, who, like herself, was a social reformer.

After getting her degree in English at Bryn Mawr College, Josephine went on for graduate study at Barnard College. At the turn of the century, she began to work as a volunteer with the National Consumers' League, which, from the 1890s through the 1930s, fought for the improvement of workers' conditions. This organization of civic-minded consumers was specifically involved in educating the public and lobbying for state laws to abolish child labor and tenement sweatshops. In 1903, Josephine became the publications secretary of the League, and she worked closely with Florence Kelley, a dynamic social activist, and the General Secretary of the League. Goldmark spearheaded a project on child labor reform which led to the publication in 1907 of her report under the title *Child Labor Legislation Handbook*. She compiled information for the legal brief that was used by her brother-in-law, Louis Brandeis, when he represented the state of Oregon before the Supreme Court in the landmark case, *Muller vs. Oregon* (1908), which upheld a state law limiting women factory workers to a 10-hour day. This was the first of the now famous "Brandeis Briefs," each one a milestone in the advancement of progressive social legislation. With these Briefs, Goldmark helped introduce a technique in legal practice which emphasized the use of factual evidence documented by copious and irrefutable medical, social, and economic data. The Supreme Court's decision in the Oregon case paved the way for the enactment of legislation by other states to protect working women, some of which had implications for nursing at that time.

With a grant from the Russell Sage Foundation, Goldmark undertook a study of working hours and the relation of fatigue to work, health, and disease. Her findings led to the publication of her book *Fatigue and Efficiency*, which became an authoritative national and international source, and brought her wide recognition in the field of American industrial hygiene.

At the outbreak of World War I, Goldmark was appointed a member of the Committee on Industrial Fatigue of the Council of National Defense. In cooperation with the United States Public Health Service, this Committee in 1917 began an intensive investigation of the working capacity in wartime. In 1918, she was appointed Special Expert by the Public Health Service and published her findings on the first section of this study, which dealt with 10-hour and 8-hour work systems.

From its inception, Goldmark's work brought her into close contact with public health nurses. She developed a profound respect for them and for their practice. Goldmark's studies that related most closely to nursing were carried out in the years immediately following World War I. In 1919 she completed a survey of health resources in Cleveland in collaboration with Dr. Haven Emerson. Her report, published in 1920, highlighted the serious lack of decent housing for nursing students, a problem which had been growing for several years. Within the following decade there was a spurt in construction of student housing at nursing schools, and many of these new residences included ample library and classroom space, marking a significant improvement in nursing education.

In 1919, Goldmark was appointed Secretary of the Committee established by the Rockefeller Foundation to organize a comprehensive study of nursing and nursing education in the United States. The Committee's original intent (Goldmark, 1923) was to investigate "the proper training of public health nurses." It soon became clear that it would be necessary to broaden the base of the inquiry to include "a study of general nursing education, with a view to developing a program for further study and for recommendation of further procedures."

When the study was completed, the findings were published in 1923 under the title *Nursing and Nursing Education in the United States,* or the "Goldmark Report." The report pointed out the need for including public health nursing as a learning experience for well-prepared nurses, and recommended that public health nurses complete special courses to supplement their basic hospital training. It called for the endowment of nursing education and strengthening of university schools for the education of nursing leaders. This was the first major study of nursing education, and a direct outgrowth was the establishment of the Yale University School of Nursing, which, from its inception, emphasized public health nursing in its curriculum.

Josephine Goldmark was one of those dedicated women of the early 20th century who sought to improve the human condition. Intellectually gifted, modest, and strongly motivated, she sprang from a liberal and humanitarian tradition which impelled her to work with others to alleviate the problems of society. She recognized and appreciated the role of public health nursing in the promotion of human welfare. As a social researcher, she made a significant contribution to the development of nursing and nursing education. As an active member of the Board of Directors of the Henry Street Visiting Nurses' Association, she worked for the advancement of public health nursing.

PUBLICATIONS BY JOSEPHINE GOLDMARK

Fatigue and efficiency: A study in industry. (1913). New York: Survey Associates.

Nursing and nursing education in the United States. (1923). Report of the Committee for the Study of Nursing Education. (Josephine Goldmark, secretary.) New York: Macmillan.

Pilgrims of '48. (1930). New Haven: Yale University Press.

Democracy in Denmark (with A. H. Hollman and A. G. Brandeis). (1936). Washington: National Home Library Foundation.

Impatient crusader. (1976). Westport, CT: Greenwood. (Originally published 1953 by University of Illinois Press, Urbana).

BIBLIOGRAPHY

Benson, E. R. (1987). Josephine Goldmark (1877–1950): A Biographic Sketch. *Public Health Nursing,* 4(1), 48, 51.

Evelyn R. Benson

EFFIE ANDERSON GRAHAM
1924–

Effie Anderson Graham devoted her career to nursing and nursing education primarily in the state of Alaska. She was instrumental in developing nursing educational programs for licensed practical nurses in Sitka, Alaska and later served as the first director of the Practical Nurse program at Anchorage Community College in Anchorage. She served as the dean of the baccalaureate-nursing program at Alaska Methodist University, completing her career as faculty member of that program when it was transferred to the University of Alaska, Anchorage.

Graham was born September 6, 1924 at home in the Spokane area. Effie Irene Anderson was the daughter of Andrew Bror Anderson and Anna Helena Brattlund, Swedish immigrants who came to Spokane, Washington, where they met and married. Effie grew up near Spokane during the Great Depression on a farm where chickens were raised for their eggs. She had three sisters and two brothers. Both brothers died in childhood; according to Effie, their death was a molding influence in her life.

Graham attended Montfort Grade School. She was a high-school sophomore in 1939 when the war in Europe began. When she graduated as salutatorian of her

Effie Anderson Graham

class in 1941, she learned that her plans to enter nursing school were accelerated due to the war. She began her new vocation just 3 weeks after high school graduation, enrolling in Deaconess Hospital School of Nursing in Spokane, Washington.

During her second year of nursing school, she became a cadet army nurse and received her diploma in June of 1945. Upon graduation she left by train for basic training at Fort Lewis, Washington. When Japan surrendered in August 1945, she was stationed at Fort Baker near San Francisco. She was discharged from the army in the fall of 1946.

Graham briefly worked in her home community of Spokane before attending the University of Washington. She received her bachelor's degree in nursing in 1949, taking courses in teaching nursing arts. She returned to Spokane, where she served as both assistant and acting director of the Deaconess Hospital School of Nursing. She remained in that position while she cared for her father who died in 1955.

She relocated to Alaska in 1956 to serve as the assistant director for the United States Public Health Service Practical Nurse Program in Mt. Edgecumbe, Alaska. The enrollment of the program was limited to Alaska Natives and American Indians. She worked in this position for 2 years, leaving to complete her master's at the University of Colorado in 1959.

Drawn to Alaska, she returned to Anchorage in 1959, shortly after statehood, and became the first professional staff person of the Alaska State Board of Nursing. She held this position for 2 years until she was recruited to become coordinator of a new practical nursing program at the Anchorage Community College in Anchorage, Alaska. She designed and implemented the program.

Feeling the need for change, she returned to graduate school as a doctoral student in social psychology and experimental social psychology at Boston University. During her matriculation there she developed her research interest in the menstrual cycle, writing her dissertation on "Cognitive Performance and Mood Change as it is Related to Menstrual Cycle and Estrogen Level." She received her Ph.D. in Social and Personality Psychology in 1972.

Even before she finished her dissertation, she received an offer to serve as the Dean of the Baccalaureate Program of Nursing at Alaska Methodist University (AMU) in Anchorage, Alaska. She assumed this role when AMU was struggling to keep its doors open. The university experienced low enrollments and declining revenues that threatened closure in each of the years Dr. Graham served as the dean. However, Graham secured substantial external funding, and the college of nursing thrived under her leadership.

It was during this time that Effie met and married her husband, Don Graham, an electrical engineer working with the air force in Anchorage. He was transferred out of the state and Graham left Alaska. In 1976 she took a position with the University of Illinois, in Chicago, and then as assistant dean at the university branch campus in Rockford, Illinois. There she was instrumental in the development of a baccalaureate completion program for registered nurses. She continued her research on the menstrual cycle. During her last year at the University of Illinois, she was on loan to Rockford College.

She and her husband returned to Alaska again in 1982. Graham assumed a position as associate professor of Nursing at the University of Alaska Anchorage. By this time the nursing program from AMU had been transferred to the state university system. She also served as the nursing education member of the Alaska State Board of Nursing. Dr. Graham retired as a full professor in 1987.

Since retirement, she has been active in nursing in the state. She has developed a research interest in writing the history of nursing in Alaska. Presently she is writing a book, *With a Dauntless Spirit: Alaska Nursing in Dog-Team Days*. She received the DeLapp Excellence Award from Theta Omicron Chapter of Sigma Theta Tau in May 1997 in recognition of her Alaskan contributions to nursing. She and her husband now live in a retirement community in Spokane, but spend their summers at their homestead in Chickaloon, Alaska.

PUBLICATIONS BY EFFIE ANDERSON GRAHAM

Graham, D., Graham, E. A., & Beecher, C. (1980) *The menstrual cycle: A synthesis of interdisciplinary research.* New York: Springer Publishing Company.

Graham, E. A., & Glasser, M. (1985). Relationship of pregnanediol level to cognitive behavior and mood. *Psychosomatic Medicine, 47*(1).

Graham, E. A. (1986). Menstrual and menopausal concerns. In J. G. Kenney (Ed.), *Contemporary women's health: An advocacy approach.* Menlo Park, CA: Addison-Wesley.

BIBLIOGRAPHY

Alaska State Board of Nursing meeting minutes
Alaska Nurse's Association State Newsletter
Oral interview with Effie Graham, June 1998, Chicka-
   loon, Alaska
University of Alaska School of Nursing

Jackie Pflaum

MILDRED MAY GRANDBOIS
1906–1997

Mildred May Grandbois was not a nurse, but she co-founded the first successful index to current nursing journals in the United States, the *Cumulative Index to Nursing Literature* print index. First published in 1961, the index grew to become the *Cumulative Index to Nursing & Allied Health Literature* (R) print index in 1977 and by the mid-1980s was available electronically as well as in bimonthly and annual print publications. Because of its distinctive red color, the index has always been known affectionately as the "Red Books."

Before becoming a medical librarian and undertaking the monumental task of indexing the nursing literature, Grandbois had already established herself as an accomplished professional in several other professions. Born in Minneapolis, Minnesota, May 26, 1906, to Anna and Arthur Grandbois, she obtained an undergraduate degree from Emmanuel Missionary College (now Andrews University), in Berrien Springs, Michigan, and a master's degree in Romance languages from the University of Michigan at Ann Arbor. After graduation, she pursued a career in education, holding a number of teaching positions in church-sponsored schools in Wisconsin and Washington state. She taught both Spanish and French, and at one school, she also served as the Girls' Dean.

She relocated to Glendale, California, where her mother had moved in 1937 after Mildred's father died. Mildred's sister had attended the Glendale Sanitarium and Hospital nursing program some years before, had married, and had settled in the area. After moving to Glendale, Grandbois took a number of positions in church community organizations. She served as secretary to the Seventh-day Adventist church's representative to South America, she taught in a church school, and she functioned as an editor and librarian for a widely known worldwide organization of her denomination, the Voice of Prophecy.

As soon as she arrived in Glendale, she began taking classes at the University of Southern California in Los Angeles to obtain a master's degree in library science. Grandbois always liked to tell the story that at the time, she was informed that she was simply "too old" to matriculate. But she kept taking courses until she was granted the degree in 1954 at the age of 48—not old at all by today's standards.

When she assumed the position of librarian at the Glendale Sanitarium and Hospital in 1956, she became aware of the need for an index to the growing body of periodical literature in nursing. At the time, librarians across the United States were creating institutional indexes for their own nursing staffs and for their hospital-affiliated schools of nursing. Because *Index Medicus*, the medical index published by the National Library of Medicine (NLM), a federal agency, focused primarily on the physician literature, there simply was no other way to access the contents of the nursing journals that were being published.

Ella Crandall, a librarian in nearby Los Angeles at another Seventh-day Adventist hospital, the White Memorial Hospital, had been overseeing the indexing of the English-language nursing literature since the 1940s—under the direction of Martha

Borg, the hospital's then-director of nurses. Hoping to publish the index nationally, Crandall had discussed this possibility with the American Journal of Nursing Company in New York, a subsidiary of the American Nurses Association at the time. The company wanted to publish an index—as did the profession, which for years had called for a unified nursing index—but was waiting for the National Library of Medicine to mount a planned-for computerized medical literature retrieval system that would include the nursing literature in its medical database (today known as Medline). Because this was still in the developmental stages, and because all indexed materials in the system would have to be organized under the aegis of the National Library of Medicine, nothing could be done with Crandall's already-completed and ongoing nursing indexing.

But the audience could not wait for official nursing and NLM. Librarians were asking for copies of Crandall's existing index, and colleagues asked to make copies of what was available. Crandall and Grandbois explored the idea of publishing the index themselves. They asked members of the Medical Library Group of Southern California (local chapter of the national organization, the Medical Library Association) if they would consider purchasing a publication of the 1956–60 indexing, some 900 pages, for a price of about $20 per copy. The answer was enthusiastically positive. Six months later, copies of the first edition of the *Cumulative Index to Nursing Literature* print index were mailed. Grandbois had asked her hospital for $300 to underwrite the project, but the amount was never needed.

The project began as a cooperative endeavor of three librarians and three hospitals—Grandbois at the Glendale Sanitarium and Hospital (now Glendale Adventist Medical Center); Mollie Sitner at the White

Memorial; and Ella Crandall, who had at that point moved to the Los Angeles County General Hospital Library with the indexing project. Within a very short time, however, Mildred and her institution had assumed the leadership to ensure that indexing and publication continued. Throughout the year, she published soft-cover current indexes, and at the end of the year produced a hardbound cumulation.

The American Journal of Nursing Company continued its planning for a nursing index via the computerized NLM system. Grandbois was invited to company headquarters in New York City twice a year as part of an advisory committee for this new index. The company then asked to buy her out, with the stipulation that she stop publishing by December 1965, 5 months before the new index was scheduled to begin. Grandbois refused, and her index continued uninterrupted. In spite of the publication of the forthcoming AJN Company-NLM index, the *International Nursing Index*, Grandbois's nursing index grew in audience and in content. It became the world's most widely used index in nursing, serving more than 5,000 customers.

Over the years, the team producing the index has consisted primarily of nurses and librarians, which has provided these professionals with a unique career opportunity. They have adapted their professional skills to indexing and publishing, with nurses in various specialties indexing the literature in their fields of expertise.

Nurses and other professionals also contribute to the development and growth of the index's essential controlled vocabulary—the first nursing-focused thesaurus for indexing the nursing literature. This tool, for which Grandbois was recognized by the profession of medical librarianship, enables searchers to pinpoint needed materials quickly and effectively. Structured in accord with the National Library of Medicine's Medical Subject Headings (MeSH) in the 1980s, the CINAHL(R) Thesaurus utilizes "medical" subject headings where appropriate and added nursing (and now allied health) subject headings when necessary to index the non-physician literature adequately. The thesaurus is the "key" to accessing the content in the database and today includes terminology for individual nursing theorists, along with the terminology from the North American Nursing Diagnosis Association and other classification systems.

In the first few years of publication, Grandbois met many challenges in her efforts to introduce the index to the nursing profession, and she had limited resources at her disposal. Typically, Grandbois traveled alone to nursing conventions, asking a local nurse to assist her at an exhibit table. Her first was the American Nurses Association meeting in Detroit in 1962. At this and every subsequent meeting, she was met with comments such as, "Where have you been all my life?" and "Why didn't I know about this in graduate school?" (comments the staff still hears today). It was a slow process to reach all the institutions, which she did through meetings and direct marketing, but in time practically every hospital and nursing school subscribed to the index.

In the 1970s, the index added allied health and today includes a wide range of allied health fields. In the 1980s, the index became available electronically, and today it can be accessed via the Internet (CINAHL direct (R) Online Service). New features and content are added regularly. For example, while the index originally included only English-language materials, it now includes journals in other languages. Materials other than journals are now indexed, including books and book chapters, audiovisuals, educational software, and dissertations. Full-text materials are now added when possible. Additionally, docu-

ments created by Cinahl Information Systems staff are indexed and included; for example, research instrument descriptions, legal cases, clinical innovations, drug records, and accreditation documents.

Glendale Adventist Medical Center continues its support of the index, which remains housed in the hospital, adjacent to the library. And as a result of the index, the library has become well-known in the library and local nursing communities because of its excellent nursing collection.

In the 1970s, Grandbois gradually turned over responsibilities to others for the hospital library and for the editorial, marketing, and business aspects of the index. But for years afterward she maintained a strong interest, working from her home telephoning customers and coordinating direct mail programs. Her home was located next to the campus of the hospital, making it convenient for her to attend management meetings and to keep up with the progress of the index.

Glendale Adventist recognized Grandbois' contribution by awarding her a place on its "Wall of Honor" outside the main entrance of the hospital. In 1989, the Nursing and Allied Health Section of the Medical Library Association honored her for being instrumental in the development of the index and for "the first subject heading list created especially for nursing." Although Grandbois dedicated herself to creating a nursing-focused index to the growing body of literature, the profession never formally or informally acknowledged her outstanding contribution. Because "official" nursing had committed its resources to another indexing system (the National Library of Medicine's literature retrieval system), Grandbois' publication never received support from any nursing organization. However, the publication earned the worldwide respect and acceptance of nurses and other health professionals who have grown to depend on its quality and comprehensiveness.

Grandbois assisted nursing in other ways. A former teacher, she helped numerous nurses who had moved from other countries pass their state boards in California. For those from Latin American countries, her command of Spanish assisted this process greatly. Frequently she took them in as borders and tutored them daily in their studies.

Handicapped for many years due to orthopedic problems, Grandbois maintained a healthy lifestyle in spite of her disability. She swam daily, adhered to a strict vegetarian diet, attended management meetings even in retirement, kept to a program of physical therapy, used a walker and her car to get around, pursued an active spiritual life, and independently maintained a home and two rental units. When she could no longer walk, she managed with an automatic cart. When she could no longer live alone, she retained live-in help. At the time of her death at age 91, she was still living in her own home.

Because of Grandbois, nursing can claim a uniquely nursing-focused index to its own literature. It has now been in publication for more than 40 years and is used worldwide in both print and electronic formats.

BIBLIOGRAPHY

Grandbois, M. (1964). The Nursing Literature Index: Its history, present needs, and future plans. *Bulletin of the Medical Library Association, 52,* 676–683.

Kilby, S. (1997). In memoriam: Mildred Grandbois, 1906–1997. *CINAHL News: The Official Newsletter of Cinahl Information Systems, 16*(3/4), and *Nursing and Allied Health Resources Section Newsletter,* (Medical Library Association), *17*(6), 1–3.

Kilby, S. (1998). In memoriam: Mildred Grandbois, 1906–1997. *Medical Library Group of Southern California and Arizona Newsletter, 30*(2), 12–13.

Many additional references exist describing the use of the index in nursing and in various allied health fields.

Sally Kilby

MABEL F. GRAY
1880–1976

Mabel Gray is remembered as the individual who kept the fledgling degree nursing program and the Department of Nursing and Health at the University of British Columbia (UBC) going during the difficult years of the Great Depression of the 1930s. Hired in 1925 as an assistant professor following Ethel Johns' resignation to join the Rockefeller Foundation, Gray was the only full-time faculty member in the department until Margaret Kerr was hired in fall 1929 to teach public health nursing. Gray remained as director for 16 years, until she retired in 1941. Despite difficult economic times, under Gray's guidance, the number of nurses who graduated with a nursing degree more than doubled, from 37 during the 1920s, to 74 during the 1930s. The number of diplomas in public health and teaching and supervision awarded graduates of hospital training programs almost doubled, from 83 during the 1920s to 154 during the 1930s. Degree and diploma nursing graduates of UBC's nursing program comprised the Western vanguard of a new cadre of public health nurses and teachers and supervisors for hospital schools of nursing.

Mabel Gray was born July 26, 1880 in Brampton, Ontario, the second child and only daughter of Samuel and Francis Gray. Mabel's father Samuel had also been born in the Brampton area, his parents having emigrated from England in the 1820s. Mabel lived as a young child for a few years in Ottawa, where her father was a civil servant, and later in Winnipeg, Manitoba, and Regina, Saskatchewan. She completed high school in Regina and obtained a teaching certificate from a normal (teacher training) school there, before teaching school in Plum Coulee, Northwest Territories and Carberry, Manitoba. In 1904, Gray decided to enter nursing and graduated from the

Mabel F. Gray

Winnipeg General Hospital training program in 1907. She stayed on at the WGH, first as a staff nurse for 2 years, later as an instructor, and then Assistant Superintendent of Nursing. Early in 1914 Gray became Superintendent of Nurses, a position she retained until 1919.

Her 5 years at the WGH were very trying for Gray. The daily patient census increased from 282 in 1913 to 365 in 1914, and within a few months of becoming superintendent, Gray found her nursing staff severely depleted by the outbreak of the First World War. Seventeen of the hospital's experienced graduate nurses joined the Canadian Army Medical Corps and left for overseas duty almost immediately. For a period of time during 1915, Gray was forced to discontinue classes for nurses in the training program so that they might spend all their time on patient care. When the 1918 influenza pandemic reached Winnipeg, the WGH cared for a record number of patients, despite the fact that more than a third of the graduate nurses and a fifth of

nurses in training also contracted the disease.

In 1919, Gray resigned as Superintendent of Nurses at the WGH and pursued an interest in public health by enrolling in Simmons College, Boston. She graduated in 1920 with a certificate in public health nursing. Soon after, Gray established a course for "nursing housekeepers" which was jointly sponsored by the Saskatchewan Registered Nurses Association, the Canadian Red Cross and the University of Saskatchewan. The 1-year program was intended to prepare a "secondary" nurse who could work in rural homes where graduate nurses were reluctant to go. As graduate nurses returned from war service, and more hospitals began nurse training programs, an oversupply of graduate nurses resulted, limiting opportunities for the nursing housekeepers. Care of ill and maternity patients shifted rapidly to hospitals after Saskatchewan passed the Union Hospital and the Rural Municipality Acts, both in 1916.

In addition to organizing and teaching in the nursing housekeepers program, Gray was also the part-time Registrar for the Saskatchewan Registered Nurses Association (SRNA). She served as Saskatchewan representative on the board of the Canadian Nurses Association (CNA) before being elected to positions as honorary secretary, and first vice-president. When CNA President Flora Shaw died in office in 1927, Gray took over the presidency for the 1927/28 term. She was CNA President when the CNA and the Canadian Medical Association (CMA) commissioned George Weir to conduct a survey of nursing education in Canada. Sometime during her Saskatchewan experience, Gray took some courses at Teacher's College, Columbia University, New York, although she did not obtain a degree.

Throughout her time in Saskatchewan, Gray maintained contact with Ethel Johns, whom she had known and interacted with professionally during Gray's time at the WGH. Like Gray and Johns, the women's mothers had also been friendly. In February 1919, Gray, Johns and four pupil nurses persuaded the Manitoba Law Amendments Committee not to include pupil nurses in proposed legislation to enforce a minimum wage and hours of work. The nurses, supported by the Manitoba Association of Registered Nurses (MARN) and the CNA, argued that pupil nurses were a student body and not a labor force. They were successful, and the prospect of a standard stipend and 8-hour work day for pupil nurses in Manitoba disappeared.

When she resigned in 1925 as Director of UBC's Department of Nursing and Health, Johns recommended Mabel Gray as her successor. UBC President Klinck interviewed Gray in Regina and offered her the position. Gray accepted, agreeing to take over both the degree nursing program and the certificate course in public health nursing. She was hired as an assistant professor, on the strength of her qualifications in public health nursing, and her experience in hospital and university teaching and administration. Because she did not possess a degree, Gray reported to Hibberd Hill, who continued as professor and titular head of the Department, while he also remained in charge of UBC's Department of Bacteriology. In 1929, Margaret Kerr was hired to teach public health nursing at UBC and Gray was able to concentrate on administration of the Department and the teaching and supervision courses. Beginning in 1931, Gray initiated a 6-year, double-degree program whereby students could be admitted to UBC at 16 years of age, and spend 3 rather than 2 years at university before beginning hospital training. Graduates received both Bachelor of Arts and a Bachelor of Applied Science (Nursing) degrees and a diploma from the VGH. The program was started because students entering hospital training had to be at least 19 years old, and some high school graduates were ready for university admission at the age of 16 years. The double-degree program was discontinued in 1951.

Throughout her tenure at UBC, Gray vigorously opposed suggestions from some nursing leaders that science courses should be adapted and specially arranged for nurses. Instead, she encouraged preclinical degree nursing students to enroll in full science courses. Gray experienced difficulty facing the challenge of the Second World War. She retired from UBC in 1941, although she was only 61 years of age and was in good health. Her unexpected retirement left the Department of Nursing and Health with no one qualified to teach the teaching and supervision courses at a time when many senior nurses were joining the armed forces. It seems likely that Gray decided she had done all that she could and recognized problems associated with her lack of academic qualifications. Two other full-time nursing academic staff both held master's degrees and perceived some need for programming changes. Following retirement, Gray stayed in Vancouver and was active in the Vancouver Graduate Nurses Association which helped place private duty nurses. She served previously as convenor of the public health committee of the Vancouver Local Council of Women, and continued after retirement as convenor of its mental health committee. Gray also learned to drive a car after retirement and was able to get more easily to golfing and lawn bowling greens. Mabel Gray died August 13, 1976 at age 96.

PUBLICATIONS BY MABEL F. GRAY

Various editorials during her CNA Presidency, 1927/ 28, in *The Canadian Nurse* journal.

BIBLIOGRAPHY

Biographical Information File. Available from the CNA Library, 50 The Driveway, Ottawa, Ontario, K2P 1E2.

Johns, E. (n.d.). *The Winnipeg General Hospital School of Nursing, 1887–1953* (Chapter 6, pp. 49–53). Winnipeg, MAN: The Alumnae association, The Winnipeg General Hospital School of Nursing.

Street, M. (1973). *Watch-fires on the mountains: The life and writings of Ethel Johns.* Toronto: University of Toronto Press.

Zilm, G., & Warbinek, E. (1994). *Legacy: History of nursing education at the University of British Columbia, 1919–1994.* Vancouver: UBC Press.

Sharon Richardson

AMELIA GREENWALD
1881–1966

Amelia Greenwald

Quietly leading the way as an international public health nurse between the two world wars best describes Amelia Greenwald. Amelia was born in Gainesville, Alabama on March 1, 1881 to Joseph and Elisha (Elise Haas) Greenwald, German-Jewish immigrants who married in Memphis, Tennessee. Joseph was a grain dealer and the mayor of Gainesville and had been a Confederate soldier. Amelia was the youngest of eight children. Her siblings were Isaac, Carrie, Jake, Morris, Sylvester, Julian, and Isadore.

After her debut in society, and over the objections of her family, Amelia entered the Touro Infirmary Training School for Nurses (TISON), in New Orleans, Louisiana and graduated in 1908. In 1909 she helped organize the Pensacola Sanitarium, Pensacola, Florida and worked in a hospital in North Carolina prior to attending a post-graduate course in psychiatric nursing at Phipps Clinic, Johns Hopkins University, Baltimore, Maryland (1913–1914). While in Baltimore, Greenwald met Henrietta Szold, who introduced her to Zionist ideas and talked to her about going to Palestine as a public health nurse.

Amelia Greenwald moved to New York, where she took private tutoring in Hebrew, Yiddish, and Jewish history, as she stated she preferred to work among the Jewish community. She also attended the nursing program at Teachers College, Columbia University. She worked for the Metropolitan Life Insurance Company and directed the New Jersey Public Health Association, Long Branch, New Jersey from 1916 until overseas service during World War I. With Greenwald's efforts, a new milk ordinance was enacted and the Association hired the first health officer in Long Branch and paid his salary until it was incorporated into the city budget.

With the American Expeditionary Forces she served as acting Chief Nurse of a hospital at Verdun, France and Night Superintendent of a hospital in Savoy, France. Her American Red Cross pin number was 5532 when she enrolled in Manhattan, New York, on January 28, 1915. She aided German war brides and helped establish the first American hospital at Coblenz, Germany. She received the Victory Medal for service at the Meuse-Argonne Defensive Sector. Greenwald joined one of the first American

Legion Posts ever organized and remained a member all her life.

In October 1919, Greenwald was asked by the National Council of Jewish Women to head its farm women program. This program was organized in cooperation with the Jewish Agricultural and Industrial Aid Society (JAIAS) of New York City. The purpose of JAIAS was to encourage immigrants to settle away from urban areas.

She began her work in the small village of Woodridge, New York, giving English lessons twice weekly, acted as public health nurse, and developed hygiene programs for the elementary public schools.

In 1923 she established the Jewish Nurses' Training School at the Jewish Hospital in Warsaw, Poland utilizing the New York State University nursing curriculum. She went at the insistence of Dr. Bernard Flexner, chairman of the Joint Distribution Committee, Dr. Lee K. Frankel, social analyst and manager of the Metropolitan Life Insurance Company Welfare Division, and Herbert Hoover, not yet president but head of the American Relief Administration which distributed food, clothing, and medical supplies to refugees in Eastern Europe. Greenwald ultimately wrote that Dr. Frankel had given her the challenge which became the greatest ambition of her life to accomplish. Lillian Wald and the Henry Street Nurses Association gave her an outfitted nurse's bag as a farewell gift. Since there were no nursing textbooks available in Polish, the students used Russian, German, and French medical books to write up permanent notes.

In November 1925, the first class of 15 students graduated. Future teaching faculty were chosen from this first class and sent for postgraduate courses to Germany and England. On their return, they received administrative training by Greenwald. According to her initial agreement, the task of maintaining the school was given to these capable women and Greenwald left Poland at the end of 4 years. The school received international accolades at the International Exhibition of Hygiene and Sanitation in Warsaw, the International Convention of Nurses in Geneva and was decorated for its standards by the Division of Public Health of the League of Nations. Greenwald was the first woman decorated with the Polish Golden Cross of Merit. She was also the first woman licensed to drive in Poland and wrote to relatives that she introduced iced tea.

On her return to the U.S. she worked briefly in Miami, FL, before returning to New York to work with the National Council's Department of Farm and Rural Work. In 1932, ostensibly to survey hospital nursing services in Palestine, she served, instead, as Director of the Nurse's Training School, Rothchild Hospital (Hadassah) for one year.

On her return to the U.S. in 1933, Greenwald retired from active nursing, and opened La Vogue Dress Shop, in Eunice, Louisiana, at the persuasion of her oldest brother, Isaac. She sold ready-to-wear clothing, but she truly preferred her beloved antiques.

Although single, in 1939, she adopted a 15-year-old distant cousin, Liselotte Levy, to save her from the Nazis. Amelia and Liselotte developed a very close friendship and love. Amelia called Liselotte "her greatest blessing." Liselotte Levy Weil and her husband remained in Eunice to care for Greenwald when she became ill with cancer.

Greenwald died on January 1, 1966, and is interred in Beth Israel Cemetery, Meridian, Louisiana. Her gravestone bears the simple inscription: "Nurse, Army Nurse Corps, World War I."

Amelia Greenwald was an extraordinary nursing leader. She served as an example of an international public health nurse leader in the period between the two world wars. She quietly led the way 70 years ago.

BIBLIOGRAPHY

Greenwald, A. (1925). Nursing education in Poland. *International Aspects of Nursing Education.* New York: Bureau of Publications, Teachers College Columbia University, pp. 72–77.

Kahn, C. (1992). From the archives. *Tourovues,* (1992, Fall): 24–27.

Mayer, S. L. (1994). Amelia Greenwald: Pioneer in international public health. *Nursing and Health Care, 15,* 74–78.

Mayer, S. L. (1996). *The Jewish experience in nursing in America: 1881 to 1955.* Ed.D. dissertation, Teachers College, Columbia University.

Sokoloff, L. (1993–1994). Amelia Greenwald (1881–1966), Pioneer American-Jewish nurse. *Korot,* 92–101.

Turitz, L. (1985). Amelia Greenwald (1881–1966). *American Jewish Archives, 37,* 291–292.

Susan Mayer

JEAN ISABEL GUNN
1882–1941

As Superintendent of Nurses at Toronto General Hospital, Jean I. Gunn demonstrated leadership in confronting various nursing issues during her long tenure (1913–1941). Her leadership style was cooperative and empowering as she worked through a large network of nursing and non-nursing colleagues to achieve nursing goals. She often had to devise strategies to circumvent political and medical opposition to such projects as student government at Toronto General, enrollment of nurses in the military in the 1914 to 1918 war, nurse registration in Ontario, a nursing department at the University of Toronto, construction of a national memorial to World War I nurses, a national survey of nursing education, and an 8-hour work day for nurses.

Jean Isabel Gunn was born on February 11, 1882, in Belleville, Ontario, Canada. She was the fifth of eight living children of a Scottish-Canadian and his wife whose family was descended from Loyalists who had emigrated from the Hudson Valley at the time of the American War of Independence. Her name registered at birth was Barbara Isobella, but she was known to her family as "Jennie" and apparently adopted "Jean" as her given name. Gunn's father was opposed to his daughter's wish to become a nurse, preferring instead that she become a teacher. Accordingly, Gunn studied at Albert College, Belleville and graduated second in her class at the age of 19. She may have taught school for a short time before doing what she was determined to do: become a nurse. She entered Presbyterian Hospital School of Nursing in New York in 1902 with the support of both her mother and of her older sister who lived in the New York area.

Her student experience occurred when Anna Maxwell was director of the school and included some "social service" or public health nursing. She received her diploma on May 16, 1905; following her graduation, she remained in the United States for 8 years, filling a variety of positions at Presbyterian Hospital, including Night Director and head nurse in a busy operating room. Some sources report that she did some "social service" work in New York City at the Henry Street Settlement. Her last position before returning to Canada was Assistant Superintendent at Morristown Hospital, Morristown, New Jersey.

Gunn was officially appointed superintendent by the Board of Trustees, Toronto General Hospital on August 8, 1913. Toronto General, which had moved into a new building in June of 1913 was Canada's largest and most modern hospital, supported by the political and social elite of Toronto. Records show that she started her position at a salary of $1,500 (CDN) per year, only a few hundred dollars less than the medical director. She headed "a staff of 22 [graduate] nurses to assist with running the hospital nursing service and school which had 119 pupil nurses, 41 probationers, 1 pupil-dietitian and 2 pupils from an affiliated school. An additional 42 probationers were admitted on September 1 and 16, before Gunn's arrival" (Riegler, 1992, p. 95). Gunn lived in a suite in the nurses' residence with her own maid for her entire career, until her death in 1941.

From this influential position and working with the Canadian National Association of Trained Nurses (CNATN), which in 1924 became the Canadian Nurses' Association, Gunn strove to incorporate education into the preparation of nurses, speaking strongly in favor of access to the university for nurses in order to gain knowledge necessary to keep up with community health and medical science and to move toward professional status. She viewed the major responsibility of organized nursing to be sure that there was an adequate supply of qualified nurses to meet the hospitals' and the public's needs. She lobbied for registration of nurses and self-regulation of nurse education and nursing by the profession itself.

Gunn and her colleagues in the Graduate Nurses Association of Ontario (GNAO) in 1915 had instituted a standard curriculum for nursing which was accepted voluntarily by Ontario schools. She also advocated short intensive courses in public health work at university level to prepare nurses returning from the military for civilian jobs and as a result of this strategy, in 1920 the Department of Public Health Nursing at the University of Toronto admitted its first students, giving nurses access to university education.

An early act as superintendent was instituting student government for nursing students, which she believed would increase the professionalism and leadership skills of the students and give them control of their residence life. She believed that participating in self-governance in the residence would lead to nurses' participation in nursing organizations. This was a first in Canada, and opposition was met from alumnae of the school and from the indifference of some of the students themselves. Gunn nurtured student responsibility in the early development of the student government and remained a strong supporter of its operations and effectiveness.

At the outset of World War I, demand for nurses increased, and Gunn was named coordinator of efforts by the CNATN to enroll trained nurses in military service. Despite many strongly worded protests from Gunn, however, the government continued its practice of enrolling untrained nurses for military duty.

During WW I, she worked closely with the Canadian Red Cross in their project to get women's groups to assemble surgical dressings for the war effort. In the last months of the war, she was involved in the testing of sphagnum moss for use in dressings when cotton became scarce. Her work with the Red Cross resulted in the development of powerful allies in her subsequent fight to raise the standards of nursing.

At the end of the war, there was a shortage of qualified trained nurses, in large part because of the double need of staffing military hospitals and nursing victims of the influenza pandemic. Gunn, as president of the CNATN, and in her own hospital struggled to keep up nursing standards by supplying the shortage by increasing enrollment in schools rather than relying on untrained nurses. She used the crisis to promote the educational interests of trained nurses and the involvement of nurses in health reform, efforts that were opposed by the medical establishment and the government.

At this same time Gunn organized the efforts of the CNATN to build a memorial to the 47 nursing sisters who died in the First World War. The idea had been proposed in 1918, but had not been acted upon until Gunn was appointed Convenor of the Memorial Committee and gave direction to the efforts which resulted in the dedication of the Nurses' Memorial in Ottawa in 1926.

In the mid-1920s, Gunn called for separation of nursing education from nursing service in order for nursing students to receive more education and to provide employment for graduate nurses. She advocated the 8-hour work day for nurses. She saw this as benefiting students by giving them more time for education in their program and graduates by increasing the number of nurses needed.

Gunn accomplished much of her work through a sometimes overlapping network of committees in many organizations. She was an active and participating member of the Canadian National Association of Trained Nurses, the Canadian Nurses' Association, the Graduate Nurses' Association of Ontario, and its successor, the Registered Nurses' Association of Ontario (from 1925 until her death), the Canadian Society of Superintendents of Training Schools (1915–1917) and the Canadian Association of Nursing Education (1917–1924). She served in many capacities with the Canadian Red Cross (National Office) and with the Ontario Division between 1917 and 1941. Gunn served the International Council of Nurses on various committees and was first vice-president from 1937–1941. She also gave her efforts to the Canadian National Council of Women and the Canadian National Council for Combating Venereal Diseases.

Gunn received numerous awards during her career including being made an Officer in the Civil Division of the Order of the British Empire in 1935 and in the same year receiving the King's Jubilee Medal from King George V. She was the first recipient of the Mary Agnes Snively Medal awarded by the Canadian Nurses' Association (1936). The University of Toronto bestowed an Honorary Doctor of Laws degree in 1938.

Jean Gunn was a strong voice advocating education and professionalism in nursing in Canada. She saw nurses as educated and equal partners with physicians in health care and throughout her career emphasized the role of the nurse in public health and home nursing as well as in hospital nursing. Gunn's health deteriorated in 1940 and she died in Toronto on June, 28, 1941 at age 59 of metastatic sarcoma. She is buried in the family plot on the family farm property.

BIBLIOGRAPHY

Reigler, N. N. (1992). *The work and networks of Jean I. Gunn, Superintendent of Nurses, Toronto General Hospital, 1913–1941: A presentation of some issues in nursing during her lifetime.* Unpublished doctoral dissertation, University of Toronto. [Available from: National Library of Canada, 395 Wellington St., Ottawa, Ont. Canada K1A 0N4].

Reigler, N. N. (1994). Portrait of leadership. Jean I. Gunn: A leader among leaders (1882–1941). *Registered Nurse, 6*(3), 32–34.

Marian Brook

LAURIE MARTIN GUNTER
1922–

Laurie Martin Gunter was one of the founders of gerontological nursing and was instrumental in developing the first geriatric certificate program of the American Nurses Association. Educationally, her major achievements came as chair of the department of nursing at Pennsylvania State University. Among other things, she facilitated the move from a hospital location in Pittsburgh to an on-campus location in University Park; revamped the curriculum and expanded the program from an enrollment of 100 to 900; and implemented a graduate degree program as well as an extended degree program.

Laurie Martin Gunter

Gunter was born in Pelham, Navarro County, Texas, on March 5, 1922, to Hollie Myrtle Carruthers and Lewis Marion Martin. The eldest of three children, she attended Pelham grade and high school and graduated at the top of her class. In 1940 she entered the school of nursing at Meharry College in Nashville and after graduating in 1943 went to work as a staff nurse at George W. Hubbard Hospital in Nashville. While there she went on to get a B.S. degree in human development from Tennessee A & I University in Nashville. In 1948 she received a Rockefeller Fellowship for advanced study of nursing and attended the

University of Toronto for a year. She then returned to Nashville where she received an M.A. from Fisk University, and from there she commuted to Chicago where she earned her Ph.D. in Human Development in 1953 from the University of Chicago. By this time she had married and had a 3-year-old daughter, Lara; her mother cared for the child while Gunter was away.

From 1948 she was an instructor in the school of nursing at Meharry Medical College, and after receiving her Ph.D. she was appointed an assistant professor there. She became acting dean in 1957 and dean from 1958 to 1961. It was at this time that she began to specialize in gerontology and in 1959 served as a fellow at the University of California, Berkeley, at the Inter University Council of Social Gerontology. While doing all these things she also gave birth to a second daughter, Margo Alyce.

From 1961 to 1965 she taught at UCLA, making a break from the segregated schools of the South. From UCLA, she moved to Indiana University Medical Center in Indianapolis, and after teaching there for a year joined the University of Washington College of Nursing in Seattle as associate professor in 1966, and was promoted to full professor in 1969. In 1971 she was appointed professor and head of nursing in the College of Human Development at Pennsylvania State University in University Park, where she radically changed the nursing school moving it from Pittsburgh to University Park, establishing a graduate program, and moving the nursing school into the front ranks of collegiate schools. After she stepped down as chair, she concentrated on research into gerontological nursing. She retired from Pennsylvania State in 1987. During her last few years there she also served as a visiting professor at the Universities of Delaware, Tulsa, and UCLA.

From 1971 until 1976 Gunter served on the executive committee of the division of

Geriatric Nursing Practice of the ANA, and among her honors was election to membership in the Institute of Medicine of the National Academy of Sciences, election as fellow of the Gerontological Society of America, and also of the American Academy of Nursing. She served an important role in organizing the first International Conference on Gerontological Nursing in 1981. She published some 50 articles or reports, mostly on gerontological nursing. Among her many honors were being made an honorary alumna of Penn State, an award from Sigma Theta Tau for outstanding contributions to nursing research. Laurie herself summed up her life by saying: "I have been interested in a lot of things and have scattered my energies over a broad area. I doubt if my mother or my children ever really knew much about my professional stature, whatever I did successfully was what was expected of me." At the time of this writing she lives in Seattle, where she keep active in the community and enjoys being a grandmother.

PUBLICATIONS BY LAURIE MARTIN GUNTER

Gunter, L. M., & Estes, C. A. (1979). *Education for gerontic nursing.* New York: Springer. [This was the first book to suggest a curricula for gerontological nursing.]

BIBLIOGRAPHY

Ebersole, P. (1998). Looking for a few good nurses. *Geriatric Nursing, 19*, 49–50.
Ebersole, P. (July, 1998). [Personal interview]. Seattle, Washington.
Gunter, L. Professional curriculum vita.

Priscilla Ebersole

H

GERTRUDE MAY HALL
1897–1960

Gertrude May Hall was one of a small cadre of second-generation Canadian nursing administrators who developed extensive practical knowledge and skills which were used to revitalize nursing practice and education during the period of national reconstruction that followed the end of the Second World War. Despite lack of a university degree, Hall was well-versed in the deficiencies of hospital nurse training, and strongly supported university education to prepare leaders of nursing. She advocated separation of nursing school budgets from hospitals' general budgets and replacement of semi-apprenticeship nurse training by sound educational programming. Hall also advocated replacement of 5-year degree nursing programs, in which 1 year of general arts and science courses at a university was followed by 3 years in a hospital training program, and a final year back at university specializing in either ward teaching and supervision or public health nursing, with 4-year programs in which nursing and general arts and science courses were conjointly offered in each year of the program, thereby facilitating "integration" of learning. Although she was unsuccessful in 1959 in convincing the University of Alberta School of Nursing to replace its 5-year segmented degree program with a 4-year integrated model, Hall was able in the mid-1950s to implement a dramatically improved curriculum and master plan for rotation of students through clinical areas at the Calgary General Hospital School of Nursing. Hall's administrative expertise, coupled with a tremendous capacity for hard work, considerable personal charm and skill as a public speaker, contributed to her national and international reputation as an expert in nursing and health care. Hall's personal integrity was unquestioned. She really cared about what she conceived to be right and was prepared to stand up and be counted rather than acquiesce to pressure.

Gertrude May Hall

Gertrude Hall was born May 6, 1897 in Winnipeg, Manitoba. Her parents were of Scottish descent and farmed near the vil-

lage of Hazel Ridge before moving into the St. Boniface district of Winnipeg. Both parents were ardent Presbyterian church and community workers. Hall was raised in a comfortable home with Victorian elegance and Victorian standards. She taught school as a substitute teacher for a year before graduating in 1916 from the one-year nurse training program sponsored by the Grace Maternity Hospital, Winnipeg.

Hall was Night Supervisor at the Grace Hospital from 1917 to 1918, before enrolling in and graduating from the Winnipeg General Hospital nurse training program in 1921. From 1912 to 1922, she was Superintendent of Nurses at Ethelbert Hospital, Manitoba, and from 1922 to 1923, Hall engaged in what she herself described as "public health nursing" at an outpost hospital in northern Manitoba. Desiring advanced nursing education, Hall enrolled in McGill University's School for Graduate Nurses, graduating in 1924 with a certificate in public health nursing. During the ensuing year, she was a staff nurse in the Social Service Department of the Winnipeg General Hospital.

In 1925, Hall began an 11-year period of employment with the Manitoba provincial government in a wide variety of roles. From 1925 to 1927, she was Supervisor of Public Health Nursing at Portage la Prairie, Manitoba, before returning to Winnipeg as health teacher and student advisor at the Manitoba Normal School (teacher training) from 1927 to 1931. In September 1931 she became a Supervisor for the Department of Health and organized health services in half the province. Beginning in September 1935, Hall undertook a year-long special project surveying nursing homes for the Department of Health and assisting to establish provincial regulations for these homes. This was followed by a survey of schools of nursing in the province and recommendations for improvements in nurse training programs. She was granted a leave of absence by the provincial Department of Health in November 1936 to guide the Manitoba Association of Registered Nurses (MARN) and subsequently became MARN's chief administrative officer and provincial nursing school advisor until 1943.

In 1943, she was appointed Director of Nurses, City Health Department in 1943, to plan the amalgamation of nursing services. During this year, she visited hospitals, university nursing programs and public health agencies, chiefly in the United States, under a 4-month Rockefeller Foundation Travelling Fellowship. In October 1944, Hall advanced from the provincial to the national nursing arena in Canada and accepted the position of chief administrative officer of the Canadian Nurses Association (CNA). She continued in that role until 1952.

Throughout her career, Hall was very closely associated with hospital and public health nursing administration and her participation in professional associations reflected this interest. As a representative of CNA, she attended board and congress meetings of the International Council of Nurses (ICN), in Great Britain, the United States, Sweden, and Belgium. In 1946, she spent 2 months surveying hospitals and nurse training programs in Great Britain and Holland to help analyze nursing problems in post-war Europe. In June 1951, Hall was appointed for a 5-year term to the World Health Organization's Expert Committee on Nursing, and was reappointed for a second 5-year term in 1957. In 1952 she became Director of Nursing Service and Nursing Education at the Calgary General Hospital, Calgary, Alberta, in September 1952. For eight years, Hall and her hand-picked senior nursing staff, supported by a sympathetic hospital board of directors, effectively planned and implemented a revamped nursing service and nurse training program for the CGH as the hospital doubled in size. Hall died unexpectedly on October 14, 1960 from a heart seizure suffered while she presided at graduation ceremonies at the Calgary General Hospital. She was buried in Winnipeg.

During her lifetime, Gertrude Hall earned a personal and professional reputation for commitment to nursing and to serving her fellow human beings through high quality patient care and education of adequate numbers of nurses to provide that care. She possessed a finely tuned sense of responsibility which manifested itself by being prepared to stand up for what she believed was right.

PUBLICATIONS BY GERTRUDE MAY HALL

Numerous editorial and articles published in *The Canadian Nurse* journal, especially during the last 20 years of her life, from 1940 to 1960.
Administrative aspects of nursing education in the clinical field, (1940). *The Canadian Nurse, 36,* 555.
Queues and waiting, (1946). *The Canadian Nurse, 42,* 1020–1022.
Who is exploiting whom? Public asked, (1947). *Montreal Daily Star.*
With Street, M. M. (1959). Survey of a hospital nursing service. *International Nursing Review, 6,* 46–54.

BIBLIOGRAPHY

Biographical File—Gertrude M. Hall. [Available from the CNA library, 50 The Driveway, Ottawa, Ontario, K2P 1E2.]
Mackie, E. J. (1983?). *Gertrude M. Hall and Margaret M. Street: Biographical information.* [Compiled to accompany the annual scholarship for a selected nursing student from a Canadian university who is entering the first year of the Master's in Nursing at the University of Calgary.] [Available from the Canadian Nurses Association library, 50 The Driveway, Ottawa, Ontario, K2P 1E2.]

Sharon Richardson

ANNE G. MONTGOMERY HARGREAVES
1923–

Anne G. Montgomery Hargreaves has been a leader in psychiatric nursing education and practice with a career that spans both academic and service delivery sectors. She was a pioneer in the development of nurse leadership of group therapy and in the movement of psychiatric nursing education from hospital to community settings. She took leadership in the care of disadvantaged populations, exemplified by her position as Assistant Deputy Commissioner of Health for the City of Boston responsible for nursing education and service at Boston City Hospital, and also by her service on four Health and Human Rights Commissions to El Salvador. She asserted the importance of professionalism for nurses in her role as President and as Executive Director of the Massachusetts Nurses Association and as a charter member of the American Academy of Nursing.

Hargreaves was born in Lexington, Massachusetts, on September 9, 1923, the daughter of Murdoch Montgomery and Dolena McLeod Montgomery. Both parents were born in Nova Scotia, where her mother was a school teacher and her father a carpenter. Her mother, who later studied nursing in Boston, died of measles complicated by pneumonia when Anne was 3 years old. Anne had one younger sister. Her father later married a nurse, and Anne acquired five stepsisters and a stepbrother whom she and her sister helped to care for. Anne's first job, when she was 15 years old, was as a ward maid for a summer at Emerson Hospital. She worked the following summer at Newton Wesley Hospital. Although she thought of becoming a doctor, for financial reasons she decided on nursing, and entered Boston City Hospital School of Nursing, where clinical preparation was good and students were paid a stipend. She graduated in 1944.

She served with the Army Nurse Corps in the European Theater in Germany with the 135th Evacuation Hospital from 1944 to 1946. Her first Army experience was a collision of the ship on which she was traveling to Europe. She later described that experience, and the experience of caring for burn victims from the Cocoanut Grove fire, as the two life experiences that had a profound effect on her. When she returned from Europe in 1946, she married Edward Hargreaves, an insurance underwriter in Boston. They had two children, Edward Jr. and George.

From 1946 to 1951 Hargreaves worked at Boston State Hospital, a psychiatric facility, where she became the Educational Director, and began studying part-time towards a baccalaureate, and then a master's degree, at Boston University. She became a Director of Nursing at Ring Sanitarium, a private psychiatric hospital from 1951 until 1953. From 1953 to 1972, she was a faculty member at Boston University School of Nursing, where she rose from instructor to full professor, teaching psychiatric nursing in the undergraduate and graduate programs.

Anne's first article, published in the AJN in 1950 while she was employed at Boston State Hospital, focused on the nurse as the leader of group psychotherapy sessions, a new role for psychiatric nursing. She continued as a leader in this role throughout her career, not only teaching but also in clinical practice, with such diverse groups as prisoners, adolescent girls, college undergraduates, mental health center day hospital patients, and elderly women in a nursing home. While on the Boston University faculty she was awarded two Danforth Teacher Grants, and during a sabbatical she was a fellow at the Harvard Medical School Laboratory of Community Psychiatry. She recognized the trend towards deinstitutionalization of psychiatric patients, and was awarded an NIMH training grant to teach undergraduate nursing students in a community mental health setting. She pioneered in and gained recognition for her work in using experiential group training for nurses, which she wrote about in a series of articles, including one in 1967 in the AJN entitled "Group Culture in Nursing Practice." She also helped develop a day hospital for psychiatric patients at Massachusetts Mental Health Center, described in a 1961 AJN article entitled "A Day Hospital for Psychiatric Patients."

From 1969 to 1974, she was Chairperson of the Massachusetts Board of Registration in Nursing. Her husband had suffered a stroke in 1970 and had a lengthy hospitalization before returning home. She left Boston University in 1972 during a time of stress and dissension in the institution. She served as Assistant Deputy Commissioner of Nursing for the City of Boston Department of Health and Hospitals, from 1972 to 1985. This position included serving as Executive Director of Nursing Service and Nursing Education at Boston City Hospital. During this time she was successful in closing out the diploma program at the hospital, in setting up a rape counseling program, a first of its kind, and in instituting a psychiatric nurse counseling program in the hospital's emergency department.

From 1983 to 1989 she served as a member of a Public Health and Human Rights Commission to El Salvador, which she wrote about in a special article for *Nursing Outlook* in July 1983. In 1985 she became Executive Director of the Massachusetts Nursing Association, a position which she held until 1989. During that time she helped strengthen the Board of Nurse Registration, worked on legislation to require continuing education for nurses, and developed definitions of expanded nursing practice.

Hargreaves was named as one of 36 charter members of the American Academy of Nursing in 1973. In 1992 she received the University of Massachusetts Urban Community Service award for her nursing leadership and her lifetime commitment to the underserved. After retiring in 1989, she returned to Boston University to obtain a certificate in gerontology. She is currently a consultant for the Mental Health Management/Bay Colony Counseling Service, doing group counseling with older women nursing home residents. She is also President of the Massachusetts Association of Older Americans, to which she was elected in 1997. She lives with her husband in Dedham, Massachusetts.

PUBLICATIONS BY ANNE HARGREAVES (SELECTED)

The nurse leader in group therapy. (1950). *American Journal of Nursing, 50,* 713–717.
A day hospital for psychiatric patients. (1961). *American Journal of Nursing, 61,* 30–33.
Group culture and nursing practice. (1967). *American Journal of Nursing, 67*: September.
Emotional problems of patients with respiratory disease. (1968). *Nursing Clinics of North America,* September.
Long-term mental illness in the community. (1970). *Nursing Clinics of North America,* March.
Maintaining academic freedom. (1971). *American Journal of Nursing, 71,* 59–92.
Special report on health care in El Salvador. (1983). *Nursing Outlook, 31* (July–August).
Coping with disaster. (1989). *American Journal of Nursing, 89,* 683.

BIBLIOGRAPHY

Fellows named to Academy of Nursing. (1973). *The American Nurse, 5.*

Lois Monteiro

MARGARET HARPER
1911–

Margaret Harper served as the 11th Chief of the Army Nurse Corps from September 1, 1959 until August 31, 1963. Her wise, farsighted leadership laid the groundwork which prepared the Army Nurse Corps to deal with the formidable challenges it would encounter during the Vietnam War.

Harper was born on July 23, 1911 and raised in her birthplace of Potomac, Illinois. As a young woman, she took delight in outdoor living and the joys of sporting activities. An expression of Harper's zest for the active life and disregard for gender restrictions can be found in documentation recorded by the superintendent of her training school. The superintendent noted that during the course of her nurse's training, Harper was accidentally shot while in the field hunting. Another example of Harper's intrepid personality was demonstrated by the fact that while on duty in New Guinea during World War II, Harper always carried a personal handgun and drove her own jeep. Such atypical behavior was then unexpected, uncommon, and rarely observed in an Army nurse. Later in her Army career, Harper also qualified on the Carbine M2 rifle. In another illustration of her unique, vigorous, and enterprising spirit, Harper revealed on one occasion that horseback riding was a lifelong avocation. As a young woman, Harper attended college for 2 years and then entered the Evanston General Hospital School of Nursing in Illinois, graduating in 1934. In the 7-year period before she joined the Army Nurse Corps, she served as superintendent of nurses at Chicago Memorial Hospital in Illinois, and at Murry Hospital in Butte, Montana.

Harper's military nursing career began as a general duty nurse at Fort Lewis, Washington, in 1941 just before the outbreak of World War II. At this time the Army was anticipating what seemed to be inevitable hostilities and consequently was looking for more Army Nurse Corps officers. Harper's next assignment was in the South Pacific. There she served as chief nurse of the 155th Station Hospital in Australia and as advance base chief nurse in New Guinea. In 1944, Harper was assigned for a short while at

Margaret Harper

Percy Jones Army Hospital in Battle Creek, Michigan. She then joined the 123rd Evacuation Hospital as chief nurse at Camp Rucker, Alabama, in 1945 and accompanied the unit to the European Theater for a period of service in the Rhineland. She subsequently served as chief nurse of the 59th Field Hospital and the 120th Station Hospital in Europe. After World War II, Harper attended Teachers College, Columbia University, and earned a bachelor of science degree in nursing education. Following her academic assignment, Harper put her newly acquired knowledge and her extensive military nursing experience to use writing and editing extension courses at the Medical Field Service School, Fort Sam Houston, Texas. In 1949, she transferred to the Army hospital at Fort Sill, Oklahoma, where she served as chief nurse for two years. In 1951, she became chief nurse of First Army in New York and followed that assignment with another stint at Columbia University, earning a Master's degree in nursing service administration in 1953. Harper then transferred to Valley Forge General Hospital in Phoenixville, Pennsylvania, where she held several supervisory positions. Her tenure there culminated in an assignment as Nursing Service Personnel Coordinator, presumably a position synonymous with that of chief nurse. In 1955, Harper became the assistant chief of the Army Nurse Corps under Colonel Inez Haynes and followed that assignment with her final position as chief of the Army Nurse Corps.

During Harper's administration, the Army Nurse Corps frequently supported small mobilizations and humanitarian or disaster relief efforts. In 1958, just before Harper became chief, several hospital units with their complements of Army nurses deployed to Lebanon. This, the first mobilization of male Army nurses, highlighted a few issues associated with the introduction of male nurses, for example, housing males in female nurses' quarters, and male nurses treating female patients. Harper faced resistance from the Army line commanders with the introduction of male nurses. She countered their objections with humor. On one occasion, she used a pancake story to illustrate that few differences existed between male and female nurses. She told a commander that male and female pancakes were "stirred up the same, but they come out just a little bit different in shape." Another mobilization occurred with the May 1960 mission to Chile after that country was struck by an earthquake and tidal wave. Army nurses participated in that relief effort as well. Additionally in September 1962, 21 Army nurses from the 8th Evacuation Hospital in Landstuhl, Germany, participated in a disaster relief effort following a tragic earthquake in Iran.

In October 1962, a number of Active, Reserve, and National Guard Army nurses mobilized to Florida as part of the defensive posture in response to the Cuban Missile Crisis—an attempt by the former USSR to establish strategic missile sites aimed at the United States. Because Army Nurse Corps officers never had been issued organizational clothing routinely in times of peace, many of the aggregate arrived in an unseemly array of uniforms. The complaints emanating from Commanding General Harper's own dismay on noting the lack of uniformity in the Army Nurse Corps complement in Florida indicated a need for change. As a result, Harper established a mandatory issue of organizational clothing. Another readiness issue surfaced when Army nurses assigned to the Strategic Army Corps (STRAC) units departed for Florida. Their home hospitals were confronted with significant staff deficits and no hopes of obtaining replacement nurses due to the chronic shortage of Army nurses. Operation NIGHTINGALE, a recruiting project initiated by Harper to increase civilian nurses' awareness of the opportunities in Army nursing, resulted. Many relief operations, albeit on a smaller scale, followed and served to provide some field preparation for Army nurses who would participate in another war on the horizon in Southeast Asia.

By all accounts, Harper's resolute leadership style featured an intriguing blend of humor and candor. One co-worker described her unmatched personal qualities as businesslike and pragmatic. After her retirement in 1963, following over 22 years of federal service, Harper moved to the state of Colorado where she again immersed herself in the pleasures of an active outdoor life. Still later, she settled in San Antonio, Texas where she resides as of this writing.

BIBLIOGRAPHY

Condon-Rall, M. E. (1994, August). U.S. Army medical relief to Chile, 1960. [Information Paper.] U.S. Army Center of Military History, Washington, DC.
The many faces of a United States Army Nurse. (1964, January 6). *Army news photo features.* [Downey Col-

lection, AMEDD Museum, Fort Sam Houston, TX.]

The many worlds of the Army Nurse. (1963, December). *Army Information Digest*, 10–19.

Margaret Harper. [DA Form 66B]. ANC Archives, U.S. Army Center of Military History, Washington, DC.

Meeting and workshop at the Historical Unit, Fort Detrick, Maryland. (1975, February 3). [Proceedings.] pp. 33–34. ANC Archives, U.S. Army Center of Military History, Washington, DC.

Oblensky, F. (1963). Eleven women—and the Army Nurse. *The Retired Officer, 19*, 32–33.

Odell, E. W. (1941, July 19). United States Army Nurse Corps, certificate from School of Nursing. ANC Archives, U.S. Army Center of Military History, Washington, DC.

Official biography: Colonel Margaret Harper. (n.d.). ANC Archives, U.S. Army Center of Military History, Washington, DC.

Potter, H. E. (1963, November 13). *The role of the Army Medical Service in the Cuban Crisis, 1961*, pp. 22, 66–70. [Unpublished manuscript.] ANC Archives, U.S. Army Center of Military History, Washington, DC.

West, I. J. (1962). Earthquake in Iran 1962: Operation IDA (Iranian Disaster Assistance). [Unpublished manuscript.] ANC Archives, U.S. Army Center of Military History, Washington, DC.

Mary T. Sarnecky

D'Lorz Inez Haynes

D'LORZ INEZ HAYNES
1909–1997

D'Lorz Inez Haynes was the 10th Chief of the Army Nurse Corps. Her tenure in this position of leadership spanned the period from October 1, 1955 until August 31, 1959. Following her retirement from the Army in 1959 with 26 years of military service, Haynes devoted the next 10 years of her professional life to several key positions with the National League for Nursing. After resigning from the National League for Nursing, Haynes held academic appointments in Texas and Oklahoma.

Haynes was the first child born to the farming family of Floyd and Lola Rampey Haynes on June 3, 1909 in Paint Rock, Texas. She and her three brothers and sister grew up in the country around San Angelo, Texas. After her 1929 graduation from Miles High School in Miles, Texas, Haynes entered nursing school at Scott and White Hospital in Temple, Texas. As a newly registered nurse, Haynes listened to the advice of friends and family who spoke of the exploits of Army nurses of World War I. Consequently, she too decided to join the Army. Haynes applied to enter the service at Fort Sam Houston in San Antonio, Texas and began her career in the Army Nurse Corps, coming to active duty in 1933. She spent 6 years as an operating room nurse at Fort Sam Houston, Texas, and 2 additional years in the same role at Sternberg General Hospital in the Philippines. Six months before the Japanese invasion, she transferred to a brief assignment at Fort Lewis, Washington, and subsequently to another posting at Fort Worden, Washington. In 1942, Haynes again served in the operating room, this time at Walter Reed Army Hospital in Washington, D.C. For the duration of World War II and in its immediate aftermath, she served as chief nurse of several general hospitals in Europe and in the Pacific. In 1947, Haynes became chief nurse of the First Army Area in New York. She attended the Army Medical Department Officers' Advanced Course in 1948 and, in 1949, she began a 4-year-tenure in the Army Nurse Corps Career Management Branch in the Surgeon General's Office in Washington, D.C. There she managed the assignments and careers of a group of Army Nurse Corps officers. From 1953 until 1955, Haynes' duty involved a return to an academic setting, at the University of Minnesota, where she earned her bachelor of science in nursing. In 1954, she became the deputy chief of the Army Nurse Corps, the second most senior position in the Corps. In October 1955, she began her 4-year term as the tenth Chief of the Army Nurse Corps.

The challenge of maintaining an adequate nurse force in the context of a decade-long national nursing shortage was a continual concern for Haynes, as it was for so many of her predecessors. In 1955, the ratio of those nurses leaving the Army to those joining the Army Nurse Corps was 2.5 to 1. In 1957, the authorized strength of the Corps was 5,000 but only 3,489 officers were on active duty. Many Army nurses had been dissatisfied with their military experiences in World War II and left the service after V-J Day, vowing never to rejoin. Others had wished to remain in the Army, but were forced out with the postwar reduction in forces. Later, these embittered groups were unwilling to return to the Army Nurse Corps and discouraged their associates, subordinates, and/or students from joining the military. Still other World War II

veterans were firmly entrenched in key civilian positions or were busy wives and mothers. The newer graduates set their sights on civilian hospital positions or marriage and were not attracted to the Army. Haynes' response to the vexing problem was to add another program of educational incentives—the Army Student Nurse Program—to the ongoing Registered Nurse Student Program. This plan recruited nursing students in their last one or two years of training. It paid the students' educational expenses and furnished them with the salary of an enlisted soldier. It required participants to join the Army Nurse Corps after graduation, serving for 2 or 3 years on active duty. In 1957 through 1959, respective totals of 150, 180 and 226 students joined the program. By the year 1960, the Army Student Nurse Program produced 54% of all professional nurses entering active duty. Another approach utilized by Haynes to attract and retain Army Nurse Corps officers was to strive to improve their living conditions. She stressed the importance of sponsoring incoming officers and providing them with an orientation to the recreational features of their assignment area. She developed a plan to furnish improved apartment style living quarters for single nurses. The buildings that served as a pilot project for these bachelor officer quarters were erected at Fort Knox, Kentucky, in 1958. Haynes additionally supported the development of a system to categorize patients' nursing care needs and thus better utilize staff. A further sign of progress occurred in 1956 when Haynes assigned three male nurses to Fort Campbell, Kentucky for airborne training. These three became the first Army nurses to earn the elite paratrooper status. Another step forward came about in that same year of 1956, when two additional Army nurses achieved the temporary rank of colonel, raising the total of Army Nurse Corps colonels to five. Haynes also can be credited with sponsoring the birth of nursing research in the Army. It was on her watch that the Department of Nursing at Walter Reed Army Institute of Research began a seminal program which educated nurses in research methods and gave these talented pioneer women the opportunity to break new ground in clinical nursing research. The much respected endeavor served as a bellwether for nursing research in the civilian community. Another of Haynes' contributions centered on her interest in awakening the profession to the importance of developing a body of nursing knowledge concerning nuclear warfare and mass casualty nursing. In 1957, she authorized the participation of a small group of Army nurses in Operation Plumbob, a classified research study which involved nuclear detonation testing in Nevada. The nurses helped to evaluate the effects of atomic weapons on swine. Finally, her ongoing, close relationships and activism within the world of civilian nursing and nursing organizations, such as the National League for Nursing and the American Nurses Association, enhanced the status and day to day operations of the Army Nurse Corps.

Colonel Inez Haynes retired from the Army Nurse Corps on August 31, 1959. She immediately began a second career as general director and secretary of the National League for Nursing on September 1, 1959 and continued in that position until June 1969. At that time, she joined the faculty of the College of Nursing at the University of Texas at Austin as an assistant professor. One year later she relocated to El Reno, Oklahoma, to care for her widowed mother and became affiliated with Oklahoma University, with a primary responsibility for assisting the faculty in obtaining grants and research funding. In her later years, Haynes finally had time to enjoy painting, art appreciation, symphonic music, and travel. At the same time, Haynes dedicated time and effort to civic endeavors as well. She actively supported the United Fund, Salvation Army, the local Junior College, the County Hearing Association, and other organizations in the community. She died on May 29, 1997 in El Reno, Oklahoma.

BIBLIOGRAPHY

Ambrose, M. E. (1975, January). A curriculum vitae of Colonel Inez Haynes, ANC. [Unpublished manuscript] ANC Archives, U.S. Army Center of Military History, Washington, DC.

Both ANA and NLN to lose executive directors. (1968). *American Journal of Nursing, 68,* 2328–2330.

Burke, C. A. (1987). [Interview with Inez Haynes]. (Project No. 87-14, 212). [Senior Officer Oral History Program] U.S. Army Military History Institute, Carlisle Barracks, PA.

Claussen, E. (1955). Categorization of patients according to nursing care needs. *Military Medicine, 116,* 209–214.

Colonel Inez Haynes (1949, July). *NLN News.*

Colonel Inez Haynes retires as Chief, Army Nurse Corps. (1959, September 3). [Press release] ANC Archives, U.S. Army Center of Military History, Washington, DC.

Inez Haynes resigns as director, June '69. *NLN News, 16,* p. 1.

Oblensky, F. (1963). Eleven women—and the Army Nurse. *The Retired Officer, 19,* 32–33.

Parade rest. (1997). *The Connection, Retired Army Nurse Corps Association, 22,* p. 9.

Mary T. Sarnecky

UNA H. HAYNES
1911–

Una H. Haynes is an instrumental and influential nurse in the field of cerebral palsy and related developmental disorders. During her 23 years as a member of the national professional program staff at the United Cerebral Palsy Associations, Inc. (UCPA), Haynes organized and directed programs of nursing education in this field; developed a protocol for enhanced nursing assessment of infants to foster earlier detection of anomalies or dysfunctions; fostered more comprehensive services to individuals with multiple disabilities in addition to significant intellectual deficits; and inaugurated, directed, and field-tested a transdisciplinary collaborative approach to provide comprehensive services for atypical infants and their families. These efforts also resulted in postgraduate courses for nurses, a number of publications, films, curriculum guides, self-directed learning modules, and other materials to assist in the education of nurses, other professionals and paraprofessionals, and families.

Una H. Haynes

Haynes was born on June 2, 1911 to Albert H. and Marie Caron Hebert in Holyoke, Massachusetts. An only child until the age of 12 years, she was overjoyed when her mother gave birth to her brother. There is no doubt that her continuing interest in and involvement with the field of child growth and development was both initiated and firmly rooted during these formative years.

Haynes graduated from the Northampton School for Girls (now Williston-Northampton Academy) in 1929. She intended to begin college as a pre-med major, but was unable to do so due to financial problems associated with the onset of the Depression. Meanwhile, she was encouraged to study nursing and enrolled in the Diploma Program at the Worcester City Hospital School of Nursing in Worcester, Massachusetts. With the aid of a scholarship, Una was later enabled to go on to Teachers College, Columbia University in New York where she received her BSN in 1934. She then stayed on to complete several postgraduate courses before moving on to Boston where she had accepted a position in public health nursing at the Boston Community Health Association.

In 1939, Haynes received a scholarship from a local women's group to medical school plus special preparation in epidemiology, but shortly after this she met her husband, B. Quincy Haynes, and she reluctantly declined to accept it. The two were married on September 18, 1939.

During her early married years, Una first worked nights in labor and delivery in Foxboro, Massachusetts, where her husband was stationed as an engineer during World War II. A friend of theirs had rubella during the first trimester of pregnancy and consequently had a baby who was severely multihandicapped. This experience greatly impacted Haynes and her husband, as did the loss of her own twins in utero.

In 1946, the shortage of nurses was still marked and Haynes accepted a part-time position on the faculty of the Holyoke Hospital School of Nursing where the couple had returned to live. She later accepted the position as Director of Outpatient Services for the medically indigent at the hospital affiliated Skinner Clinic.

In 1953, Haynes received a visit from the program service director at National UCPA headquarters in New York who was helping the local chapter study existing services and determine how UCPA might assist most effectively in meeting unmet needs. Una was offered a UCPA stipend shortly thereafter to study the programs of service available for patients with cerebral palsy in Massachusetts. Granted a 3-week leave of absence to do so, Haynes found that most of the services currently enrolling children with cerebral palsy were orthopedic clinics with adjunctive physical, speech, and occupational therapy. Haynes also found that the current therapeutic modalities being used on behalf of the children with cerebral palsy was to use techniques evolved for the care of post-polio patients. She reasoned that these two groups of children were very different, as the children with cerebral palsy had never experienced "normalcy;" they had no idea what it felt like, nor how to work toward regaining normal posture, tone, and movement. She recommended and helped the UCPA affiliate to activate a professional services committee to assist them in continuing the study of program possibilities, aid with program planning, and implementation.

Not long thereafter, Una joined the staff of UCPA in order to replicate and expand throughout New England the type of program consultation she had provided for the local affiliate. Her first title was "Regional Program Services Consultant."

In 1956 Haynes joined the National UCPA staff as Associate Director of Professional Program Services. She was soon to realize that the role of nursing had not yet surfaced to any appreciable degree in cerebral palsy programming. Her search of the nursing literature had revealed but one book on cerebral palsy published by a nurse (Jessie Stevenson West) back in the 1940s when she was a public health nurse with the Henry Street Visiting Nurse Association. Outlining what she felt nursing might

be able to accomplish, Haynes then developed a job description, applied for, and received the adjunctive role and title of Nurse Consultant.

One of her first priorities in this role was the activation of a nursing advisory committee with representation on the overall national UCPA Program Services Committee. Many distinguished nurses served on the committee and both the American Nurses Association and the National League for Nursing designated various nurses to attend committee meetings from time to time during the ensuing years.

Initial discussion focused upon the need to educate nurses about cerebral palsy and to further explore the role of nursing. With the committee's help and guidance, Haynes organized and implemented a nationwide series of seminars on these topics cosponsored by UCPA affiliates on the state and local levels in collaboration with Schools of Nursing, Public Health and Visiting Nurse Agencies along with other official and voluntary organizations. By the 1970s, a little over 20,000 nurses had participated in these seminars.

In 1966, Haynes consulted with Patricia McNelly, Director of Nursing at Central Wisconsin Center near Madison, Wisconsin, in conducting a pilot study involving the "transdisciplinary care" of children who were severely disabled. This concept was originally conceived as a "mini-team" in which a nurse, physical therapist, and an occupational therapist met to discuss the care of a select group of children. After the specific disciplinary care was outlined, each member of the team was then educated and trained in the care given by the other disciplines. The idea was to provide care encompassing each discipline. A member of the research team for the consequent demonstration project, Dorothy Hutchinson of the University of Wisconsin Extension, later coined the term "transdisciplinary care" to describe this cross-disciplinary, cross-modality form of care.

In 1967, Haynes wrote the *Developmental Approach to Casefinding* which was published by the Children's Bureau. Accompanying this book was the "wheel of development." This wheel was a handy tool that a nurse could keep with him or her and use to assess for normal development and presence of reflexes when assessing an infant, up to 36 months of age. Haynes' husband assisted her in developing the concept of a wheel to cover the normal 3-month range of variability. This book was last published in 1980 and has been translated into French, Spanish, German, Italian, Japanese, and Portuguese. A film was also made where Haynes demonstrated the proper assessment of an infant during a bath using knowledge of normal growth and development, the wheel, and other common standardized screening instruments, such as the Denver Developmental Screening Test.

In 1968, Haynes and her national nursing advisory committee were involved in the development and initiation of a postgraduate nursing course at Indiana University School of Nursing in cerebral palsy and related disorders. This program was supported in part by UCPA and adjunctive federal funds. It was an intensive, 5-day course that taught nursing leaders in the field about the theoretical and clinical aspects of cerebral palsy and related disorders in order for them to return home and teach other nurses and paraprofessionals in their geographical area.

From 1971 through 1977, Haynes directed the development and implementation of the "Nationally Organized Collaborative Project to Provide Comprehensive Services for Atypical Infants and their Families." This project initially involved five centers from across the country that were serving children, 2 years and younger, with cerebral palsy and related disorders. These centers collaborated to develop a more comprehensive curriculum and establish better services to the community. Staff from the original centers helped to train staff from the next round of "ripple" centers. At the end of the project, 65 agencies from 26 states were collaborating and a total of nearly 10,000 infants and their families had been served. A multitude of curriculum guides, films, self-directed learning modules, and publications resulted from this project. She retired from UCP in 1977.

Haynes is a Fellow of the American Public Health Association, and a member of many organizations. She has also received five national awards from various groups.

Nursing in the field of mental retardation and developmental disabilities has been an unglorified nursing specialty. There have been few nurses before Haynes or nurses since her that have given so much of their talent and energy to this population of children and their families that she has. Her accomplishments and publications attest to this important contribution to nursing history.

PUBLICATIONS BY UNA H. HAYNES (SELECTED)

Haynes, U. (1967). *A developmental approach to casefinding among infants and young children.* U.S. Dept. of Health, Education and Welfare, HEW No. (HSA) 79-5210 (reprinted in 1969 and 1980).

Haynes, U. (1979). Basic considerations of health and safety in developmental programs for young disabled children. In M. K. McCormack (Ed.), *Prevention of mental retardation and other developmental disabilities* (pp. 511–536). New York: Marcel Dekker.

Haynes, U. (1977). Evolvement of the transdisciplinary approach. In B. Frankel & R. Smith (Eds.), *Making the difference now: Programs for developmentally delayed infants* (pp. 11–19). Trenton, NJ: Division of Mental Retardation.

Haynes, U. (1983). *Holistic health care for children with developmental disabilities.* Baltimore: University Park Press.

Haynes, U. H. (1968). Nursing approaches in cerebral dysfunction. *American Journal of Nursing, 68,* 2170–2176.

Haynes, U. (Contributor). (1978). In F. P. Connor, G. G. Williamson, & J. M. Siepp (Eds.), *Program guide for infants and toddlers with neuromotor and other developmental disabilities.* New York: Teachers College Press.

Haynes, U. (Project Director) (1976–1977) for *Programming for atypical infants and their families* (Monographs 1-6) (1976–1977). New York: United Cerebral Palsy Associations.

Haynes, U. (1974). The cross disciplinary-cross modality approach to services for the developmentally disabled who have physical handicaps. In F. J. Menolascino & P. H. Pearson (Eds.), *Beyond the limits* (pp. 44–81). Seattle, WA: Special Child Publications.

Haynes, U. (1963). *The role of nursing in programs for patients with cerebral palsy and related disorders.* New York: United Cerebral Palsy Associations.

Haynes, U., Bumbalo, J., Cook, C., Haar, D., Krajicek, M., Slamar, C. F., & Smith, L. L. (1978). *Guidelines for continuing education in developmental disabilities* (NP-58). Kansas City, MO: American Nurses' Association.

Haynes, U., Patterson, G., D'Wolf, N., Hutchison, D. J., Lowry, M., Schilling, M., & Siepp, J. (1976). *Staff development handbook: A resource for the transdisciplinary process.* New York: United Cerebral Palsy Associations.

Wendy M. Nehring

ANNA MAE McCABE HAYS
1920–

Anna Mae V. McCabe Hays was the 13th Chief of the Army Nurse Corps. She served in this capacity from September 1, 1967 until August 31, 1971. Hays was the first woman in all of the United States military services to be promoted to general or flag officer status.

Hays was born on February 16, 1920, in Buffalo, New York to parents who both were Salvation Army officers. Religion, music, and a spirit of service were guiding lights in the family enclave. The nature of the elder McCabes' calling dictated the need for frequent moves, and the household resettled in a number of locations in Western New York State and Eastern Pennsylvania

during the period of Hays' childhood. After graduating from high school in Allentown, Pennsylvania, Hays attended the Allentown General Hospital School of Nursing and graduated from that institution with a diploma in nursing in 1941 as World War II was looming on the horizon.

Anna Mae McCabe Hays

Hays joined the Army Nurse Corps and went on active duty early in 1942, traveling by train with her unit to a staging area, Camp Claiborne, Louisiana. In January 1943, Hays' unit proceeded to Ledo, Assam, India, 1,000 miles above Calcutta at the site of the origin of the famous Ledo Road which cut through the jungles into Burma. She served in this challenging and austere milieu for 2 1/2 years and subsequently returned to the states on leave. While she was home on furlough, World War II ended. After the war, Hays served as an operating room nurse and later as a head nurse at Tilton General Hospital at Fort Dix, New

Jersey; as obstetrics supervisor at Valley Forge General Hospital in Phoenixville, Pennsylvania; and as head nurse of the outpatient clinic at Fort Myer, Virginia. In the summer of 1950, Hays traveled with the 4th Field Hospital to Inchon, Korea, landing shortly after MacArthur's strategic invasion at Inchon. Her stint in this combat setting again involved long, arduous hours of service. Nonetheless, during both of her combat tours in World War II and the Korean War, Hays devoted part of her off duty time to assisting chaplains by playing a field pump organ for weddings and church services, often on the front lines. After earning enough service points to depart Korea during her 7-month combat tour, Hays transferred to Tokyo Army Hospital and spent a year there as a management nurse in the comptroller's office. For her next assignment, she returned to Pennsylvania to be the obstetric/pediatric supervisor at the U.S. Army Hospital, Indiantown Gap. Her subsequent assignment as a student in the Nursing Service Administration Course at Fort Sam Houston Texas was followed by 3 years' duty at Walter Reed General Hospital. During that time, Hays served as a private duty nurse for President Dwight D. Eisenhower for about 30 days when he suffered an ileitis attack in 1956. Hays married in 1956, but was widowed in 1962. In 1957, she matriculated at Teachers College, Columbia University and in 1958 was awarded a bachelor's degree in nursing education. Her next assignment was as Head Nurse of the Nuclear Medicine and Radioisotope Clinic at Walter Reed Army Institute of Research (WRAIR). A return trip to Korea in 1960 as chief nurse of the 11th Evacuation Hospital in Pusan, another tour at Walter Reed General Hospital, and a short assignment in the Office of the Surgeon General as a special assistant to the Chief of the Army Nurse Corps preceded her selection as Assistant Chief of the Army Nurse Corps

from 1963 to 1966. In 1968, Hays earned her master of science in nursing degree from The Catholic University of America in Washington, D.C. From 1967 until 1971 she served as the 13th Chief of the Army Nurse Corps.

In order to relieve the acute shortage of Army nurses precipitated by the Vietnam War in 1968 and 1969, Hays assigned over 30 Army Nurse Corps officers to recruiting duty. She justified sending more Army nurses to civilian schools for graduate and doctoral education, another incentive that encouraged graduate nurses to join the Army Nurse Corps. She set up a number of clinical specialty courses and instituted a master's program in anesthesia nursing sponsored jointly by Tripler Army Medical Center, Hawaii, and the University of Hawaii. In 1967, she fostered the selection of the first Army nurse, Major Doris S. Frazier, to attend in residence a senior service school—the Command and General Staff College at Fort Leavenworth, Kansas. Hays also increased the number of appointed nursing consultants, both military and civilian. She recommended that the Surgeon General support a proposed Department of the Army policy that would change regulations and allow certain pregnant Army Nurse Corps officers to remain on active duty after the birth of a child. This goal was realized in January 1970. One year later, she worked to reverse the ruling that denied male spouses of Army nurses the privilege of shopping in the commissary and post exchange. In a groundbreaking move in 1970, she assigned Major Susan Phillips as the first female Army officer to become a White House social aide. Phillips worked on the day shift at Walter Reed and in the evening represented the Corps at the White House. In that role, she was able to showcase the Army Nurse Corps in a highly publicized forum and thus facilitate recruitment efforts. Hays also sponsored an analysis of and instituted changes in the Army Nurse Corps military occupation specialty (MOS) structure to enhance utilization of Army nurses. She transformed the nursing sections in Army hospitals from a nursing service structure to a department of nursing, thereby giving nursing more peer recognition, even greater control over assets, and significant input into decisions affecting nursing concerns. Hays was the guiding force behind the Army Nursing Contemporary Practice Program which, in 1968, first expanded the practice of pediatric nurses, and later developed the roles of nurse midwives and ambulatory care practitioners in the Army. She assigned more Army Nurse Corps officers to serve as instructors for enlisted medics in the increasing numbers of enlisted courses such as the nine Clinical Specialist (Practical Nurse) Courses at various medical treatment facilities, the renal dialysis course, the operating room courses, and other educational opportunities offered to paraprofessional personnel. Hays managed all of these and many other issues while simultaneously answering the unrelenting demands for nurses to support the war in Vietnam. On May 15, 1970, President Richard M. Nixon gave rise to a watershed event for women in the military when he nominated Colonel Anna Mae Hays for promotion to the grade of brigadier general.

Thus on June 11, 1970, Colonel Anna Mae Hays was promoted and became the first woman in the United States Armed Forces to wear the insignia of a brigadier general. The Army Chief of Staff, General William C. Westmoreland, and the Secretary of the Army, Stanley C. Resor, officiated at the ceremony. Army Surgeon General Hal B. Jennings pinned the stars on Hays' uniform.

On August 31, 1971, Hays retired from the Army and was awarded the Distinguished Service Medal for her many contributions. Other honors garnered during her career included the Legion of Merit; the 1971 Daughters of the American Revolution Anita Newcomb McGee Nurse of the Year Award; an honorary Doctor of Science Degree from Cedar Crest College in Allentown, Pennsylvania; and alumni awards from Teachers College, Columbia University and Catholic University of America. After her retirement, Hays took up residence in her home in Arlington, Virginia. Additionally, for many years, she spent 4 to 5 months annually in Marbella, Spain. In retirement, she maintained some involvement in Army Nurse Corps affairs, but added other activities and interests in professional circles, hometown issues, her condominium association, and an array of retiree groups. Brigadier General Anna Mae McCabe Hays led the Army Nurse Corps through one of its most stressful eras. She did so with grace, dignity, and wisdom.

BIBLIOGRAPHY

Biographical summary (Anna Mae Hays). (1994, December 17). ANC Archives, U.S. Army Center of Military History, Washington, DC.

BG Dunlap sworn in; BG Hays retires. (1971, September 1). *News SGO/R&D, 1* 1, 7.

Carson, A. J. (1983). [Interview with Anna Mae Hays.] transcript, 106, Project 83-10, 1983, Senior Officers Oral History Program, U.S. Army Military History Institute, Carlisle Barracks, PA.

Day, J. A. (1971, August 31). BG Hays retires. *News From the US Army Medical Department, No. 233.*

General Hays honored by DAR. (1971, April 16). OTSG News Release No. 69 JD.

Moore, C. J. (1997, January 28). [Interview with Anna Mae Hays.] Tape 4, Side 2 and Tape 5, Side 1.

Recent regulation changes affecting ANC Officers. (1971, April 27). News Release No. 76JD, Office of the Surgeon General, U.S. Army.

Mary T. Sarnecky

BENA HENDERSON
?–1939

Bena Henderson was a nurse administrator who devoted most of her career to the care of sick children in hospitals. She made outstanding contributions to several nursing organizations and to the American Journal of Nursing Company.

Canadian-born, she eventually became a naturalized American citizen. An 1897 graduate of the school of nursing at Toronto General Hospital, she was a superintendent of a hospital in British Columbia, where her outstanding work led to membership in the Victorian Order of Nurses.

Henderson came to the U.S. to take a postgraduate course at the Presbyterian Hospital in Chicago. Such courses were offered by large institutions to assist nurses gain knowledge and skill in specialized areas of nursing; they were usually 3 or 4 months in length. After completing the course, she joined the staff of the Chicago Visiting Nurse Association, and in 1908 was appointed superintendent of Children's Memorial Hospital in Chicago, where she served for 15 years. While in Chicago, she was president of the Illinois State Board of Nurse Examiners and secretary of the Illinois Nurses Association. From 1920 to 1924, she was treasurer of the National League for Nursing Education.

In 1923, Henderson came to Milwaukee as superintendent of the Children's Hospital. Initially titled the Children's Free Hospital, it was founded in 1894 by seven civic-minded Milwaukee women, established largely to address the needs of immigrant children. It had occupied a series of different houses in various locations until 1923, when it moved to a new building.

Henderson organized and opened the new hospital, and her 10-year tenure was a period of great expansion and a growing demand for services. Three years after she arrived, the hospital merged with the Milwaukee Infant's Hospital, an institution that cared for babies under 2 years of age. In addition to the hospital, a 50-bed convalescent home was opened in 1930, to provide care for children requiring long recuperation periods.

Bena Henderson

Henderson served as president of the American Journal of Nursing Company from 1926 to 1931. In this role she recommended a revision and modernization of the Company's business procedures. During her tenure as president, the business offices of the *Journal* moved from Rochester, New York, where they had been from the time the company started in 1900, to New York City. This timely move was appropriate, since the three major nursing organizations were located here.

Her contributions to national nursing organizations did not interfere with her work at the Milwaukee Children's Hospital (now titled The Children's Hospital of Wisconsin), and she played a major role in making it one of the leading hospitals of its kind in the country. It was said that "her warm humanity and capacity for friendship" made for harmonious relationships with the staff.

She resigned in March 1933. Her physician ordered her to take a long rest, and she went to Vermont where she lived quietly for some time. She returned to Wisconsin in 1937, but the next year she suffered a heart attack and never completely recovered.

After a long and dedicated career, Bena Henderson died January 25, 1939, at her home in Putney, Vermont. She is buried in Putney.

BIBLIOGRAPHY

100 years of caring, 1894–1994. Milwaukee: Children's Hospital of Wisconsin.

Bena Henderson (obituary). *American Journal of Nursing, 39,* 331.

Bena Henderson (obituary). *Bulletin of the Wisconsin State Nurses Association, 7,* 26.

Hospital manager quits; Must rest. (1933, March 24). *Milwaukee Leader.*

Long sickness fatal to nurse. (1939, January 28). *Milwaukee Journal.*

Signe S. Cooper

FRANC FLORENCE HENDERSON
1874–1956

Florence Henderson, an early 20th-century nurse anesthetist, administered anesthetics to the patients of Dr. Charles H. Mayo at St. Mary's Hospital in Rochester, Minnesota from 1904 until 1917. Henderson was the pupil and successor of Alice Magaw (Kessel), the nurse anesthetist granted the title "The Mother of Anesthesia" by Dr. Charles H. Mayo. Under the guidance of Alice Magaw, Henderson established herself as an exceptional clinician, a creditable author, and a teacher whose influence was carried unknown distances by those nurses and physicians sent from various parts of the world to St. Mary's Hospital to learn how to administer open-drop ether. Henderson was an early advocate for the development of the specialty of nurse anesthesia. Never a politically active woman, she remained

steadfast to her principles, and quietly supported those of her peers who were on the forefront of the political scene. The standards of patient care and the principles of practice to which she devoted herself are presented in her publications.

Franc Florence Henderson

Henderson was born in Illinois on February 14, 1874, to John and Josephine Henderson. The marriage may not have been Mr. Henderson's first, as he was 46 years old at the time of the birth and 21 years older than his wife. Henderson relocated his wife and two young daughters, Kate and Florence, to the farming community of Seward, Nebraska in 1876. Although her legal first name was Franc, Ms. Henderson was addressed as Florence casually as well as on most documents and records. The family was completed with the birth of Margaret in September of 1876.

Henderson attended local schools and graduated from Seward High School. She attended Knox College in Galesburg, Illinois, for less than one year in 1892. Little is known concerning her activities between 1892 and 1898 except that she taught school for a period of time.

In 1898, at the age of 23, Henderson entered Bishop Clarkson Memorial Hospital Training School for Nurses in Omaha, Nebraska. Following graduation in 1900, she assumed the duties of Superintendent of Nurses at Bishop Clarkson Hospital. Her role as superintendent was unique for the time. Not only did she supervise patient care and teach nursing students, but she also learned to administer chloroform and ether anesthetics. Henderson resigned from Bishop Clarkson Hospital in 1903 to accept employment at St. Mary's Hospital in Rochester, Minnesota.

With Magaw as her instructor, Henderson quickly excelled at the clinical practice of anesthesia. Henderson successfully implemented her belief that the relationship between the anesthetist and the patient was a vital component to the success of an anesthetic. The application of the psychotherapeutic technique known as suggestion, the use of interpersonal skills, as well as the ability to deliver an anesthetic tailored to meet the individual patient's needs while still fulfilling the surgeon's demands were all factors that contributed to the level of skill she attained. At a time when brute force was often used to control the excitement phase of anesthesia, visiting physicians and nurses were said to be charmed and instructed while they watched Henderson and Magaw gently talk their patients to sleep. Henderson's skill at the use of suggestion during the induction of anesthesia was documented by Dr. Henry S. Munro (1913) who said it was quite common for an anesthetist who does not understand the use of suggestion to use from ten to twenty times the amount of ether in anesthetizing a patient that was used by Magaw and Henderson, who made use of suggestion in every possible way in a given operation.

To accommodate the ever growing surgical practice of Dr. William J. Mayo and Dr. Charles H. Mayo, additional operating rooms were built and surgeons were added to the staff. The resulting increased demand for anesthesia services mandated an increase in the number of anesthesia providers. The Mayo doctors, believing in the quality of the practice of their nurse anesthetists, selected individuals from the available pool of staff nurses to be trained by Henderson and Magaw to provide anesthesia.

It was during her years at St. Mary's Hospital that Henderson wrote, published, and presented papers before national audiences. In 1909, she presented "The Nurse as an Anaesthetist" to the 12th Annual Convention of the Nurses' Associated Alumnae of the United States. In 1913, "Ether Anesthesia" was presented to the Southern Minnesota Medical Association and published in the St. Paul *Medical Journal.*

Following the death of her father in 1908, Henderson's mother moved to Rochester, Minnesota, and bought a home in which she and her daughter accepted boarders. In 1911, her widowed sister Margaret joined them. Then, in 1917, Henderson retired from St. Mary's Hospital and moved with her mother to Los Angeles, California in 1917 to join her sister Margaret, who had moved to Los Angeles by 1915. Subtle phrases in her letters reveal that the decision to leave St. Mary's was not an easy one for her to make.

Upon arrival in Los Angeles, Henderson administered anesthetics for several surgeons, although primarily for Dr. E. C. Moore, and at various Los Angeles Hospitals. Henderson bought and ran a boarding house in Los Angeles which functioned as a retreat for professional women. She continued her practice of anesthesia in Los

Angeles until she retired in 1923 at the age of 49.

Many factors may have influenced her decision to retire from the practice of anesthesia. Her retirement coincided with the growing effort of physicians to terminate the practice of anesthesia by nurses. That her decision was not entirely of free choice was alluded to by Ella Deitrich (1926): "Without venturing an opinion on the justice or injustice of the act which limited the field of anaesthetist to the physician, one must admire immensely the noble fortitude and courage with which this skilled and capable woman laid down the lucrative practice of years, and uncomplainingly bowing to necessity, entered into new activities to support herself and her dear old mother to whom she has been such a devoted daughter." Without supplying details, Henderson simply wrote to Dr. William J. Mayo "they stopped my work out here." Upon being informed of Ms. Henderson's situation, Dr. William J. Mayo offered her employment if she would move back to Rochester, Minnesota. She kindly declined the offer, citing her mother's health as the reason she could not return.

During the years following her retirement, Henderson continued to support herself and her mother by operating her boarding house. Throughout her years in California she remained active in the American Red Cross, the California State Nurse's Association, and the Los Angeles Nurse's Club. In November of 1929, after renting her house in Los Angeles to a nurse, Ms. Henderson fulfilled a lifetime dream by embarking on a world tour that included extended visits to India, Japan, France, and Italy.

In 1934, the efforts of a group of California physician anesthetists culminated when charges were brought against Dagmar Nelson, a nurse anesthetist, for violation of the California State Medical Practice Act. Henderson was called upon to testify during the William V. Chalmers-Francis vs. Dagmar A. Nelson trial. An attempt was made to implicate her in violation of the State Medical Practice Act; however, this effort was aborted, since she had already retired from the practice of anesthesia. It was the William V. Chalmers-Francis vs. Dagmar A. Nelson trial that established the precedent for the legal practice of nurse anesthesia and continues to preserve it.

Henderson died at St. Vincent's Hospital, Los Angeles, California, on December 17, 1956, following a period of poor health complicated by thrombosis of carotid arteries and bronchopneumonia. Her body was returned to her childhood home of Seward, Nebraska, and buried in the family plot at Greenwood Cemetery beside her parents and sisters. There are no living descendents of the family produced by John and Josephine Henderson.

PUBLICATIONS BY FRANC FLORENCE HENDERSON

The nurse as an anaesthetist. (1909). *American Journal of Nursing, 9,* 947–954.
Ether anesthesia. (1914). *St. Paul Medical Journal,* 74–82.

BIBLIOGRAPHY

Bankert, M. (1989). *Watchful care: A history of America's nurse anesthetists.* New York: Continuum.
Deitrich, E. G. (1926). Three women leaders of the South. *The Pacific Coast Journal of Nursing, 22,* 477–478.
Hamric, A. B., Spross, J. A., & Hanson, C. M. (1996). *Advanced nursing practice. An integrative approach.* Philadelphia: Saunders.
Harris, N. A., & Hunziker-Dean, J. (1997). *The art of Florence Henderson: Pioneer nurse and anesthetist.* Unpublished manuscript, Mayo School of Health-Related Sciences, Rochester, MN.
Munro, H. S. (1993). *Handbook of suggestive therapeutics* (3rd ed.). St. Louis: Mosby.
Oderkirk, W. W. *Learning to Care A Century of Nursing Education At Bishop Clarkson College, 1988.*
Pougiales, J. (1970). The first anesthetizers of the Mayo Clinic. *Journal of American Nurse Anesthetists,* 237–241.

Thatcher, V. (1953). *History of anesthesia with emphasis on the nurse specialist.* New York: Garland.

William V. Chalmers-Francis, Dewey Wightman, George P. Waller, Jr., and Anesthesia Section of the Los Angeles County Medical Association, a Corporation, vs. Dagmar A. Nelson, and St. Vincent's Hospital, a Corporation. (1934). Agnes McGarrell, official reporter, Superior Court, notary public, Dept no 2, 611 Hall of Records, Mutual 9211, Sta 2609, Los Angeles, California.

Worthington, L. (1921). The nurse anaesthetist. *The Pacific Coast Journal of Nursing, 15,* 408.

Nancy A. Harris

MABEL FRANCES HERSEY
1872–1943

Mabel Frances Hersey was a unique member of an early cadre of Canadian-born hospital nursing superintendents who, without university education, herself, nonetheless actively promoted university postgraduate education for others.

Mabel Hersey was born in 1872, in Lucan, Ontario, of Irish-Canadian parentage. In 1902 she entered the Royal Victoria Hospital (RVH) nurse training program in Montreal, and shortly after her graduation in 1905, became a staff nurse in the hospital's operating room. Three years later, Hersey was chosen to be the hospital's fourth Superintendent of Nursing, a position which she retained until retirement in 1938.

Little is known of Hersey's private life; her public life centered on three major areas of endeavor—overseeing the nursing department of the Victoria General Hospital, which included responsibility for its nurse training program; advancing nursing as a profession; and promoting university education for graduates of hospital training programs. As the Superintendent of Nurses at the RVH, Hersey recruited and organized nursing staff for an increasing number of new departments and administered

Mabel Frances Hersey

its school of nursing. During her tenure, she increased the number of pupil nurses, introduced new teaching methods, and increased content in the curriculum. A supporter of advanced education for teachers of pupil nurses, Hersey implemented scholarships for promising young graduates to undertake postgraduate study and return to teach in the RVH school of nursing.

Much of Hersey's spare time was given to advancing nursing as a profession by working toward provincial registration and improved standards in small hospitals. In July 1917, Hersey and Grace Fairley, then Lady Superintendent of the Alexandra Hospital, organized the Graduate Nurses' Association of Montreal. This became in 1920 the Association of Registered Nurses of the Province of Quebec (ARNPQ) which lobbied for registration for nurses in the province. In the early days, when ARNPQ had little financial backing, Hersey and Lillian Phillips put up their own life insurance policies as collateral to meet legal fees. From 1928 to 1930, Hersey was President of the Canadian Nurses Association (CNA) and in that capacity hosted the July 1929 Congress of the International Council of Nurses in Montreal. The Congress had originally been scheduled to take place in China, but civil war required a change of venue. Although the CNA accepted responsibility as host on very short notice, herculean efforts by Hersey, other members of the CNA executive, and Montreal nursing organizations resulted in a very successful Congress, attended by nearly 7,000 nurses from around the world. When the Great Depression hit Canada in 1929, as CNA President, Hersey advocated raising entrance requirements to hospital nurse training programs and making them uniform throughout Canada. This strategy was intended to reduce the overproduction of nursing graduates, and alleviate unemployment among private duty nurses.

Perhaps Mabel Hersey's greatest contribution to Canadian nursing was her sponsorship and unflagging support for McGill University's School for Graduate Nurses. Hersey and her colleague, Grace Fairley, were personally responsible for persuading the Faculty of Medicine at McGill University, Montreal, to consider establishing a school of nursing to offer advanced education to graduates of Canadian hospital training programs. They began by personally visiting the Secretary of the Medical Faculty in fall 1917 and followed up by inviting Adelaide Nutting, Dean of the Columbia School, to meet with representatives of McGill University. In May 1918, the Dean of the Faculty of Medicine asked Hersey and Fairley to draw up a program plan for

submission to the Medical Education Committee. When Fairley left Montreal to assume a hospital superintendency in Ontario, Hersey soldiered on with a committee of six leading nurses from Montreal hospital training schools to prepare a syllabus. On June 8, 1920, formal approval was given and lectures for 15 students enrolled in McGill University's School for Graduate Nurses began October 4, 1920. Courses were of 8 months' duration and prepared specialists in either public health nursing or teaching and supervision in schools of nursing. Hersey continued to facilitate postgraduate programming for nurses at McGill University by serving on the school's advisory committee for 18 years, her last 6 years as chairman. In this capacity, she also participated in subcommittees, such as the one that appointed Bertha Harmer, Assistant Professor of Nursing at Yale University School of Nursing, as the new director in fall 1927. When the University Board of Governors threatened closure of McGill's School for Graduate Nurses in 1932 for budgetary reasons, Hersey actively worked to raise money for an endowment to keep programming alive for graduate nurses. At the time, McGill School for Graduate Nurses served not only Central and Eastern Canada, but also an increasing number of nurses from the four Western provinces. There was a pervasive fear among nurse leaders that if it closed, Canadian graduate nurses would again be forced to seek higher education in the United States, and a large number would be unlikely to return. Hersey and other members of the Advisory Committee engaged in a fundraising campaign which garnered nearly $20,000 and ensured continuation of the school. Until it was disbanded in December 1945, Hersey continued as a member of a Special Finance Committee which battled continuously to keep the School fiscally afloat. The School's deficit was finally relieved by the unprecedented expansion in university postgraduate nursing courses during the period of reconstruction which followed the Second World War.

In recognition of her outstanding service to Canadian nursing, Hersey received the Order of the British Empire from King George V in 1935, and the Mary Agnes Snively Medal from the CNA in 1936. She was one of the first three recipients of the Snively Award, instigated in 1936 as the CNA's highest award in honor of its founder and first president. Two years later, she was the first nurse ever to receive the Honorary Degree of Doctor of Laws from McGill University. Hersey retired from the RVH in 1938 and died December 21, 1943 after a lengthy illness.

PUBLICATIONS BY MABEL FRANCES HERSEY

Numerous editorials and presidential addresses published in *The Canadian Nurse* journal, especially during the late 1920s and early 1930s.

BIBLIOGRAPHY

Biographical File—Mabel Hersey. Available from the CNA library, 50 The Driveway, Ottawa, Ontario, K2P 1E2.

Gibbon, J. M., & Mathewson, M. S. (1947). *Three centuries of Canadian nursing.* Toronto: Macmillan.

Logan, B. T. (1966). *In caps and gowns: The story of the School for Graduate Nurses, McGill University, 1920–1964.* Montreal: McGill University Press.

Mabel Frances Hersey: Obituary. (1944). *The Canadian Nurse, 40*(2), 101–102.

Miss M. F. Hersey, of R.V.H. resigns. (1938, March 30). *The Gazette, Montreal.*

Sharon Richardson

RENILDA E. HILKEMEYER
1915–

Renilda E. Hilkemeyer is known as an internationally recognized pioneer in the specialty of cancer nursing, having worked in the field since 1950. She fostered excellence in cancer nursing as a practitioner, administrator, author, educator, and consultant in private and public sectors. She was at the forefront as an advocate for cancer patients, facing many challenges in the early days of oncology nursing.

Hilkemeyer was born on July 29, 1915, in Martinsburg, Missouri. Her father, Henry Gerard Hilkemeyer, was a carpenter and builder. Her mother, Anna Marie Bertels Hilkemeyer, was a seamstress. Renilda was the second child among two brothers and one sister. She was raised in a home that respected hard work and commitments to values of the Catholic church.

Renilda E. Hilkemeyer

Hilkemeyer received her diploma from St. Louis University School of Nursing and St. Mary's Hospital in St. Louis, Missouri in 1936. She obtained a B.S. in Nursing Education from George Peabody College for Teachers in Nashville, Tennessee in 1947. She began her career in nursing as an operating room staff nurse at St. Mary's

Hospital in Jefferson City, Missouri (1936–1937) and had varied experiences as a District Public Health Nurse in the Missouri Division of Health (1937–1940), Assistant Director of the School of Nursing at General Hospital No.1 in Kansas City, Missouri (1947–1949), and as Assistant Executive Secretary in the Missouri State Nurses Association (1949–1950). In 1940, she was ill with tuberculosis and was hospitalized at a sanatorium on two different occasions. Her long-term recovery, during a time when bed rest was the major treatment for tuberculosis, temporarily interrupted her nursing career. She became active in professional organizations on both local and national committees. She held elected offices in the Missouri State Nurses Association and served as president, vice-president, and on multiple committees in the Missouri League for Nursing. She continued to be active in the professional organizations on a district and state level in Texas. These activities included serving as first vice president of the Houston Area League of Nursing (1958–1960) and president of the Texas Graduate Nurses Association (1962–1964). She was appointed as a member of the Texas Governor's Committee on Aging from 1962 to 1963 and as a member of the Governor's Emergency Resource Planning Committee in 1963.

In 1950, she began her career in cancer nursing as a consultant in nursing education in the Bureau of Cancer Control in the Missouri Division of Health. In 1955, she became the Director of the Department of Nursing and Professor in Oncology Nursing at the University of Texas System Cancer Center (UTSCC) M.D. Anderson Hospital and Tumor Institute in Houston, Texas and was in this position until 1977. From 1977 to 1979, she was the Assistant to the President for Nursing Resources at M.D. Anderson and from 1979 to 1984, she was staff assistant to the President of the University of Texas M.D. Anderson Cancer Center. Her leadership during her long tenure at M.D. Anderson until her retirement in 1984 was a major factor in the cancer center's reputation for high standards of nursing care.

Hilkemeyer also had a solid reputation in national organizations that influenced the development of cancer nursing. She was one of the original 20 oncology nurses who founded the Oncology Nursing Society in 1973–1975, which has grown today to a membership of over 20,000 nurses. She was recognized as an expert in cancer nursing and was an asset in committee work; thus, she was retained as an active member for extended appointments for both public and private agencies. In 1954, she began serving as a member of the Nursing Advisory Committee for the American Cancer Society (ACS) and continued in this capacity until 1960. Hilkemeyer was a member of the Professional Nurse Education Committee of the ACS, and other committees of the ACS on the national level, as well as on the local Houston level. She was the chair of the ACS subcommittee to establish ACS scholarships for master's and doctoral education in cancer nursing. She was the chairperson of the ACS Subcommittee to develop the proposal for clinical professorships in oncology nursing. These scholarships and professorships were subsequently influential in developing leaders in oncology nursing and in improving education on cancer nursing in schools of nursing across the country. She served as a member of the Planning Committee for the ANA and ACS National Conference on Cancer Nursing; this conference continues to be offered periodically. Hilkemeyer was also asked to serve on a number of committees for health organizations in the federal agencies concerned with cancer. As early as 1952 through 1960, she was a special consultant to the Nursing Section, Field Investigation and Demonstration Branch of the National Cancer Institute (NCI), DHEW. She served as a member of the Cancer Special Review Committee in the Division of Extramural Activities of NCI of the National Institutes of Health (NIH) in 1985 to 1986 and then served as a consultant in the Occupational Cancer Branch, Division of Cancer Prevention and Control at NIH. She was a member of the Cancer Control Grant Review Committee and Chairperson and/or member of site visit teams for NCI, NIH. In 1983, she also served as consultant at NIH to the National Heart, Lung and Blood Institute.

Hilkemeyer was the first nurse to receive the American Cancer Society's Distinguished Service Award in 1981. She was honored as she said in an interview as "an internationally recognized pioneer whose sensitivity and extraordinary effort helped to create the specialty of cancer nursing." In 1989, Hilkemeyer was the first recipient of the American Cancer Society's National Nursing Leadership Award. In 1986, she was one of the two first recipients of the Distinguished Merit Award for national and international contributions from the International Society of Nursing in Cancer Care. In 1981, the Board of Directors of the Texas Medical Center Inc. dedicated and named its new child care center, the Renilda Hilkemeyer Child Care Center, in her honor. She had conceived the idea of the original child care center in 1969 to serve children of the nurses and later other personnel of the hospitals at the Texas Medical Center. In 1979, Hilkemeyer was the third recipient of the Texas Nurses' Association Nurse of the Year Award, which read "for achievements in and contributions to oncology nursing and oncology health care, not only in Texas, but nationally and internationally." She received an honorary degree of Doctor of Public Service from St. Louis University in May 1988 in recognition of her

"splendid work in oncology nursing." In 1983, she was recognized "for outstanding contributions to Programs of the Division of Extramural Activities of the National Cancer Institute from 1979 to 1983. Other honors included election into the Beta Beta Chapter of Sigma Theta Tau National Honor Society at the Texas Woman's University in Houston in 1971 and an award for honorary membership from the Oncology Nursing Society in 1991. She has also been honored by organizations outside of nursing, such as receiving an Outstanding Houston Professional Women Award from the Federation of Houston Professional Women in 1983. A certificate of appreciation "for unselfish service to education" was awarded by the Houston Community College System in 1983.

Hilkemeyer was a prolific writer and is credited with 49 publications from 1956–1996 and three media publications on cancer topics. She presented papers on cancer nursing in the national and international arena. Her articles and presentations were at the forefront with new concepts and new content in cancer nursing practice and education. She was also successful in writing grant proposals, and obtained a contract award to establish an enterostomal therapy education program from NIH NCI, Division of Cancer Control and Rehabilitation in 1974–1977 (a program which still exists currently). Another contract from the same division was awarded in 1974–1976 to establish "Oncology Nursing Programs in Cancer Centers." These are only two of the seven financial awards she obtained to further improve cancer nursing education and practice.

As of this writing, Hilkemeyer continues to receive honors. In 1997, she received a Volunteer of the Year Award from the Braes Interfaith Ministries (BIM) for "more than 6000 hours of faithful service meeting the needs of families and individuals in crisis."

She has volunteered for this organization for over 10 years, and has served on the board of directors as well as its president in 1990, 1995, and 1998. She continues to volunteer with the BIM Food Pantry. Renilda Hilkemeyer continues to live in Houston.

PUBLICATIONS BY
RENILDA E. HILKEMEYER (SELECTED)

Alston, F., Hilkemeyer, R., White, M., & Schmolke, H. (1960). Perfusion. *American Journal of Nursing, 60,* 1603–1607.

Hilkemeyer, R., & Kinney, H. (1956). Teaching cancer nursing. *Nursing Outlook, 4,* 77–180.

Hilkemeyer, R. (1958). Nursing care of the cancer patient in the hospital and home. *Cancer: A Bulletin of Progress, 8,* 122–125.

Hilkemeyer, R. (1958). Exchange for education: Program director speaks. *American Journal of Nursing, 58,* 1688–1690.

Hilkemeyer, R. (1962). Sickness at home. In R. L. Clark & R. Cumley (Eds.), *Book of health* (2nd ed., pp. 615–621). Princeton: D. Van Nostrand.

Hilkemeyer, R., Fleming, E., & Kincaid, M. (1964). Nursing care of the patient with brain tumor. *American Journal of Nursing, 64,* 81–83,

Hilkemeyer, R. (1966). Intra-arterial chemotherapy. *The Nursing Clinics of North America, 1,* 295–307.

Hilkemeyer, R. (1967). Nursing care in radiation therapy. *The Nursing Clinics of North America, 2,* 83–95.

Hilkemeyer, R. (1967). *Guidelines for cancer content in refresher courses for registered nurses.* New York: American Cancer Society.

Hilkemeyer, R. (1971). *Guidelines for cancer care: Nursing.* Chicago: American College of Surgeons.

Hilkemeyer, R., & Rodriguez, D. (1976). Development of an enterostomal therapy education program. *Nursing Clinics of North America, 11,* 469–478.

Hilkemeyer, R. (1982). A historical perspective in cancer nursing. *Oncology Nursing Forum, 9,* 47–66.

Hilkemeyer, R. (1991). A glimpse into the past of cancer nursing. *Dimensions in Oncology Nursing, 5,* 5–8.

Hilkemeyer, R. (1955). In B. Nevidjon (Ed.), *Building a legacy, voices of oncology nurses.* Boston: Jones & Bartlett.

Hilkemeyer, R. (1996). Foreword. *Cancer nursing: A comprehensive textbook* (2nd ed.). R. McCorkle, M. Grant, M. Stromberg, & S. Baird. Philadelphia: Saunders.

BIBLIOGRAPHY

Curriculum vitae, R. E. Hilkemeyer.
Personal telephone interviews with R. Hilkemeyer.
Cancer Nursing News, 11(4), 20.

Susan Dudas

KATHERINE J. HOFFMAN
1910–1984

An expert in curriculum development and program evaluation, Katherine Hoffman was a consultant to many nursing schools across the country. The first nurse in the state of Washington to earn a Ph.D., she was an early proponent of nursing research and graduate education for nurses, and served as a mentor to countless students and colleagues. She was inducted into the Hall of Fame of the American Nurses Association in 1996.

Katherine Janet Hoffman was born on April 18, 1910, in Grand Forks, British Columbia, and moved to Tacoma, Washington, with her family in 1923. She received a bachelor's degree in English Literature in 1929 and a nursing diploma from Tacoma General Hospital School of Nursing in 1934. While completing an advanced certificate in obstetrical nursing, she worked as a night supervisor. In 1937, she joined the faculty at the College of Puget Sound and Pacific Lutheran College. She received a master's degree in nursing from the University of Washington in 1941 and, in 1956, became the first nurse in the state of Washington to earn a Ph.D.

Hoffman was affiliated with University of Washington for more than 30 years. She served as professor in the School of Nursing, and as assistant dean, associate dean, and assistant vice-president for health affairs, the first woman or nurse to be named to that post. Keenly aware of the importance of research, she established a nurse-scientist program in 1963 which enabled nurses in doctoral program to pursue research in scientific disciplines.

Hoffman was an active participant in the American Nurses Association, the National League for Nursing, and the Washington State Nurses Association. She served on the board of the American Nurses Foundation, as vice-chair of the American Nurses Association's Committee on Research and Studies, and on the editorial board of *Nursing Research*. She was one of the founders of the Western Society for Research in Nursing and assisted in the establishment of the Western Council for Higher Education in Nursing In 1973, she was named a Charter Fellow of the newly founded Academy of Nursing, joining 35 other nursing leaders chosen by the American Academy of Nursing as founding members.

When she retired in 1975, she was named professor emerita in recognition of her many years of service and outstanding contributions to the University of Washington. She died in 1984.

PUBLICATIONS BY
KATHERINE J. HOFFMAN (SELECTED)

A study of post-graduate curricula in teaching and administration of the clinical nursing services. (1941). St. Louis: Washington University.

A suggested method for the development of a tool to aid in the evaluation of performance in nursing. (1956). Ph.D. dissertation, University of Washington.

An overview of the Nurse-Scientist Program at the University of Washington. (1968). New York: National League of Nursing.

BIBLIOGRAPHY

Sentz, L. Interview with Dannenhold, K. (July 1998).

Dr. Hoffman named charter fellow of new National Academy of Nursing. (1973). *Washington State Journal of Nursing, 45,* 11.

Lilli Sentz

EDITH FOLSOM HONEYCUTT
1916–

Edith Folsom Honeycutt graduated from Emory University Hospital School of Nursing, Atlanta, Georgia, in 1939, with a strong dedication to excellence in patient care. Her entire career was dedicated to that principle which she shared generously with numerous nursing students and other staff nurses. Over the years, Honeycutt provided nursing care to many patients in several departments of Emory University Hospital. Finally, she entered the hematology and oncology service, where she spent the majority of her career. The majority of her practice was at Emory University Hospital, where she remained a staff nurse with special arrangements to serve as a private duty nurse to members of the Woodruff family.

Edith Folsom was born to Inez Sykes Folsom and Bryon V. Folsom on September 3, 1916, in Quincy, Florida. One of six children, she spent most of her youth in Florida. As a child, Honeycutt had the opportunity to observe actual nursing care. When her brother had pneumonia, his recovery was attributed to the good care received from a private duty nurse. Later, after the stock market crash in 1929, Honeycutt's father left home and never returned. Her mother, who had studied nursing, began caring for patients in their home in order to earn money. The strong, positive exposure to nursing led her into nursing as a career.

After graduating from Monteverde Academy near Orlando, Florida, she entered

Edith Folsom Honeycutt

Tennessee College near Murfhreesboro on a music scholarship. Her great ability to share information and assist others was readily evident when she became an assistant in the chemistry department. In addition to excelling in music, Honeycutt had mastered much college-level chemistry in her preparatory school. After one year in Tennessee, Edith Folsom entered Emory University Hospital School of Nursing in 1936 and graduated in 1939. She married Paul Honeycutt in 1939 and they had two children, Dianne and Danny.

Honeycutt was employed primarily as a private duty nurse during these first years after graduation and began working as a private duty nurse for Mr. Ernest Woodruff in 1941. Ernest Woodruff was the patriarch of the family and architect of the Woodruff takeover of the Coca-cola Company. During the war years, Honeycutt worked closely with Nell Hodgson Woodruff, who served patients as a Red Cross Volunteer nurse's

aide. There was a tremendous shortage of nurses at that time, and the volunteers led by Mrs. Woodruff greatly enhanced patient care quality. When her children became older, Honeycutt took a staff nurse position at Emory University Hospital, where she worked the remainder of her career. Her employment had a special caveat: she was always available to provide private duty nursing to members of the Woodruff family. Through the years, she cared for four generations of the family. In 1946, Honeycutt was elected President of the Nurses' Alumni Association and held the first dance ever held on Emory campus, as a fundraiser for the Nurses Alumni Association. She served nurses in the state in many ways and, in 1958, she served the nurses of Georgia as President of the 5th District of the Georgia Nurses Association.

Through these years, Honeycutt worked as a staff nurse in many patient care units of Emory University Hospital before she became a permanent member of the nursing staff on the hematology and oncology unit. Within the system, she became an agent of change by combining the best in scientific findings with clinical data from her own patients. She questioned practices that could have negative outcomes, and demonstrated ways to work within the system to make changes.

Many have recognized and honored Honeycutt and her devotion to the best in patient care and to the school where she studied. Her dedication to Emory is unparalleled. In 1980, the Nurses Alumni Association presented her with its Award of Honor. Her support and dedication clearly extends from the School of Nursing, named after her dear friend, Nell Hodgson Woodruff, in 1968, to the entire university. At the university's sesquicentennial commencement ceremonies in 1986, a special declaration was made in honor of Honeycutt's "enduring loyalty." Her dedication to excellence in nursing care was publicly recognized in 1990 when the Atlanta Community Foundation honored Honeycutt by endowing a Chair in Nursing at the Nell Hodgson Woodruff School of Nursing at Emory University. It is exceptional to have a chair endowed for a staff nurse, and exemplifies the continued influence of Honeycutt on the education and practice of nursing. As of this writing, Honeycutt still is active in music and dancing. She belongs to a small group of dancers who provide special presentations for her residential community. Her interest in the Nurses Alumni Association continues and she still serves on its Executive Board. She is an active member of her church, and enjoys the company of her two children and their families. She is busy, and gives generously of her time and talents for the School of Nursing and its students for whom she regularly makes the history of Atlanta and Emory nursing come alive.

BIBLIOGRAPHY

Baviar, A. Personal interviews with E. F. Honeycutt.

Anne Baviar

JACQUELINE ROSE HOTT
1925–

Jacqueline Rose Hott is a prominent nurse clinician, educator, researcher, and author of books, articles, and research publications. A recognized leader in sex education and sex therapy and a distinguished lecturer in nursing, she continues her practice as a clinical specialist in adult psychiatric/mental health nursing. Her lifelong commitment to the professional is evident in each of her varied endeavors.

Jacqueline Rose Hott was born on March 27, 1925, in Jersey City, New Jersey. Her parents, Ida and Morris Rose, migrated

Jacqueline Rose Hott

from Minsk, Russia. She had one sister Miriam, seven and a half years older than she, who died in 1993. Jackie, after graduating as valedictorian of her high school class, entered the New Jersey College for Women (Douglas College), working all the time to support herself. In 1943 she enlisted in the newly established Cadet Nurse Corps, selecting New York University Bellevue Hospital for her nurse's training and concentrated her efforts in psychiatric nursing because Bellevue was famous for its psychiatric service.

While a student nurse at Bellevue hospital she met her husband to be, Louis Randell Hott, M.D. a psychiatric resident. They were married December 27, 1947. They had two sons and two daughters and currently ten grandchildren. Her husband died March 18, 1980.

She received her R.N., B.S. in 1946 from New York University-Bellevue School of

Nursing. During her senior year she completed a 6-month intensive training period on the Psychiatric Unit at Bellevue and after graduation, she accepted a position there as a clinical instructor in Psychiatric Nursing, the position she left 3 years later when she gave birth to her first son, in 1949. Four years later she enrolled in the Master's of Arts at the School of Education, Division of Nursing, NYU School of Education, in 1953, completing the degree after the birth of her second and third children in 1950 and 1952. She later returned to her alma mater, NYU, for her Ph.D. in parent-child nursing, her dissertation was *An Investigation of the Relationship between Psychoprophylaxis in Childbirth, and Changes in Self-Concept of the Participant Husband and His Concept of His Wife.*

In 1976, she became a Certified Sex Therapist, American Association of Sex Educators, Counselors and Therapists, after a sabbatical at the New York Medical College Sex Therapy Program. Dr. Hott also worked as a consultant in Sex Therapy for the Family Service Association of Hempstead, N.Y. She is certified by ANA as a clinical specialist in Adult Psychiatric/Mental Health Nursing, and maintains a private practice as a sex therapist and psychotherapist in Great Neck, New York. Certified by the Adelphi University Derner Institute in 1982 in psychoanalysis and psychotherapy, she served as president of the Northeast Psychological Associates, Vice President Visiting Nurses Association of Long Island, N.Y., Hadassah Nurses Nassau County Council, L'Chaim, and as a clinician for NYU Behavioral Health Program. While serving as Dean of Adelphi University School of Nursing, she was the coordinator of *Project Talk with Me* on a $140,00 grant collaborative effort between Adelphi University and Winthrop University Hospital to detect early hearing impairment in newborns.

Hott holds membership in numerous professional and scholarly organizations. She was elected as Fellow, American Academy of Nursing, 1978; ANA Council of Nurse Researchers (Chairperson, 1985–1987); Nurses Association of American Colleges of Obstetricians and Gynecologists (AWHONN); Sigma Theta Tau, including Alpha Omega Chapter, charter member, American Psychiatric Nurses Association (APNA); Society for Research and Education in Psychiatric Nursing (SERPN); Society for the Scientific Study of Sexuality (SSSS); Society for Sex Therapy and Research (SSTAR); and American Association of Sex Educators Counselor and Therapists (ASSECT).

Hott has served as reviewer and consulting editor for many nursing journals and has been the recipient of many honors and awards, including the first Mentor Award (1986) presented at Chapter level from Alpha Omega Chapter, Sigma Theta Tau; (1986) NYU Distinguished Alumni Award (1981); Distinguished Alumnae Award from Douglass College (1978); Who's Who In Women of Education (1972); Distinguished Outstanding Educator: Kappa Delta Pi, National Honor Society of Education, Sigma Theta Tau, Upsilon Chapter, New York University, Sigma XI, Scientific Research society of North America, and fellow American Academy of Nursing.

From 1967 onward, Hott had taken particular interest in the development of new nurses at Adelphi University, teaching as an assistant professor and associate professor, and received early promotion to Professor of Parent-Child Nursing. In 1975 she was the commencement speaker, International Year of the Woman, Adelphi University. In 1983, she accepted early retirement as professor emerita at Adelphi University to become the Executive Director of MARNA, the Mid Atlantic Regional Nursing Association. Her commitment to the academic setting of nursing has always been to "recognize its scholarship, clinical expertise, and research productivity." She returned to the School of Nursing at Adelphi to serve as Dean, 1986–1989, and then she became special assistant to the Provost at Adelphi for two years.

On numerous editorial and professional boards among her offices was chairperson of the American Nurses Association Council of Nurse Researchers (1985–1987). As executive director of MARNA, Hott promoted collaboration and integration of research into practice, education and administration. She has received USHHS federal funding for MARNA and for her NIMH research on "the pregnant father."

Hott's research interests have focused on sexuality across the life span as it relates to pregnancy, parenting, maturation, chronic illness, and loss. Currently, in private practice as a clinical nurse specialist in adult psychiatric mental health nursing and sex therapy, she continues to serve as consultant for graduate students with similar research interests.

Hott is the perfect example of how a nurse can utilize her background in a variety of career alternatives. As author, researcher, administrator, therapist, mentor, professor, and advisor to professional nursing organizations, she has been actively involved in expanding the role of the nurse and creating opportunities for those in the profession.

PUBLICATIONS BY JACQUELINE ROSE HOTT

Books

With Lucille E. Notter, *Essentials of Nursing Research* (5th ed.). (1994). New York: Springer Publishing Company. Translated into Finnish, Japanese, Spanish, Swedish, German, and U.K. Adaptation.
With P. Bailey (1993). Policy, politic and foundations. In D. Mason, S. W. Talbott, & J. K. Leavitt

(Eds), *Policy and politics for nurses: Action and the workplace* (pp. 653–663). Philadelphia: Saunders.

Book Chapters

Sexuality. In S. S. Gorin & J. H. Arnold (Eds.), *The health promotion handbook*. St. Louis: Mosby Year Book.
Is there sex after death? Five widows. W. F. Finn, et al., *Women in loss: Psychobiological perspectives* (pp. 50–57). New York: Praeger.
Best laid plans: Pre- and postpartum comparison or self and spouse in primiparous Lamaze couples who share delivery and those who do not. (1981). In B. S. Raff (Ed.), *Perinatal parental behavior: Nursing research and implications for newborn health*. New York: Alan R. Liss.

Articles (Selected)

The telephone rape: Crisis intervention for an obscene phone call. (1983). *Issues in Health Care of Women, 4,* 107–113.
To see ourselves as others see us: The public image of the nurse on the get well card. (1984). *Imprint, 31*(1), 45–48.
(With Marybeth Ryan-Merrit). A national study of nursing research in human sexuality. (1982). *Nursing Clinics of North America, 17*(3), 429–447.

BIBLIOGRAPHY

Lagerman, L. Personal interviews with Jacqueline Rose Hott.

Lois Lagerman

DOROTHY JONES HUTCHINSON
1914–1997

Dorothy Jones Hutchinson was a pioneer in continuing nursing education and a distinguished nurse educator. She was the founding editor of the *Journal of Continuing Education in Nursing*, and edited it for its first 7 years.

Dorothy Lenore Jones was born July 10, 1914, in Granville, Ohio. Her parents were E. Clifford and Lora Mabel Wallace Jones. She and her older sister, Lora Mabel, were their only children.

Dorothy Jones Hutchinson

After graduating from Granville High School, she enrolled in the Ohio State University School of Nursing in Columbus. In a unique 5-year program, she majored in nursing and education simultaneously, earning her B.Sc. in 1936. The next year she was awarded an M.A. in education, also from Ohio State University. She later enrolled in the doctoral program at (Case) Western Reserve University in Cleveland.

Hutchison began her nursing career as a staff nurse in obstetrics at the Ohio State University Hospital, and then she enrolled in a 4-month postgraduate course at the Chicago Lying-In Hospital. She was appointed an administrative assistant to Dean Ruth Perkins Kuehn and instructor of maternal and child health nursing at the Ohio State University School of Nursing. In 1940, she served as director of the Fairview Park Hospital School of Nursing in Cleveland, and the next year she became a lecturer and consultant in health and parent educa-

tion for the Family Health Association of Cleveland.

She married Joseph Shields Hutchison on December 23, 1937, at Columbus. Their children are Jon Kendall, Paula Browyn (who is now also a nurse), and Linden Ann (Spear). A developmentally disabled baby, Bruce Wallace, died at 6 months.

During World War II and the Korean Conflict, Hutchison was an army wife, living in Texas, Washington, D.C., Kansas, and Maine. During these years, she held various short-term positions, teaching in hospital schools of nursing, instituting training programs for auxiliary workers, teaching American Red Cross first aid and home nursing courses. In 1954, she taught obstetric nursing at the Akron City Hospital School of Nursing in Akron, Ohio and then served as an occasional consultant and lecturer in adult and health education, family living, and mental retardation in a variety of locations.

When the family moved to Madison, Wisconsin in 1963, Hutchison was appointed to the faculty of the Department of Nursing in the University of Wisconsin-Extension. This unit was responsible for conducting statewide continuing education programs in nursing, and her primary duties were preparing inservice education coordinators in hospital and nursing homes.

Hutchison was awarded tenure at the University in 1970, and 6 years later was promoted to full professor. During her employment at University Extension, she engaged in a number of educational activities and projects. In the 1960s, she was one of a cadre of teachers of inservice education workshops offered in various parts of the country and sponsored by the National League for Nursing and the American Hospital Association.

In 1970 Hutchison became the founding editor of the *Journal of Continuing Education in Nursing*. She convinced the publisher,

Charles Slack, of the need for a journal for educators in the field to communicate their concerns, describe their roles, share their ideas, publish their research, and learn from colleagues. She selected the title of the journal, believing it to encompass all aspects of continuing education, including inservice education and staff development. She edited the *Journal* for 7 years, solicited and edited manuscripts, selected landmark statements, and wrote features and many book and media reviews. As editor, she was particularly supportive of unpublished writers.

Hutchison was widely sought as a speaker, and she spoke at many national meetings, including American Nurses Association (ANA) and National League for Nursing Conventions (NLN). She also presented papers at the Congress of the International Society for Scientific Study of Mental Deficiency held in Washington, DC, in 1976.

Active in many nursing-, adult education-, and health-related organizations, she chaired the Awards Committee of the NLN (1969–1970) and the ANA's Mary Mahoney award committee (1972–1973).

Hutchison was presented an "Into Life" Medallion at the 1975 Centenary Celebration, Hospital for Sick Children, Toronto, Canada, where she had conducted a number of workshops. Upon her retirement as editor she was presented a recognition plaque for outstanding service in "successful formulation, growth and development of *the Journal of Continuing Education in Nursing*" by Charles B. Slack, Inc.

Her husband, Joseph Hutchison, died of amyotrophic lateral sclerosis in January 1995. Hutchison herself developed Alzheimer's Disease and lived in Las Vegas, Nevada, with her daughter Paula for the last years of her life. She died March 30, 1997.

An innovate and inspiring teacher of nursing and a skillful editor, Dorothy Hutchison touched the lives of many. She understood and articulated the importance of continued learning for effective practice.

PUBLICATIONS BY DOROTHY JONES HUTCHISON

Articles (Selected)

The supportive role of the nurse in relation to health service workers. (1968). *Nursing Clinics of North America, 3,* 153–163.

In-service education: Is it really "in"? (1970). *Journal of Continuing Education in Nursing, 1,* 33–35.

The process of planning continuing education for health manpower. (1974). In R. Blakely & A. Charters (Eds.), *Fostering the growing need to learn.* Washington, DC: DHEW Pub. HRA 74-3112.

A decade of progress in continuing education in nursing. (1980). *Journal of Continuing Education in Nursing, 11,* 60–66.

Thirty editorials and other items for the *Journal of Continuing Education in Nursing,* 1970–1976.

BIBLIOGRAPHY

Hutchison, D. J. (1986). Curriculum vita. School of Nursing files, University of Wisconsin-Madison.

Hutchison, D. J. Papers. Archives, University of Wisconsin-Madison.

Hutchison, D. J. Personal conversations with author, 1963–1985.

Kuehn, R. P. (1970). Introducing the *Journal of Continuing Education in Nursing* and the editor. *Journal of Continuing Education in Nursing, 1,* 7–8.

Wise, P. S. Y. (1983). Living history series: Dorothy Hutchison. *Journal of Continuing Education in Nursing, 14,* 28–34.

Signe S. Cooper

J

EILEEN M. JACOBI
1918–1996

Eileen M. Jacobi was a dedicated nurse and educator who held the position of Dean and Professor of the College of Nursing and Allied Health at the University of Texas, El Paso, as well as the position of Dean and Professor at the School of Nursing at Adelphi University in New York.

Jacobi was born on May 7, 1918, in Meath, Ireland, to Patrick and Marion (Mahon) Ahern and emigrated to the U.S. as a child. She graduated from high school in 1936 with the aspiration of becoming an attorney, but due to the Great Depression, was unable to insist on a college education and decided to enter nursing. She obtained her nursing education at Cumberland Hospital in Brooklyn, New York in 1940. On August 2, 1941, she married A. Francis Jacobi. During World War II, she did various volunteer work which included assisting with the examinations of the pre-inductees to the armed forces, and concentrating on raising her two children, Francis and Virginia.

In 1950, she started her baccalaureate degree at Adelphi College in Garden City, New York. After finishing her B.A. in 1954, she immediately continued her education and received a master's degree in psychiatric nursing in 1956. She had already been teaching at Adelphi College for a few years when she accepted the position of Acting Dean, and then Dean of the College of Nursing in 1959. In 1968, she earned a Doctorate in Education from the Teachers College at Columbia University, New York.

During this period, Jacobi also served on the New York Board of Nurse Examiners.

After 12 years at Adelphi, Jacobi decided to move on. She agreed to be the Executive Director of the American Nurses Association in 1970. After her husband died in 1975, Jacobi decided to leave ANA and took the position as Dean of the School of Nursing at the University of Texas, El Paso. While there, she was appointed to the Texas Board of Nurse Examiners and served for 6 years and for a time served as its President. In 1986, Jacobi retired from the University of Texas, but remained an active participant in the nursing field. She was active in the International Council of Nurses for which she served as the Vice President.

She was awarded the Outstanding Alumni Award at Adelphi University and the Merit Award for Distinguished Service in Nursing from Boston University. She was also a Fellow of the American Academy of Nursing.

Her research through the years had been most notably on the topics of simulation and stimulation in nursing laboratories and academic freedom. She also had been involved in psychiatric mental health, nursing group therapy and international nursing.

Eileen Jacobi died on December 26, 1996, in Orange, California.

PUBLICATIONS BY EILEEN M. JACOBI

Books

Academic freedom in baccalaureate programs in nursing. (1968). New York: Columbia University Press.

With Annette J. Craddock (1988). *Accreditation and nursing education.* Kansas City, MO: American Nurses' Association.

Articles

The American Nurses' Association in a time of change. (1972a). *Alabama Nurse, 26*(4), 2–4.

ANA takes stand on national health plan. (1972b). *Maryland Nurse, 2*(4), 1–3.

Statement on National Health Insurance to the Committee on Ways and Means, U.S. House of Representatives. (1972c). *Florida Nurse, 20*(1), 5–12.

Changing role of nursing to meet societal needs. (1974). *Australian Nurses Journal, 4*(5), 17–18.

Perinatal care in the United States. (1975). *New Zealand Nursing Journal, 68*(3), 7–8.

The moral leadership of the nursing profession. (1977). *Journal of Advanced Nursing, 2*(6), 561–569.

Professional accountability. (1978). *Occupational Health Nursing, 26*(6), 7–11.

The changing of the guard. (1986a). *Journal of Professional Nursing, 2*(4), 205.

Nurses must share in resolving health care crisis. (1986b). *American Nurse, 18*(9), 4.

With Walsh, M. E., & Leedham, C. L. (1970). The physician's assistants: Officially speaking . . . *RN, 33*(10), 57.

BIBLIOGRAPHY

Franz, J. (Ed.). (1989). *Who's Who in American Nursing 1988–1989.* Washington, DC: Society of Nursing Professionals.

Lavenson, B. D. (1990). Managing your academic career: Interview with a dean . . . Eileen M. Jacobi. *Nurse Educator, 15*, 3–5.

Jeanne Fielding

DOROTHY E. JOHNSON
1919–

Dorothy Johnson influenced a generation of nurses through her work, some directly through her teaching at the University of California at Los Angeles, and some though invited lectures and presentations; and others came to know her indirectly through her writings. She has continued to have an important impact upon subsequent generations of nurses again, through her articles and monographs, and also through lectures to various groups in the United States and internationally. She is considered to be one of the pioneers in theoretical thinking in nursing (Botha, 1989; Meleis, 1985; Newman, 1994) and the model she developed has been tested and applied extensively in nursing practice, education, and research (Thibodeau, 1983). Johnson introduced the concept of nursing diagnosis in 1959, when she differentiated the work of nursing from medicine (Johnson, 1959). She also introduced the concept of nursing problems as distinct from medical problems (Newman, 1994).

Born in Savannah, Georgia, on August 21, 1919, she was the seventh and youngest child of Annie Bryce Johnson, born in 1883, and Charles-Leroy Johnson, born in 1881. Like other children in her family, Dorothy was a voracious reader, and she was taken regularly to the public library as a child by her brothers. She graduated at 17 from Senior High School in Savannah and then went on to junior college there for 2 years. Between junior college and university, Dorothy went to Florida and became a live-in nanny for two little girls at Miami Beach. She credits this experience with her later choice of pediatric nursing as an area of specialty. Her undergraduate nursing education was taken at one of the few baccalaureate programs in nursing in the United States at the time, Vanderbilt University School of Nursing in Tennessee. Here she met Lulu K. Wolff, who was her teacher and became her mentor throughout her career. She graduated from Vanderbilt on June 8, 1942.

Following her studies at Vanderbilt, Dorothy took a position as Instructor of Nursing at Vanderbilt University from January to July 1943. From here she went on to do staff nursing in Savannah, Georgia at the Chatham-Savannah Health Council. She returned to Vanderbilt in 1944 to continue her position as Instructor in Pediatric Nursing until 1948.

She came to realize that she needed more preparation, and she returned to

Dorothy E. Johnson

school to pursue a master's degree from the Harvard University School of Public Health. Following convocation on June 10, 1948, she returned to Vanderbilt University as an Assistant Professor of Pediatric Nursing (Johnson, 1989).

In 1949, Dorothy Johnson accepted a position as Assistant Professor of Pediatric Nursing at the University of California at Los Angeles, where she became well-respected for her clinical expertise and knowledge. Over time she became a highly significant mentor to students and faculty. The undergraduate curriculum at UCLA was eventually based upon her model.

In 1955, Professor Johnson was invited to go to Vellore, India, to assist with the development of a baccalaureate program in nursing, a challenge she enjoyed immensely and where she had the opportunity to meet then Prime Minister Nehru. This international experience had a profound effect upon her and after returning to UCLA, Dorothy maintained her international contacts with nurses in India, and a number of Vellore faculty colleagues subsequently came to UCLA to do graduate work.

Throughout her career at UCLA, where she was an important role model and men-

tor to students, Johnson did innovative and pioneering work in developing her own theoretical framework—the behavioral systems model. Teacher *par excellence* and one of the first to develop a theoretical nursing framework, Johnson wanted to communicate to others the need for, and importance of, identifying the scientific bases of nursing practice. At the core of Johnson's work was her belief that nursing has important scientific foundations which require study and thought in order to understand their application in nursing practice. In one of her early publications (1961), she referred to "the achievement and maintenance of a stable state" as "nursing's distinctive contribution to patient welfare and the specific purpose of nursing care" (p. 64). She developed and honed her ideas, and she was particularly articulate in putting them forward, whether in person or in writing. At an early stage of her thinking, she was able to delineate her beliefs about nursing's unique responsibility in health care and the ultimate goals of nursing in a rational and detailed manner (Johnson, 1959).

Johnson believed that theory development in nursing was a critical and essential matter for the profession, and her teaching and writing began to reflect this as early as 1959 (Johnson, 1959a, 1959b). She noted in 1974 that "if nursing's social responsibility had been clearly and precisely formulated as an ideal goal in patient care many years ago, perhaps, we, too would have been building upon previously established theory" (p. 373). She emphasized the need to build conceptual systems and the criteria by which these might be evaluated. Her graduate classes in theory development had great impact upon the students who took them and a number developed their initial theoretical frameworks while students in her classes. Sister Callista Roy is an example of a major nursing theorist who was stimulated to think about and to express her own beliefs about nursing in Professor Johnson's classes (P. J. Brink, July 1998, personal communication). Johnson's ideas were creative and unique, and the profession welcomed her contributions. She stressed the importance of knowledge based upon research findings as the basis of nursing science and emphasized the importance of research and theory in developing a body of knowledge that would have important implications for nursing practice.

Johnson took an early retirement from UCLA in 1978 following open heart surgery. She retired at the height of her career, just as her theoretical work was beginning to be recognized more widely for the significant contribution it was. She retired having earned a reputation as a first-rate theorist, scholar, and teacher. Her retirement was an occasion for a number of honours, of which the Lulu Hassenplug Award for distinguished achievements conferred by the California Nurses Association was but one. She has maintained her home in Florida since her retirement, and continues to occasionally travel nationally and abroad to present her work at the invitation of those who recognize the importance of her work. Dorothy Johnson's contribution was indeed unique, for few nurses in the modern era had previously done any work in knowledge development and theory. Her influence continues to be strong and her enduring legacy is to be found in her students, her colleagues, and professional nurses who have read her work.

PUBLICATIONS BY
DOROTHY E. JOHNSON (SELECTED)

Johnson, D. E. (1943). Learning to know people. *American Journal of Nursing, 43*, 248–252.

Johnson, D. E. (1949). The nursing of children. In A. F. Brown (Ed.), *Clinical instruction*. Philadelphia: Saunders.

Johnson, D. E. (1959). A philosophy of nursing. *Nursing Outlook, 7*, 198–200.

Johnson, D. E. (1959). The nature of a science of nursing. *Nursing Outlook, 7*, 291–294.

Johnson, D. E., Sheldon, E., & Slusher, M. (1959). An experimental program in nursing research. *Nursing Research, 8*, 169–171.

Johnson, D. E. (1961). The significance of nursing care. *American Journal of Nursing, 61*, 63–66.

Johnson, D. (1961). Patterns in professional nursing education. *Nursing Outlook, 9*, 608–611.

Johnson, D. E. (1962). Consequences for patients and personnel. *American Journal of Nursing, 62*, 96–100.

Johnson, D. E. (1962). Professional education for pediatric nursing. *Children, 9*(4), 153–156.

Johnson, D. E. (1964). Post-master's education. *Nursing Outlook, 12*(1), 33–35.

Johnson, D. E. (1964). Nursing and higher education. *International Journal of Nursing Studies, 1*, 219–225.

Johnson, D. E. (1965). Today's actions will determine tomorrow's nursing. *Nursing Outlook, 13*(9), 38–41.

Johnson, D. E. (1965). Competence in practice: Technical and professional. *Nursing Outlook, 14*(10), 30–33.

Johnson, D. E. (1966). The meaning of maternal deprivation and separation anxiety for nursing practice. In B. Bullough & V. Bullough (Eds.), *Issues in nursing* (pp. 145–152). New York. Springer Publishing Company.

Johnson, D. E. (1967). Powerlessness: Significant determinant in patient behavior? *Journal of Nursing Education, 6*(2), 39–44.

Johnson, D. E. (1968). Theory in nursing: Borrowed and unique. *Nursing Research 17*(3), 206–209.

Johnson, D. E. (1968). Professional practice and specialization in nursing. *Image, 2*(3), 2–7.

Johnson, D. E. (1974). Development of theory: A requisite for nursing as a primary health profession. *Nursing Research, 23*(5), 372–377.

Johnson, D. E. (1980). The behavioural systems model. In C. Roy & J. Riehl (Eds.), *Conceptual models for nursing practice* (2nd ed.). New York: Appleton-Century-Crofts.

Johnson, D. E. (1987). Evaluating conceptual models for use in critical care nursing practice. *Dimensions of Critical Care Nursing, 6*(4), 195–197.

Johnson, D. E. (1989). Some thoughts on nursing. *Clinical Nurse Specialist, 3*(1), 1–4.

Johnson, D. E., & McCaffrey, M. (1965). Crying in the newborn infant. *Nursing Science, 3*(5), 339–355.

Johnson, D. E., & McCaffery, M. (1967). The effect of parent group discussion upon epistemic responses. *Nursing Research, 6*(2), 352–358.

Johnson, D. E., Wilcox, J., & Moidel, H. (1967). The clinical nurse specialist as a practitioner. *American Journal of Nursing, 67*(11), 2298–2303.

BIBLIOGRAPHY

Botha, M. A. (1989). Theory development in perspective: The role of conceptual frameworks and models in theory development. *Journal of Advanced Nursing, 14,* 49–55.

Johnson, D. E. (1959a). The nature of a science of nursing. *Nursing Outlook, 7*(5), 291–294.

Johnson, D. E. (1959b). A philosophy of nursing. *Nursing Outlook, 7*(4), 198–200.

Johnson, D. E. (1974). Development of theory: A requisite for nursing as a primary health profession. *Nursing Research, 23*(5), 372–377.

Johnson, D. E. (1978). *Application of the behavioral system model to nursing practice, education and research.* Videotape available through Nursing Resources, Inc., 12 Lakeside Park, 607 North Avenue, Wakefield, MA, 01880.

Johnson, D. E. (1978). *The behavioral systems model for nursing.* Videotape available through Nursing Resources Inc., 12 Lakeside Park, 607 North Avenue, Wakefield, MA, 01880.

Johnson, D. E. (1989). *Exploring nursing theory: Dorothy Johnson: The behavioural system model: An orientation to nursing practice.* [videotaped interview with Dorothy Johnson during her visit to the Faculty of Nursing, University of Alberta, Edmonton, Alberta, October 27, 1989. Available at the library of the Faculty of Nursing.]

In A. I. Meleis (Ed.). (1985). *Theoretical nursing: Development and progress* (pp. 195–206). Philadelphia: J. B. Lippincott Co.

Newman, M. A. (1994). Theory for nursing practice. *Nursing Science Quarterly, 7*(4), 153–157.

Thibodeau, J. A. (1983). *Nursing models: Analysis and evaluation.* Monterey, CA: Wadsworth.

Janet Ross-Kerr
Pamela J. Brink

HELEN R. JOHNSON
1914–

No books, no instructors, no students, no curriculum, just a sketchy plan for a nursing program that would provide quality nurses at a time when there was a staggering need for more. That's what Helen R. Johnson,

R.N., Ed.D., started with when she came to Purdue in the fall of 1962 as the sole nursing faculty member. For 18 years, she was the driving force behind the development and growth of nursing education at Purdue University.

Helen R. Johnson

Johnson, daughter of Earl and Blanche Snyder, was born on November 15, 1914. With her five brothers and one sister, she grew up in the small Indiana town of Fritchton, helping her parents run their general merchandise store. During a hospital stay with a broken leg, the 7-year-old Helen watched in awe as the nurses cared for patients. She started reading all the Clara Barton and Florence Nightingale books she could find and decided to become a nurse with strong caring skills and a solid education.

Johnson left her small-town life for the large Indianapolis campus of Indiana University, where she earned a General Nursing Degree in 1936. She then worked at the

Indiana University Medical Center, where she moved from staff nurse to head nurse in 6 years.

She met her future husband, Gordon, at Indiana University. They were married in 1938, and had two children, Jim and Earl.

From 1942 to 1949, she worked at the Indianapolis Chapter of the American Red Cross. During World War II, she instructed volunteer nurse aides. After she earned a baccalaureate nursing degree from Indiana University in 1949, she went to work as the assistant chief of nursing education at the Veterans' Administration Hospitals at Fort Benjamin Harrison in Indianapolis. Three years later, she earned a master's degree in education from Butler University and was named chief of nursing services for the Veterans' Administration Hospital.

Her husband, a teacher at Shortridge High School in Indianapolis, died suddenly from a heart attack in 1954, and Johnson was left to raise her two sons alone. Still she remained active in community and professional organizations. She was president of the Indiana State Nurses Association in 1952, and served on the Indiana State Board of Health for 16 years. In 1957, she returned to Indiana University Medical Center as associate director of nursing services and assistant professor of nursing. During a trip to the Purdue West Lafayette campus for her son's college orientation in 1962, Johnson decided to investigate the rumors that Purdue wanted to start a nursing program. With demand for nurses at an all-time high, health care organizations and hospitals were asking universities to design curriculums that would provide well-educated nurses. Johnson's savvy leadership style, impressive resume, and fiery, yet generous, spirit won over the Purdue administrators, who hired her almost on the spot.

A down-to-earth, optimistic, and forward-thinking woman, she was charged with initiating a 2-year associate degree nursing program for the entire Purdue nursing program, not just on the West Lafayette (Indiana) campus, but on the four regional campuses as well.

With strong support from Purdue administrators who said she was "manna from heaven," Johnson began to hire faculty, arrange clinical experiences in local health care agencies, develop a curriculum, network with health care organizations statewide, and earn state approval of the new program. Most important, she made the appropriate national, state, and local contacts that continue to contribute to Purdue nursing's success.

From the W.K. Kellogg Foundation, she secured a $126,033 grant to provide educational programs for new faculty members, many of whom had never taught in an associate degree program. This grant also allowed hundreds of nurses from across the United States to attend summer seminars at Purdue on developing and teaching associate degree nursing programs.

Over the next 3 years, Johnson initiated associate degree nursing programs on all four Purdue campuses. By May 1969, each Purdue nursing program had successfully graduated a class and was accredited by the National League of Nursing. By 1970, the students on the main campus had grown from 30 to 172, and 611 nurses had graduated with associate degrees from all of the Purdue campuses.

Johnson, who won the 1968 Indiana Nurse of the Year Award, then unveiled her next vision for Purdue Nursing: baccalaureate degree programs. Again, the W.K. Kellogg Foundation supplied a grant to aid in developing an upper-division baccalaureate program designed to provide a career ladder opportunity for registered nurses who had graduated from an associate degree or diploma program. The first baccalaureate degree students in Purdue's "2 +

2" program were admitted in the fall of 1970. One of her crowning achievements at Purdue was a $1.3 million grant from the United States Public Health Service, which funded the majority of the construction of a nursing facility at Purdue's main campus. Johnson was instrumental in the design of the building, using the knowledge she gained as a member of the National Institutes of Health's Construction of Nurse Training Facilities Review Committee. Upon its completion in 1977, the new facility was a major impetus in upgrading the nursing program from a department in the School of Technology to a separate school with its own operating budget with Johnson at its head. Purdue then decided to place the health professions programs— pharmacy, health sciences, and nursing— under one administrative unit to provide cohesion and the opportunity for interdisciplinary education.

As a champion of high-quality nursing education, Johnson was a review panel member and site visitor for the National League of Nursing, a survey visitor for the Oklahoma State Board of Nurses' Registration and Nursing Education, and a member of the Panel on Nursing Education of the Committee on Institutional Cooperation (CIC). She participated in statewide planning for nursing education with the Indiana Regional Medical Programs and the Indiana Higher Education Telecommunications System. She also consulted to numerous nursing education programs in Indiana and throughout the Big 10.

Johnson earned a doctorate in higher education administration from Indiana University in 1975. She was the Indiana Nurse of the Year Award in 1968, and won the Distinguished Alumnus Award from the Indiana University School of Nursing in 1977.

Those who worked for her still vividly remember her charisma. She was a powerful communicator who could effectively impart to all audiences just where she felt Purdue Nursing should go and the steps to get there. She also was a strong leader who had wisdom, interpersonal skills, and vision far ahead of her time. Johnson also genuinely cared for and respected those she served and those who served her.

In 1989, the School of Nursing building was named the Helen R. Johnson Hall of Nursing. This was a fitting tribute to the woman whose name will always be synonymous with Purdue Nursing.

PUBLICATIONS BY HELEN R. JOHNSON (SELECTED)

A training program for hospital aides. (1953). *Hospital Progress*, 64–65.

Structuring a longitudinal study in longitudinal and graduate follow-up studies in associate degree education. (1978). In *Associate Degree Education* (pp. 1–13). New York: NLN Press.

(With Edmund Shea). Another administrative role: Building unity of purpose. (1960). *Hospitals, 34*, 55–56, 60, 116,118.

BIBLIOGRAPHY

A down-to-Earth optimist. (1968, June). *Purdue People, 17*.

Brooks, J. A., & Lohman, B. (1997, October 26). Johnson, H. R. Interview with authors.

Johnson, H. R. (1975). *A history of Purdue University's nursing education programs.* Doctoral thesis, Purdue University, West Lafayette, IN.

Johnson, H. R., & Lohmann, J. (1976). New patterns of nursing education: Associate degree and baccalaureate degree programs at Purdue University. West Lafayette, IN: Purdue University.

New route to the R.N. (1968, May). *Campus Copy* [Purdue University], 2–5.

Nursing: "House" that Helen built. (1989). *Perspective* [Purdue University], 6.

Schleman Award goes to Johnson. (1977, April 19). Lafayette (IN) *Journal & Courier.*

Johnson, H. R. Personal files (1962–1980).

Jo A. Brooks
Becky Lohman

K

ANNA KAPLAN
c. 1888–1960

The American nurse Anna Kaplan was a pioneer who made a prodigious contribution to implementation of the idea of nursing as a profession in early 20th-century Palestine. She was also one of the major founders and directors of the first modern school for Jewish nurses in this then-backward province.

Anna Kaplan

Anna Kaplan was a member of the American Zionist Medical Unit for Palestine (A.Z.M.U), subsequently, Hadassah Medical Organization, of the Zionist Organization of America (Z.O.A). The Z.O.A., foremost its division for American women Zionists, established a modern hospital in 1918—an institution that remains one of the best in Israel and in the Near East. Hadassah also laid the foundations for the organization of health services in Palestine. The Hadassah Training School for Nurses, established as part of this enterprise, was the only facility of its kind in Palestine until 1936 and was considered the leader in its field for many years.

Kaplan was born in Bialystok, Poland (then under Russian rule), circa 1888. As a girl, she left her home town and emigrated to America (Hadassak Bulletin, 1927). Several years later, having acquired a command of English, she enrolled in the school for registered nurses at Lebanon Hospital (today Lebanon-Bronx) in New York, which had been founded as a Jewish general hospital for members of all faiths in 1890 (Lebanon Hospital Assn., 1891). In 1909, by which time Lebanon Hospital was owned by the City of New York and situated on West Chester Avenue, 12 physicians lectured to 59 students at the hospital's nursing school. The school was headed by a superintendent—the head of nursing services—and her assistant.

Anna Kaplan was one of 14 members of the graduating class of 1910. In July of that year, the New York State Board for Nursing issued her with registered nurse's license No. 007254.

Kaplan's first position was the night supervisor at this hospital. She also spent two years as the head nurse at Liberty Sanitarium and from 1914 to 1918 worked in public health, evidently in New York. In 1918, she set out for Palestine as a member of a Z.O.A. medical mission.

The activity of American nurses in Palestine, including that of Anna Kaplan, should be examined in the context of the 19th-century tradition of worldwide dissemination of nursing ideas. In 1918, a Red Cross mission spent about one year in the country while the Z.O.A. sent a medical team of its own. The inhabitants of Palestine suffered from malaria, trachoma, dysentery, tuberculosis, skin diseases, and high infant mortality. The nurses in these missions, most of whom were registered nurses, brought the "gospel" of modern nursing to this area, where appropriate health services had not yet developed. In the Jewish society of Palestine, nursing work had been done until then by pharmacists or women whom doctors trained haphazardly for specific tasks, such as treatment of ophthalmologic disorders. A school following the model that Florence Nightingale was unknown. The Hadassah school for registered nurses was the first post-secondary vocational school for Jewish women in Palestine!

The mission set up its headquarters in Rothschild Hospital in Jerusalem, which had been upgraded to function as a 110-bed general hospital. At this time, Hadassah was establishing hospitals and clinics elsewhere in Palestine—in Jaffa (subsequently Tel Aviv) in the central district, and in Haifa, Tiberias, and Safed in the north.

Kaplan had to wear several hats simultaneously—director of the nursing school and superintendent of nursing at Rothschild Hospital, its outpatient clinics, the other Hadassah hospitals in Palestine, and clinics in small localities. Her job description was "Chief Nurse in the hospitals and dispensary system of the Hadassah Medical Organization in Palestine." Kaplan organized the work of Jerusalem's midwives and dealt with equipment and supplies. As the chief nurse, she helped organize the Hadassah hygienic department for the schools of Palestine, a country where eye and skin diseases were rampant among children. In 1923, a project for nursing services in the

community, by means of health centers in Jerusalem and elsewhere, was introduced along the lines of the Henry Street Settlement, which Lillian Wald founded in New York in 1895. The developers of this endeavor in Palestine were Kaplan and another American nurse, Bertha Landsman. In 1927, Kaplan supervised the work of the 300 nurses in these institutions. The registered nurses' school began to coalesce as soon as the mission arrived and quickly received 400 applications for admission. The admission requirements were "a high school education, general cultural background, and good moral character." Only 35 applicants were enrolled in the 3-year course of study. The language of instruction was Hebrew, reflecting the ideology of the time, although Hebrew-speaking teacher-physicians were hard to find. Most of the bedside instruction took place in English, but since some students were not fluent in this language, some of this instruction was in Yiddish. There were no textbooks; students took notes during the lectures. Kaplan lectured in Hebrew and wrote a pamphlet on nursing principles in this language, based mainly on the textbook by A. C. Maxwell and A. E. Pope (Maxwell & Pope, 1914).

In 1924, Kaplan, helped by Hadassah Schedrovitzky, a member of the first graduating class, (who also completed a year of study at the Columbia University Teachers' College and the Henry Street Settlement), introduced a curriculum that had been proposed in 1917 by the National League for Nursing Education, including a 3-month preparatory course. Kaplan also extended the basic curriculum by 6 months by adding a course in public health and midwifery for all students, thereby expanding the program to 3 years and 3 months.

Kaplan and Henrietta Szold, the founder of Hadassah in New York, made special efforts to send additional graduates to American nursing education institutions for training. The main destination was the Columbia University Teachers College, with which the Hadassah nursing school had special connections from its inception until the 1940s through one of the leading figures at the Teachers College, Isabel M. Stewart. During a 5-month leave of absence in 1924, Kaplan personally studied several courses in hospital administration and public health at the Columbia University Teachers College.

Kaplan also obtained authorization to have the graduates of her school take the State Board Examinations for registered nurses of New York State, since she was an American administrator and her school was run by American standards. The British government in Palestine recognized the school as an institution for the training of registered nurses, on the basis of the requirements of the General Nursing Council in Great Britain.

In 1927, as part of her years of struggle to professionalize nursing, Kaplan presented the Hadassah administration with a detailed proposal to merge the school into the newly founded Hebrew University of Jerusalem. As she explained, the proposal was influenced, among other things, by the process—newly under way at the time—of such mergers, e.g., the Connecticut Training School for Nurses into Yale University in New Haven, by Annie W. Goodrich in 1924 (Kalisch & Kalisch, 1995). In Jerusalem, however, the proposal was not accepted at that point in time. Kaplan left Palestine and returned to New York in 1927. From 1928 to 1937, Kaplan was the directress of nurses at Beth Moses Hospital in Brooklyn and published an article in the *American Journal of Nursing* about the job-sharing method that she had implemented for registered nurses there (Kaplan, 1933). The editor of the *Journal* in her introduction noted that Kaplan "has worked out one of the most practical 'share the work' plans yet seen."

Kaplan never married. In 1959, at the end of her life and living in Manhattan,

Kaplan sent a letter to the director of the Hadassah Nursing School, Etiya Margalit-Kohan, stating that she was disabled and could not write with her right hand because of a stroke. The tenor of the letter suggests that Kaplan was on the verge of death and she died soon after.

Today, the Hadassah-Hebrew University academic school for nurses in Jerusalem still rests on a firm foundation, laid in the early 1920s by the American nurse Anna Kaplan.

PUBLICATIONS BY ANNA KAPLAN

Nurses and their work in Hadassah institutions in 1926. (1926). *Hadassah Bulletin, 4–5*, 7–9.
Work sharing at the Beth Moses Hospital. (1933). *American Journal of Nursing, 33*(1), 36, 70.
The first nine years. (1938, April). *Hadassah News Letter*, pp. 127–129, 138.
The Hadassah Nursing School in Jerusalem. (1960). *The Nurse in Israel, 36*, 25–27. Original published in 1924.

BIBLIOGRAPHY

The bibliography is based mainly on the archives of the Hadassah Nursing School (J113) and of the Hadassah Medical Organization (J113), the Central Zionist Archives in Jerusalem, and the archives of the Hadassah Medical Organization in New York (record group #2).
Hadassah Bulletin, 10–12, 14–15. "On the resignation of Anna Kaplan." (1927).
Kalisch, P. A., & Kalisch, B. J. (1995). *The advance of American nursing*. Philadelphia: Lippincott.
Kaplan, A. (1933). Work sharing at the Beth Moses Hospital. (1933). *American Journal of Nursing, 33*(1), 36, 70.
Lebanon Hospital Association of the City of New York. *Constitution and Charter*. (1891), [Microform], 592-7311, and Annuals, 1893–1910, New York Public Library, New York City.
Maxwell, A. C., & Pope, A. E. (1914). *Practical nursing: A text-book for nurses*. New York: G. P. Putnam's Sons.

Nira Bartal

REGINA KAPLAN
1887–1957

"Woman of valor." "A tiny dynamo." These words describe Regina Kaplan. Regina was born to Gershon and Adella (Hannah) Traube Kaplan (German-born immigrants) in Memphis, Tennessee, on May 12, 1887. She was the third of five children: Sally, Belle, Regina, Louis G., and Dora.

The health problems of Adella Kaplan caused the family to move to Denver, Colorado. Kaplan wanted to become a physician but the financing of such an education was not available to her. Instead, she entered Mercy Hospital Training School for Nurses, Denver, Colorado, graduating in 1908. She was at the head of her class of 12: five religious and seven lay nurses. Her height was just under 5 feet tall and her weight was barely 90 pounds.

Regina Kaplan

In the style of the times, Miss Kaplan first began work as a private duty nurse, planning to enlist in the army: to this end she enrolled in the American Red Cross (which furnished Army nurses) on January 14, 1915 in Denver, but the army turned her down because of short stature. She con-

tinued her private duty practice until relatives told her of the need for a superintendent at the Leo N. Levi Hospital in Hot Springs, Arkansas.

For the next 35 years, from January 16, 1916 to January 16, 1951, Regina Kaplan was superintendent and also administrator at the Leo N. Levi Hospital, Hot Springs, Arkansas. She was issued license number 515 by reciprocity, by the Arkansas State Board of Nurse Examiners.

Regina either reorganized or newly opened the Leo Levi Hospital School of Nursing. She designed the pin and the cap. Regina herself appears to have taught many of the classes. Her students remember that she especially reserved teaching the ethics class for herself. After the necessary funds were obtained to expand the nurses' residence, Regina chose candidates for the School of Nursing who had obtained some college credits.

In 1923, the Arkansas State Board of Nurse Examiners conducted a survey of the Training School for Nurses and issued an unflattering report. Kaplan was cited as not being familiar with the Standard Curriculum and her record keeping was described as poor. Living quarters for the student nurses required that they go to the women's bath house for their baths. There was no library. The examiner found that "the pupils wore very short skirts, a good deal of rouge, and all sorts of shoes and stockings and that the discipline is lax" (LeMaster, 1987). There is no record of Regina Kaplan responding to this report but the school continued to exist until 1952.

In 1917, Kaplan, as part of the war effort, organized and directed an outpatient dispensary, organized a local Red Cross chapter, taught the nurse aide classes, and home nursing and first aid classes for adults and high school students. She hired the first school nurse for Hot Springs and encouraged the establishment of a free public health nursing program.

In 1927, Kaplan, after attending the birth of a baby girl set up for adoption, convinced a judge to allow her, an unmarried women, to adopt the child.

Regina belonged to the American Nurses Association (1918 onward), the Arkansas Nurses Association and the Colorado State Nurses Association. She was named chairman of the National Rehabilitation Association in the State Hospitals (1928) and was a member of the American College of Hospital Administrators. She attended a hospital administrators institute (Purdue University, 1940), belonged to the American Hospital Association (vice-president 1945–1946) and urged Levi's participation in Blue Cross. Regina felt so positively about Blue Cross that she became a member of the Board of Trustees of the Arkansas Blue Cross, Blue Shield. She continued serving the Garland County Red Cross as executive secretary (1917–1945). In 1944, she was honored with brunch at the White House. Miss Kaplan attended a hospital administrator's institute, Colorado University (1945) and founded the Lakewood Convalescent Home for "old age indigents" of Garland County (president 1946–1953). She served as president of the Arkansas Hospital Association (1947–1948), was a member of the Mid-West Hospital Association (1948–1949), and a member of the advisory consultant board of hospitals for Arkansas, State Board of Health (1949–1953). She listed herself as organizer and director of the National Arthritis Research Foundation (NARF) (1942–1951), an organization in competition with the American Rheumatism Association. They funded several projects at the University of Arkansas, before it ceased to exist. She contributed to professional journals and read papers before sectional meetings of the American College of Surgeons.

Regina served as director, sang soprano, and was chairperson of the Temple Beth Israel choir. She also served on Beth Israel's board of directors. Miss Kaplan was a member of most of the women's clubs and community betterment groups in Hot Springs.

Regina Kaplan retired on January 16, 1951 but remained as consultant to Levi Hospital until dying from cancer, she left Hot Springs to return to Denver. She died at the Jewish Hospital, Denver on October 8, 1957, her daughter, Betty Uzick, at her side.

BIBLIOGRAPHY

De Kruif, P. (1949). *Life among the doctors*. New York: Harcourt, Brace & Co.

Kaplan, R. (1955). *Who's who in world Jewry*. New York: Who's Who in World Jewry, in cooperation with Monde Publishers. Entry by Betty & Louis Uzick.

LeMaster, C. (1987). *Regina Kaplan: Arkansas' 'lady with the lamp.'* Cincinnati, OH: American Jewish Archives, Hebrew Union College, Jewish Institute of Religion. Unpublished.

Mayer, S. L. (1996). *The Jewish experience in nursing in America: 1881 to 1955*. Ed.D. dissertation, Teachers College, Columbia University.

Susan Mayer

LUCIE S. KELLY
1925–

Lucie S. Kelly is a distinguished nurse educator and mentor who has had a profound impact on nursing and public health in this country and abroad. Among her many contributions, she developed and implemented an interdisciplinary program for nurse administrators at Columbia University, served in leadership roles in state and national organizations, and bridged the disciplines of nursing and public health. The author of two major textbooks and subsequent revisions and more than 150 other publications, she was editor of *Nursing Outlook* for 9 years.

Lucie Stirm Young Kelly was born in Stuttgart, Germany, on May 2, 1925, the

Lucie S. Kelly

daughter of Hugo Karl and Emilie Rosa (Engel) Stirm. She came to the United States at the age of 4. Fleeing the devastating inflation of the 1920s in Germany, the family arrived in this country at the start of the Great Depression. Kelly was raised to the standards of hard work, thrift, and achievement. She was an exceptional student who loved to read, played the cello, and edited the high school magazine. Without the knowledge of her parents, she applied for a scholarship at the University of Pittsburgh and was awarded a senatorial scholarship providing her with partial tuition. She persuaded her father to cover the balance and, in 1943, entered the university as a nursing major.

Kelly graduated in 1947 with a bachelor of science degree. Married, with a young daughter, she worked in psychiatric, occupational health, and private duty nursing for a number of years. The turning point in her professional career came in 1953,

when a night supervisor at McKeesport Hospital, Pennsylvania, suggested to the director of nursing that Kelly would make a good faculty member. Kelly realized that she had a talent for teaching, both in the clinical area and in the classroom, and, in 1956, she returned to the University of Pittsburgh for full-time graduate work. Towards the end of her masters program, she was invited to become a member of the nursing faculty. During this time, Kelly also became involved in local and state activities of the American Nurses Association and the National League of Nursing (NLN) and was listed with the speaker's bureau of the NLN. She also continued her education while teaching, receiving her Ph.D. in 1965.

She returned briefly to Pittsburgh as assistant dean, before moving to McKeesport Hospital to become director of its school of nursing in 1966. There, she made a number of major changes that were well received, including the acceptance of married students and men in the accredited nursing education program. Later, she persuaded the board, the administration, the faculty and the alumni association to work toward closing the diploma program and affiliating with a community college. She also became president of the Pennsylvania Nurses' Association. As the only nurse with a Ph.D. to head a community hospital nursing service, Kelly was in demand nationally as a speaker. In 1969, she was offered and accepted the position of professor and chair of the nursing department at California State College, Los Angeles. A strong advocate of the nurse practitioner role, she initiated and implemented one of the first nurse practitioner master's programs in the nation.

After remarrying in 1972, Kelly returned to the East Coast. She taught at Teacher's College, wrote the third edition of *Dimensions of Professional Nursing*, and became involved in the New Jersey State Nurses' Association. She also headed the office of Consumer Health Education at the University of Medicine and Dentistry of New Jersey and taught medical students about nursing at Rutgers Medical School.

In 1975, Kelly was invited to join the School of Public Health at Columbia University by the dean who wanted a nationally recognized nurse to represent the school and someone who could also have an impact on the public health faculty and students. Kelly asked for and received a joint appointment in the School of Nursing. Within a year, she submitted a proposal for an interdisciplinary program for nurse administrators to the Kellogg Foundation which was funded. Kelly considers the development and implementation of that program one of her most satisfying professional experiences. At Columbia University, she also served as associate dean of academic affairs in the School of Public Health and honorary professor of nursing education at Teachers College.

Her 15-year tenure at Columbia University was interrupted only once by a leave, during which she served as the first executive director of the Mid-Atlantic Regional Nursing Association. She continued her participation in professional organizations and was elected to the boards of ANA and NLN and president of Sigma Theta Tau. She also led delegations, consulted, and presented papers in many parts of the world.

The recipient of six honorary doctorates, Kelly has received numerous awards throughout her career, including the Distinguished Alumna Award, University of Pittsburgh School of Nursing Education (in 1981), the Bicentennial Medallion of Distinction, the highest alumni honor from the University of Pittsburgh (in 1987), the Louise R. McManus Medal for Distinguished Service to Nursing, Teacher's College Nursing Education Alumni (in 1987),

the Ruth Freeman Public Health Nursing Award of the Public Health Association (in 1993), the Dean's Distinguished Service Award, Columbia School of Public Health (in 1995), and the Second Century Award for Contributions to Health Care, Columbia University School of Nursing (in 1996). She was elected Fellow of the American Academy of Nursing in 1976 and, in 1993, received the ANA Honorary Recognition Award. After first presenting the International Mentor Award of Sigma Theta Tau to her mentor, Ruth Kuehn, in 1993, Kelly herself received the award at the same meeting. The award has since been named the Lucie S. Kelly Mentor Award, and Kelly has been its recipient on two other occasions.

Kelly has published more than 150 articles and editorials in addition to books and book chapters. From 1978 to 1981, she served as senior editor of *Image*, the refereed journal of Sigma Theta Tau, and, from 1982 to 1991, as editor of *Nursing Outlook*, a peer-reviewed journal that provided a forum for presenting a diversity of ideas on professional trends and concepts in nursing education and administration. She served on a number of editorial advisory boards, including the *American Journal of Public Health* and *American Health*. Her superior communications skills also lead to frequent newspaper, radio, and television interviews as well as to many speaking engagements. Over the years, she served on the boards of many community organizations as well.

In 1990, Lucie S. Kelly retired from Columbia University. She has continued to be an advocate for issues related to health care and serves on the boards and executive committees of Palisades Medical Center in New Jersey and the Visiting Nurse Service of New York.

Identified as one of the 50 most influential nurses in the country in two surveys,

Kelly has demonstrated courage, creativity, and commitment throughout her distinguished career. She has been a strong advocate for patients' rights and for consumers. Grateful to her own mentor, Ruth Kuehn, Kelly has mentored numerous students and believes that the concept of mentoring, which involves the philosophy of caring, is the heart of nursing.

PUBLICATIONS BY LUCIE S. KELLY

Books and Book Chapters

Physician's assistants and the law. (1973a). In M. H. Browning & E. P. Lewis (Eds.), *The expanded role of the nurse.* (Contemporary Nursing Series) (pp. 104–114). New York: American Journal of Nursing Company.

What the patient needs as seen by the nurse. (1973b). In M. E. Auld & L. Hulthen Birum (Eds.), *The challenge of nursing: A book of readings* (pp. 17–23). St. Louis: Mosby.

Dimensions of professional nursing. (1975). New York: Macmillan. Successive editions in 1981, 1985, 1991, and (with Lucille Joel) 1995 and 1999.

The impact of social trends and legislative action. (1975b). In C. B. Lenburg (Ed.), *Open learning and career mobility in nursing* (pp. 105–110). St. Louis, MO: Mosby.

Institutional licensure. (1975). In B. Bullough (Ed.), *The law and the expanding nurse role* (pp. 109–123). New York: Appleton-Century-Crofts.

The Nurse Training Act: How legislation is formulated, adopted and implemented. (1976). In *People, Power, Politics for Health Care.* New York: National League of Nursing.

Reference sources for research and continuing education. (1977). In *Nursing.* Kansas City, MO: American Nurses Association.

Community health involvement: How and where? (1978a). In *Community health today and tomorrow* (pp. 37–46). New York: National League for Nursing.

External constraints on nursing education. (1978b). In J. A. Williamson (Ed.), *Current perspectives in nursing education: The changing scene.* Vol. 2. St. Louis: Mosby.

Women and power: Means to attainment. (1979). In *Nursing's influence on health policy for the eighties.* Kansas City, MO: American Academy of Nursing.

Institutional licensure: Panic or panacea. (1980). In B. Bullough (Ed.), *The law and the expanding nurs-*

ing role (2nd ed., pp. 109–123). New York: Appleton-Century-Crofts.

The nursing experience: Trends, challenges, transitions. (1987). New York: Macmillan. Further editions published in 1992, and (with Lucille Joel) in 1996.

Articles (Selected)

The role of the baccalaureate graduate in nursing service. (1966). *Nursing Outlook, 14,* 49–52.

The modern nurse administrator. (1969). *Journal of Nursing Education, 8,* 13–23.

Room at the top: A place for the nurse administrator. (1972). *Journal of Nursing Administration, 2,* 81–86.

Open curriculum: What and why. (1974). *American Journal of Nursing, 74,* 2232–2238.

End Paper, *Nursing Outlook,* 1978–1982.

Reflections on a (sort of) retirement. (1990). *Nursing Outlook, 38,* 167.

Editorials, *Nursing Outlook* 1982–1991.

BIBLIOGRAPHY

Lucie Young Kelly Collection, Nursing Archives, Mugar Memorial Library, Boston University.

Schorr, T., & Zimmerman, A. (1988). *Making choices, taking chances: Nurse leaders tell their stories* (pp. 136–145). St. Louis: Mosby.

Sentz, L. Personal interview with L. S. Kelly. July, 1997. Unpublished.

Who's Who in America. Chicago: Marquis, 1975 and successive volumes.

Who's Who in American Nursing. Washington, DC: Society of Nursing Professionals, 1985 and subsequent editions.

Who's Who in Medicine and Healthcare. New Providence, NJ: Marquis, 1996 and subsequent volumes.

Who's Who of American Women. Chicago: Marquis, 1996.

The World's Who's Who of Women. Chicago: Marquis, 1997.

Lilli Sentz

MARGARET E. KERR
1900–1976

Margaret E. Kerr, editor of *The Canadian Nurse* for 21 years, helped shape the thinking and understanding of generations of Canadian nurses as editor, educator, and as an active participant in professional organizations.

Margaret Kerr was born in Ontario, Canada, of Scottish and Irish parentage at the turn of the century. She graduated from the Vancouver General Hospital School of Nursing, and received a baccalaureate degree in nursing from the University of British Columbia and a master's degree from Columbia University. She then returned to the University of British Columbia, where she was assistant professor from 1929 to 1944 in the Department of Nursing and Health. As chair of the Public Health Nursing Section of the Canadian Nurses Association for 6 years, she gained a national reputation. She was elected president of the Registered Nurses Association of British Columbia from 1943 to 1944.

Margaret E. Kerr

On May 1, 1944, Kerr became editor and executive director of *The Canadian Nurse*. She developed the publication from a newsletter to a national professional journal, with a French edition equal to the English counterpart. When she assumed the editorship, the mailing list showed 5,000 subscribers. In September 1957, there were more than 37,000 subscribers, and by the time she died in 1976, the journal had a combined circulation of 120,000, in great part due to her leadership.

When Kerr took over as editor in 1944, she discussed the idea of subscription through association fees with the editorial board of the journal. She believed that this approach would stimulate interest in and understanding of professional developments for Canadian nurses. By 1949, the editorial board had approved her plan and she started her campaign to gain the support of each provincial association. Traveling across Canada, she made formal presentations and participated in numerous meetings and discussions. Eventually, she was able to obtain the official approval of nursing associations in all the provinces. An astute businesswoman, Kerr was also able to turn the journal around financially. Nursing editors around the world recognized the phenomenal growth and success of the journal under her leadership and asked her for advice.

When Kerr retired as editor in August of 1965, she was made an honorary member of the Canadian Nurses Association. She returned to Vancouver, British Columbia, where she continued her involvement in the nursing community and engaged in an active social life until her death on June 27, 1976.

Kerr's objective as educator and editor was to further the cause of her profession and to develop a body of well-informed nurses. She was an inspiring, forceful teacher, a skilled parliamentarian, and an engaging speaker who had a keen mind and a wonderful sense of humor. Many of her former students consider themselves members of a club "F.S.O.M."—Former Student of Margaret, a badge of great distinction.

PUBLICATIONS BY MARGARET E. KERR

Editorials. *The Canadian Nurse*, 1944–1965.

BIBLIOGRAPHY

Canadian Nurses Association. Clippings File, Archives, CNA.

Lindeburgh, M. (1944). The new editor of the Journal. *The Canadian Nurse, 40*(5), 310.

Obituary. (1976). *The Canadian Nurse, 72*(8), 10.

A tribute to our Editor and Executive Director on her retirement. (1965). *The Canadian Nurse, 61*(9), 703–707.

Lilli Sentz

Imogene M. King

IMOGENE M. KING
1923–

King is a pioneer nursing theorist and an internationally known scholar whose ideas have influenced nursing theory advancement worldwide. King's nursing experiences have fostered scientific theory-research knowledge development in nursing, while her professional activities have supported intellectual pursuits for nurse educators, practitioners, administrators, and researchers. King's Theory of Goal Attainment continues to be used worldwide and has impacted education, research, and practice in many countries, including Canada, Germany, Japan, Sweden and U.S.A.

Imogene M. King was born on January 30, 1923 in West Point, Iowa, the youngest of three children of Mary and Dan King.

During the depression, King's family moved to Fort Madison, Iowa, where King attended high school (1936–40). King learned to play golf and tennis from her brother and is still an avid golfer playing at least twice a week. Following graduation from high school in 1940, King worked as a secretary at the Schaeffer Pen Company. When the Second World War began, her uncle, a surgeon, suggested she consider enrolling in a school of nursing. She was admitted to St. John's Hospital School of Nursing, St. Louis, Missouri, where her aunt worked as a private duty nurse. King graduated from St. John's Hospital Nursing School in 1945, one week after the war ended. One month later, she enrolled in Maryville College of the Sacred Heart, a girl's boarding school, and worked as a nurse for the out-of-town students while at the same time pursuing college courses toward a bachelor of science degree. After a year of study, King transferred to St. Louis University where she completed requirements and received a Bachelor of Science Degree in Nursing Education in 1948. Her bachelor's thesis was titled "Designing a Clinical Instruction Program for St. John's Hospital School of Nursing." From 1945 to 1947, King practiced as a staff nurse, college health nurse, physician's office nurse, and a private duty nurse. This was known at that time as "working your way through college."

King returned to St. John's Hospital School of Nursing as a clinical instructor in medical-surgical nursing from 1947–51, where she helped to change the curriculum from a medical model to a nursing model. In 1951, she took a leave of absence to care for her father, who was dying. Upon his death, she moved her mother to St. Louis with her and returned to St. John's Hospital as a teacher and assistant director of nursing (1952–1958). While working at St. John's, King completed a Master of Science Degree in Nursing at St. Louis University in 1957. Soon after, King was admitted to the doctoral program at Teachers College, Columbia University, N.Y. and graduated in 1961 with a Doctor of Education (Ed.D).

King is recognized as one of the early nurse theorists through her publications, *Toward a Theory for Nursing* (1971) and *A Theory for Nursing: Systems, Concepts and Processes* (1981). King's Theory of Goal Attainment is considered a major contribution to the discipline of nursing. The 1971 book was translated into Japanese; the 1981 book was translated into Japanese and Spanish. The influence of her work is further exemplified in Frey and Seiloff's book, *Advancing King's Systems Framework and Theory of Nursing* (1995).

King's position in several different universities provided a broad educational and experiential background. King was Assistant Professor and Chairman of the Undergraduate Nursing Program (1961–1963) and Associate Professor and Director of the Graduate Nursing Program (1963–1966) at Loyola University of Chicago.

From 1966–68, King served as Assistant Chief, Research Grants Branch, Division of Nursing Bureau of Health Manpower, Department of Health Education and Welfare (HEW) in Washington, DC. In 1969, King was selected by the World Health Organization to conduct a research seminar for nurses in the Western Pacific Region in Manila. King served on the Defense Advisory Committee on Women in the Services, US Department of Defense from 1972 to 1975.

In 1968, King was appointed Professor and Director, School of Nursing at Ohio State University in Columbus, Ohio. In 1972, King returned to Loyola University as a professor and teacher in the graduate nursing program. She served as Coordinator for Research in Clinical Nursing at Loyola University Medical Center (1977–1980).

In 1980, King was appointed professor in the College of Nursing at the University of South Florida in Tampa and was appointed Director of Research (1984–1987). She also served as program consultant to the University of Miami PhD Nursing program and was Principal Investigator for a statewide project "Florida Concept Validation Project" funded by Florida Nurses Association, District V Charitable Trust (1985–87). During this time, she facilitated a group of nurse researchers at the University of South Florida studying circadian rhythms.

In every state in which she taught, King was active in the nurse's association, at both the local and state level. King was also active in Sigma Theta Tau International, serving as President of Delta Beta Chapter, and served as co-chair for the 1991 Sigma Theta Tau International Biennial Convention held in Tampa and served as a Sigma Theta Tau International distinguished lecturer (1989–91). She has been a recipient of numerous honors in every state in which she lived.

Among her honors is being elected one of the initial Sigma Theta Tau International Virginia Henderson fellows in 1993. The University of South Florida College of Nursing dedicated the Imogene King Works in the Special Collection of University of South Florida Library in 1996; American Nurses Association's Jessie Scott Award at the 100th American Nurses Association Anniversary Convention in 1996; a gold medallion from Governor Chiles for advancing the nursing profession at the 1997 Florida Nurses Association Convention, and at the Sigma Theta Tau International 75th Anniversary Convention, 1997 American Nurses Association/Sigma Theta Tau International grant was re-named in her honor. An organization, King International Nursing Group (KING) has been incorporated to improve nursing care and contribute to the science of nursing through the advancement of King's Interacting Systems Framework and related theories.

King further develops nursing science by active participation in professional activities at the district, regional, state, national and international levels and mentors practicing nurses in the academic and clinical settings. King has had a major influence on the development and direction of theoretical/conceptual thinking in nursing education, research and practice over the past five decades. King provided an early and strong link between academics and practice. Her work in developing the Theory of Goal Attainment is an excellent example of the integration of theory and research in knowledge development for the nursing profession. King gave the keynote address, "A Theoretical Basis for Nursing Informatics," at the 6th International Congress on Nursing Informatics, in Stockholm, Sweden, September 26–October 1, 1997.

King continues to be active in the profession of nursing and is now involved in nursing informatics, the cutting edge of nursing as it moves in to the 21st century. She was awarded an honorary doctorate from Loyola University, Chicago in May, 1998.

PUBLICATIONS BY IMOGENE M. KING

Books (Selected)

King, I. (1971). *Toward a theory for nursing.* New York: Wiley.

King, I. (1981). *A theory for nursing: Systems, concepts, process.* New York: Wiley.

King, I. (1986). *Curriculum and instruction in nursing: Concepts and processes.* Norwalk, CT: Appleton-Century-Crofts.

King, I., & Fawcett, J. (Eds.). (1997). *The language of nursing theory and metatheory.* Indianapolis, IN: Sigma Theta Tau International.

Book Chapters (Selected)

King, I. (1975). The decision-maker's perspective: Patient care aspects. In L. Shuman, R. D. Spears, & J. P. Young (Eds.), *Operations research in health care: A critical analysis* (pp. 3–20). Baltimore, MD: The John Hopkins University Press.

King, I. (1983). Application of King's theory of goal attainment in family health care. In I. Clements & F. Roberts (Eds.), *Family health: A theoretical approach to nursing care* (pp. 177–188; 342–347; 383–384). New York: Wiley.

King, I. (1988). Measuring health goal attainment of patients. In C. Waltz & O. Strikland (Eds.), *Measurement of nursing outcomes: Measuring clinical skills and professional development in education and practice* (Vol. II, pp. 109–123). New York: Springer Publishing Company.

King, I. (1989a). King's general systems framework and theory. In J. Riehl-Sisca (Ed.), *Conceptual models for nursing practice* (3rd ed., pp. 149–158). Norwalk, CT: Appleton-Lange.

King, I. (1989b). King's systems framework for nursing administration. In B. Henry, C. Arndt, M. Vincenti, & A. Marriner-Tomey (Eds.), *Dimensions of nursing administration* (pp. 25–46). Cambridge, MA: Blackwell.

King, I. (1995a). A systems framework for nursing. In M. Frey & C. Sieloff (Eds.), *Advancing systems framework and theory of nursing* (pp. 14–22). Thousand Oaks, CA: Sage.

King, I. (1995b). The theory of goal attainment. In M. Frey & C. Sieloff (Eds.), *King's systems framework and theory of nursing* (pp. 23–32). Thousand Oaks, CA: Sage.

King, I. (1995). In M. Mischo-Kelling & K. Wittneben, *Pledgebilding und plegetheorien* (Chapters 2 & 3). Germany: Urban & Schwarzwenberg.

Articles (Selected)

Gulitz, E., & King, I. (1988). King's general systems model: Application to curriculum development. *Nursing Science Quarterly, 3*(2), 128–132.

King, I. (1963). Junior college education for nursing: An urgent necessity. *Illness Medical Journal, 23*(1), 88–89.

King, I. (1964). Nursing theory: Problems and prospect. *Nursing Science, 2*(5), 394–403.

King, I. (1968). A conceptual frame of reference for nursing. *Nursing Research, 17*(1), 29–31.

King, I., & Daubenmire, J. (1973). Nursing process models: A systems approach. *Nursing Outlook, 13*(10), 50–51.

King, I. (1974). [Letter.] *The Journal of Nursing Administration, 5*(1), 40–41.

King, I., & Tarsitano, B. (1982). The effects of structured and unstructured preoperative teaching. *Nursing Research, 31*(6), 324–329.

King, I. (1985). Philosophies of nursing education: A national survey. *Western Journal of Nursing Research, 6*(4), 377–379.

King, I. (1987). Translating research into practice. *The Journal of Neuroscience Nursing, 19*(1), 44–48.

King, I. (1988). Concepts: Essential of theories. *Nursing Science Quarterly, 1*(1), 22–5, 11.

King, I. (1990). Health as the goal of nursing. *Nursing Science Quarterly, 3*(3), 123–128.

King, I. (1991). Nursing theory 25 years later. *Nursing Science Quarterly, 4*(3), 94–5, 12.

King, I. (1992). King's theory of goal attainment. *Nursing Science Quarterly, 5*(1), 19–26, 22.

King, I. (1994). Quality of life and goal attainment. *Nursing Science Quarterly, 7*(1), 29–32.

King, I. (1996). The theory of goal attainment in research and practice. *Nursing Science Quarterly, 9*(2), 61–6, 16.

King, I. M. (1997). Reflections on the past and a vision for the future. *Nursing Science Quarterly, 10*(1), 15–7.

King, I. M. (1998). Nursing informatics: A universal nursing language. *The Florida Nurse, 46*(1), 1, 2, 3, 5, 9.

BIBLIOGRAPHY

Messmer, P. (1997). Imogene King, Ed.D., EN, FAAN receives gold medallion from Governor. *Florida Nurse, 45*(9), 10.

Schorr, T., & Zimmerman, A. (1988). *Making choices: Taking chances* (pp. 146–150). St. Louis: Mosby.

Schorr, T., & Zimmerman, A. (1988). *The nurse theorists: Portraits of excellence. Imogene King.* [Videotape series.] Athens, OH: Helene Fuld Health Trust. Fuld Institute for Technology.

Schorr, T., & Zimmerman, A. (1997). *The nurse theorists: Portraits of excellence: Imogene King: Interacting systems framework.* Nurse Theorists CD-ROMs FITNE Athens, OH.

Patricia Messmer

ALICE YOUNG KOHLER
1911–1992

Alice Young Kohler, a Chinese-American woman from Honolulu, was Hawaii's first nurse-midwife. Kohler's career in public health covered many of the key themes in the field at mid-century. She worked on the island of Molokai, where people with Hansen's Disease (or leprosy) were sent to live in isolation in the name of public protection. She worked for the Palama Settlement in Honolulu, which provided health and welfare services to the poor, including tuberculosis and well-baby clinics. Finally, she worked for the Territorial Board of Health in maternal and child health. Trained as a public health nurse and nurse-midwife, she became the supervisor of midwives during the 1930s and 1940s, placed in charge of every lay midwife on the islands of Hawaii.

Born Alice Hing Tong Young, she grew up in Honolulu's Chinatown. Her father, Wah Kam Young, was a Chinese immigrant who worked as a fish merchant. He travelled to China often for his business and he died there on a visit when Alice was a young girl. Her mother, Bow Ngan Sum, was of Chinese and Hawaiian descent.

After graduating from high school Kohler had wanted to become a doctor but since her mother was a widow with 9 children, there was no money to spare for tuition. Thus, she became a nurse because she could get an education without having to pay tuition fees. At age 18 she went to California, where she attended St. Luke's Hospital School of Nursing in San Francisco. After graduating with basic nurse training, she returned to Hawaii where she enrolled in a 1-year public health nursing program at the University of Hawaii.

Kohler began her public health nursing work with the Palama Settlement, a social welfare program on Oahu. After 2 years, the Board of Health for the Territory of Hawaii hired her as a public health nurse for the island of Molokai, known for its "leper colony." She worked there with the general public for almost 2 years, although probably not directly with people with leprosy.

Her notoriety in the history of health work in Hawaii came when she was selected to become Hawaii's first supervisor of midwives. Drawing on Social Security Funds designed to improve maternal and child health, the Territorial Board of Health sent her to New York City in 1936 to become a nurse-midwife. She attended the nurse-midwifery program set up by the Maternity Center Association of New York and the Teacher's College at Columbia University. As part of the program, students conducted midwifery field service at the Lobenstine Clinic in Harlem. She returned to Hawaii in 1937.

Hawaii's Board of Health first began to regulate midwifery in 1931, at a time when midwives delivered 40% of all babies born in Honolulu and 25% of all babies born in the islands. The board registered nearly 200 midwives, most of whom were Japanese immigrants, although there were also Filipino, Hawaiian, and Portuguese women, as well as one Chinese woman. Over half of the women had formal midwifery schooling, ranging from 6 months to several years. As supervisor, Kohler was to maintain regular contact with the women. Although she spoke English, Cantonese, and pidgin English, which was used throughout the islands, she did not speak Japanese. Nevertheless, with the help of translators, she organized educational programs, inspected midwife bags, and attended deliveries with midwives as part of Hawaii's regulation of midwifery. In 1940, she developed a manual for midwives, drawing on other state midwife manuals as a guide. She became the liaison between the midwives and government officials as she attempted to ease tensions when the midwives objected to ever-increasing restrictions imposed by the board.

In 1942, Kohler married Drew Kohler, a Caucasian from Minnesota who worked as a linguist for Naval Intelligence. They met in Hawaii during World War II when he was a member of the 14th Naval District Combat Intelligence Unit at Pearl Harbor. Although she initially continued her position as midwife supervisor, she resigned in 1943 when she became pregnant. She raised three children, Katharine, Stephanie, and Paul, but still found new ways to continue nursing. During her pregnancy, for example, she wondered why there were no parent education classes available. After discussing this fact with her obstetrician, Dr. Richard Sakamoto, she convinced him to hire her to offer education classes for his patients. Her courses were similar to the childbirth education and prenatal classes offered by hospitals and midwives today. From 1950 to 1952 she provided expectant mothers with seven 2-hour classes and eventually evening classes for fathers. Thus, as she explained in her 1953 article in *Nursing Outlook*, she brought public health nursing to the practice of obstetrics.

Kohler continued to find ways to perform nursing work even as she and her family lived in several different places, including Japan, Taiwan, and Washington, D.C., as required by Drew's work. In Taiwan, for example, she assisted women with prenatal care, delivery, and postnatal care at the U.S. Navy Hospital. Finally, in the mid-1960s she and her husband retired and returned to Hawaii. After several decades back in their beloved Hawaii, Drew Kohler died in 1985, and Alice Kohler died a few years later in 1992. However, they both lived long enough to see her selected to be among the first Distinguished Alumna of the School of Nursing at the University of Hawaii. This honor in 1983 paid tribute to her lifelong commitment to the people of Hawaii and the field of nursing.

PUBLICATIONS BY ALICE YOUNG KOHLER

The place of the public health nurse in private medical practice. *Nursing Outlook, 1*(9), 528–529.

BIBLIOGRAPHY

Ambrose, J. (1984, March 23). Midwifery declined after wartime role changed. *Honolulu Star-Bulletin*, p. A-12.

Foster, D., & Coleman, T. (1986, November 1). Nurse-Midwifery Week proclaimed. *Molokai News.*

Unprocessed papers of Alice Young Kohler, possession of Katherine Kohler, Honolulu, Hawaii.

Records of the Department of Health, Director's Office, Hawaii State Archives, Honolulu, HI.

Record Group 90, United States Public Health Service, Group III-States, 1936–1944, Box 205 and 206, National Archives, Washington, DC.

Record Group 102, U.S. Children's Bureau, Central Files, 1937–1940, Box 754, National Archives, Washington, DC.

Smith, R., & Riznik, B. Interview with Alice Young Kohler. (1985, August 6). Oral history project: *Public health Services and family health on Kauai, 1920–1955*. Written transcript, Grove Farm Homestead Museum, Kauai, Hawaii.

Susan L. Smith

L

MARGARET BRYDON LAIRD
1871–1968

Margaret B. Laird was a considerable presence in women's suffrage and New Jersey politics, yet she has been lost in obscurity. One of the first two women elected to the New Jersey legislature, her nursing background was subsumed by larger issues.

Very little is known of Laird's early life: she was born in Newark, New Jersey, on March 28, 1871, the daughter of James Brydon and Frances McDonald Brydon. Her mother, a contemporary of Susan B. Anthony, had been very active in the women's suffrage movement. Her maternal grandfather, an Anglican minister in Scotland during the early part of the 19th century, had been an outspoken advocate for women's rights.

She entered nurse's training at Newark City Hospital and graduated in 1895 at the age of 24. It is not known whether she ever practiced as a nurse. She married a pharmacist, Reginald Laird, sometime after completing her training and they had two children, Robert and Margaret. She designed her own house plans, according to her ideas of making housekeeping simple and efficient.

This efficiency was essential because she was very active outside the home, belonging to the YWCA, the women's auxiliary of the YMCA, the Red Cross, the Order of the Eastern Star, and the New Jersey State Nurses Association. A trustee of the Contemporary Club, she served on its legislative and civic committees and chaired the Liberty Loan committee.

Like her mother and grandfather, Laird was actively involved in the women's suffrage movement. From 1915 to 1920 she served as the New Jersey treasurer of the National Woman's Party, was secretary of the Essex County (NJ) Suffrage Association, chairman for Newark for the National American Woman's Suffrage Association and was the vice-president of the Women's Political Union.

Decades later she recalled how "rowdies, beating on pans, would try to shout her down during demonstrations . . . shouting

'Go home and wash dishes'" (Moran, 1968). During the administration of Woodrow Wilson (for whom she had little regard), she picketed the White House and was disappointed that she wasn't arrested. She claimed her husband "was tickled to death" with her political activities.

She was also involved with Newark political and civic activities. Appointed to the Newark Board of Health in 1916, the Democratic majority in the Common Council refused to confirm the appointment. But further Newark city appointments followed: the Committee of Ten for "Bundle Day" early in the First World War and the committee to plan and celebrate Newark's 250th anniversary.

Once the vote for women was assured, she ran for the state assembly as a "dry" Republican from Essex County in 1920, and received the second highest vote out of 12 candidates. She and another Republican from Essex County, Mrs. Jennie C. Van Ness, were thus the first two women elected to the New Jersey state assembly, and Laird, at the age of 49, was apparently the first nurse elected to the state legislature in the U.S.

She recalled that the legislators were "delighted" to have a woman among them and Democratic Governor Edward I. Edwards, along with many members of the Assembly, vowed to vote for "any bill I introduced."

Early during her term she sponsored a bill which was part of the prohibition legislation. Over the course of her two terms, she made her mark by sponsoring groundbreaking liberal legislation in two areas: equal pay for women employed by the state (including teachers), and the establishment of juvenile courts. Reelected in 1921, she declined to run for a third term because of the night hours of the assembly. She continued her political involvement and founded the Newark Women's Republican Club in 1926. After her husband retired

and they left Newark, she became very active in local public health organizations in Monmouth County, New Jersey.

At the age of 97, only 3 months before her death, she gave a newspaper interview, which focused on her remarkable past. Laird was still so engrossed in politics that the interview had to be scheduled during a break in the Republican National Convention.

Margaret B. Laird, New Jersey's first woman and apparently first nurse elected to the state legislature in the U.S., died November 30, 1968. She was survived by a daughter, Margaret L. Cross, two grandchildren, and four great-grandchildren.

BIBLIOGRAPHY

Morgan, M. (1968, August 10). First assemblywoman recalls past. *Asbury Park Press*.

Mrs. R. Laird, 97, First assemblywoman. (1968, November 30). [Obituary]. *Newark Evening News*.

Mrs. Laird, 97, first woman in Jersey legislature, dead. (1968, December 1). [Obituary]. *New York Times*.

Mrs. Margaret B. Laird. (1921). *Manual of the Legislature of New Jersey, 21*, 293–294.

State's first woman legislator is dead. (1968, November 30). [Obituary]. *Asbury Park Press*.

Janet L. Fickeissen

SISTER MARIE DENISE LEFEBVRE
1907–1993

Lefebvre pioneered the movement to doctoral preparation for Canadian nurses. The first Canadian nurse to obtain a doctoral degree, Lefebvre devoted her nursing career to the advancement of nursing science and the improvement of teaching methods in nursing. A member of the Grey Nun Community for 67 years, she lived to see the first doctoral nursing program open in Canada in January 1991 at the University of Alberta.

Sister Marie Denise Lefebvre

Marie Denise Lefebvre was born in 1907 in Saint-Benoit, Quebec. With several family members already in the Grey Nuns Community, she followed their path and in 1926 was admitted to the novitiate at the Mother House of the Grey Nuns of Montreal when she was 19 years old. Wishing to provide service as a nurse, Lefebvre studied at St. Boniface Hospital School in Manitoba and graduated in 1932. In 1935 she received her Bachelor of Arts degree from the University of Montreal. Furthering her education in the United States, Lefebvre received her Bachelor of Science degree in Nursing from St. Louis University in Missouri in 1938. A year later she received her Master of Science degree in Nursing Education from the Catholic University of America in Washington, DC.

Lefebvre returned to Canada in 1939, where she became Director of the Institut Marguerite d'Youville, a French-language nursing school in Montreal. During her 20-year tenure there she developed a baccalaureate program in conjunction with the University of Montreal, in addition to teaching nursing education and psychology. As a traveling instructor she helped to organize clinical teaching programs and improve the curriculum in several French-speaking schools of nursing. The Institute later closed in 1967, after 33 years, when the baccalaureate program was integrated into the newly created Nursing Sciences program at the University of Montreal.

A strong contributor to professional nursing organizations throughout her career, Lefebvre took on leadership roles with the Registered Nurses Association of the Province of Quebec and convened the French division of the Hospital and School of Nursing Section. In 1946 she served as Secretary of the Canadian Nurses Association in addition to co-authoring a book on nursing principles and procedures. Her experience in demand, she participated in evaluating 24 schools in the Canadian Conference of Catholic Schools of Nursing in 1950. Still she found time to enhance her education, and at age 48, Lefebvre received her doctoral degree, Docteur de Pedagogie, from the University of Montreal in 1955. Well-qualified, she served on several committees of the World Health Organization.

From 1973 to 1981, Lefebvre served as Superior General of the Order of Grey Nuns of Montreal. In 1981 she began to prepare the case for canonization of the founder of the Order, Marguerite d'Youville, which was realized in 1991.

Lefebvre received numerous awards during her lifetime for outstanding contributions. In 1967 she was awarded the Centennial Medal of Confederation from the Government of Canada. In 1984 she again was recognized by the Canadian Government and appointed to the Order of Canada and presented with the Marie Therese Casgrain

Prize, named for the Canadian feminist and politician who had successfully fought to attain full suffrage for women in Quebec. That same year Lefebvre also received the Jeanne Mance Award, the highest honor of the Canadian Nurses Association. In addition, she received an honorary doctorate from the University of Moncton in New Brunswick.

Lefebvre died at the age of 86 in 1993. A Grey Nun for nearly 70 years and a nurse for 61, she devoted her life to God and to advancing nursing education in Canada.

PUBLICATIONS BY SISTER MARIE DENISE LEFEBVRE

Books

(With A. Levasseur, G. Dessureau, & F. Bellemare). (1947). *Le soin des malades: Principes et techniques.* Montreal: Institute Marguerite d'Youville.

Articles

Jeanne Mance. (1942). *Canadian Nurse, 38,* 164–167.
Evaluation of schools of nursing. (1950). *Canadian Nurse, 46,* 278–285.
First National Work Conference on Catholic Nursing Education. (1954). *Canadian Hospital, 31,* 60–104.

BIBLIOGRAPHY

Du Gas, B. W., & Knor, E. R. (1995). *Nursing foundations: A Canadian perspective.* Scarborough, Ontario: Appleton & Lange Canada.
Interesting people. [Sister Marie Denise Lefebvre]. (1946). *Canadian Nurse, 42,* 883.

Sharon C. Murphy

MADELEINE LEININGER
1925–

Madeleine Leininger has been a pioneer and an initiator throughout her career in nursing. She is best known as founder and leader of transcultural nursing and for her work in human care theory and research. Her Theory of Culture Care Diversity and

Universality is the hallmark of her contributions. Her work has included articulation of a theory of transcultural nursing and development of a nursing research method, namely ethnonursing, to support her theory. She has written and taught extensively about qualitative methods of research and has demonstrated the applicability of these methods to nursing. Leininger is a pioneer in research on care and caring and has focused on care as the essence and central domain of nursing.

Madeleine Leininger

Leininger was born the daughter of George and Irene Sheedy Leininger on a farm homestead in Sutton, Nebraska, on July 13, 1925. She grew up in a household that included her own five siblings and, in addition, five boy cousins of whom her parents were guardians. While attending Sutton High School, Leininger worked her way through and took a normal school course which enabled her to teach for a time in a country school. Money from teaching and a scholarship award enabled her to attend Benedictine College (formerly Mt. St. Scholastica College), Atchinson, Kansas for 2 years to take liberal arts courses.

She entered nursing school with her sister at St. Anthony's Hospital in Denver through the Cadet Nurse Corps, and was president of her class. Leininger's first nursing employment was in a general hospital in Denver, where she gained experience in a number of clinical areas and became aware of the importance and power of care. She returned to Benedictine College and completed a science degree in 1950, majoring in biology and with a minor in philosophy and humanistic studies.

Upon completion of her B.S. degree, Leininger worked at St. Joseph's Hospital, Omaha in a variety of roles: medical-surgical staff nurse, instructor, and head nurse. She became the first director of a new psychiatric unit opened in the hospital. During this time she continued advanced education in nursing, nursing administration, and education at Creighton, University, Omaha and finally completed her M.S. in psychiatric nursing at Catholic University of America in 1954.

She then joined the faculty of the School of Nursing at the University of Cincinnati, Ohio, where she was the initiator and director of the nation's first graduate child psychiatric nursing program. In 1960 she published (with Hofling) *Basic Psychiatric Nursing Concepts*, one of the first texts in this field. It was published in 11 languages and used worldwide.

While working with children in a child guidance setting in Cincinnati during the 1950s, Leininger became aware of the lack of staff understanding of cultural factors in children's behavior. She noted that existing psychoanalytic theories and therapy did not address cultural behavior and needs of children raised within different cultures. During this time, Dr. Margaret Mead was Visiting Professor in Anthropology at University of Cincinnati; Leininger discussed her emerging ideas with Mead about the incorporation of cultural values and beliefs into nursing and health care programs and services. Determined to develop her ideas, Leininger enrolled in the University of Washington, Seattle for graduate study in cultural and psychological anthropology, and became the first nurse to complete a Ph.D. in this discipline.

After receiving a Ph.D., Leininger became Professor of Nursing and Anthropology at the University of Colorado. This was the first joint academic appointment in nursing and anthropology, carrying expectations for Leininger to teach and conduct research in both disciplines. Accordingly, she developed and taught courses in both nursing and anthropology and developed the first graduate transcultural nursing course at Colorado. While in Colorado, she initiated and became Director of the first Nurse Scientist Ph.D. program in Nursing in the United States. In 1969 she was appointed Dean and Professor of the School of Nursing and Lecturer in Anthropology at the University of Washington (Seattle). She took the leadership to establish the first academic nursing departments in five areas. She gave support to establish master's courses and a doctoral program in nursing. Under her leadership, and with active support from a cadre of Ph.D. nurse faculty, the Research Facilitation Office was instituted, one of the first in the United States. While at the University of Washington, she was instrumental in bringing the School into first position as an outstanding public nursing educational institution. During this time, she wrote *Nursing and Anthropology: Two Worlds to Blend* (1970), the first book to support the transcultural nursing field.

From 1974 to 1981 Leininger was Dean and Professor of Nursing at the University of Utah. At this institution, she initiated master's courses and a Ph.D. program in transcultural nursing. Again she initiated a Research Facilitation Office and, with the faculty, reorganized the College into new areas of study, research, and clinical practices. During this time she further refined her thoughts about transcultural nursing and care phenomena and published the first text for the field, *Transcultural Nursing: Concepts, Theories and Practices,* in 1978.

Early in 1981, Leininger was chosen as Distinguished Nurse Scholar at Troy State University, Troy, Alabama. While there she gave campus and community lectures and did a major research investigation on two Southern villages. From late 1982 until the present (1998), Leininger has been associated with Wayne State University, Detroit, Michigan as Professor of Nursing and Adjunct Professor of Anthropology, Director of Transcultural Nursing; currently she is Professor Emeritus. At Wayne State University she actively and creatively developed a master's degree program in transcultural nursing and human caring, and also seminars for Ph.D. students in the College.

In her career of 48 years in higher education, she has guided 52 students with their Ph.D. dissertations, and 45 master's-bound students. A dynamic speaker, she has been frequently sought as a public speaker in different disciplines. She has given over 700 public addresses and many workshops and conferences worldwide. Presently she is semi-retired in Omaha, Nebraska, remaining active in research, teaching and consultation.

Leininger spearheaded the foundation of the *Journal of Transcultural Nursing* and in 1989 became its first editor. She continues to be active in publishing. She launched the "Human Health and Care Series" published by the Wayne State University Press in the early 1970s. She has authored or edited more than 27 books, has published approximately 200 articles, and 45 book chapters. Leininger has been a peer reviewer for several national and international publications and remains an active consultant to several nursing schools in the Caribbean, Europe, Africa, Australia, Japan, Scandinavia, and Russia.

Throughout her career, Leininger has been an involved leader with many professional organizational activities in nursing and anthropology. Among them is a term as full-time President of the American Association of Colleges of Nursing. Leininger was founder and first President of the Transcultural Nursing Society in 1974. She established the National Research Caring conference in 1978, which later became the International Association of Human Caring. She also initiated the Committee on Nursing and Anthropology in 1968 with the American Anthropological Association, and has served as a member of the Commission on Nursing Education for the American Nurses Association.

Some of Leininger's awards include an honorary Doctor of Science (D.S.) degree from Indiana State University and a Ph.D. from the University of Kuopio, Finland, which was the first honorary doctorate for a nurse and anthropologist. She also holds the honorary degree of Doctor of Human Letters (L.H.D.) from Scholastica College, Atchinson, Kansas. She was the first nurse and health professional to receive the Trotter Distinguished Lecturer Award from the University of Texas Health Center (Houston). Wayne State University also has honored her with several awards.

Leininger's unique contributions to nursing have been many; however, she is known worldwide for establishing and maintaining transcultural nursing, developing the Theory of Culture Care, promoting the use of qualitative research methods (including development of the ethnonursing method) and speaking to the future of nursing. Through her teaching, writing, and speaking career, she has influenced many nurses and health professionals to value and to seek ways to provide culturally congruent and safe care to people in our multicultural world.

PUBLICATIONS BY MADELEINE LEININGER (SELECTED)

Books

Leininger, M. (1970). *Nursing and anthropology: Two worlds to blend.* New York: John Wiley and Sons.

Leininger, M. (Ed.). (1974). *Health care dimensions* (3 volumes). Philadelphia: F. A. Davis.

Leininger, M. (1978). *Transcultural nursing: Concepts, theories and practices.* New York: John Wiley & Sons. (2nd ed. published 1995 by McGraw-Hill).

Leininger, M. (1984). *Care: The essence of nursing and health.* Thorofare, NJ: Charles B. Slack.

Leininger, M. (1985). *Qualitative research methods in nursing.* New York: Grune & Stratton.

Leininger, M. M. (Ed.). (1991). *Culture, care, diversity, and universality* (Pub. No. 15-2402). New York: National League for Nursing.

Leininger, M. (1995). *Transcultural nursing: Concepts, theories, research and practices* (2nd Ed.) New York: McGraw-Hill.

Articles

Leininger, M. (1972). Two strange health tribes: Gnisrun and Enicidem. *Human Organization, 35,* 253–261.

Leininger, M. (1984). Transcultural nursing: An essential knowledge and practice field for today. *Canadian Nurse, 80*(11), 41–45.

Leininger, M. (1991a). Becoming aware of types of health practitioners and cultural imposition. *Journal of Transcultural Nursing, 2*(2), 32–39.

Leininger, M. (1991b). Leininger's acculturation health care assessment tool for cultural patterns in traditional and non-traditional lifeways. *Journal of Transcultural Nursing, 2*(2), 40–42.

Leininger, M. (1994). The tribes of nursing in the USA culture of nursing. *Journal of Transcultural Nursing, 6*(1), 18–22.

Leininger, M. (1996a). Culture care theory, research and practice. *Nursing Science Quarterly, 9*(2), 71–78.

Leininger, M. (1996b). Transcultural nursing: Meaning, relevance and concerns in a world without boundaries. *Asian Journal of Nursing Science, 2*(4) 26–34.

Leininger, M. (1997a). Ethnonursing research method: Essential to discover and advance Asian nursing knowledge. *Japanese Journal of Nursing Research, 8*(2), 20–32.

Leininger, M. (1997b). Future directions in transcultural nursing in the 21st century. *International Nursing Review, 44*(1), 12–23.

Leininger, M. (1997c). Overview of the theory of culture care with the ethnonursing research method. *Journal of Transcultural Nursing, 8*(2), 32–52.

Leininger, M. (1997d). Quality of life from a transcultural nursing perspective. *Nursing Science Quarterly, 9*(2), 71–78.

Leininger, M. (1997e). Transcultural nursing research to transform nursing education and practice. *Image: Journal of Nursing Scholarship, 29*(4), 341–347.

Leininger, M. (1997f). Transcultural nursing: Scientific and humanistic care discipline. *Journal of Transcultural Nursing, 8*(2), 54–55.

BIBLIOGRAPHY

Alexander, J. E., Beagle, C. J., Butler, P., Dougherty, D. A., Andrews Robards, K. D., Solotkin, K.C., & Velotta, C. (1994). In A. Marriner-Tomey (Ed.), *Nursing theorists and their work* (3rd ed.) (pp. 423–444). St. Louis: Mosby.

Leininger, M. (1978). *Transcultural nursing: Concepts, theories and practices.* New York: John Wiley & Sons. Second edition (1995) published by McGraw-Hill.

Leininger, M. (1997). Transcultural nursing research to transform nursing education and practice: 40 years. *Image: Journal of Nursing Scholarship, 29,* 341–345.

Leininger, M. (1997, January 14). Personal communication (telephone).

Madeleine Leininger. *Who's who in America* (1994). Madeline Leininger. (p. 2050). New Providence, NJ: Marquis.

Leininger, M. [Curriculum vitae, 1990, 1997]

Marian Brook

AMELIA LEINO
1912–1985

Wyoming is known for having the first woman governor and for being the first state to allow women to vote. It is characteristic then, that Wyoming would have a baccalaureate degree program for nurses when they were just becoming in vogue. Amelia Leino was asked to establish a program at the University of Wyoming in 1951. This was, and still is, the first and only nursing program in a university in Wyoming. Leino planned the program, selected the first faculty members, administered and taught in the program until 1968.

Amelia Leino

The youngest of the three daughters of Hilma Leino, Amelia was born on September 18, 1912, in Three Town, Wyoming, a town named for a coal mine. John and Hilma Leino emigrated from Finland, met, and married in Dietz, Wyoming, then moved to Hanna.

In 1914, the family moved to Finland, their native country, believing that running their own business would be better than working for the coal mines. However, with the breaking out of World War I in Europe, they quickly realized that citizenship papers for America were a prized possession, and the family returned to Dietz within the year. Leino's mother did not speak English, so her daughters learned from their teachers at school. There were many nationalities in Hanna, as the mines attracted hard-working people. The Finns tended to stay together, following the culture they knew from the old country.

The family moved to West Frankfort, Illinois, where Leino started school. After Hilma Leino died in 1920, the family shared their home with two families from Finland. Once those families returned to Hanna, the Leino family decided to try it on their own. When the Depression hit, John Leino bought a Ford, drove it to Chicago and met the girls, who had traveled by train. They then drove to Detroit, where Mr. Leino worked for the Fisher Auto Body Plant. In 1924, the family moved back to Hanna. Leino and her sister Meimi went to school while their oldest sister Saima assumed the role of housekeeper. Amelia, being a tall girl, became quite a basketball player, won a medal, and was selected to play in a tournament in the Midwest.

Upon completion of high school, Leino took a train to Chicago and enrolled in the nursing program at Cook County Hospital. After receiving her diploma in 1934, she became a teacher at Cook County. She taught nursing arts from 1935–1937 and was a clinical instructor from 1937–1940. Her next teaching job was in Portland, Oregon. When the war broke out in 1942, Leino went back to Cook County Medical Hospital and joined Group 209, a unit of the U.S. Army Nurse Corps. When VE day arrived, Leino was a major. At this point, she recognized the need for more education, so started school at the University of Washington. After one semester, she moved to New York and completed her bachelor's and master's degrees at Columbia University, Teachers College. A Mrs. Newman, head of the department of nursing at Columbia, told Leino that she had received a notice that the University of Wyoming was looking for a Dean of the School of Nursing. Amelia applied, interviewed, and was hired in 1951 as the Director of the Division of Nursing. In 1957, she became the first woman dean at the University of Wyoming. At the time of her retirement from the Reserve Officers Association, she was a Lieutenant Colonel. She returned to Columbia to complete her Doctorate of Education, her degree being awarded August 25, 1955.

Through her involvement in national organizations, Amelia had an influence on the development of education throughout the country. Graduates of her programs received excellent scores on the national licensing exams. At one point, the scores of the University of Wyoming graduates were the highest in the nation.

Leino was a member of the American Association of University Professors, American Association of University Women, American Nurses Association, National League for Nursing, Pi Lambda Theta, Kappa Delta Pi, Chi Gamma Iota (Honorary Educational Societies), and Gamma Phi Beta sorority. She was a frequently sought speaker in Wyoming and Colorado, served as an officer in many organizations, and initiated the formation of Alpha Pi Chapter of Sigma Theta Tau in 1966. She was listed in *Who's Who in America, Who's Who in the West* and *Who's Who of American Women*. She was one of the first six nurses designated as Western Council of Higher Education in Nursing emeriti.

Dr. Amelia Leino died April 14, 1985 at Ivinson Memorial Hospital in Laramie, Wyoming. She is buried in Cheyenne, Wyoming.

PUBLICATIONS BY AMELIA LEINO

Leino, A. (1951). Team organization of nursing service personnel. *American Journal of Nursing, 51,* 665–667.

Leino, A. (1952a). A new basic program. *American Journal of Nursing, 52,* 834–835.
Leino, A. (1952b). Planning patient-centered care. *American Journal of Nursing, 52,* 324–325.
Leino, A. (1956). University of Wyoming program. In *The yearbook of modern nursing.* New York: G. P. Putnam's Sons.

BIBLIOGRAPHY

Watts, P. (1985). *The Finn's daughter: An oral history prepared for women's studies.* Unpublished manuscript, The University of Wyoming.

Marcia L. Dale

MYRA ESTRIN LEVINE
1920–1996

Myra Estrin Levine was best known as an innovative teacher, an ethicist, an intellectual, and creator of the four "Conservation Principles." She was born in Chicago, on December 12, 1920, the daughter of Julius Jay and Celia Bluma Estrin. Levine was the surviving child of a pair of twin girls; there was a younger boy and a younger girl in the family. Mr. Estrin was the owner of a hardware store, but the family often struggled financially because of his ill health.

As a girl, Levine experienced anti-Semitism from her schoolmates and was aware of the subtle and not-so-subtle anti-Semitic messages from the community at large. In spite of this, Myra excelled at a high school which offered an intellectually stimulating atmosphere, placing fifth in a class of 700 students. She also enjoyed sports and music activities. Just before her high school graduation, Levine had an emergency appendectomy, and became aware of the world of nursing through the student nurses she encountered.

In 1938, she entered the University of Chicago on a scholarship provided by a women's group, but was only able to stay for 2 years because of financial problems. In 1940 she entered Cook County Hospital School of Nursing, her second choice, because her first choice school had filled its quota of Jewish students. Her nursing course was completed in 1944, the same year she married Edwin Burton Levine, a classics scholar then serving in the Army.

The next several years offered work experiences in Minneapolis and Chicago, as her husband completed his education following his discharge. During their time in Chicago, Levine herself completed her Bachelor of Science degree at the University of Chicago (in 1949) while beginning her own teaching career at Cook County Hospital School of Nursing. Here she introduced a course called "Physical Sciences for Nurses," establishing a pattern of innovation and revision "to make a course better by allowing it to grow and change each time it was taught" (Schorr & Zimmerman, 1988, p. 224). Completion of the degree brought an offer of a better-paying job as Director of the Drexel Home, a geriatric facility in Chicago. Here she found opportunities to be a pioneer in care of the aged, staffing the facility with registered nurses and licensed practical nurses and instituting practices that were a model for care of the aged for the next generation. The experience clarified for her that her real love was for teaching rather than administration.

Levine's husband began his teaching career as a lecturer in Lincoln, Nebraska in 1951. There, their first child, a son, was born and died at 3 days of age. The couple returned to Chicago at the end of the academic year where their second son, Bill, was born in 1952, and her husband completed his Ph.D. in 1953. Their next move was to Detroit, where his next academic appointment was at Wayne State University. Daughter Patricia was born and Levine was content as a homemaker. However, in order to fill the financial gap that occurred during the summers with her husband's academic position, she returned to nursing as a clinical instructor in the summer at Henry Ford Hospital, continuing during the academic year as a part-time supervisor. She continued this pattern for 7 years and at the same time earned a Master of Science in Nursing at Wayne State.

In 1962, her husband returned to the University of Chicago where he would stay, as lecturer, professor, chair of the Department of Classics, and, finally, Professor Emeritus until his death in 1997. Levine was appointed at the University of Illinois College of Nursing to create a Fundamentals of Nursing course and from there moved back to Cook County Hospital School of Nursing as coordinator of clinical nursing. From 1963 until 1967 she worked with the faculty at Cook County Hospital to produce a new curriculum for nursing education, adding much new material based on research in nursing and other sciences, particularly in the concepts of stress of Hans Selye. The syllabus become *An Introduction to Clinical Nursing Practice* published in 1969 with a revised second edition in 1973. The American Journal of Nursing named it "Book of the Year" in both years.

Loyola University offered her a position as Assistant Professor of Nursing in 1967, teaching in their master's program. She left Loyola, an Associate Professor, in 1973 in order to accept an invitation to teach for a year at Tel Aviv University in Israel. This experience, and subsequent visits to Israel, helped the Levines to rediscover and affirm their Jewish heritage.

Upon her return to the United States, Levine acted as a consultant to the Evanston Hospital Department of Continuing Education for 2 years. She then was associated with Rush University as Associate Professor and coordinator of the graduate program in oncology until 1977, when she became Associate Professor of Nursing at the University of Illinois, Chicago. She remained there as Professor of Nursing and Adjunct Professor of Humanistic Studies until her retirement as Professor Emerita in 1987. Myra Levine was awarded an honorary doctorate (LHD) by Loyola University in 1992.

Throughout her career, Levine was an activist for nurses and for human justice. She was a negotiator in contract talks between nurses and Cook County in 1966. She was instrumental in the admission of the first African-American student to Cook County School of Nursing and was the innovator of the Tutorial and Cultural Program for underprivileged students there. From 1974–1979 she served as a member of the advisory board for the American Nurses Association Minority Ethnic Fellowship Program. She was an invited participant at the Third Annual Joseph P. Kennedy, Jr. Foundation Intensive Workshop on Medical Bioethics in 1976 and spoke and wrote frequently about ethical issues in nursing and nursing care.

Levine is known as a nurse theorist for her "Conservation Principles of Nursing," first discussed comprehensively in *An Introduction to Clinical Nursing* although she had been developing the model in previous articles. The model evolved from her own thinking as she sought a structure for teaching nursing students at the University of Illinois. Levine conceptualized the four conservation principles as a way to organize nursing knowledge in order to teach science principles upon which to base professional decision making and intervention. She wrote in 1988, "I never dreamed that others would see in it a new nursing theory. I was certain it would educate good nurses. That is all I ever wanted to do" (Schorr & Zimmerman, 1988, p. 227).

Levine began her scholarly activities as author and principal investigator of a surgical dressings project at the University of Chicago in 1952–1953. In 1966 she contributed to nursing the concept of "trophicognosis," a term she coined to replace "diagnosis," which she felt to be incorrect and legally unsound when applied to nursing. She defined trophicognosis as "a nursing care judgment arrived at by the scientific method" (Levine, 1991, p. 24).

Subsequent contributions included her textbook, numerous articles about the Conservation Principles, nursing education and ethics and several chapters in books. For more than 40 years she wrote for practicing nurses, for educators, and for nurse scholars and students at all levels. A much-sought-after speaker, Levine originated and presented workshops or seminars on clinical subjects for nursing faculty and practicing nurses from the beginning of her career until 1994.

Myra Levine was an active member of the Illinois Nurses Association throughout her career. She served as a Board member, Chairman of various committees and delegate to INA conventions. She served on the American Nurses' Association Committee on Ethical, Legal and Professional Standards from 1966–1968, participating in the revision of the Code for Nurses. She was ANA representative to joint committees and conferences on health care and population issues. In addition, she served as Chairman of the Council for Baccalaureate and Higher Degree Programs of the Illinois League for Nursing from 1970 to 1972.

Levine died in Chicago on March 20, 1996. A gifted intellectual and humanist, she influenced countless students with her scholarly, innovative teaching, urging them and inspiring them to use research and scientific principles to provide nursing care that would protect the wholeness of patients. A strong participant in nursing organizations, Levine modeled collective action to strengthen the profession. She provided for the nursing profession not only a model for organizing nursing knowledge, but also a model for intellectual, ethical, and spiritual life and growth.

PUBLICATIONS BY MYRA ESTRIN LEVINE (SELECTED)

Books

Levine, M. E. (1969a). *Instructor's guide to introduction to clinical nursing.* Philadelphia: F. A. Davis.

Levine, M. E. (1969b). *Introduction to clinical nursing.* Philadelphia: F. A. Davis.

Levine, M. E. (1973a). *Instructor's guide to introduction to clinical nursing* (2nd ed.). Philadelphia: F. A. Davis.

Levine, M. E. (1973b). *Introduction to clinical nursing* (2nd ed.). Philadelphia: F. A. Davis.

Book Chapters

Levine, M. E. (1989). The conservation principles: Twenty years later. In J. Riehl-Sisca (Ed.), *Conceptual models for nursing* (3rd ed.). Norwalk, CT: Appleton & Lange.

Levine, M. E. (1991). The conservation principles: A model for health. In K. M. Schaefer & J. B. Pond (Eds.), *Levine's conservation model: A framework for nursing practice* (pp. 1–11). Philadelphia: F. A. Davis.

Articles

Levine, M. E. (1966a). Adaptation and assessment: A rationale for nursing intervention. *American Journal of Nursing, 66,* 2450–2453.

Levine, M. E. (1966b). Trophicognosis: An alternative to nursing diagnosis. In *American Nurses' Association Regional Clinical Conference* (Vol. 2, pp. 55–70). New York: American Nurses' Association.

Levine, M. E. (1967). The four conservation principles of nursing. *Nursing Forum, 6,* 45–69.

Levine, M. E. (1969). The pursuit of wholeness. *American Journal of Nursing, 69,* 93–98.

Levine, M. E. (1973). On creativity in nursing. *Image, 5*(3), 15–19. (Reprinted in 10th anniversary collection, *The best of Image* (1983) and in *Classic Image* (1997) (*Image, 29*(3), 216–217.)

Levine, M. E. (1988a). Antecedents from adjunctive disciplines: Creation of nursing theory. *Nursing Science Quarterly, 4,* 16–21.

Levine, M. E. (1988b). Review of Parse's nursing science: Major paradigms, theories and critiques. *Nursing Science Quarterly, 4,* 184–185.

Levine, M. E. (1995). The rhetoric of nursing theory. *Image: The Journal of Nursing Scholarship, 27,* 11–14.

BIBLIOGRAPHY

Arlique, G. S., Foli, K. J., Johnson, T., Marriner-Tomey, A., Poat, M. C., Poppa, L., Woeste, R., &

Soretich, S. T. (1994). Myra Estrin Levine: Four conservation principles. In A. Marriner-Tomey (Ed.), *Nursing theorists and their work* (3rd ed.) (pp. 199–210). St. Louis: Mosby.

Edwin Burton Levine. (1997). *Who's who in America* (51st ed., vol. 2) (p. 2545). New Providence, NJ: Marquis.

Fawcett, J. (1991). Analysis and evaluation of Levine's Conservation Model. In K. M. Schaefer & J. B. Pond (Eds.), *Levine's conservation model: A framework for nursing practice* (pp. 13–43). Philadelphia: F. A. Davis.

Levine, M. E. (1991). The conservation principles: A model for health. In K. M. Schaefer & J. B. Pond (Eds.), *Levine's conservation model: A framework for nursing practice* (pp. 1–11). Philadelphia: F. A. Davis.

Levine, M. E. (1995). Curriculum vitae. Unpublished.

Levine, M. E. (1996–1997). *Who's who in American nursing* (p. 372). New Providence, NJ: Marquis.

Levine, Patricia. Personal Interview. July 1997. Unpublished.

Schaefer, K. M., & Fawcett, J. (1991). *Levine's conservation model: A framework for nursing practice.* Philadelphia: F. A. Davis.

Schorr, T. M., & Zimmerman, A. (1988). *Making choices, taking chances: Nurse leaders tell their stories.* St. Louis: Mosby.

Stafford, M. (1996, May/June). In tribute to Myra Estrin Levine, Professor Emerita, MSN, RN, FAAN. *Chart,* 5–6.

Marian J. Brook

MARION LINDEBURGH
1887–1955

Marion Lindeburgh was a vital force in raising the standards of nursing education and service in Canada during the 1930's and 40's. A renowned leader, her 30-year career spanned two world wars. She served as President of the Canadian Nurses Association and for over a decade was Director of the McGill School for Graduate Nurses in Montreal. A strong proponent of quality nursing and patient-centered care, she devoted her adult life to advancing the art and science of nursing in Canada.

Marion Lindeburgh

Lindeburgh was born in Kutawa, Saskatchewan in 1887. Five years earlier, her father had opened a telegraph office in this isolated spot, then part of the Northwest Territories. Alfred von Lindeburgh was American-born of Swedish parents. He married an Irish woman, Margaret Ligget, and together they had five children. The family lived in the homestead built by Lindeburgh's father in a community that had an Anglican church but no school. Lindeburgh and her siblings were privately tutored until 1899, when a one-room school was built on the family property. There they received their high school education. At age 16, Lindeburgh enrolled in the Regina Normal School and obtained her teaching certificate. For the next 12 years, from 1904 until 1916, she taught in rural and urban Saskatchewan schools. From this, she obtained a depth of teaching experience that

would serve her extremely well in her second career.

Lindeburgh decided to enter nursing in her late 20s. She enrolled in St. Luke's Hospital School of Nursing in New York City in 1916, in the midst of World War I. After graduating in 1919, she spent the next 3 years at St. Luke's. Positions held included head nurse of the medical and surgical wards, clinical supervisor, and for 2 1/2 years, night superintendent. In 1922, Lindeburgh returned to Saskatchewan. For the next 7 years she pioneered the field of school health and was Director of the Health Education Department in the Provincial Normal School in Regina. One summer she conducted a survey of health conditions in the remote northern part of Saskatchewan, hiking and traveling by canoe with a guide as her only companion. This outdoor experience matched her interests.

In 1929 she was recruited to join the nursing faculty at McGill University as Assistant Director to Miss Bertha Harmer, its Director. A year earlier, Harmer had succeeded Flora Madeline Shaw, first Director of the school. The school had opened in 1920 to educate nurses in public health as well as management and teaching in schools of nursing and hospital administration. Lindeburgh's association with the school was to extend for over two decades. Lindeburgh served as Acting Director at McGill after Harmer's death in 1934 and in 1939, as the university recovered from the economic effects of the depression, Lindeburgh was appointed Director and Associate Professor of the School.

Lindeburgh was in great demand as an instructor of refresher courses given by provincial associations across Canada. Despite this and her strenuous schedule at McGill, Lindeburgh still managed to take courses herself, primarily during the summers. She obtained her Bachelor of Science degree from Teachers College, Columbia University in 1936, followed by her Master of Arts degree, also from Columbia, in 1940.

Lindeburgh was active in professional nursing organizations. She convened the Public Health Section of the Saskatchewan Registered Nurses Association for 7 years. Following the publication in 1932 of the *Weir Report*, a survey of nursing education in Canada, Lindeburgh was appointed Chair of the Standing Committee on Curriculum of the Canadian Nurses Association. Due in large part to her efforts over the next 8 years, the Committee produced two significant and long-lasting contributions. The *Proposed Curriculum for Schools of Nursing in Canada* was published by the Canadian Nurses Association in 1936. The committee included representatives of all of the provinces and each field of nursing service and marked a turning point in educational planning. This provided the framework for the creation of the permanent Committee on Nursing Education that replaced the original Curriculum Committee. As first Chair of the Committee on Nursing Education, Lindeburgh strengthened this earlier work on the undergraduate curriculum by the publication of a supplement, *The Improvement of Nursing Education in the Clinical Field*, published in 1940.

Lindeburgh was President of the Canadian Nurses Association in 1942 after serving as second vice-president from 1938 to 1940, and first vice-president from 1940 to 1942. Lindeburgh was a contributing member of the International Committee on Nursing Education. She represented Canadian nurses at meetings of the American Nurses Association, the National League of Nursing Education, and the International Council of Nurses. In addition, she authored numerous columns and journal articles in professional nursing publications.

In 1943, Lindeburgh was made an Officer of the Order of the British Empire by the King's Honor List, a tribute to her outstanding professional contributions. In 1944, she received one of the Canadian Nurses Association's highest awards, the Mary Agnes Snively Memorial Medal. In recognition of her lifetime achievements, the University of British Columbia conferred upon her the degree of Doctor of Science (honoris causa) in May of 1950. In May 1953, she was appointed Professor Emeritus in Nursing at McGill.

Although physical health problems began to surface in 1939, with surgery in 1940 and the diagnosis of a diabetic condition at age 53, Lindeburgh remained vital and active. However, in 1946 she experienced a series of illnesses resulting in a noticeable decline in her health. She was forced to cut short an extended and successful Canadian tour in 1950 undertaken to solicit alumni donations for the Flora Madeline Shaw Memorial Fund. In August 1950 she suffered a heart attack at age 63. Lindeburgh officially retired from the McGill School for Graduate Nurses in August 1951 due to continuing poor health. She left Montreal to make her home in Victoria, British Columbia the following year.

Lindeburgh died in her sleep in Victoria on March 19, 1955. She was noted for her enthusiasm, warm personality, and kind and generous nature. After her death, the Alumnae Association of the McGill School for Graduate Nurses initiated the annual Dr. Marion Lindeburgh Memorial Scholarship. In her will, Lindeburgh left $1000.00 to the Flora Madeline Shaw Memorial Fund. Although she didn't live to see it, the successful culmination of the fund and endowment to McGill resulted in the establishment of the Flora Madeline Shaw Chair of Nursing in 1957.

PUBLICATIONS BY MARION LINDEBURGH (SELECTED)

Teaching of Health in High Schools. (1929). *Canadian Public Health Journal, 20*, 294–298.

The educational objective of public health nursing. (1934). *Canadian Public Health Journal, 25,* 443–447.

Nursing yesterday and today. (1935). *Canadian Hospital, 12,* 7–9.

Curriculum study [Progress reports]. *Canadian Nurse, 30* (February 1934): 63; (October 1934): 476–9; (December 1934): 564–5; 31 (March 1935): 115–6; (June 1935): 259–60; 32 (September 1936): 405–08.

Canadian Nurses Association. (1936). *Nursing Education Section: A Proposed Curriculum for Schools of Nursing in Canada.* Montreal: Canadian Nurses Association; and Supplement, *The Improvement of Nursing Education in the Clinical Field,* 1940. [Lindeburgh chaired the committees that produced these documents.]

The school for Graduate Nurses, McGill University. (1939). *Canadian Nurse, 35,* 85–86.

The role of the student nurse. (1940). *Hospitals, 14,* 128–131.

The fundamentals of professional leadership. (1942). *Canadian Nurse, 38,* 375–382.

A friendly hearing. [Report to Special Committee on Social Security, House of Commons]. (1943). *Canadian Nurse, 39,* 387–391.

BIBLIOGRAPHY

Beamish, R. (1970). *Fifty years a Canadian nurse: Devotion, opportunities and duty.* New York: Vantage Press.

Chittick, R. (1944). Marion Lindeburgh, O.B.E. *Canadian Nurse, 40,* 388–389.

Mathewson, M. S. (1942). Marion Lindeburgh: The New President of the C.N.A. *Canadian Nurse, 38,* 540–542.

Obituary. (1955). *Canadian Nurse, 51,* 376–377.

Tunis, B. L. (1966). *In caps and gowns: The story of the School for Graduate Nurses, McGill University, 1920–1964.* Montreal: McGill University Press.

Sharon Murphy

EVELYN C. LUNDEEN
1900–1963

Evelyn Lundeen was the first supervisor of the largest, if not the first, premature infant station in the United States. For 38 years, Lundeen ran the Hortense Schoen Joseph Premature Station housed in Sarah Morris Children's Hospital, the pediatric department of Chicago's Michael Reese Hospital. The methods she devised to keep premature babies alive eventually became standard medical practice nationwide. Regional supervisors for the United States Children's Bureau and nurses from around the country routinely attended her 3-week training seminars for the care and maintenance of premature babies. Lundeen's approach to premature infant care was so successful that it was instrumental in changing the medical prognosis for premature babies from invariably hopeless causes and a waste of precious medical resources to infants with the same potential for healthy minds and bodies as full-term infants.

Evelyn C. Lundeen

Born in Rockford, Illinois on February 15, 1900, of Scandinavian parents, Lundeen grew up in a home characterized by order, cleanliness, and discipline. It is likely no coincidence that these attributes eventually became her trademark as a nurse. Lundeen's mother died when Lundeen was three. Consequently, she and her sister lived in California for the next several years with their grandparents. When their father remarried, the sisters returned to their father's new home in Rock Island, Illinois.

Lundeen graduated from Augustana College in Rock Island before entering the School of Nursing at Lutheran Hospital in Moline, Illinois. After her graduation from nursing school in 1922 she worked at Lutheran Hospital. Her supervisors declared her performance outstanding and she came to the attention of Julius Hess, a prominent Chicago pediatrician later known as the father of neonatal medicine. Hess was the first medical director of the Premature Station at Sarah Morris. He established the station in 1922 after Hortense Schoen Joseph—a wealthy, young society matron and founder of the Chicago Infant's Aid Society—died suddenly and left a bequest of more than $65,000 to build the facility. By 1924 Hess had outfitted the Station with eight heated beds, a heated table, and three wet nurses who guaranteed that premature infants would have a steady supply of human milk. That year he hired Lundeen to run the Station.

In 1924 many women and doctors in Chicago still favored home birth, so there was a desperate need for hospitals willing to care for premature babies born at home. Sarah Morris was the first hospital in the city to accept premature infants who were either born at home or born at another hospital unable to cope with their special needs. In 1930, Cook County Hospital, the city's publicly funded hospital, opened a facility modeled on the Premature Station at Sarah Morris in order to augment Lundeen's work.

In 1935—as part of an effort to lower the city's infant mortality rate and to take advantage of the unique facilities for premature infants available at Sarah Morris

and Cook County—the Chicago Board of Health instituted the City-Wide Plan for the Care of Premature Babies, which required that all premature births be reported to the Board of Health within 1 hour. As part of the Plan, the city acquired its own Hess ambulance (specially heated ones) and Board of Health public health nurses proceeded to aid Lundeen and her nursing staff in conveying premature babies to either Sarah Morris or Cook County.

In caring for premature babies, Lundeen in her books and articles placed fanatic emphasis on aseptic practices. A sterile environment, scrubbing hands and arms up to the elbow before handling each infant in turn, isolation of sick infants, separation of diapering and feeding areas, and the more elusive qualities of enthusiasm, conscientiousness, constant vigilance, and "an understanding of the fact that care of premature infants always constitutes an emergency" were mainstays of her method. She continually explained that "the most minute detail" of premature nursing care was important, and told all the nurses that she trained that they alone were responsible for preventing infection in the nursery. Preventing an infection, Lundeen argued, was a far greater victory than curing one.

At least as important as a sterile environment, Lundeen contended, were the questions of how, what, and how much to feed a premature baby. Because most premature infants were too weak to swallow, let alone suck, she avoided feeding them immediately after birth in order to prevent aspiration pneumonia. Instead, to prevent dehydration, she injected a salt solution into babies' thighs for the first 12 to 48 hours after birth. When babies were a bit stronger, if they were still too weak to suck, Lundeen laboriously fed them human milk with a dropper. She fed the weakest infants by gavage. She also kept these infants' caloric intake down because she found that reducing the amount of food presumed adequate for a newborn decreased the chance of a premature baby having diarrhea.

Lundeen considered breast milk vital to these infants' survival. Thus, all babies cared for at the Premature Station consumed only human milk until they weighed 4 to 4 1/2 pounds. Lundeen found that wholly breastfed infants could be released from the hospital much sooner than the babies fed artificially after they gained sufficient weight. If a mother did not supply her baby with breast milk or did not supply enough milk—and 40 to 50 percent of mothers did not—Sarah Morris's resident wet nurses furnished it for as long as Lundeen deemed necessary. After the Chicago Board of Health opened its Mothers' Breast Milk Station in 1938 to supply pasteurized human milk in bottles to the city's sick and premature infants, Lundeen came to depend on the Breast Milk Station for human milk as well. She preferred, however, that mothers supply their own milk. She taught and encouraged them to express their milk manually four or five times each day and to deliver their cache once daily to the Premature Station. When a baby was strong enough, Lundeen urged a mother who had persisted in supplying her own milk to come to the station and breastfeed her infant directly. In encouraging mothers to pump and eventually breastfeed, Lundeen not only helped women maintain their milk supply while they were separated from their babies, she also learned who failed to do so. Cognizant of the mothers who were no longer lactating, she could provide babies who needed it with an adequate formula before their release.

Lundeen's efforts decreased the mortality rate of premature infants at Sarah Morris dramatically, from 60 percent in 1925 to 24.1 percent in 1928. She nonetheless remained dissatisfied. Babies discharged in good condition from the Station often deteriorated rapidly at home, and had to be readmitted to the hospital within a week or two. Lundeen attributed these chronic relapses to poverty. Because most of the babies cared for at the Station came from destitute homes, Lundeen argued in her writing that "naturally the home environment was not inducive [sic] to the welfare of the premature infant." To rectify the problem, Lundeen hired a nurse in 1930 to help mothers ready their homes for their babies' arrival, to assist mothers in maintaining their breast milk, to accompany infants home when they were ready for discharge, and to continue to visit infants' homes at regular intervals to monitor parents' infant care practices. The number of readmissions to the Station dropped dramatically.

Lundeen's myriad efforts bucked prevailing trends. When she began her work with premature infants in 1924, doctors intensely debated whether or not premature babies were worth saving. In an era when eugenics was a fashionable notion, physicians and assorted social critics voiced concern that premature infants were unlikely to ever become useful citizens. To counteract the worry, Lundeen conducted a study of 250 premature babies born between 1928 and 1933 which demonstrated that premature babies who had not suffered brain damage at birth eventually developed comparably to full-term infants. She also collaborated with Hess on a study of anemia in premature infants and devised a better way to regulate the flow of oxygen into incubators.

In 1933, the Sarah Morris Premature Station closed temporarily and moved its personnel and babies to the Incubator Building at Chicago's Century of Progress World's Fair. There the public paid 25 cents to gawk at the tiny infants lying in incubators. The Infant Incubator Company and the Infant's Aid Society split the proceeds.

Julius Hess attributed the country's increased interest in bettering the care of premature infants to the exhibit at the Fair. Lundeen was less enthusiastic. Although the mortality of babies on display at the Fair was only 18.3 percent, Lundeen was relieved when the Fair ended and she could return to Sarah Morris where she was able "to care for the babies in a more normal manner." In 1937, due to increased demand, Sarah Morris expanded its Premature Station to accommodate 22 babies.

In 1954, Michael Reese Hospital drastically enlarged and redesigned the Hortense Schoen Joseph Premature Station according to Lundeen's specifications. The new unit contained Lundeen's personal laboratory where she tailored infant formulas to a baby's needs, an admitting room, a scrub room, a large room to house the weakest babies, a smaller room for older babies weighing more than 1,800 grams, an isolation room for sick babies, a nurses' station with a view of all three nurseries, private rooms where mothers could breastfeed, a storage room, a utility room, and a nurses' lounge.

During Lundeen's tenure, the Premature Station at Sarah Morris was the almost exclusive domain of nurses. Because premature infants required such constant and labor-intensive care, neonatal nursing, as devised by Lundeen, became one of the rare places in a hospital where all medical personnel deemed nurses at least as important as doctors, if not more so. Lundeen herself ran the Hortense Schoen Joseph Premature Station with singular authority.

Lundeen never married. She was the recipient of the Illinois State Nurses' Association Nurse of the Year Award in 1958. She retired from her position as supervising nurse at the Hortense Schoen Joseph Premature Station in 1962. She died of a chronic heart ailment in the Michael Reese Hospital Nursing Home on January 29, 1963.

PUBLICATIONS BY EVELYN C. LUNDEEN

Books

Hess, J. H., & Lundeen, E. C. (1958). *The premature infant: Medical and nursing care.* Philadelphia: J. B. Lippincott Company.

Lundeen, E. C., & Kunstadter, R. H. (1958). *Care of the premature infant.* Philadelphia: J. B. Lippincott Company.

Articles

History of the Hortense Schoen Joseph Premature Station. (1937). *The Voice of the Clinic, 2,* 8–11.

Feeding the premature baby. (1939). *American Journal of Nursing, 39,* 596–604.

Safe hospital care of the premature baby. (1940). *Hospitals, 14,* 110–115.

Prematures present special problems: Basic factors in nursing care. (1954). *The Modern Hospital, 82,* 60–65.

Newer trends in the care of premature infants. (1959). *Nursing World, 133,* 9–11.

BIBLIOGRAPHY

Baker, J. P. (1996). *The machine in the nursery: Incubator technology and the origins of newborn intensive care.* Baltimore: The Johns Hopkins University Press.

Evelyn Lundeen. (1963). *American Journal of Nursing, 63,* 130–131.

Gordon, S. (Ed.). (1981). *A centennial history of Michael Reese Hospital and Medical Center: 1881–1981.* Chicago: Michael Reese Hospital and Medical Center.

Hess, J. H. (1936). The Chicago city-wide plan for the care of premature infants. *Journal of the American Medical Association, 107,* 400–404.

Hess, J. H. (1951). Chicago plan for care of premature infants. *Journal of the American Medical Association, 146,* 891–893.

Julius Hess. Papers, Special Collections, Regenstein Library, The University of Chicago.

MacMullen, N. J., & Bruckner, M. C. (1986). Evelyn Lundeen: Perinatal pioneer. *Neonatal Network, 4,* 20–23.

Michael Reese Hospital. Papers, Chicago Jewish Archives, Spertus College of Judaica, Chicago, IL.

Miss Lundeen, infant nurse expert, dies. (1963, January 30). *Chicago Tribune,* F(2).

Jacqueline H. Wolf

THERESA I. LYNCH
1898–1994

Theresa I. Lynch, educator and administrator, was instrumental in establishing an independent school of nursing at the University of Pennsylvania. As its first dean, she initiated master's and doctoral programs which served as models throughout the country.

Theresa Inez Lynch was born in Winchester, Virginia, on August 9, 1896, one of five children. Her father, Maurice M. Lynch, was a lawyer and her mother, Theresa B. (Ahren) Lynch, a civic leader. Responding to the horrors of World War I, she decided to take up a career in nursing over the objections of her parents, who believed that nursing was inappropriate for a young woman of good family. She graduated from the Hospital of the University of Pennsylvania School of Nurses in 1920. In 1929, she received a baccalaureate degree in education from George Washington University and a master's degree in education from Columbia University in 1934, followed by a Ed.D. from New York University in 1940.

She was an instructor in microbiology and nursing arts at the Sydenham Hospital in New York City, before accepting, in 1930, the position of education director and later director of nursing at Willard Parker Hospital of Communicable Diseases, also in New York City. She left Willard Parker Hospital in 1936 to become director of the nursing program at New York University, which focused on teaching nursing theory.

Six years later, Lynch was invited by her alma mater, the University of Pennsylvania, to direct its nursing program. She was instrumental in establishing the School of Nursing as a Division of Medical Affairs in 1944. Realizing the importance of an independent nursing school, she fought the male-dominated leadership opposed to an independent school. Lynch prevailed and, in 1950, the School of Nursing of the University of Pennsylvania was founded and she became its first dean. During her tenure, the School of Nursing established both a master's and a doctoral program which became models for other such programs in the country.

Throughout her career, Lynch was active in many nursing organizations and chaired the National Recruitment Committee for the National League for Nursing, the first committee on careers in nursing. A consultant to nursing schools throughout the country, she was named Honorary Citizen of New Orleans for her contributions to nursing education. In 1971, she received the Distinguished Alumnus Award from the School of Nursing, Hospital of the University of Pennsylvania. Lynch was the author of a widely used textbook *Communicable Disease Nursing,* published in 1942 and in 1949. The book was translated into many languages including Japanese.

Lynch retired as dean in 1965. Shortly thereafter, she was asked to establish a nursing school at Widener University, Chester, Pennsylvania. In 1972, she moved to Washington, D.C. From 1980 until her death on February 3, 1994, she lived at Saunders House, a retirement home in suburban Philadelphia.

A pioneer in nursing education, Lynch was described as ahead of her time in accomplishments, but of the previous generation in grace and social skills.

PUBLICATIONS BY THERESA I. LYNCH

Communicable disease nursing. St. Louis: Mosby, 1942 (second edition, 1949).

BIBLIOGRAPHY

Obituary. *Alumni Newsletter.* School of Nursing, University of Pennsylvania.

Papers. Center for The Study of the History of Nursing, University of Pennsylvania.

Who's Who in America. Chicago: Marquis, 1966 and subsequent editions.

Who's Who of American Women. Chicago: Marquis, 1958 and subsequent editions.

Lilli Sentz

M

MARY ARDCHRONIE MACKENZIE
1869–1948

Mary Ardchronie MacKenzie[1] was a foremost leader in Canada's early professional nursing associations and an early advocate for education for visiting nurses beyond that offered in hospital training programs. She must have been proud, therefore, to close her career by becoming the first lecturer in public health nursing in Canada's first university nursing degree program. Despite her major contributions, little information is available about her life.

She was born in Toronto, Ontario, Canada, on October 25, 1869, one of at least two daughters of Campbell MacKenzie. She received a Bachelor of Arts from the University of Toronto in 1892 and in 1893 an Ontario Higher School Teacher's Certificate, with specialist standing in modern languages. She then taught in various high schools in Ontario and Quebec before moving to Boston to enter the Massachusetts General Hospital Training School for Nurses, with 3 additional months at the Sloan Maternity Hospital in New York. She graduated in 1901. A period of work in hospitals in Boston and Concord, NH, followed, and she was Superintendent of the Brooklyn (NY) City Hospital Training School before taking positions as visiting nurse in Washington, DC, and Chicago.

In 1907, she returned to Canada to take up the top administrative position with the Victorian Order of Nurses.[2] The VON, established in 1897, was Canada's premier national, voluntary, nonprofit organization of visiting home nurses, especially important for Canada's remote rural areas. The VON also established small outpost hospitals, and Chief Superintendent MacKenzie drew on her experiences as a visiting nurse to enhance and expand VON's mandatory post-hospital training program for its nurses at VON headquarters in Ottawa and other centres.

During her years in Ottawa, she became active in provincial and national professional nurses' associations and was elected second president (1912–1914) of the Canadian National Association for Trained Nurses (forerunner of Canadian Nurses Association); she had headed the Association's committee that advocated that nursing education, particularly public health nursing education, should be at universities. The chief issues she identified during her term of office related to advancement of nursing education, especially education for public health, and nursing registration.

"Mary Ard" (as she usually signed herself and frequently was called by her nursing colleagues) left the VON in 1917. During her years as Chief Superintendent, the VON had become a model for agencies in other countries. Her final year, however, was marred by a dispute in which she protected nursing standards of the VON against board proposals that the Order should offer what she called "substandard nursing services" by lesser-educated nurses and lay midwives in selected parts of the country. Following her resignation and a public outcry, those board proposals were withdrawn, but this was too late for MacKenzie.

After leaving the VON, MacKenzie spent 2 years in what might be termed short-term consultancy positions related to public health nursing in the United States. For example, she was Superintendent of Nurses, University of California, San Francisco; State Supervisor, Tuberculosis Nurses, Oklahoma; and Superintendent, Visiting Nurse Association, Denver, Colorado.

In 1920, she returned again to Canada to become Red Cross Instructor in the new Department of Public Health at the University of British Columbia (UBC). UBC was one of four Canadian universities that received Red Cross funding ($5,000 annually for 3 years at UBC) to establish post-diploma courses to prepare public health nurses to fill the increased demands for qualified care for this expanding field. MacKenzie directed the short-term certificate program at UBC until its funding term was complete in 1923. During this time, she also taught the public health nursing courses in Canada's first university nursing degree program, which had opened at UBC in 1919.

She apparently retired from nursing in 1923 and no record is available yet of her

later years. She died in Victoria, B.C., April 6, 1948.

NOTES

1. The spelling of both "Ardchronie/Ardcronie" and "MacKenzie/Mackenzie" varies in documents. The use of MacKenzie is based on her signatures on the RNABC (1920) registration records. University of Toronto Alumnae card and one presidential address published in *The Canadian Nurse* shows "Mackenzie," but most other published sources (e.g., CNA, Gibbon, Street) show it with a capital K. The use of "Ardchronie" is based on the University of Toronto Alumnae card (verified personal communication, G. Lowes, June 30, 1998).

2. Gibbon (1947) and VON (1996) indicate her tenure as beginning in 1907, but other notes indicate she started March 15, 1908.

PUBLICATIONS BY MARY ARDCHRONIE MACKENZIE

MacKenzie, M. A. (1913). President's Address. *The Canadian Nurse, 9*(5), 588–590.

MacKenzie, M. A. (1914). President's Address. *The Canadian Nurse, 10*(10), 561–563.

BIBLIOGRAPHY

B.C. Association Report. (1921). *The Canadian Nurse, 17* (February), 85.

Canadian Nurses Association. *Mary Ard. Mackenzie Vertical File.* (This file contains no primary data. File originally contained one typewritten sheet copied November 1967 by Forster, McGuire & Company from a summary sheet on Mary Ardohronie [*sic*] Mackenzie from the "History of Nursing, Canada Folder 19: Biographies Canadian Nurses" available in the Mathewson files, Library School for Graduate Nurses, McGill University. No sources were indicated on this summary sheet.)

Gibbon, J. M. (1947). *The Victorian Order of Nurses for Canada: 50th Anniversary 1897–1947.* Montreal: Southam Press.

Lowes, G. (1998, June 30). Personal communication (telephone call). (University of Toronto Alumnae Office.)

Meilicke, D. (n.d.). *CNA presidents, 1908–80: Beginning biographies and presidential themes.* Unpublished manuscript. Available CNA Library, Ottawa.

Meilicke, D., & Larsen, J. (1992). Leadership and the leaders of the Canadian Nurses Association. In A. J. Baumgart & J. Larsen (Eds.), *Canadian nursing faces the future* (2nd ed.). St. Louis: Mosby Year Book.

Riegler, N. (1991, September 5). Personal communication [letter].

Riegler, N. (1997). *Jean I. Gunn: Nursing leader.* Toronto: Associated Medical Services and Fitzhenry & Whiteside.

Registered Nurses Association of B.C. (1921). *Mary Ard MacKenzie Registration Record RNABC #1424.* Vancouver: Author. (RNABC Registration Archival Records. Microfiche.)

Street, M. M. (1973). *Watch-fires on the mountains: The life and writings of Ethel Johns.* Toronto: University of Toronto Press.

Victorian Order of Nurses for Canada. (1996). *A century of caring 1897–1997: The history of the Victorian Order of Nurses for Canada.* Ottawa: Author.

University of British Columbia. (1919–1925). *Calendars.* Vancouver: Author.

University of Toronto, Department of Development. (n.d.) *Mackenzie [sic], Mary Ardchronie; UofT Alumnae Card.* (Photocopy). Toronto: University of Toronto Archives, Faculty of Arts Student Transcript Cards, Box 19.

Zilm, G., & Warbinek, E. (1994). *Legacy: History of nursing education at the University of British Columbia 1919–1994.* Vancouver: University of British Columbia School of Nursing/University of British Columbia Press.

Glennis Zilm

HAZELLE BAIRD MACQUIN
1898–1989

Hazelle B. Macquin was the first Dean of the College of Nursing at the University of Utah. An "outlander" from the East Coast, she was hired in 1942 as an instructor for a projected nursing education program at the University. Within a year she was appointed to chair the effort to organize a program to educate nurses to meet critical needs of a nation at war. In 1948 she became the first Dean of a new, autonomous College. Stepping down from the deanship in 1954 she served as Director of Graduate Education at the College until her retirement in 1964.

Hazelle Baird Macquin

Macquin was born on June 11, 1898, near Stanford, Illinois to Tearly Clayton and Julia Etta Wilson. Macquin described herself as one who gave the appearance of being "frivolous and changeable" as a young women because she was interested in so many things and made several false starts in career choice (Clayton, 1983). She studied acting and graphic arts and maintained an interest in marine biology throughout her long, rich life. Macquin completed a baccalaureate degree at the University of Cincinnati in 1925, majoring in Nursing and Biology. She became a teaching assistant at Mt. Sinai Hospital School of Nursing in New York City from 1925 to 1927, simultaneously continuing her studies at Columbia.

The young woman's obviously keen mind led to her involvement as an assistant to Isabel Stewart in writing the *Standard Curriculum of 1927*, one of three curricula (1917, 1927, 1937), published by the National League for Nursing Education to provide standardization and the basis for national accreditation for schools of nursing. This experience provided a strong foundation in the mechanics and architecture of nursing education.

At some time during this period Hazelle married Robert S. Douglas and gave birth to a daughter, Gabriella. Douglas died in 1929. The years 1932–1940 were spent in England, France, and Italy. Macquin served in staff and head nurse positions, supervised an orphanage and a home for aged women, and taught civil defense. She incidentally became fluent in French and Italian and gained a fair mastery of German. However, her personal life was marred with tragedy. She was married again, to Captain Edmond Macquin, and had a son, Steven. Captain Macquin died in 1937. Macquin returned to the States and was employed as a teaching assistant, 1940–1942, at Teachers College, Columbia, where she completed the Master of Arts in 1941, majoring in Nursing Education and Administration. She was 37 years old.

Late in 1941, Macquin was hired by the University of Utah to develop its fledging nursery program. There were four diploma hospital schools of Nursing, where university professors had been involved in teaching science courses since 1913. The professors welcomed the extra money. Years later Macquin wryly speculated that the notoriously low salaries in higher education in Utah accounted for the eagerness of faculty to moonlight.

There was a critical nursing shortage in Utah, particularly in supervisory, administrative, and teaching positions. World War II compounded the problem and encour-

aged the University to act to increase the numbers of nurses available for the military. Nursing was established as the Department of Nursing Education in the School of Education in 1941. The entire faculty of the new department was made up of Hazelle Macquin and Mildred Dericott Rordame, later Quinn, who would succeed Macquin as the second Dean of Nursing. Money initially was a crushing problem, however the program was finally funded in 1942 by the USPHS. In 1943, the cadet nurse corps funding helped the school get on a firm financial footing. Still, the transitional nature of the Department was apparent. Two curricula were offered: a new 4-year baccalaureate degree and a 3-year diploma offered in cooperation with three Salt Lake hospital schools and one in Ogden, 40 miles from the campus. Partial responsibility for the 3-year program was retained by the hospitals, which continued to issue their own diploma, complementing a certificate from the University of Utah.

Most of the 200 students who graduated annually elected the 3-year program. The Cadet program was terminated in 1948 and so was the 3-year curriculum. Nurses returning from military service took advantage of the G.I. Bill, and 30 or 40 students a year registered under that program, preventing probable crisis in enrollment.

In 1948 Nursing became a college, thereby gaining recognition as a professional discipline at the University.

Achieving college status for nursing and successfully launching the baccalaureate program were crowning achievements of Hazelle Macquin's career. She elected to step down as Dean in 1953 and accepted the position as Director of Graduate Programs in Nursing. She used her considerable writing skills in preparing the College for League accreditation (achieved in 1955), in writing justification for the graduate program (initiated in 1958), and in assisting with grant applications for federal funding of undergraduate and graduate initiatives. She added wisdom and depth of understanding of the philosophy and theory of nursing to the graduate program. Dean Macquin was a powerful resource in preparation of the grant application that secured federal funding for a new five-story building for the College, completed in 1969.

Macquin retired in 1964. She pursued coursework in marine biology and in mal-ecology at the Universities of Hawaii and Guam, then worked as a visiting scientist on several research projects in Bimini, Heron Island and in Australia. Her special interest was the huge crown-of-thorns starfish, a ma-licious creature endangering the coral reefs of the South Pacific. Regarding herself as a volunteer, she nevertheless was paid hon-oraria by the research laboratories. A nice compliment, she said. Serendipitous to her marine biology research, she had the joy of gathering a museum-quality collection of exotic seashells.

The academic portrait of Macquin was painted by Utah's Alvin Gittins, commis-sioned by Dean Quinn and the faculty.

Hazelle Macquin died December 18, 1989, and is buried in Bountiful, Utah.

BIBLIOGRAPHY

Clayton, B. (1983). Oral History of Hazelle Macquin. (Part of the E. L. Cooley Oral History Project. Tapes and Transcripts archived at the Marriott Library, University of Utah, Salt Lake City, UT).
Obituary, *Salt Lake Tribune*, Dec. 21, 1989, p. 4E.

Bonnie C. Clayton

ELSIE S. OTT MANDOT
1913–

During the early 1940s, Army Air Force nurses were demonstrating that their vitally needed skills were providing a lifesaving service to the nation. Second Lieutenant Elsie S. Ott Mandot was a pioneer in the air evacuations of military casualties. She was born November 5, 1913 in Long Island, New York, and graduated from Smithtown High School in 1933. Following her gradua-tion she entered Lenox Hill Hospital, School of Nursing in New York and gradua-ted in 1936. Her first nursing positions were at Kings Park Hospital, Long Island, New York and St. Francis Hospital, Miami, Flor-ida. Following these nursing experiences, Mandot joined the Army Air Force Nurse Corps in September of 1941 and was com-missioned a Second Lieutenant. Her first military took her to Barksdale Army Air Field Station Hospital, Louisiana and later to Fort Storey, Virginia. In February of 1942 she received orders assigning her to the 159th Station Hospital located in the desert of Karachi, India. At that time, she had no preparation for or experience in trans-porting patients by air.

As World War II progressed in the early 1940s on all fronts, evacuation of the sick and wounded was of prime concern to med-ical officials. Recognizing the necessity of moving troops rapidly from the front to the Zone of Interior was considered expedient in order to save lives. As aerial flight became a feasible method of transportation, the War Department began to seriously con-sider moving patients rapidly by air. The Army Air Force was enthusiastic about or-ganizing a battalion of so called "Air Ambu-lances." Patients could thus bypass terrain obstacles, thus increasing speed and effi-ciency. However, aeromedical evacua-tion—especially the use of female nurses— was not regarded as feasible or economical by many. Although the Air Transport Com-mand was far from ready to undertake any ambitious program of intercontinental air evacuation, Army medical authorities de-cided to do an experimental test on the intercontinental application of aeromedical evacuation and planned a 11,000-mile flight from Karachi, India to Washington, D.C.

Mandot was selected to make this historic experimental flight, with only 24 hours notice during which time she had to supply and equip the plane. On the morning of January 17, 1943, Mandot and five patients boarded a DC-3 transport at Karachi, India. The plane arrived in Washington, D.C. on the evening of January 23 after making stops at Salala and Aden in Saudi Arabia; Khartoum and El Fasher in the Egyptian Sudan; Ascension Islands; Natal and Belem in Brazil; Morrison Army Air Field in Florida and finally Washington, D.C. Of her five patients, two litter patients were paralyzed of their lower extremities, one from poliomyelitis and the other from multiple fractures with deep ulcerated bedsores. The other three ambulatory patients had respective diagnosis of early active tuberculosis, glaucoma and manic-depressive psychosis and considered nonviolent for the trip.

In recognition of her meritorious achievement, on March 26, 1943 at Bowman Air Field in Kentucky, Mandot received the first Air Medal ever awarded to a woman in the history of the United States Army. Although some opposition continued in regard to placing nurses on air ambulances, General Davis N. Grant rapidly overrode this and on October 7, 1943, established an official program for the training of flight nurses at Bowman Army Air Field, Kentucky.

Mandot returned to India in October as a member of the 803rd Military Air Evaluation Squadron. Later she was promoted to Captain before being discharged in 1946. She then married Larry Mandot and settled down in Wheaton, Illinois. In August 1965, Mandot was selected to "christen" a specially developed C-9 known as the "Nightingale," the first of a new type of air ambulance.

Air evacuation was a successful endeavor due to the pioneer flight of Second Lieutenant Elsie S. Ott Mandot and the skill of many competent flight nurses that followed. Many distinguished themselves in their efforts to save lives and some gave their lives in the performance of their military duty. Their many sacrifices are documented in the historical literature.

BIBLIOGRAPHY

Books

Aerospace Studies Institute, Washington, D.C. (1961). Development of Aeromedical Evacuation in the U.S. Air Force 1909–1960.

Craven, W. F. (Ed.). The Army Air Forces in World War II. (1983). Washington, DC: U.S. Government Printing Office.

The Story of Air Evacuation: 1942–1989. Taylor Publishing Co.

Wings Over America. (n.d.). The Army and Navy Publishing Co. of Louisiana.

Articles

Army Air Force flight nursing. (1980). *Aviation, Space, and Environmental Medicine, 51*(4), 414–416.

Air Force Flight Nurses: The world is their ward. (1969). *RN, 32*(10), 36–41.

Air surgeon's letter. (1945). *Bulletin, 2*(2), 49.

Air transport of the man who needs everything. (1980). *Aviation, Space, and Environmental Medicine,* 725–728.

Army nurses in the air. (1943). *American Journal of Nursing, 43*(4), 342–343.

Flight nurse. (1945). *Douglas Airview,* 18–19.

Historical perspectives of the U.S. Air Force, Army, Navy, Public Health Services, and Veteran's Administration nursing services. (1978). *Military Medicine,* 457–463.

The history making event of Flight Nurse Elsie S. Ott becoming the first women to win the Air Medal. (1943). *American Journal of Nursing, 43*(5), 443–444.

The history and significance of the Air Medal. (1944). *Army Nurse, 1*(5), 8–9.

The U.S. Flight Nurse: An annotated bibliography. (1981). *Aviation, Space, and Environmental Medicine,* 707–708.

Nightingale chosen as name for aeromedical evacuation twinjets. (1968). *Command Post,* 10–11.

Origin of flight nursing in the United States Army Air Force. (1979). *Aviation, Space, and Environmental Medicine,* 1176–1178.

U.S. Army Air Force flight nurse training and pioneer flight. (1980). *American Journal of Nursing,* 414–415.

D. Haritos

FRANCES LUCILLE MAST
1919–

Frances Mast was one of the architects of the Arizona State Premature Transport Project, the first in the nation to have statewide coverage for premature infant transport. She participated in writing perinatal nursing standards for the Arizona Nurses Association and she was responsible for establishing standards of maternal and child health care in Arizona. Under her direction, Arizona became the first state to have a program for monitoring of maternal and child health program activities statewide by public health nursing. Mast was the first in Arizona to involve nurses in yearly proposals for county funding for maternal and child health. Through this system, counties developed uniform records, adopted one method of medical recording, implemented an organized plan of program review, received county health department manuals, and had full nurse participation in planning. Evaluation programs were put into place and regular inservice programs were provided based on the needs observed through the monitoring process.

Frances Mast was born at home in rural Marshall County, Indiana, on March 18, 1919. Her parents were Charles and Dean Martin Mast. She had one brother, 18 months older. Frances graduated from Plymouth High School in Plymouth, in 1936.

In May 1940, Mast graduated from Epworth Hospital School of Nursing, South Bend, IN. She worked as a staff nurse in

Frances Lucille Mast

the newborn nursery in Epworth Hospital from 1940 to 1942. She attended St. Mary's College, Notre Dame, IN, part-time in 1942, and in 1942 and 1943 she attended a postgraduate course in pediatric nursing at Cook County Hospital, Chicago, IL, and then worked in the premature infant transport program for the Chicago Board of Health from 1943 to 1944. In August 1945, she was awarded a Bachelor of Science in Education with a major in Public Health Nursing from Indiana University, Bloomington, IN. She was a Visiting Public Health Nurse, Indianapolis, IN, from 1945 to 1946 and a staff Public Health Nurse for the Johnson County Health Department in Franklin, IN, from 1946 to 1948. From 1949 to 1950, she studied Supervision in Public Health Nursing at George Peabody College for Teachers, Nashville, TN. During that time she was employed by the Nashville City Health Department. From 1951 to 1956, she was a staff nurse and then supervising nurse for the Visiting Nurse Service, Terre

Haute, IN. From 1956 to 1958, she was employed by the Phoenix City and Maricopa County Health Departments, Phoenix, AZ. In June 1959, she was awarded a Master in Public Health degree from the University of Michigan in Ann Arbor, MI. She then served as the Maternal and Child Health Nursing Consultant for the Arizona State Department of Health, Phoenix, AZ, from 1956 until her retirement in 1981.

As Maternal and Child Health Nursing Consultant, Mast made her greatest contributions. In 1961, she and Sister Alice Montgomery, a neonatal nurse at St. Joseph's Hospital and Medical Center in Phoenix, AZ, developed the idea of a system of regionalization of neonatal intensive care. However, it was not until 1967 that the Arizona State Premature Transport Project was initiated by the two. Initially inservice education on the care of the premature infant was provided. Teams of physicians and nurses were sent out of state for courses in the care of premature infants. Nurseries were redesigned and a neonatologist was recruited. Through the efforts of Mast and Sister Alice, residents of the community, health departments, nurses and physicians, social workers, insurance agencies and transport companies cooperated to provide services. Initially, two hospitals in Phoenix had centers; later two hospitals in Tucson were added. These efforts had significant effects on the neonatal mortality rate in Arizona, which dropped to 11.8 in 1971 from 19.7 in 1961. Arizona rose to third in the nation in infant mortality rate from its previous 37th place.

Once the regionalization of premature infant transport was in place, Mast turned her attention to the monitoring of statewide maternal and child health program activities. She was instrumental in developing Maternal Child Health Minimum Standards for the Arizona Department of Health Services in 1974, as well as Perinatal Nursing Standards published by the Arizona Nurses Association in 1977.

While Maternal and Child Health Nursing Consultant, Mast attended numerous short-term courses. Mast used the information she obtained in these courses to enhance the care of mothers and infants and of family planning.

Mast received numerous awards from neonatal and state groups including the American Public Health Association, the Arizona State Department of Health, the Arizona State Nurses Association, Arizona State University School of Nursing, the Arizona League for Nursing, the National Foundation March of Dimes, and the Nurses Association of the American College of Obstetricians and Gynecologists.

Through her efforts, the care of mothers and infants in the State of Arizona was improved and public health nursing reached a new level in monitoring of maternal and child health activities. Her goal-oriented approach served her and served Arizona well.

Mast retired in 1981 and lives in Phoenix, AZ. In retirement, she returned to an early interest in music; she had played piano and clarinet in high school. One week after she retired, she enrolled in a music theory class at Phoenix Community College as well as starting private piano and clarinet lessons. She rang in her church handbell choir and is currently taking lessons on the recorder and playing with a small recorder group of senior citizens.

PUBLICATIONS BY FRANCES L. MAST

Will they be saved? (1961). *Arizona Nurse*, 16–19.

The nurse in family planning. (1966). *Arizona Nurse*, 6–10.

Babes in flight. (1968). *Arizona Nurse*, 12–14.

Overall maternal child health trends in Arizona. (1969). *Arizona Nurse*, 18–19.

Turn your patient on. (1969). *Arizona Nurse*, 8–9.

Flight to life . . . Part I: The take off. (1974). *JOGN Nursing, 3*(2), 15–18.

Monitoring statewide maternal and child health program activities. (1978). *MCN, the American Journal of Maternal Child Nursing, 3*(3), 139–142.

Houden, M., Mast, F., Maurice, S., Rose, M., & Warrick, L. (1977). *Perinatal nursing standards.* Phoenix, AZ: Arizona Nurses Association Division on Maternal-Child Health Nursing Practice.

BIBLIOGRAPHY

Moore, W. J. (1976). From the director's desk. *Arizona Perinatal Program News, 1*(1), 1, 3.

Schwenn, J., & Hayes, T. (1975, February). Arizona: No. 1 baby state in a great new sense. *Arizona Highways,* pp. 40, 41, 43, 44.

Mast, F. M. (1998). Telephone interviews and letters, February, April, and May, 1998.

Shannon E. Perry

HELEN GRIFFITH McARTHUR
1911–1974

Helen Griffin McArthur made significant contributions to the wide field of public health nursing at provincial, national, and international levels through her leadership as a district nurse, university educator and director of public health nursing in Alberta, and as the first national Director of Red Cross Nursing Services in Canada, with special responsibilities as associate coordinator of the League of Red Cross Societies and advisor to the Korean Red Cross during the Korean War. Capitalizing on her early public health and district nursing experience in rural and isolated communities in Alberta, McArthur quickly identified opportunities for what is now described as "expanded role nursing" or the "Northern nurse practitioner." She carried her experience with program innovations in Alberta to the national and then international arenas in her 24 years with the Red Cross. The recognition McArthur received for her international nursing contributions raised the profile of Canadian nursing and nurses.

Helen Griffith McArthur

Born in the rural Alberta community of Stettler in 1911, Helen McArthur represented the fourth generation of her family to be born in Canada since the original ancestors immigrated from Scotland. She enrolled in the University of Alberta's School of Nursing, graduating in 1934 with a B.Sc.N. with specialization in public health. From 1930 to 1937, all University of Alberta degree nursing students completed their fifth and final year in public health by affiliating at another Canadian university. McArthur took her one year of public health at the University of British Columbia.

McArthur's first employment in 1934 was as senior public health nurse with the Okotoks/High River Rural Health Unit, one of Alberta's first two experimental rural health units begun in 1931 with significant funding from the Rockefeller Foundation. Serving an area of 1,800 square miles with a widely dispersed population of ranchers and grain growers, and only five small communities, McArthur supervised a generalized public health program focused on physical inspection of school children, immunization against communicable diseases, infant and preschool child welfare clinics and pre- and post-natal education. In 1937, McArthur joined the provincial Division of Public Health Nursing, serving for the next two years as a district nurse stationed at Stanmore, Peers, Valleyview, Kinuso and Bow Island. District nurses provided midwifery and emergency medical services in sparsely populated regions which had neither a physician nor a hospital. Realizing from first-hand experience the need for increased midwifery training for district nurses, McArthur sought a Rockefeller Fellowship which enabled her to graduate in 1940 with an M.A. in supervision and teaching in nursing, from Teacher's College, Columbia University, New York. As her thesis, she planned a midwifery course to meet the needs of Alberta's district nursing. This became the basis of the 4-month Advanced Practical Obstetrics (APO) Course begun in 1943 under the auspices of the University of Alberta School of Nursing.

On her return from Columbia, McArthur was the Acting Director of the University of Alberta School of Nursing from 1940 to 1943. She implemented the APO course, planned and mounted a successful Summer School For Graduate Nurses with financing channelled through the Alberta Association of Registered Nurses (AARN) from the Canadian Nurses Association federal government "War Emergency" grant, and taught public health nursing to 5th-year degree students. In 1944, she took the opportunity to expand the provincial nursing service when she became Director of the Public Health Nursing Division of the Alberta Department of Public Health. Two years later, in 1946, McArthur moved into a wider sphere of public health by becoming the first national Director of Red Cross Nursing Services, serving with distinction in this capacity until retirement in 1970.

It was during her almost quarter century with the Red Cross that McArthur made her most significant national and international contributions to nursing. Nationally, in addition to supervising the Red Cross's outpost hospitals and nursing stations, home nursing program, sickroom loan cupboards and other nursing services, McArthur promoted coordination of divisional nursing which led to unification and expansion of Red Cross nursing throughout Canada. She was also one of the representatives of the Canadian Red Cross Society which worked with the CNA to sponsor the Metropolitan Demonstration School in 1948, in Windsor, Ontario. Independent of hospital control, the school's purpose was to demonstrate that professional nurses could be prepared adequately in less than 3 years if they were not used for labor in the hospital during their educational program. The project was successful and provided a prototype for other 2-year diploma programs. Internationally, McArthur served in Korea and Japan, from June 1954 until December 1955 as associate coordinator of the League of Red Cross Societies and advisor to the Korean Red Cross, with responsibility for channelling all relief assistance sent to Korea by Red Cross Societies throughout the world. Her major concern was the care and placement of 100,000 war orphans, many suffering from tuberculosis. On returning from Korea, McArthur was appointed member, and then chairman, of the nursing advisory committee to the International Red Cross. One of the first projects undertaken by her committee was selection and special training of Red Cross personnel on a standby basis for service as Chief Nurses during international disaster operation.

McArthur contributed significantly to professional nursing associations at both the provincial and national levels. She served in Alberta as first vice-president of the Alberta Association of Registered Nurses (AARN) in 1946, and in Ontario as the first president of the Council of the College of Nurses of Ontario, the provincial licensing body for registered nurses and registered nursing assistants. Nationally, in 1944 McArthur became simultaneously chairman of the public health section of CNA and the public health nursing section of the Canadian Public Health Association (CPHA). In 1948, she was appointed convenor of CNA's public relations committee, before being elected CNA President for two consecutive terms, from 1950 to 1954. Her priorities as CNA President centered on strategies to ameliorate the shortage of nurses in hospitals and to separate nursing education from hospital control.

As an outcome of her contributions to Red Cross nursing, and nursing as a whole, McArthur received numerous honors. In recognition of her services in Korea, the Republic of Korea awarded her a scroll and a pin and the Korean Red Cross presented her their highest service award, the Coronation Medal, in 1953. Additionally, in 1955, the new nurses' residence at the Seoul Red Cross Hospital was named "McArthur Hall" in her honor. In 1957, the International Committee of the Red Cross presented her their highest nursing award, The Florence Nightingale Medal, awarded biennially in recognition of outstanding contributions to the development and prestige of the nursing profession. In 1964, McArthur received the honorary degree of Doctor of Laws from her Alma Mater, the University of Alberta, and shortly before her death, she was named an Officer of the order of Canada. As Florence Emory concluded in early 1975, "Helen McArthur's success flowed from two sources: a warm dynamic personality with a fine presence and special flair for effective public relations with national groups, professional and lay, and in particular with organized nursing, provincial and national. With acute perception, she knew that the establishment of such relationships would benefit the Red Cross, the nursing profession and the Canadian community" (Emory, 1975).

McArthur married Dr. W. Watson around the time of her retirement from the Red Cross in 1970, and was thereafter identified as Dr. Helen McArthur Watson. She died December 15, 1974 in Guelph, Ontario.

PUBLICATIONS BY HELEN GRIFFITH McARTHUR

Numerous editorials and CNA Presidential addresses published in *The Canadian Nurse* journal in the late 1940s and early 1950s; for example,

Open a Better Way. *The Canadian Nurse, 48*(7), 543–546.

Measuring progress. *The Canadian Nurse, 50*(9), 701–702.

BIBLIOGRAPHY

Biographical File: Helen McArthur Watson. Available from the CNA library, 50 The Driveway, Ottawa, Ontario, K2P 1E2.

Emory, F. H. M. (1975). *An appreciation of Helen G. McArthur Watson.* Available from the CNA library, 50 The Driveway, Ottawa, Ontario, K2P 1E2.

Helen McArthur, President. (1950). *The Canadian Nurse, 46,* 620–621.

Meilicke, D., & Larsen, J. (1992). Leadership and the leaders of the Canadian Nurses Association. In A. Baumgart & J. Larsen (Eds.), *Canadian nursing faces the future* (2nd ed., pp. 519–555). Toronto, ON: Mosby Year Book.

Stewart, I. (1979). *These were our yesterdays: A history of district nursing in Alberta.* Altona, MAN: D.W. Friesen & Sons.

Sharon Richardson

R. FAYE McCAIN
1917–1982

During her tenure at The University of Michigan, R. Faye McCain developed the Systematic Nursing Assessment and was widely respected for her pioneering work in the development of the Clinical Nurse Specialist concept. Her vision and her dedication to the idea of graduate education in nursing and the role which clinical nurse specialists would play in realizing that idea were highly regarded. To implement her ideas, she provided the leadership that established the University of Michigan School of Nursing's medical-surgical graduate program. Her landmark 1965 article "Nursing by Assessment—Not Intuition" in the *American Journal of Nursing* is still being quoted over 30 years later. It set a foundation for the development of the scientific basis of nursing practice.

R. Faye McCain

R. Faye McCain, a native of Texas, was a very private and modest individual in re-

gard to her personal life, so much so that little is known about her life prior to entering nursing. She was born September 16, 1917 in Texas and received her diploma in 1937 from Parkland Hospital School of Nursing in Dallas, Texas. She worked as a staff nurse for 4 years before spending 4 years in the Army Nurse Corps as a Head Nurse and a Flight Nurse in World War II. After the War, she worked as a Head Nurse and as a Supervisor at the San Francisco Veterans Administration Hospital. She received her B.S. in Nursing Education from the San Francisco College for Women in 1949 and her M.A. from Teachers College, Columbia University in 1951. She returned to San Francisco to teach for 2 years at the San Francisco College for Women.

She moved to Ann Arbor in 1953 to become the Supervisor of Medical-Surgical Nursing at the University Hospital and as the Chairperson of Medical-Surgical Nursing in the School of Nursing. She continued a joint role with the University Hospital as an Assistant Director of Nursing Service for Medical-Surgical Nursing and until 1968, as a Clinical Nursing Specialist.

In the School of Nursing, she was quickly promoted from Assistant Professor to Associate Professor and in 1959 to Professor. She continued to chair Medical-Surgical Nursing in the School for more than 20 years. Under her leadership the Master's degree program in Medical-Surgical Nursing was initiated in 1962. She served as its Director for 12 years. From 1974 to 1976, she was Acting Director of Graduate Study in Nursing.

At the heart of her academic work was the development of the clinical nurse specialist role. Integral was the development of a precise method of determining when nursing intervention was needed. McCain outlined the nursing assessment process that evolved from the work of the graduate students in medical-surgical nursing in her hallmark article, "Nursing by Assessment—Not Intuition" in 1965. The assessment tool as outlined by McCain in that article represented one of the first successful attempts to make data collection systematic. McCain was concerned that nurses base their practice on a firm scientific footing. Her article has continued to be cited 30 years after its publication.

McCain was also instrumental in developing another element of the scholarly evolution of the graduate program in medical-surgical nursing. This was a method by which students in the program could learn to systematically investigate medical-surgical nursing content. Organizing investigation around the major functions or most common types of behavior exhibited by patients provided the basis for a "Nursing Symptom" framework. The patients' functional disabilities or symptoms were identified and classified into the broad functional areas of respiration, metabolism, circulation of body fluids, and integration. Once the symptoms were categorized, four aspects were identified: the description of the symptom mechanism, the types of causative factors that initiated the mechanism, the nursing concepts and principles concerned with the symptom, and the principles from the related sciences fundamental to the nursing concept and principle. Then the student identified some nursing propositions related to the symptom requiring research. Along with her work on nursing assessment Miss McCain laid the foundation for the profession's eventual development and refinement of nursing diagnoses and interventions. At the end of her career, she participated in the early national meetings to begin development of a common nursing diagnostic classification system, the roots of which were embedded in her pioneering nursing assessment work.

She spoke widely on university campuses and was active in a number of nursing organizations. Within the National League for Nursing, she served as an alternate member on the Board of Review for the Department of Baccalaureate and Higher Degree Programs (1966–69) and starting in 1966 she served for many years as an Accreditation visitor. She was a charter member of Rho Chapter, Sigma Theta Tau and a member of Phi Kappa Phi national honor society.

Personally, although McCain's roots were embedded in Texas and she never lost her Southern drawl, she became one of the most loyal fans of the "Maize and Blue"—especially of the University of Michigan Wolverine football teams, and she attended all home basketball and football games and tailgate parties.

She retired from the University on January 1, 1981 and was honored with a symposium in which her former students gave papers honoring her work. A graduate scholarship in medical-surgical nursing was established in her name. Following her retirement she moved to Washington, D.C., to be closer to one of her three sisters. She died on June 26, 1982, in the Washington, D.C. area.

PUBLICATIONS BY R. FAYE McCAIN

Articles

Nursing care in the prevention and management of acute renal failure. (1964). *The University of Michigan Medical Center Journal, 30*(5), 216–219.

Nursing by assessment—Not intuition. (1965a). *American Journal of Nursing, 65*(4), 82–84.

Systematic investigation of medical-surgical nursing content. (1965b). *The Journal of Nursing Education, 4*(2), 23–31.

Boyle, R. E., MacVicar, J., Szigeti, E., McCain, R. F., & Brophy, S. (1970). Proposition 6: A supervised practicum in the functional and clinical areas should be part of every master's program. *NLN Publications,* (15-1397), 33–6.

BIBLIOGRAPHY

Strodtman, L. K. Banquet Program for R. Faye McCain [personal notes], 1981.

Centennial Brochure. (1991). *The University of Michigan School of Nursing: 1891–1991.*

Emeritus Professors Remembered . . . " (1984). *Alumni Association News Bulletin,* The University of Michigan, *5*(8), 1, 12.

R. Faye McCain. Personnel file and the biographical vertical file. Bentley Historical Library, The University of Michigan, Ann Arbor, MI.

Mallick, M. J. (1981). Patient assessment—Based on data, not intuition. *Nursing Outlook, 29,* 600–605.

Linda K. Strodtman

AGNES LOUISE BARLAND McDANIEL
1891–1982

Agnes Louise Barland McDaniel was a nurse missionary in Siam (now Thailand) in the 1920s and 30s. She also taught at the Presbyterian Hospital School of Nursing in San Juan, Puerto Rico.

McDaniel was born in Eau Claire, Wisconsin on April 21, 1891, the daughter of John Clarkson Barland and Dora Schlegelmilch Barland. Her grandparents were early settlers in the Eau Claire area. The second of six children, her sister Dorothea was older, and they had four younger brothers: Gordon, Herman, Howard, and George. She grew up on a farm near Eau Claire.

Hers was a devout Presbyterian family. In a brief unpublished article about her early years, she wrote, "My mother and father dedicated me to become the Family Missionary to the Orient, if the opportunity should present itself" (Barland, *Archives*).

She attended the Eau Claire State Normal School (now the University of Wisconsin-Eau Claire) and taught in a rural school in the area. She then went to Oberlin College in Ohio, graduating in 1914. After teaching English at the Fergus Falls, Minnesota High School for 2 years, she left for New York and earned a master's degree at Columbia University.

Agnes Louise Barland McDaniel

World War I influenced McDaniel's decision to become a nurse. In an undated letter to her Aunt Emelia, she wrote, "If it (the war) does come, I believe that I shall take up nursing at Johns Hopkins instead of work at Columbia." But she went to Columbia, then enrolled in the Vassar Training Camp the summer of 1918. This intensive preliminary nursing course was offered at Vassar College, Poughkeepsie, New York. It was designed so that those completing it could then finish a nursing program in 2 years.

When the program ended, she then entered the Johns Hopkins Hospital Training School for Nurses in Baltimore. McDaniel completed the nursing program in 1921. Her first nursing employment was at Luther Hospital in Eau Claire.

The next year, she was invited to go to Chiengmoi, Siam, under the auspices of the Presbyterian Board of Foreign Missions, to help a missionary doctor establish the first school of nursing in the northern part of that country. She was the first nurse to serve at the McCormick Hospital, where she helped establish its school of nursing. Returning home after 5 years, she took the opportunity to do postgraduate work at Cook County Hospital in Chicago.

In 1933, she returned to Siam to marry Dr. Edwin McDaniel, a medical missionary. For the next 5 years she helped him in his mission hospital and leprosarium in Nakon Sritamarat in southern Siam.

While there, McDaniel and her husband furnished author Margaret Landon with the writings of Anna Leonowens, an English widow who went as a governess to the court of King Mongkut in the 1860s. Her two books, published in the 1870s, described her personal experiences, and became the basis of Landon's novel, *Anna and the King of Siam*, and later for the musical, *The King and I*.

After her husband's death in 1938, McDaniel left Siam. She then taught at the Presbyterian Hospital School of Nursing, San Juan, Puerto Rico, for 5 years. Later she served as a housemother in a dormitory at Wheaton College in Illinois.

She returned to Eau Claire and after her brother Gordon's death, she operated the T.G. Barland Agency in that city.

In her later years, she lived at the W.B. Syvesson Lutheran Home in Eau Claire, where she died on June 9, 1982. She was survived by a niece, three nephews, two stepdaughters and a stepson.

BIBLIOGRAPHY

Barland, A. Correspondence. Archives, State Historical Society of Wisconsin, Madison, WI.

Clappsion, G. B. (1964). *Vassar's Rainbow Division, 1918.* Lake Mills, IA: The Graphic Publishing Company.

Fitzgerald, A. (1929). Nursing in Siam. *American Journal of Nursing, 29,* 817–821.

Former missionary to Siam Agnes Barland McDaniel dies. (1982, June 10). *Eau Claire Leader-Telegram.*

News item. (1933). *Bulletin Wisconsin State Nurses Association, 1,* p. 14.

Signe S. Cooper

MARY LUCIEL McGORKEY
1903–1990

Although not well known in contemporary nursing circles, Mary Luciel McGorkey achieved both notoriety and success in attempting to found a labor union for nurses. She fought the ANA and the nursing establishment during much of her career. Her independent spirit was exhibited even as a young girl, which eventually contributed to a strong determination to improve working environments for nurses. She was involved in a number of movements to benefit nurses such as lobbying for the 8-hour day, elimination of the practice of using clerks as nurses, higher pay, and alleviation of a nursing shortage. McGorkey emerged as a prominent influence in the labor movement in New York as she attempted to formally organize nurses and push for improved working conditions. As with other nurses who tried to change nursing, she got into difficulty with mainstream nursing organizations, whose leadership at the time was composed of a very narrow group centered primarily at Columbia Teachers College and New York University.

McGorkey was born April 11, 1903, in Venice, Ohio. She and her identical twin, Laurene, were the middle of 12 children of Bernard and Mary Olive (Ollie) O'Rourke McGookey. The early descendants of the family used the name MacGuckin when they emigrated from Northern Ireland (Ulster) to the United States in the Sandusky area of Ohio. The McGookey name first appeared in Ohio in the early 1840s, and the majority of the family members retained that name. Luciel and Laurene, however, changed their name to McGorkey

Mary Luciel McGorkey

when they relocated to New York, since they believed that New Yorkers "butchered" the sound of the name.

The McGookey family were Irish Catholics. Her father, Bernard, was a saloon keeper among other things, and her mother, Mary Olive, took in laundry. "The Twins" received at least part of their primary and secondary education in a Catholic school. Upon finishing high school, they traveled East to Pennsylvania to attend the nursing school in Dixmont State Hospital in 1924 and were granted RN licensure by exam in the state of Pennsylvania on May 8, 1925. Luciel's Pennsylvania license expired in 1938; she was never registered in the state of New York.

Following graduation from nurses' training, McGorkey went to New York City, where she practiced as a private duty nurse caring for patients in French Hospital and

in their homes. She soon became involved with a number of unions. This was consistent with her belief that unionization was one vehicle that could facilitate the treatment of nurses as "human beings." She was also keenly aware that nurses were reticent to join unions, due to traditions established early in nursing's history. This did not, however, deter her and she eventually headed a group of approximately 3,500 nurses. Although not politically inclined in terms of a specific party involvement, her union activities enabled her to develop a network comprised of councilmen and other politicians who often supported her efforts. In addition, she was frequently pictured in newspapers with Mayor LaGuardia whenever nursing issues were reported.

McGorkey's union activities occurred mainly between 1937 and 1942. They originated with her involvement as head of the Association of Hospital and Medical Professions, an affiliate of the American Federation of Labor (AFL). Records indicate that by 1938 she was president of the nurses' union of the Hospital Division of the State, County and Municipal Workers of America (Local 230), an affiliate of the Committee for Industrial Organization (CIO) which eventually became known as AFSCME. This nurses' union was comprised of nurses employed in the Department of Hospitals in New York City.

Numerous legislative bills relative to working conditions in New York City hospitals, which directly or indirectly affected nurses and other city personnel, were being considered during this time period and beyond. McGorkey represented the union's position at frequent hearings as these bills progressed through the system. Among these was the Burke bill which provided a *consecutive* 8-hour day (nurses in many hospitals worked 10-hour split shifts at this time) for 20,000 city hospital employees in greater New York. The bill was opposed by the State Hospital Association on the basis that three 8-hour shifts would incur additional expense to hospitals. This bill was drafted, campaigned for with McGorkey leading the fight, and won by the Association of Hospital and Medical Employees. It went into effect on July 1, 1937. A push was then started to establish the 8-hour day throughout the State of New York.

Other concerns being addressed by McGorkey and the union were overcrowded hospitals, the hiring of unskilled nurses because they were "cheap," low salaries, inadequate hospital budgets, and vermin-infested hospitals. In hearings before the New York Temporary Commission to Formulate a Health Program, McGorkey revealed that clerks were employed as nurses, that incompetent persons administered drugs, and that it was not uncommon for one nurse to care for 50 children. She claimed that in one instance one nurse had 101 City Hospital patients under her care from 11:00 p.m. to 7:00 a.m.

The Nurse Practice Act was also being reviewed during this time, with three bills introduced into the legislation. Nurses agreed that there were difficulties with the current act, but did not agree on all points of a new law. The NYSNA supported one bill, McGorkey and the Association of Hospital and Medical Employees supported another; and the National Nurses Association, an organization founded by a New York attorney, Lillian Rock, and comprised of both registered and practical nurses, supported still another. After several amendments, eventually two bills remained: the Feld-Todd and the Livingston-Wagner. Both of these bills contained similar proposals related to requiring licenses of all nurses for hire, but the Feld-Todd, supported by the NYSNA, provided for the licensing of practical nurses. McGorkey and the Association for Hospital and Medical Employees favored the latter bill on the

basis that practical nurses would be used as a source of "cheap labor" and would replace the registered nurse in hospitals.

Perhaps a greater source of conflict between McGorkey and the NYSNA arose in 1940 as the union struggled to obtain representation on the State Nurse Examiners' Board at Albany. At that time, all nine incumbents on the Board were members of the powerful NYSNA, appointed by the Board of Regents from lists of members submitted by the Association. McGorkey's position was that union representation on the Board would provide a mechanism for information relative to difficulties and injustices in the rank and file of the profession. Clearly, there was a struggle for power in the ranks of the New York State's nurses, with horror expressed by nursing conservatives at the suggestion of union members sitting on the Board

In the early 1940s, Luciel married William G. Mulligan, a corporate lawyer, and became less active in nursing politics. A previous marriage to Harry Liss in the 1920s had ended in divorce. The Mulligans adopted a son, Don Mulligan after unsuccessfully attempting to have a child of their own, but a daughter Luciel Laurene Mulligan ("Cielie") was born in 1948. Cielie was approximately 16 years old when her parents' marriage also ended in divorce. In time McGorkey moved to San Francisco with her daughter and died there in February 1990, within five days of her twin sister.

McGorkey, although active in nursing for a relatively short period of time, focused her energies primarily on two areas. She strongly advocated for "public protection" through the use of qualified nurses and promoted those strategies she believed would provide nurses with decent working conditions. She used the union and union activities as the vehicle to achieve those ends. She held fast to the notion that unions could be effective at a time when the idea of unions was not particularly popular in nursing circles and she fought the nursing establishment to make them so.

PUBLICATIONS BY MARY LUCIEL McGORKEY

A redhead grows up. (1939). *The New Nurse, 1,* 3–4.
Pie-man, let me taste your wares: Analysis of the Harmon Plan. (1939). *The New Nurse,*6–9, 12.

BIBLIOGRAPHY

Hollander, R. B. (nephew of Luciel McGorkey). (1997, April). E-mail correspondence. Princeton, New Jersey.
Donahue, M. P. (1997, August 31). Interview with Edythe McGorkey (sister-in-law of Luciel McGorkey). San Diego, California.
Nurses Association of the Counties of Long Island Archives (MC 9). Subject Files, Boxes 7 and 19, and Scrapbooks, Box 26. Foundation of NYSNA Center for History, Guilderland, New York.
Rhoades, C. Clerical Supervisor, State Board of Nursing, Bureau of Professional and Occupational Affairs, Commonwealth of Pennsylvania, Harrisburg, Pennsylvania. (1998, June 8). (Letter).

M. Patricia Donahue

JUNE MELLOW
1924–

Investigating other nurses' and her own experiences of caring for individuals experiencing schizophrenia, Mellow developed the concept of nursing therapy. Her framework of care then became the focus for the development of the first Doctor of Nursing Science degree program, which opened at Boston University in 1959.

Mellow was born in Gloucester, Massachusetts, on December 19, 1924. Her parents were Joseph and Alta (Reed) Mellow.

Receiving her diploma from the Salem Hospital School of Nursing in 1946, Mellow next earned a bachelor of science degree in psychology from the University of Rochester in 1949. Then, while working as a head nurse at the Boston State Hospital, Mellow

began to focus on the delineation of the concept of nursing therapy as she cared for patients with schizophrenia. This project was formalized further as she wrote her thesis, *An Exploratory Study of Nursing Therapy with 2 Persons with Psychoses,* for her master of science degree in psychiatric nursing, which was granted by Boston University in 1953.

Collaborating with Alice Robinson, Director of Nurses, Phyllis Hurteau, a nurse who was an apprentice-observer, and Marc Fried, a psychologist, Mellow was the research nurse on a project conducted at Boston State Hospital. This research, which was funded by a grant from the National Institutes of Health, examined the relationships of nurses and patients with psychiatric illnesses.

Mellow's perspective of nursing therapy integrated two specific components of "genuine human caring" (Mellow, 1968, p. 2365). The first aspect was creatively using the nurse's daily contacts of helping patients meet their daily needs. Mellow advocated that nurses needed to emphasize the "therapeutic potential . . . of what are considered mundane activities associated with women's sphere of work—feeding, bathing, dressing, granting privileges, teaching, comforting, scolding, joking, socializing, counseling" (Mellow, 1986, p. 183). The second part of the process was using verbal skills to help the patients gain knowledge of their health problems. Mellow emphasized that nursing therapy was needed for patients, especially during the acute phase of a psychotic illness, both to prevent the problem from becoming a chronic one and to promote improvement in the person's condition so that they might benefit from psychotherapy.

Mellow refined this concept further as she acquired a doctor of education in social foundations degree from Boston University in 1965. Her dissertation was *The Evolution of Nursing Therapy and Its Implications for Education.* Her doctoral studies were partially funded by a scholarship award from the National League for Nursing.

Mellow was employed as an educator in a wide variety of clinical settings and institutions of higher education. Some of these positions included being the Director of Nursing Therapy Education at Boston State Hospital, an Assistant in Psychiatry at Tufts University, Director of Staff Development in the Nursing Department at the Massachusetts Mental Health Center, and a lecturer in psychiatric education at the Harvard Medical School. Mellow also served as a member of the Editorial Review Board of *Perspectives in Psychiatric Care* from 1967 through 1977.

Most importantly, Mellow was the Director of the Clinical Laboratory in the Boston University Doctor of Nursing Science Program at Massachusetts Mental Health Center from its inception in 1959 through its closing in 1965. Within this role, Mellow influenced approximately 20 psychiatric nurses. Some of these nurses then branched out across the country as educators who taught Mellow's philosophy of care to their students.

Mellow firmly believed in the necessity of multidisciplinary collaboration, especially between nurses and physicians, as the means to provide the care needed for individuals suffering from psychoses. This perspective was advanced when Mellow addressed both national and international conferences.

As of this writing, Mellow was living in Massachusetts.

PUBLICATIONS BY JUNE MELLOW (SELECTED)

Books, Monographs, Chapters, and Proceedings

Graduate education in psychiatric nursing: The one-to-one relationship. (1958). In *Aspects of Psychiatric Nursing: 1956 Regional Conferences: Part B* (pp. 54–56). New York: National League for Nursing.

Nursing therapy in the acute and post-acute phases: An atypical case. (1959). In *Three reports on nurse-patient interactions in psychiatric nursing* (pp. 15–20). New York: National League for Nursing.

Research in nursing therapy. (1959). In L. E. Heidgerken (Ed.), *Proceedings of the Workshop on the Improvement of Nursing Through Research Conducted at the Catholic University of America, June 14–24, 1958* (pp. 100–112). Washington, DC: Catholic University Press.

The importance of the arts and sciences in the education of the nurse therapist on the doctoral level. (1961). (Boston: Boston University School of Nursing Alumni University Publication Series).

The evolution of nursing therapy and its implications for education. (1965). (Ed.D dissertation). Ann Arbor, MI: University Microfilms.

The experiential order of nursing therapy in acute schizophrenia. (1969). In G. F. D. Helestine (Ed.), *Psychiatric research in our changing world* (pp. 148–154). Amsterdam: Excerpta Medica Foundation.

Burwell, D., Gemeroy, H., Jones, M., Mellow, J., & Pelletier, I. O. (1969). Confrontation. In G. F. D. Helestine (Ed.), *Psychiatric research in our changing world* (pp. 166–170). Amsterdam: Excerpta Medica Foundation.

Articles

Nursing therapy as a treatment and clinical investigative approach to emotional illness. (1966). *Nursing Forum, 5*(3), 64–73.

Evolution of nursing therapy through research. (1967). *Psychiatric Opinion, 4*(1), 15–21.

The experiential order of nursing therapy in acute schizophrenia. (1968). *Perspectives in Psychiatric Care, 6*(6), 249–255.

Nursing therapy. (1968). *American Journal of Nursing, 68*(11), 2365–2369.

A personal perspective of nursing therapy. (1986). *Hospital and Community Psychiatry, 37*(2), 182–183.

Robinson, A. M., Mellow, J., Hurteau, P., & Fried, M. (1955). Research in psychiatric nursing: 1. The role of the nurse-therapist in a large public mental hospital. *American Journal of Nursing, 55*(4), 441–444.

Mellow, J., Robinson, A. M., Hurteau, P., & Fried, M. (1955). Research in psychiatric nursing: 2. Nursing therapy with individual patients. *American Journal of Nursing, 55*(5), 572–575.

Robinson, A. M., Mellow, J., Hurteau, P., & Fried, M. (1955). Research in psychiatric nursing: 3. The psychiatric head nurse. *American Journal of Nursing, 55*(6), 704–707.

BIBLIOGRAPHY

Colliton, M. (1965). The history of nursing therapy: A reactionnaire to the work of June Mellow. *Perspectives in Psychiatric Care, 3*(2), 10–18.

Dumas, R. G. (1994). Psychiatric nursing in an era of change. *Journal of Psychosocial Nursing, 32*(1), 11–14.

Franz, J. (Ed.). (1989). Mellow, June. In *Who's Who In American Nursing, 1988–1989* (3rd ed., p. 311). Owing Mills, MD: Society of Nursing Professionals.

Moxley, C. F. (Ed.). (1997). Mellow, June. In *Who's Who In American Nursing, 1996–1997* (6th ed., p. 426). New Providence, NJ: Marquis Who's Who.

Janice Cooke Feigenbaum

HANNAH D. MITCHELL
1907–

Hannah D. Mitchell

Hannah D. Mitchell's life is an example of ardent faith and conscientious work. She utilized her education to create good for others, while she attributed much of her success to reliance on a higher power. Born and raised in rural Missouri, she later became a nurse on horseback at the Frontier Nursing Service in Hyden, Kentucky, and completed her career as a midwife consultant in the Department of Health for the State of Georgia.

The eldest of six children, Mitchell was born on a farm near Norwood, Missouri. Her father, educated through high school, became a successful printer, carpenter, and farmer. Her mother, who completed grade school, listed herself as a housewife. Because Mitchell's local country school had only 10 grades, she was sent to Neosho, Missouri to live with her grandmother, where she completed high school.

When her father died tragically in a construction accident, Mitchell and her oldest brother chose a college where they could both study and work, John Brown University in Siloam Springs, Arkansas. Mitchell earned her money for school by working each summer as a scout and campfire leader for the college summer program, and 4 hours a day during the school year as house mother to the younger girls. In 1932, at the age of 25, Mitchell completed her B.A. degree at John Brown University. After graduation from college, she taught history for a time, then in 1935 she entered the nurse training school at St. Luke's Hospital in Kansas City, Missouri from where she received her diploma in 1938 at the age of 31. In 1939 she moved to Kentucky, where in 1940 she became the first American nurse to both graduate from the midwifery program at the Frontier Nursing Service and to teach courses in the program. During the next 4 years she was first assigned to a district called Bull Creek, and later to Red Bird, both accessible only by horseback. Mitchell was well suited for the work in Kentucky, for as a child growing up on a farm her father kept two large plow horses, and one saddle horse which she especially loved to ride.

In 1946 Mitchell, encouraged by Mary Breckinridge, accepted a special assignment to Panama to establish a nurse-midwifery school under the auspices of the Pan American Sanitary Bureau in Washington, D.C. After 2 years in Panama, Mitchell flew directly to New York for her next educational adventure.

At Columbia University in New York in 1946, Mitchell earned a B.S. degree. While still in the program, she was actively recruited to come south to establish a demonstration nurse midwife program for the State of Georgia. After several years in this leadership position, she requested an educational leave to complete a master of Public Health degree at the University of Michigan at Ann Arbor. She graduated on June 11, 1949.

After returning to her position in Georgia, her most famous assignment was as nurse consultant for the film "All My Babies" completed in 1952. The Georgia Department of Public Health, with funds from the United States Children's Bureau, sponsored the making of this film, intended to improve the skills of the many granny midwives still delivery the majority of babies in the rural sections of Georgia. George Stoney, the filmmaker, credited Mitchell's contributions in building community relationships, and her special bond with Miss Mary, the Black granny-midwife featured in the film, for much of the success of the project.

The film won the Flaherty Award, the equivalent of an Oscar in the documentary category. What pleased Mitchell most, however, was the good that the film accomplished around the world. This outcome was party related to the unexpected reception she and the film received in Geneva, Switzerland at a World Health Organiza-

tion meeting. After superb accolades from the viewing audience, the film was widely distributed as a training film for birth attendants in many underdeveloped countries. In the United States the film became a classic work for its outstanding artistic treatment and cultural relevance in communicating the miracle of birth.

Mitchell is also credited for assisting with the *Mother and Baby Book* for expectant mothers, distributed throughout Georgia, and for the *School Health Guide*, a classic outline for school health programs. She also assisted with another documentary film aimed at controlling venereal diseases.

Hannah Mitchell retired due to ill health in 1967. Between 1967 and 1990 she continued to teach Sunday School, tend her garden, and photograph birds around her home in Atlanta and in the nearby mountains. In 1990 she relocated to Louisiana to be near relatives. Mitchell never married. She led a full and productive life as a nurse and nurse-midwife laboring among underserved populations.

BIBLIOGRAPHY

Mitchell, H. D. (1989). [Oral history interview and private papers.] In Georgia Public Health Oral History Collection, Special Collections, Robert W. Woodruff Library, Emory University, Atlanta, GA.

Stoney, G. (1959). All my babies. In R. Hughes (Ed.), *Film Book 1: The Audience and the Film Maker.* New York: Grove.

Untitled and undated tribute to Hannah Mitchell at the time of her retirement provided by Jane McCombs, Georgia Division of Public Health.

Rose Cannon

IDA V. MOFFETT
1905–1996

The Ida V. Moffett School of Nursing is part of Samford University, a Baptist-related institution in Birmingham, Alabama. The school bears the name of one of its early graduates, its long-time leader, and its continuing symbol.

Ida Vines Moffett was born April 9, 1905, in Toadvine, a small rural family village in the western part of Jefferson County, Alabama. Her parents, Mary and Perry Vines, named her Lou Ida Verla Vines. She was educated by community tutors and graduated from the Alliance High School in 1923.

Inspired, recruited, and aided by public health nurses who worked in her remote community, Ida enrolled in the Birmingham Baptist Hospital School of Nursing in June 1923. Its school of nursing had been one of the first accredited by the Alabama State Board of Nurses' Examiners when nurse registration was enacted by state law in 1915.

Ida V. Moffett

According to the custom of the day, Ida immediately went to work as a bedside nurse, with instruction from older students and three registered nurses. Physicians taught a few informal classes. After completing the required 1,095 days of hands-on training, Ida passed the state examination and became Registered Nurse number 1830 in Alabama on June 3, 1926.

Upon graduation, she worked in a physician's office and did private duty nursing at Baptist Hospital. Local physicians arranged for her to go away for a year's post-graduate study. She trained in orthopedic nursing at University of Iowa Hospital and then studied surgical nursing at the University of Cincinnati. Back in Birmingham in June 1928, she became operating room supervisor for Birmingham Baptist Hospital, serving until her marriage to Howard D. Moffett on June 29, 1929.

She followed her husband to his work in Atlanta, Georgia, where she did private duty nursing in homes. In 1934, Birmingham Baptist Hospital acquired a second branch by purchasing the Gorgas Hospital-Hotel and Moffett was invited to return to Birmingham as a head nurse in what became known as the Highland Avenue Baptist Hospital.

In September 1941 she was given a temporary appointment as director of nursing for the two Baptist hospitals and their School of Nursing. Her first duty was to manage enrollment for a new class of students. The temporary job lasted until her first official retirement at age 65 in 1970.

In the years between, she led several major steps in the development of nursing as a profession and nurse education as an accredited degree. In 1943, she organized the first unit of the Cadet Nurse Corps to be set up in Alabama. She led in building a lavish second building for the School of Nursing, this one located adjacent to the Highland Avenue Baptist Hospital.

In 1946, she attended the first nationwide biennial conference of the major professional nursing organizations, which convened in Atlantic City. She became committed to the concept aired there, that nurses should be educated in a university classroom setting. Immediately after the convention she was named to the Alabama State Board of Nurses' Examiners and Registration and was elected chairman at her first meeting. She plunged into a historic issues concerning training and status of Black nurses. She led in closing several substandard training programs, and she helped arrange the state's first 4-year collegiate nursing program—one which served Black students—at Tuskegee University. She dealt with several minor issues which won professional rights and courtesies for Black nurses.

She led in implementation of 1945 legislation which led to licensure for practical nurses. She guided development of the state's first training program for licensed practical nurses and placed Annelle Collins Bishop, one of her Baptist Hospital nursing graduates, in charge of the program in Gadsden, Alabama. The first class graduated in 1948 and was thought to be one of the first two such groups trained in the Southeast United States.

In 1948 she began serving on a committee of the Alabama State Nurses Association which advised the University of Alabama in setting up a school of nursing. After obtaining legislative approval in 1949, she served on a committee to select the first dean of nursing. The school began functioning in September 1950 at the University campus in Tuscaloosa and was later relocated in Birmingham.

At the same time, Moffett was making provisions for her own Birmingham Baptist Hospital School of Nursing to offer college courses in conjunction with the Birmingham campus of the University of Alabama. The arrangement extended into 1971, giving BBH nursing students approximately 2 years of university credits in addition to their nursing diplomas.

Ida Moffett was appointed to the first state licensing board for hospitals and other health care institutions in Alabama, and she served 10 years. By the 1950s, she was recognized as one of the state's leading arbiters of quality in health care, and she was named Birmingham's Woman of the Year in professions in 1953. She was a founder of the Birmingham Regional Hospital Council.

From 1949 until 1955, national accreditation of the Baptist School of Nursing was the driving issue of Ida Moffett's life. Her school was the first in the state and the first of many Baptist-related schools in the nation to receive national accreditation. At the time, only 21 percent of schools were nationally accredited. She was soon in demand as a consultant for other schools seeking accreditation, and she was named for 10 years to the national Board of Review for Accreditation of Associate and Diploma Degree schools of nursing, one of the first two Southerners on that board.

Closely linked to the accreditation movement was the push for faculty to have advanced degrees in nursing. Briefly Ida Moffett attempted to enroll in college herself, but her hospital duties were too pressing. Instead she sponsored her faculty members in their pursuit of degrees.

In 1961, Moffett was appointed to the U.S. Surgeon General's Consulting Group on Nursing. During this period she was involved in several changes in nurse education in response to a shortage of nurses. The 3-year diploma program of her school was reorganized with a 2-year curriculum, and the 2-year associate degree program was implemented in state junior colleges. Moffett advised at Jefferson State Junior College in the set-up of the first associate degree program and arranged clinical experience at Baptist Hospitals.

Nursing service in the two Baptist hospitals grew as buildings expanded rapidly and bed capacity of the hospitals rapidly grew to approximately 1,000.

Until this time, Ida Moffett had directed operations of almost every department of the hospital, functioning in the old "hospital superintendent" model of organization. Now, she moved to a corporate model of leadership. She was named chief of nursing for the Baptist system, with associates heading each of the hospitals and the school of nursing.

In 1968 the Board of Trustees of Baptist Medical Centers of Birmingham announced the renaming of the school as the Ida V. Moffett School of Nursing. That name was retained in 1973 when the school became a part of Samford University.

In her retirement, Mrs. Moffett occasionally lectured and advised at the school, helped to organize one of the first racially integrated Baptist churches in Alabama, and worked occasionally as a volunteer at Baptist hospitals. But she was unhappy and depressed unless working constantly. In 1978 she agreed to consult with a new for-profit hospital, Brookwood Medical Center, in reorganization of its nursing service. The job stretched into the early 1980s, when the Baptist Medical Centers brought her back into active employment with the title Chief of Nursing Emeritus. She was to work at the corporate level advising in varied aspects of nurse education and nursing service, as the Baptist system branched into many locations statewide. Although frequently involved in executive issues of health care institutions, she was happiest when in direct contact with patients. Until she was almost 90 years old she made rounds to see patients with special needs in one or more hospitals each day.

She was chosen a member of Sigma Theta Tau nurse honor society, one of the few non-college graduates specially inducted at the national level. She was named by Samford University to membership in Phi Kappa Phi honor fraternity. She was recognized nationally by the American Protestant Health Care Association and she received dozens of local, state, and regional honors in health care and charity.

In final retirement, she set up an apartment at the Baptist Health System's Galleria Woods Retirement Community. She was a deacon and active Baptist church member. She continued to administer the Nightingale Pledge to graduate nurses in traditional pinning ceremonies of the Ida V. Moffett School of Nursing until a few weeks before her death. More than 4,000 nursing students had graduated under her direct influence.

She died at Montclair Baptist Hospital November 17, 1996 from heart failure and related complications, having survived nearly 15 years since having bypass surgery at Princeton Baptist Hospital.

Moffett was a reluctant writer, preferring to demonstrate her messages in action with sick people. Numerous papers and memorabilia of her life are archived at the Samford University Special Collections Library and in a museum display at the Ida V. Moffett School of Nursing. Moffett was in the first group inducted into the Alabama Healthcare Hall of Fame in 1998.

BIBLIOGRAPHY

Allen, L. N., & Allen C. B. (1988). *Courage to care: The story of Ida V. Moffett.* Birmingham: Samford University Press.

Catherine B. Allen

SISTER ALICE MONTGOMERY, (RELIGIOUS SISTER OF MERCY) 1918–

Sister Alice was one of the architects of the Arizona State Premature Transport Project. She organized, with the obstetric education chief and the Directors of the Nursery, the Division of Reproductive Medicine at St. Joseph's Hospital and Medical Center,

Phoenix, AZ; this was probably the first division of reproductive medicine at a private teaching hospital. She initiated the Family Childbirth Center at St. Joseph's Hospital and Medical Center, the first of its kind in the State of Arizona.

Sister Alice Montgomery

Sister Alice was instrumental in convening a group of health care providers, in sending nurse-physician teams to other states for education in care of the premature infant, and in developing a statewide seminar on care of the premature infant that was offered to nurses and physicians. Two intensive care nurseries and a system of neonatal transport in Arizona were created through these efforts. Through this regionalization of the care of premature infants, the neonatal mortality rate in Arizona dropped from 19.7 in 1961 to 11.8 in 1971. Arizona rose from 37th in the nation in infant mortality to third. Maternal and infant care was greatly improved in Arizona

through the vision of Sister Alice. She provided extensive consultation to hospitals in Arizona and California in remodeling units serving mothers and infants and revising policies and protocols.

Alice Montgomery was born in Ferndale, CA, on April 15, 1918, the youngest of 11 children of Felix A. Montgomery and Margaret A. Friel. She attended grades 1 and 2 in Jacoby Creek School in Bayside, CA, 1924–1925, and grades 3 to 8 in Nazareth Academy in Eureka, CA, 1925 to 1932. She attended Eureka High School in Eureka, CA, and graduated in 1936. She attended Humboldt State College in Arcata, CA, 1936–1937. She received a diploma in nursing from St. Mary's College of Nursing in San Francisco, CA, in 1940.

Six months after graduating from nursing school, Montgomery felt a call to the religious life and entered the congregation of the Sisters of Mercy, Burlingame, CA, and took the name of Pius (after Pope Pius X, a saint in the Roman Catholic Church). She describes her family as devout and encouraging of her choice to enter the religious life. Two of her sisters were also religious sisters and a number of her relatives were members of other religious congregations. Her oldest sister entered the convent at age 19 before Montgomery was born and was the one who named her Alice. Another sister entered the convent when Montgomery was 2. Around 1966, Sister Pius stopped wearing a religious habit and took back her birth name and has been known as Sister Alice since.

Sister Alice received a bachelor's degree from Lone Mountain College, San Francisco, CA, in 1953, and attended Arizona State University, Tempe, AZ, from 1969 to 1972, earning 21 units in postgraduate study.

Sister Alice's nursing experience includes being Surgical Nursing Supervisor, Mercy Hospital and Medical Center, San

Diego, CA, 1943–1944; Pediatric Nursing Supervisor, Mercy Hospital and Medical Center, San Diego, CA from 1944–1946; Obstetrical Nursing Supervisor, St. Mary's Hospital and Medical Center, San Francisco, CA, 1946–1948 and 1956–1957; Administrator, St. Joseph's Hospital and Medical Center, Phoenix, AZ, 1948–1951; and Surgical Nursing Supervisor, Mercy Hospital and Medical Center, San Diego, CA, 1951–1952. From 1953 to 1964, she served as director of planning and construction for the Sisters of Mercy in San Diego, Bakersfield, and San Francisco, all in California. In 1964–1965, she was Medical Nursing Supervisor, Notre Dame Hospital, San Francisco, CA. She spent the next 18 years at St. Joseph's Hospital and Medical Center, Phoenix, AZ, as Obstetrical, Gynecological and Neonatal Nursing Manager, 1965 to 1980, and as Perinatal Nurse Consultant, 1980 to 1983.

Sister Alice was a member of a number of professional nursing associations and was National Treasurer of the Nurses Association of the American College of Obstetricians and Gynecologists (NAACOG). She received a March of Dimes Service Award in 1973, was NAACOG Arizona Nurse of the Year in 1979, and in 1980, for her volunteer work, was awarded the Arizona Hon Kachina as one of "12 Who Care."

From 1984 to 1994, Sister Alice initiated and coordinated the Lifeline Personal Response System at St. Mary's Medical Center, San Francisco, CA. The Lifeline Personal Response System provides a way for those who live alone or have need of assistance to obtain help in an emergency. The client wears a button which when depressed activates a box on the telephone. At a centralized receiving line, the operator ascertains if the client needs assistance and notifies a "responder" (a relative, friend or neighbor who has volunteered to check on the client and has a key to the home). The operator

has local fire, ambulance and police telephone numbers and can notify them as necessary.

Now officially retired, Sister Alice lives in Burlingame, CA, but continues to volunteer 2 days a week at St. Mary's Medical Center in the Lifeline Personal Response System.

Sister Alice's achievements in a lifetime of dedication to the care of women and infants are significant. Through her vision and action, premature care in Arizona was transformed, neonatal mortality significantly decreased, and the lives of those she touched made better. She continues her good works through her volunteer activities.

PUBLICATIONS BY SISTER ALICE MONTGOMERY

Montgomery, A. (1974). Flight to life. Part II: Ground operations. *JOGN Nursing, 3*(2), 18–22.
Montgomery, A. (1974). Regional maternity health services in Aberdeen, Scotland: A WHO fellowship study. *JOGN Nursing, 3*(6), 29–34.

BIBLIOGRAPHY

Curriculum vitae, Sister Alice Montgomery.
Montgomery, A. (n.d.). *Regional maternity health services in Aberdeen, Scotland, U. K.* Unpublished manuscript.
Perry S. (1998). Personal interviews with Sister Alice Montgomery. February, 1998; April, 1998.

Shannon E. Perry

RUTH NEIL MURRY
1913–1995

Ruth Neil Murry has been described as a pioneer nurse educator in the South, a role model, and leader in professional nursing. For 33 years, she was responsible for the nursing educational program at the University of Tennessee (UT), Memphis. She provided the leadership to develop the first state supported baccalaureate and master's programs in nursing for Tennessee and the Midsouth area.

Murry was born June 26, 1913, in Hattiesburg, Mississippi, the oldest of five children of Jasper and Lois Hartzog Murry. Because of her father's work, the family lived in several cities in both Mississippi and Georgia. Murry graduated from high school in Hattiesburg. In June 1932, she graduated from Pearl River Junior College in Poplarville, Mississippi. She also attended Mississippi Southern College for the academic school year 1932–1933 and then enrolled at the University of Tennessee School of Nursing in Memphis, graduating in June 1936.

Ruth Neil Murry

Following graduation in 1936, Murry was employed as a staff nurse in obstetrics at John Gaston Hospital in Memphis. She completed an 8-month postgraduate certificate program in obstetric nursing at the New York Hospital, Cornell University Med-

ical Center in 1937. She returned to Memphis and became the University of Tennessee School of Nursing's first clinical instructor in obstetrical nursing in January 1938. Murry received her bachelor of science in nursing degree from UT School of Nursing in 1940 and her master of arts in nursing education administration from the University of Chicago in 1953. She also completed additional coursework at Case Western Reserve University in Cleveland, Ohio, and the University of Tennessee Graduate Center in Memphis.

The University of Tennessee School of Nursing was established in 1926 as a division of the College of Medicine, having previously operated as a clinical training program through the Memphis General Hospital. Most of the graduates received a certificate or diploma, unless they had 2 years of college and could be awarded a degree. In 1944 Murry was named educational director of the school, serving until 1946 when she was named director of the school which continued to operate as a division of the College of Medicine. Murry was responsible for influencing the university administration to establish the School of Nursing as an academic unit separate from the other professional education units and was named the first Dean of the school in July 1949. Murry transformed a mediocre diploma program with limited university resources to one of the top diploma programs in the country. In *Nursing Schools at the Mid-Century* (1950), UT was rated in Group I, or the upper 25% of basic programs. The school attracted students from Mississippi and Arkansas as well as all of Tennessee. Murry led the difficult transition from a diploma to a baccalaureate program with the establishment of the first state supported 4-year BSN program in 1950. The diploma program was phased out by 1954.

Murry spearheaded the effort to establish the first state-supported graduate program in nursing which began in 1973. One of the first areas of specialization offered at the master's level was the family nurse practitioner program, which supplied the Midsouth with these expanded role graduates. Another career highlight was the application and selection of UT in 1975 to implement an experimental accelerated nursing program to provide an opportunity for those with non-nursing degrees to earn the baccalaureate in nursing. Murry retired from UT in December 1977 and was named Emeritus Dean.

Some of Murry's other professional activities included a term as president of the Tennessee Nurses Association, member of the Tennessee Board of Nursing from 1956–1960, and as a committee chair of the Southern Region Education Board (SREB). She served as an accreditation visitor for the National League for Nursing and as a member of the Commission on Colleges of the Southern Association of Colleges and Secondary Schools. Honors included Memphis Professional Woman of the Year in 1966 and Outstanding Alumnus of UT College of Nursing in 1974. She was selected for membership in Sigma Theta Tau International, Phi Lambda Theta, and Delta Kappa Gamma honor societies.

She died September 7, 1995 and is buried in Hattiesburg, Mississippi. The Ruth Neil Murry Scholarship Fund and the Ruth Neil Murry Distinguished Visiting Professorship were established in recognition of her commitment to nursing education.

PUBLICATIONS BY RUTH NEIL MURRY

From a diploma to a baccalaureate program in nursing. (1961). *Nursing Outlook, 9,* 503–504.

BIBLIOGRAPHY

A tribute to Ruth Neil Murry. (1996). *UT Memphis Nursing Magazine,* Summer, 15–17.
West, M., & Hawkins, C. (1950). *Nursing schools at the mid-century.* New York: National Committee for the Improvement of Nursing Services.

E. Dianne Greenhill

N

JOSEPHINE MAY NESBIT
1894–1993

Josephine Nesbit was second in command of the Army nurses stationed in the Philippine Islands in World War II. Her humane, dynamic leadership style during the evacuation of Manila in 1941, as head nurse of General Hospital #2 in the Bataan jungles in 1942, and as a senior nurse in Santo Tomas Internment Camp in Manila from 1942 until 1945, provided the framework which allowed American and Filipinos nurses to effectively care for themselves and thousands of war casualties and prisoners of war. She was much beloved among these women. Earlier, in 1919, Nesbit met Colonel Kermit Roosevelt, President Theodore Roosevelt's son, became a charter member of the American Legion, and embarked on a lifelong advocacy for veteran's rights.

Josephine Nesbit was born on the family farm near Butler, Missouri on December 23, 1894, the seventh of ten children. By the age of 12, she was an orphan, living first with a grandmother and later with a cousin in Kansas. She left high school, and after meeting her sister's nursing superintendent in a local bank, decided to enter nurse's training. Four years after her graduation in 1914, an army recruiter came to Kansas City looking for nurses to help with the influenza epidemic that was decimating the military. On October 1, 1918, Nesbit became Reserve Army Nurse N700 665 at Camp Logan Hospital, Houston, Texas. On July 7, 1922, she was sworn into the Regular Army with the rank of 2nd Lieutenant, relative rank.

For the next two decades, Nesbit lived the good life that could be found in military nursing, enjoying post amenities from Fort Sam Houston, Texas to Oahu, Hawaii. She became an indomitable traveler who hiked the American Rockies and rode a camel through the Valley of the Kings in Egypt past the as-yet unopened King Tutankamen's Tomb.

Nesbit arrived for her second tour in the Philippine Islands in January 1940, about the same time that strategists were beginning to address the growing aggression of the Japanese military. In October 1941, she became Chief Nurse of the premier Army facility in the islands, Sternberg Hospital, and the second in command of all Army nurses. Working with her superior, Captain Maude Davison, she helped organize the growing nursing presence in various military posts throughout the Philippines. At that time, Nesbit was a 2nd Lieutenant, relative rank, with 25 years of military service.

Although she and Maude Davison were loyal friends who shared a demand for steadfast work from their nurses, in many ways, the two were opposites. In an era when workplace formality was the norm, everyone called Nesbit "Josie"; she referred to the staff as, "my girls." Filipino nurses called her "Mama Josie." In contrast, none

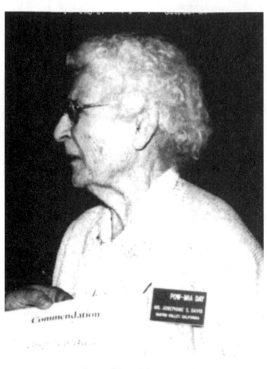

Josephine May Nesbit

would dream of referring to Davison as anything but "Miss." Josie enjoyed drinking coffee and socializing with her staff; Davison was remote and firm. When a personal matter arose, the nurses always sought out Josie for advice, not Davison.

Nesbit's kind, soft voice and approachable style offset a formidable appearance; she was a tall, big Missourian with brown hair and wire-rimmed glasses who wore a size 13 shoe.

After Davison was injured in a bombing raid, Nesbit coordinated the activities of the almost 100 Army nurses in Manila during the initial Japanese assaults of December 1941 and the subsequent allied military retreat from the city. Once her staff was safely out of the city, she volunteered to remain behind with a skeletal crew to care for the patients too ill to be moved. Her request was denied and she soon assumed responsibilities for Bataan General Hospital #2, a huge frontline hospital without buildings, set up under the jungle canopy and eventually holding over 6,000 patients.

Nesbit was in her first battle. Walking the narrow jungle paths, the 48-year-old woman confessed privately to friends that she was tired, but she never flagged. She ran 18 wards and bolstered her staff with her leadership and her own labor. The nurses looked after their patients while Nesbit looked after them. She ordered sick nurses to bed and found shoes, clothes, and underwear for women without these essentials.

On the evening of April 8, 1942, her commanding officer ordered her to have the 53 Army nurses on her staff prepare to evacuate Bataan for Corregidor. The enemy was less than two kilometers from General Hospital #2. Surrender was inevitable. Nesbit inquired about the fate of the 26 Filipino nurses at the hospital. The officer told her the order applied only to the Americans. Nesbit, in an unusually bold voice, told her commander that if every nurse was not allowed to leave, she would not evacuate. A few minutes later, the order was changed and every nurse safely left the jungle.

Later, on May 3, 1942 on Corregidor, Nesbit was offered the chance to escape surrender and imprisonment by leaving on the last allied submarine to run the Japanese blockade of the islands. She flatly refused and reasoned that her nursing experience was more valuable with the doomed patients in the Philippine Islands than elsewhere.

On the afternoon of May 6, 1942 when the Japanese captured Malinta Tunnel on Corregidor, Nesbit marshalled the 26 frightened Filipino nurses to her side. The Japanese stormed the island and invaded the tunnel, but did not interfere with the tall Missouri nurse who stood between them and the other women.

From August 1942 through February 1945, Nesbit and Davison ran the Santo Tomas Internment Camp prison hospital. Although sick from disease and starvation, none of the Army nurses died in POW camp.

After liberation, Nesbit returned home and retired from the military on November 30, 1946 as a 52-year-old Major with 28 years of service. In June 1949, she married a fellow internee, William Davis, and lived a quiet life in California. Nesbit, however, never stopped advocating for her nurses. When she felt the Veterans Administration failed to meet the needs of the former POW nurses, she wrote excoriating letters outlining the nurses' sacrifices and the government's responsibility to them.

During the long years after the war until her death on August 16, 1993, 4 months short of her 100th birthday, Nesbit never forgot "her girls." Each Christmas and birthday for almost 50 years, Nesbit mailed cards and brief notes to each woman on her Philippine staff.

Although failing health prevented her from attending the 1992 ceremony in Washington D.C. celebrating the 50th anniversary of their capture, the 97-year-old nurse wrote a note for the dinner program telling her former staff that her heart and spirit remained young and both were big enough to still embrace her girls.

Her remains were cremated and scattered off the San Francisco coast.

MILITARY AWARDS

Bronze Star Medal, 1941–1945

World War II Victory Medal, 1941–1945

American Defense Service Medal with one Bronze Star and Foreign Service Clasp, 1941–1945

Asiatic-Pacific Campaign Medal with two Bronze Battle Stars, 1941–1945

Distinguished Unit Badge, Presidential Unit Emblem with two Oak Leaf Clusters on Blue Ribbon, 1941–1945

Philippine Defense Ribbon with one
  Bronze Service Star, 1941–1945
Philippine Liberation Ribbon with one
  Bronze Service Star, 1941–1945
American Campaign Medal and American
  Theater Ribbon, 1941–1945
Philippine Independence Ribbon, 1941–
  1945
Legion of Merit, 1941–1942
United States Army Armed Forces Reserve
  Medal with one 10-year service device
World War I Victory Medal, 1918

BIBLIOGRAPHY

Graski, S. (1983, April 9). *Army Nurse Corps Oral History Program Interview. J. Nesbit Davis.* Washington, DC: Center for Military History, Army Nurse Corps Archives, Uncataloged files.

Nesbit Davis, J. (1980, February 21). [Letter to a Colonel Nichols. Seven-page handwritten biographical sketch.] Located in Washington, DC: Center for Military History, Army Nurse Corps Archives, Uncataloged files.

Nesbit, J. (1945). *History of the Army Nurse Corps in the Philippine Islands September 1940–February 1945.* Unpublished manuscript. Located in Washington, DC: Center for Military History, Army Nurse Corps Archives, Uncataloged files.

Elizabeth M. Norman

BETTY NEUMAN
1924–

Dr. Betty Neuman is best known for her contribution of the "Neuman Systems Model" to the body of knowledge of the nursing profession. Her diverse professional nursing contributions have been in organizational development, administrative activities, educational programming after consultation, and continuing education programming and facilitation. Her most recent activities have been related to further development of and consultation for Neuman Systems Model implementation. For most of her professional life she

has maintained a limited independent practice as a Licensed Marriage and Family Counselor while pursuing an active schedule of international speaking and consulting. Her R.N. was earned as a diploma graduate of People's Hospital School of Nursing in Akron, Ohio (now General Hospital) in 1947. In 1957 she graduated with a B.S.N. and in 1966 with an M.S., both from UCLA. In 1985 she received a Ph.D. in Clinical Psychology from Pacific Western University in Los Angeles.

Betty Neuman

Betty Neuman was born Betty Maxine Reynolds in Lowell, Ohio on September 11, 1924, at home on the 100-acre farm of her parents, Zelpha and Lewis Reynolds. She had two brothers, Adrian, 5 years older, and Larry, 5 years younger. Her father, a farmer, suffered from Bright's Disease, spending increasing amounts of time in treatment in a Columbus hospital; he died there at age 36 when Neuman was 11 years old.

When Neuman was a junior in high school, her mother moved with the two youngest children to Marietta, Ohio, leaving the oldest son to manage the farm. Since there was no money for college, after completing high school Neuman found work in Dayton in a defense plant drawing blueprints. When the Cadet Nurse Corps began offering accelerated nurse training to fill the wartime demand for nurses, she enrolled in a 2 1/2-year program at People's Hospital School of Nursing, now General Hospital Medical Center in Akron. She finished the program in 1947. Shortly after graduation, Neuman, her mother and younger brother visited relatives in Florida and a favorite uncle in California.

Neuman decided to remain in California, accepting a position as staff nurse at Los Angeles County General Hospital. She left hospital nursing for a period and worked as a school nurse, and later in an occupational health setting, and then returned to Los Angeles County General Hospital as a private duty nurse.

Betty Reynolds married Richard Neuman in 1954 when he was a resident physician in Ob-Gyn. Later, she helped Dr. Neuman establish his Ob-Gyn practice and acted as manager. During that time she had begun to take evening courses at Los Angeles [County] College and East Los Angeles Junior College, finally accruing enough credits to transfer to UCLA to complete the B.S.N. with academic honors.

Her interest became focused on community mental health and public health, and she began work in 1964 on a Master of Science degree in Mental Health and Public Health Consultation at UCLA which she completed in 1966. Upon completion of her M.S. degree, she assumed the chairmanship of the Community Mental Health post-master's program from which she had graduated. In 1970, she obtained a California certification as a Marriage, Family and Child Counselor and later became an American certified (AAMFT) Marriage and Family Counselor. She currently maintains these active licenses and is also a State of Ohio Social Work board certified counselor.

While Neuman was Chairperson for the UCLA Community Mental Health program she developed, validated, and published a teaching and practice model for mental health consultation. Her 1970 teaching and practice "tool," then entitled "The Whole Person Approach to Patient Problems" is the same diagram/model now known as The Neuman Systems Model. The Model was first presented at a UCLA-sponsored workshop on nursing models in 1971 and first published in 1972. Neuman quickly developed the schematic representation of the model at home to facilitate utilization of its concepts by students in the "overview" course mentioned above. The holistic Model is based on Systems Theory and introduced nurses early to the concept of prevention as intervention.

In 1973, Neuman returned to Ohio to care for her mother and there, in 1974, she implemented a clergy counseling grant for the Washington County (Ohio) Mental Health Services, for both teaching and field supervision of lay and clergy counselors. During this time period she also served as Mental Health Consultant for the State Department of Mental Health in West Virginia and continued to establish herself as lecturer, facilitator and consultant at many staff development workshops for mental health, leadership and organizational skills in Ohio, West Virginia, and California.

In the mid-1970s, more schools of nursing began to adopt the Neuman Systems Model as a basis for curricula, with first actual implementation in 1978. Neuman became increasingly involved in curriculum consultation to assist with the design, implementation, and evaluation of her work at schools in several states.

In 1982 the first book edition of utilization of the Model was published with a second edition following in 1989; a third edition continuing the same theme appeared in 1995. Other publications during the 1980s included chapters and articles, primarily on various applications of the Neuman Systems Model.

In 1986 the first International Neuman Systems Model Symposium was sponsored by Neuman College of Aston, Pennsylvania. The second symposium was convened in Kansas City, Missouri in 1988, at which time the Neuman Trustee Group was formed as an incorporated body to assist Dr. Neuman with the increasing need for information, support, research, development, and travel. Trustees travel extensively, consulting with universities and health care facilities to develop programs in various countries and handbooks explaining the Model in several different languages.

In the 1990s, the Model is being used extensively for practice, teaching and research in more than 175 locations worldwide. In the Netherlands, it has been widely used clinically and for research since the early 1990s. The Model is the basis for the continuity of care program in social psychiatric nursing care delivery in that country. The International Neuman Systems Model Association of the Netherlands began publishing the biennial "Neuman Newsletter" in February 1997. Peter Murray in London, England has created a site on the world wide web for the Neuman Model and Marco Antonini of the Netherlands also maintains a site.

At present, in 1998, Neuman maintains the pattern of private practice as a Marriage and Family Counselor; she is also a licensed real estate agent in Ohio and California. She continues national and international engagements in writing, consulting, and speaking. She has participated in many workshops, and research and theory conferences as panelist or keynoter in many states and many countries.

Dr. Neuman received an Honorary Doctorate of Letters from Neumann College, Aston, Pennsylvania in May, 1992. She has received numerous other awards and honors.

Neuman's second husband, Kree Dicklich, died in 1995. She continues her involvement in personal primary preventive activities which help to facilitate her work and visits with her daughter, Nancy and grand-daughter, Alissa in California.

PUBLICATIONS BY BETTY NEUMAN (SELECTED)

Books

The Neuman systems model: Application to nursing education and practice. (1982). East Norwalk, CT: Appleton-Century-Crofts.

The Neuman systems model (2nd ed.). (1987). East Norwalk, CT: Appleton & Lange.

The Neuman systems model (3rd ed.). (1996). East Norwalk, CT: Appleton & Lange.

Neuman, B., Deloughery, G., & Gebbie, K. M. (1971). Consultation and community organization in community mental health. Baltimore: Williams and Wilkins.

Neuman, B., & Walker, P. (Eds.). (1996). Blueprint for use of nursing models. New York: NLN Press.

Book Chapters

The Betty Neuman health care systems model: A total person approach to patient problems. (1974). In J. Riehl & C. Roy (Eds.), Conceptual models for nursing practice. New York: Appleton-Century-Crofts. (2nd edition published in 1980.)

Family interaction using the Betty Neuman health care systems model. (1986). In I. W. Clements & F. B. Roberts (Eds.), Family health: A theoretical approach to nursing care. New York: John Wiley & Sons.

The Neuman nursing process format: Adapted to a family case study. (1989). In J. Reihl (Ed.), Conceptual models for nursing practice (3rd ed.). East Norwalk, CT: Appleton & Lange.

Articles

Deloughery, G., Gebbie, K. M., & Neuman. B. (1974). Teaching organizational concepts to nurses in community mental health. *Journal of Nursing Education, 13*(1), 8–14.

Neuman, B. (1985). The Neuman Systems Model: Its importance for nursing. *Senior Nurse, 3*(3).

Neuman, B. (1986). The Neuman Systems Model explanation: Its relevance to emerging trends toward holism in nursing. *OMVARNAD* (Nursing Care Book).

Neuman, B. (1990). Health as a continuum based on The Neuman Systems Model. *Nursing Science Quarterly, 3*, 129–135.

Neuman, B. (1996). The Neuman Systems Model in research and practice. *Nursing Science Quarterly, 9*(2), 67–70.

Neuman, B., Gebbie, K. M., & Deloughery, G. (1970). Levels of utilization: Nursing specialists in community mental health. *Journal of Psychiatric Nursing and Mental Health Services, 8*, 37–39.

Neuman, B., Deloughery, G., & Gebbie, K. M. (1970). Changes in problem-solving ability among nurses receiving mental consultation: A pilot study. *Communicating Nursing Research, 3*, 41–53.

Neuman, B., & Young, R. J. (1972). A model for teaching total person approach to patient problems. *Nursing Research, 21*(2), 264–269.

Other Resources

Neuman Newsletter. Santpoort, Netherlands: International Neuman Systems Model Association. Contact: antoni@worldonline.nl

Website maintained by Peter Murray Open University School of Health and Social Welfare, London, UK. http:\\www.lemmus.demon.co.uk/newmodel.htm#book.

The Neuman Systems Model Trustees Group, Inc. Contact: Dr. Rosalie Mirenda, Neumann College, Aston, PA.

Archives for the Neuman Systems Model. Neumann College, Aston, PA. Contact: Dr. Eleanor Repp or Dr. Rosalie Mirenda (see above).

BIBLIOGRAPHY

Brook, M. (1997, October 30). (Telephone interview with Betty Neuman).

Brook, M. (1998, January 16). (Telephone interview with Betty Neuman).

The Helene Fuld Health Trust. (1988). *The nurse theorists: Portraits of excellence. Betty Neuman.* [Videotape]. (Available from Fuld Institute of Technology in Nursing Education, 5 Depot St., Athens, OH 45701).

Marriner-Tomey, A. (1994). *Nursing theorists and their work* (3rd ed.). St. Louis: C. V. Mosby.

Neuman, B. (1987). *The Neuman systems model* (2nd ed.). East Norwalk, CT: Appleton & Lange.

Neuman, B. (1995). *The Neuman systems model* (3rd ed.). East Norwalk, CT: Appleton & Lange.

Neuman, B. Curriculum Vitae. (Unpublished).

Marian Brook

O

VERONICA CAULFIELD O'DAY
1925–

Veronica Caulfield O'Day, second daughter of Benedict James Caulfield and Veronica Martin Caulfield, was born on April 4, 1925 in Yonkers, Westchester County, New York. Both parents and grandparents were of Irish ethnicity and staunchly Roman Catholic. All were born and lived in Yonkers, making Veronica a third-generation Westchesterite. Although retired in 1996, she continues to be a civic leader and an active participant in the affairs of The New York State Nurses Association, as well as continuing her research and assisting at Pace University in the development of a local historical nursing archive

O'Day attended public schools in Yonkers, graduating from the Charles E. Gorton High School in 1943 with honors and a scholarship award from the Athletic Association. As she attempted to continue her education, she learned that the Cochran School of Nursing of St. John's Riverside Hospital in Yonkers had waived tuition because of a severe shortage of nursing staff. She enrolled in the School on August 30, 1943 and when the Cadet Nurse Corps was established shortly after her enrollment, she became a Cadet Nurse.

Veronica Caulfield O'Day

To her surprise, she found the vigorous and demanding schedule of diploma education in the mid-1940s both satisfying and intellectually stimulating. She especially liked the interaction with adult and older patients and the satisfaction of assisting them to recovery and discharge. At that time, cholecystectomy patients were hospitalized for a minimum of 3 weeks and prostatectomy patients usually for 6 weeks. On the medical units, some patients with cardiac problems were hospitalized for 2 to 3 months. These long hospitalization periods

provided time to establish rapport and get to know these people very well.

After working 1 year as a staff nurse on rotating shifts, O'Day enrolled in the nursing program at New York University (NYU), one of the few students who was not on the G.I. Bill. Over the next 3 years, she attended NYU part time and continued working nights, earning a B.S. in Nursing Education in 1950. Degree in hand she was quickly appointed to the faculty of the Cochran School of Nursing and shortly after she was appointed Assistant Director of Nursing.

On November 3, 1951, Veronica and William M. O'Day were married. They adopted two children, James Martin O'Day in 1958 and Anne Maureen O'Day in April, 1962. After these adoptions, O'Day devoted herself to her family and enjoyed life at home with her young children.

In 1970 she enrolled at Hunter College in New York City to earn her master's degree. On her completion of the degree, she joined the faculty of Bronx Community College as Assistant Professor to teach medical/surgical nursing. In 1977 she was appointed Assistant Professor at the Lienhard School of Nursing, Pace University, and at the same time entered the Ph.D. program at New York University. She received her Ph.D. in Nursing in 1981. In 1983 she was appointed chairperson of the Generic Master's Department. She served in this role until 1987 when reorganization changed her title to Program Director of the Combined Degree Program. She held this position as Associate Professor and Professor until she made the decision to retire.

During O'Day's tenure as chairperson of the Generic Master's Program, it expanded and was reorganized into a combined degree program. In 1995–96 she represented Pace University in the activities of an international organization, Consortium of Institutes of Higher Education in Health and Rehabilitation in Europe. She continues her international nursing education interests as a member of the newly formed North American Consortium of Nursing and Allied Health.

Completion of the doctoral program freed O'Day to assume a dynamic leadership role in local professional affairs. A staunch believer in the efficacy of professional organization, she was elected delegate to the American Nurses Association conventions from New York State District 16. She filled this post until 1997. She also served District 16 as president and board member as well as actively participating in numerous activities of the New York State Nurses Association.

One of O'Day's most significant contributions was her founder's role in the establishment of the first four-school at-large chapters of Sigma Theta Tau International as member of the executive committee and chairperson of the establishment planning committee.

Community service has been a significant part of O'Day's professional life. This intensified after husband Bill died in 1986. As consultant and reviewer of fundable nursing research for the American Heart Association, Westchester/Putnam Counties and as member of the Research Committee of Montrose Veteran's Administration Hospital, Montrose, NY, she encouraged nursing research. Her work with the Westchester Health Action Coalition has included leadership on various committees. This, as well as her service on the Board of Directors of the Westchester/Putnam Adult Day Care Center of Peekskill, NY, earned her the honor of being named to the Senior Citizen Hall of Fame by the Westchester County Office for the Aging.

O'Day's twin professional passions, the importance of nursing organizations and the significance of nursing history stimulated her to conduct a major historical research project on the history of District 16

of the New York State Nurses Association. Interest in nursing history has been a strong theme in her life. She served as Archivist for the early Westchester Nursing History Committee, contributed to a prior publication of *Biographical Dictionary of American Nurses*, and continues as Chairperson of the Zeta Omega Chapter-At-Large Heritage Committee. Her post-retirement project is to work on the development of an archive of local nursing history housed at Pace University. In addition, she continues to guide students who write master's theses on nursing history. In 1997 she was the recipient of the first Mae J. Pepper Award for her contributions to nursing.

PUBLICATIONS BY VERONICA CAULFIELD O'DAY

May Ayres Burgess, Ph.D. 1925–1945. (1988). In V. L. Bullough & O. M. Church (Eds.), *Biographical dictionary of American nurses* (pp. 52–54). New York: Garland.

Directory of innovative nursing practices in Westchester County. (1989). New York: Office of Assembly Speaker Mel Miller.

Breaking away: How District 16, NYSNA got started. (1990). *Journal of the New York State Nurses Association.*

An investigation of membership characteristics throughout the development and history of the Nurses' Association of Westchester County, 1938–1992. (1994a). Author.

Zeta Omega, Westchester/Rockland at Large Chapter of Sigma Theta Tau, International Honor Society of Nursing, past, present, and future. (1994b). [Videotape. Narrated by the founder, Veronica C. O'Day, PhD. R.N.]

Hiestand, W., & O'Day, V. (1993). Access to graduate education for registered nurses with non-nursing baccalaureate degrees. *Journal of Professional Nursing, 9,* 220–227.

Wanda C. Hiestand

JEROME EDWIN OLMSTED
1943–1967

The name of First Lieutenant Jerome Olmsted is among the names of ten nurses inscribed in "The Wall"—the Vietnam War Memorial in Washington, DC (Panel 31E, Line 15). He died in a plane crash while on active duty with the Army Nurse Corps in Vietnam.

Jerome Edwin Olmsted

Olmsted was born in Clintonville, Wisconsin, May 11, 1943, to Mr. and Mrs. Arlyn Olmsted. After graduating from the Clintonville High School, he entered the Alexian Brothers School for Male Nurses in Chicago, receiving his diploma in 1964. Two years later, he completed the nurse anesthesia course at the St. Francis Hospital School of Anesthesia in LaCrosse, Wisconsin.

He worked for a short time at the Medford (Wisconsin) Hospital before entering the Army Nurse Corps in May 1966. His basic training was at Fort Sill, Oklahoma, where he remained until May the following year, when he was sent to Vietnam.

Before entering the service, Olmsted married Elizabeth Hanson of Galesville,

Wisconsin, on May 12, 1966. Their daughter Sherry was born in May 1967, just before he left for Vietnam.

Olmsted was killed November 30, 1967, along with three other nurses, when their C-47 transport plane crashed. They were returning from Pleiku to the 67th Evacuation Hospital in Que Nhon, where he had been stationed since his arrival in Vietnam.

His body was flown home and military rites were conducted at St. Rose Catholic Church. He was buried at the Graceland Cemetery in Clintonville. In addition to his wife and daughter, Olmsted was survived by his parents, a sister Barbara, and four brothers, William, John, Tom, and Kenneth.

A memorial to Jerome Olmsted, with a rubbing of his name from the Vietnam wall, hangs at the headquarters of the Wisconsin Nurses Association in Madison.

BIBLIOGRAPHY

Archives. Alexian Brothers Immaculate Conception Province. Elk Grove Village, IL.

Jerome Olmsted reported missing. (1967, December 7). *Clintonville* (Wisconsin) *Tribune Gazette.*

Spelts, D. (1986). Nurses who served—and did not return. *American Journal of Nursing, 86,* 1037–1038.

Son's body to be flown home. (1967, December 14). *Clintonville Tribune Gazette.*

Signe S. Cooper

MARY D. OSBORNE
1875–1946

Mary D. Osborne served as Director of Public Health Nursing with the Mississippi State Department of Health from 1921 through 1946. Early in her new career, Osborne assessed the major public health problems in Mississippi as infectious diseases, including tuberculosis, and the highest infant and maternal mortality rates in the nation. Osborne's vision of public health nursing as a teacher of health with a duty to prevent sickness ushered in a new institution within the Mississippi Department of Health. Osborne's endeavors to establish the focus of public health nursing are considered extraordinary, and became integral to the mission of the department to provide for the protection of life and health and to prevent the spread of disease.

Mary D. Osborne

Osborne was a native of Ohio. Little is known about her early life or family. Osborne never married nor had children. While it is known that she continued to visit family in Ohio, no family has been located for further information about her.

The first documented history of Osborne is in 1902 with her graduation from the Akron City Hospital School of Nursing in Akron, Ohio. In 1906, Osborne was appointed Assistant Director of Nurses, Akron City Hospital. Osborne left this position to expand her education completing 6 months of postgraduate work at Woman's

Hospital in New York City. Following this educational opportunity, Osborne became an Assistant Director of Nurses at Woman's Hospital. In 1912, Osborne became Supervisor of Nurses with the Association for Improving the Condition of the Poor, New York which was later called the Community Service Society.

While in New York, Osborne became acquainted with Harry Hopkins, a close associate of Franklin D. Roosevelt. She also became associated with the American Red Cross during her stay in New York and it was this association which eventually led her to Mississippi.

On February 27, 1920, the American Red Cross approached the Mississippi Board of Health with the request to form a cooperative relation that would place a state nurse in the Office of the Board of Health to head up public health nursing activities. Nannie J. Lackland was the first appointment though she resigned in late 1920. In April, 1921, Osborne was appointed by the Atlanta office of the American Red Cross as Director of Public Health Nursing for the Mississippi Department of Health. Osborne's appointment to Mississippi was intended to be an interim period to address the multitude of maternal and child health problems being identified in the state. Within months, Osborne accepted a permanent appointment by Dr. Felix J. Underwood, Mississippi State Board of Health Secretary and Executive Officer, as the Director of Public Health Nursing and Supervisor of the Division of Maternal and Child Health.

Osborne was acutely aware from her postgraduate work at Woman's Hospital and work experiences in New York of the problems related to infant and maternal mortality in Mississippi. She felt improvements had to be made in home delivery techniques, in access to prenatal care, and to teach basic nutrition and personal hygiene.

One of Osborne's first missions was to recruit and train public health nurses and in this she was aided by the Maternity and Infant Act, also known as the Sheppard-Towner Act, enacted in 1921. This act set a precedent for federal grant-in-aid programs to states for child and maternal care and education of personnel. Although nurses in Mississippi were registered at this time, they often lacked instruction and experience in the areas of communicable diseases and maternal and infant care. She set up educational sessions for public health nurses and this gave Osborne an opportunity to share and emulate her philosophy and the qualities she deemed essential in public health nursing.

Mississippi depended heavily on lay midwives, most of whom were in need of instruction and supervision in prenatal care, personal hygiene, and delivery techniques. By 1922, Osborne had gained support, though reluctantly, from private physicians for public health nursing supervision of midwives, completed the *Manual for Midwives* to use as a teaching guide and reference for the midwife, established policies for midwives' participation in educational programs, and received approval from the Board of Health for midwives who met select requirements to be issued permits. Within 2 years, the Mississippi physicians recognized the value of Osborne's efforts and responded in a follow-up survey to keep the public health nurses and their supervisional work with the lay midwives.

National and international recognition was bestowed upon Osborne at the International Council of Nursing in Montreal in 1929. This recognition was based on Osborne's accomplishments in lowering maternal and infant mortality rates through improved midwife practice and in forging a strong network of public health nurses in the state. In 1937, Dr. Felix J. Underwood, State Health Officer at the time, recognized Osborne for the midwifery supervision program and her development of the *Manual for Midwives* stating "the Mississippi midwife program attracted attention of workers in other states and countries, and more requests have come from foreign countries for the midwife manual than for all other health bulletins combined" (Underwood & Whitfield, 1937).

During the period she was developing public health nursing focus and activities within the state, Osborne attended maternal and infant hygiene conferences in Washington, D.C.; participated in meetings of the three national nursing bodies located in Detroit at that time; attended the regional meeting of the National Organization for Public Health Nursing in Atlanta; and accompanied representatives from the American Red Cross, the National Organization for Public Health Nursing, and the Federal Children's Bureau on field visits throughout the state.

Osborne also recognized the independent practice of the public health nurse in these early formation years. While Osborne acknowledged working with and for the physician as a primary responsibility of public health nursing, she equally promoted public health nursing as a distinct and specialized art which required a higher degree of initiative and judgment by the nurse. In 1932, Osborne was elected president of the Mississippi Nurses Association. Since Osborne had made membership to the state association a requirement for nurses entering public health, Osborne established a special interest group for public health nursing, only the second special interest group to be formed within the state association.

The Great Depression years resulted in extremely adverse public health effects, including unemployment, homelessness, hunger, general ill health and malnutrition, and increased communicable disease rates. In 1934, to create jobs and a sense of hope for the public, President Franklin D. Roosevelt initiated a government expansion known as the New Deal. Harry Hopkins, a friend of Osborne's, was appointed administrator of Roosevelt's New Deal programs. The Federal Emergency Relief Administration, the Civil Works Administration, the Works Progress Administration, and the Social Security Act brought forth funding for public health initiatives and nursing positions. Osborne, having developed many national and state relationships, seized the moment to fulfill her intent of securing funds to assure at least one public health nursing position in all 82 Mississippi counties. While in 1921 only seven public health nurses worked in the state, this number increased to 165 by 1940.

While Osborne succeeded in her goals to strengthen the public health nursing work force, recruiting qualified public health nurses in Mississippi was difficult. The Commonwealth Fund provided scholarships for public health practitioners in Mississippi. Interviewed and selected by Osborne, 12 nurses were given scholarships for public health nursing education and training in 1931–1933 and eleven in 1933–35. Nurses attended Vanderbilt University, Columbia Teacher's College, and Western Reserve University for education and training specifically for public health nurses in maternal and child health and in communicable diseases. By 1936 federal funding became available for this purpose, and an additional 60 public health nurses received scholarship opportunities from 1937 through 1940.

Osborne held the position as Director of Public Health Nursing until her retirement on June 30, 1946, due to illness. She immediately returned to Ohio to reside with a sister. Osborne died within her first week of retirement on July 7, 1946, and is buried in Jackson, Mississippi.

The Mississippi Public Health Association, Nursing Section, established the Mary D. Osborne Public Health Nurse of the Year award in 1980. The award is presented annually to a public health nurse who has made significant contributions and service in public health nursing through quality patient care and strengthening the professional public health nursing image.

Osborne contributed much to the development of professional nursing and to the caliber of public health nursing. Her induction into the 1996 American Nurses Association Hall of Fame is an honor to all public health nurses. The newest building addition to the Mississippi Department of Health complex in Jackson, Mississippi, completed in 1999, was named for Mary D. Osborne, giving enduring recognition to Osborne's achievements.

BIBLIOGRAPHY

Morton, M., Roberts, E., & Bender, K. (1993). *Celebrating public health nursing: Caring for Mississippi's communities with courage and compassion, 1920–1993.* Jackson, MS: Mississippi Department of Health.

Underwood, F. J., & Whitfield, R. N. (1938). *Public health and medical licensure in the State of Mississippi, 1798–1937.* Jackson, MS: The Tucker Printing House.

Underwood, F. J., & Whitfield, R. N. (1948). *Public health and medical licensure in the State of Mississippi, 1938–1947.* Jackson, MS: The Tucker Printing House.

Waits, J., Roberts, E., & McGrew, W. (1986). *Passing on the flame: The history of the Mississippi Nurses Association.* Jackson, MS: Mississippi Nurses Association.

Margaret Morton

P

EDITH M. PARTRIDGE
1884–1981

The strength of the Wisconsin State Nurses Association and the success of its legislative efforts is due greatly to the efforts of Edith M. Partridge. Partridge served as Executive Secretary for the Wisconsin State Nurses Association from 1924 to 1956. During that time, important legislation concerning nursing practice as well as the establishment of a State Department of Nurses was created. Partridge made numerous 90-mile trips between Milwaukee and Madison to promote legislative efforts on behalf of nursing while raising two daughters and assisting her physician husband with his practice.

Partridge was born Edith Maude Cowie on June 8, 1884 in Sindlesham, Berkshire, England in 1884 to Charles and Hannah (Creamer) Cowie. She was educated through the 8th grade in England. Although Partridge wanted to pursue a nursing career, further educational opportunities were limited because she was the child of a servant; her father was the chief butler of the country estate of the owner of the *London Times*. It was arranged that Partridge visit her uncle in Detroit, Michigan in 1903 at the age of 19. During that visit, her uncle reassured her that he would see to it that she got a nursing education, a goal that she could not accomplish in England. She enrolled in the nursing program at Grace Hospital in Detroit and graduated at the top of her class in 1906.

She initially worked as a private duty nurse, then was appointed superintendent at Bronson Hospital at Kalamazoo, Michi-

Edith M. Partridge

gan from 1912 to 1916. During Partridge's employment in Michigan, she became active in several organizations. She served as president of the Kalamazoo Graduate Nurse Association. She also served as a member of the Board of Directors of the Michigan State Nurses Association.

Partridge met her future husband, Dr. Carroll Dunham Partridge, a general practitioner who was doing research for Upjohn, pharmaceutical manufacturer in Michigan. They were married in 1916 and moved to Milwaukee in 1917, just prior to the United States' involvement in World War I. Although Partridge did not intend to continue with nursing following her marriage, with the onset of World War I, she became a supervisor of Red Cross home nursing classes in Milwaukee. Following the war, the Partridges moved to Wausau, Wisconsin, where Partridge served as city health officer until 1924. While in Wausau, Partridge organized the 8th district of the Wisconsin State Nurses Association and became its first secretary. She was elected to the Board of Directors of the Wisconsin State Nurses Association in 1920 and elected secretary in 1924.

In 1924, the Partridges moved to Cudahy, Wisconsin, a city close to Milwaukee where she and Dr. Partridge operated the Cudahy Hospital, a small maternity and emergency hospital out of their home until the early 1950s. One of the bedrooms in their home was made up as a hospital room for overnight patients. Police would often bring accident victims to the hospital because there was nowhere else to take them. Her nursing practice was more of a nurse practitioner role, soaking wounds to prevent infection prior to the advent of antibiotics, suturing lacerations when her husband was unavailable, and assisting with surgeries and deliveries.

Partridge was an energetic, determined individual who maintained the state nursing office in her home for 23 years before moving it to downtown Milwaukee in 1947. Her commitment to nursing, along with her organizational skills, played a significant role in the success of many hallmark legislative efforts. During her tenure as executive secretary, the Wisconsin legislature enacted laws that provided state money for nursing scholarships, created a state Department of Nurses, and defined professional nursing, a definition that is currently being used. Often, the legislative committee of the Wisconsin State Nurses Association, along with Partridge, would make daily pilgrimages to Madison when the legislators were in session. Minutes of the WSNA legislative committee recorded by Partridge reflect the ongoing battles with the Medical Society and legislators. Another responsibility of her job as executive secretary was to publish the monthly newsletter, *Bulletin of the Wisconsin State Nurses Association.*

In addition to being secretary for the state nursing association, Ms. Partridge was active in the Milwaukee District Nursing Association, serving as its president from 1924–1926 and as a member of the Board of Directors for 25 years. Partridge chaired the Wisconsin Council for Improvement of Patient Care. On the national level, she was involved in the American Nurses Association serving on its Bylaws and Nominating Committees for many years. She also served on the Board of Directors for the *American Journal of Nursing.*

Partridge's life as a wife of a physician and mother of two girls, Mary (Christ) Becker and Nancy (Arden) Eichsteadt, led to her very active participation in organizations outside of nursing. Partridge retired from her job as executive secretary at the age of 72, a year after her husband died. She worked as executive secretary for the Wisconsin Association of Licensed Practical Nurses for 2 years after her retirement. At age 80, she was featured in the *Milwaukee Journal* for successfully passing the 6-hour examination to become a registered parliamentarian.

Partridge died on March 6, 1981 at the age of 96 in West Allis, Wisconsin. She was alert and animated up until her death. The success of the Wisconsin Nurses Association is indebted to her early efforts and perseverance.

PUBLICATIONS BY EDITH M. PARTRIDGE

Wisconsin Scholarship Program for Graduate Nurses. (1956). *American Journal of Nursing, 56,* 1562–1563.

BIBLIOGRAPHY

Cooper, S. S. (1991, October 22). Edith Partridge. *NURSINGmatters.*

Mirr, M. (1998, June 1). Telephone interview with M. Becker.

Mirr, M. (1998, May 28). Telephone interview with N. Eichsteadt.

Mirr, M. P. (1980, October 1). Interview with E. Partridge.

Mrs. Partridge calls halt to long nursing career. (1956, June 28). *The Milwaukee Journal.*

New career called to order. (1964, June 14). *The Milwaukee Journal.*

M. Mirr

META RUTTER PENNOCK (NEWMAN)
ca. 1892–1959

Meta Rutter Pennock (Newman)

Although she was not a nurse, Meta Pennock (Newman) made important contributions to the nursing literature. She was an editor of the *Trained Nurse and Hospital Review* for over 20 years, and edited several nursing books.

Pennock was a 1917 graduate of Barnard College in New York City. In 1941, she was awarded an M.A. in public health education from Columbia University. Two years after leaving Barnard, she married Athol Newman, but professionally she used her maiden name, somewhat unusually for the time.

In 1921, she was appointed managing editor of the *Trained Nurse and Hospital Review* (later titled *Nursing World*; it ceased publication in 1960). Seven years later, she was named Editor-in-Chief.

During the time Pennock was editor, there were few nursing periodicals. The *Trained Nurse* was widely read, perhaps because it was somewhat less formal than its major competitor, the *American Journal of Nursing* (AJN). Begun in 1888, it preceded the AJN by 12 years. A commercial venture, it was published by the Lakeside Publishing Company in New York City. Its masthead identified it as a "monthly magazine devoted to professional nursing in Private Practice, Hospitals and Public Health," but it also included articles on nursing education. During Pennock's tenure, a section on anesthesia was added for nurses in the field, and later a number of articles on industrial nursing appeared.

Authorship of much of the content in the early issues Pennock edited is not identified, but since she was the sole editor, presumably she wrote it. An introductory page titled, "Just a Word with You" was signed "Your editor," without a name. A section "Editorially Speaking" was not signed; it usually addressed current issues in nursing.

Major articles were on a wide range of topics. Clinical content was limited; this may have been because Pennock was not a nurse and could not identify appropriate clinical content, but also this was at a time when few nurses were writing. Pennock's interest in international affairs is evident in the frequent articles describing nursing and hospitals in other countries.

It appears that Pennock also wrote the book reviews in the early issues she edited; later on they are signed by the reviewers, and she noted the ones she wrote with her initials "M.P." On the few occasions when she wrote a major article, she is listed as author.

Pennock made a special contribution to nursing history by editing two books on nursing biography, *Makers of Nursing History*, the second an expansion of the first. The brief biographies with photographs identify contributions of many nursing leaders that might otherwise have been lost.

In 1940, both Pennock and Janet Geister, who had previously contributed numerous articles to the publication, were listed as editors. Pennock resigned in August of the next year and Geister became editor-in-chief.

Pennock later served as assistant director of health education for the National Foundation for Infantile Paralysis (now the National Foundation—March of Dimes). She helped organize the Planned Parenthood Association of New Jersey, and served as president of the American Association of Women in Public Health. In 1953, the Newmans moved to Williamsburg, Virginia. Here she worked on behalf of the mentally ill at Eastern State Hospital.

Meta Pennock Newman died at age 61 on January 8, 1959 in Cambridge, England, while visiting her daughter. She was survived by her daughter, Priscilla Newman Nagel, her husband, her sister, Priscilla Fisher, and two grandsons. The journal ceased publication the year following her death.

PUBLICATIONS BY META RUTTER PENNOCK (NEWMAN)

Books

Makers of nursing history (Ed.). (1928). New York: Lakeside Publishing Company (Revised and expanded, 1940).

Articles (Selected)

Behind the veil in Europe: The plight of the small democracies. *Trained Nurse and Hospital Review, 106,* 177–185; 227.

Editorials. *Trained Nurse and Hospital Review* (1921–1941).

New ethics in publicity. (1931). *Trained Nurse and Hospital Review, 87,* 752–757; 800.

BIBLIOGRAPHY

In memoriam: Meta Pennock Newman and Mary M. Roberts. (1959). *Nursing World, 133,* 18.

Meta Pennock Newman [obituary]. (1959). *American Journal of Nursing, 59,* 402, 404.

Moss, J. R. (1987). *Walking the tightrope: The story of nursing as told by 19th century nursing journals.* Doctoral dissertation, University of Iowa.

Signe S. Cooper

ELIZA FARISH PILLARS
1892–1970

Eliza Farish Pillars was a major trailblazer for minorities in nursing in the South, and she worked effortlessly to reduce sickness and death among Blacks in Mississippi. She was a leader in public health nursing and the first Black registered nurse in the state of Mississippi to work for the Mississippi State Board of Health.

Eliza Farish Pillars was born in Jackson, Mississippi on April 26, 1892, to Walter L. Farish and Ella Manuel Farish. She was one of seven children and the oldest girl. She attended Smith Robertson School in Jackson, then studied at Utica Institute, in Utica, Mississippi. From there she received a diploma from Walden University in Nashville, Tennessee in 1909. Pillars wanted to be a nurse, but had to travel out of the state because Blacks were not allowed to attend nursing school in Mississippi. She entered the School of Nursing-Hubbard Hospital at Meharry Medical College in Nashville, Tennessee, graduating as a registered nurse in 1912.

Eliza Farish Pillars

After graduation, she worked as an office nurse, and as a private duty nurse in homes and as well as a staff nurse at the Jackson Infirmary Charity Hospital, the only hospital to admit Blacks in Jackson. Pillars and her sister, Anna Farish, a licensed practical nurse, and as a owned and operated her own 12-bed hospital, the Mercy Hospital, in Jackson, Mississippi on Farish Street from 1919 to 1925. Farish Street was named in honor of her family. Today, the area is designated as the Farish Street Neighborhood Historical District. Pillars and her sister later renovated the old family home on East Davis Street in this historic area as a place to care for Black patients.

Discrimination was pervasive in America, especially in the South. Eighty percent of Black women in the 1920s had their babies at home with the assistance of "granny midwives." At that time, Mississippi had the highest infant morbidity rate among Blacks in America. On February 1, 1926, the Missis-

sippi State Board of Health hired Pillars as an assistant to Mary D. Osborne, director of public health nursing. Her responsibilities were largely in midwifery supervision and health education in Negro schools and colleges throughout the state of Mississippi. She held countywide meetings to renew permits and provided individual and group teachings, and supervision of non-nurse midwives to make them more efficient and safe. She taught these midwives prenatal, postnatal, and actual deliveries. The Sheppard-Towner Act and the Rosenwald Fund (Rockefeller Foundation) provided educational scholarships to nurses for maternal and infant care. Because of dire poverty, ignorance, superstition, and the indifference of the authorities, funds were not provided for health care centers; consequently, Pillars converted rooms in rural shanties into delivery rooms in each community.

Pillars not only worked with midwives, but conducted health and hygiene classes for students, teachers, and community leaders, working closely with them in improving the health of school children. She gave vaccines and inoculations against communicable disease in schools, churches, and private homes. Wherever there was a health problem, she developed a program to meet the needs of her race. Through her services many young women were inspired to enter the nursing profession. She contributed greatly to public health work during her 19 years tenure with the Mississippi State Board of Health.

Pillars played a prominent role after Mississippi's historic 1927 flood. She worked diligently with the American Red Cross in setting up first-aid stations in Vicksburg and Natchez to take care of flood refugees as they were brought in by boat down the Mississippi River from the Delta section of the state. At the outbreak of World War II, there was a need for nurse's aides. Pillars taught the first nurse's aide class at the Baptist Hospital in Jackson, Mississippi.

In 1936, Pillars completed 4 months of postgraduate work at the Medical College of Virginia in Richmond, Virginia. Pillars actively participated in Lambda Pi Alpha Sorority (Medical) and served as president and financial secretary of the Southern Region of the National Association of Colored Graduate Nurses. During this time period, she married Euclid Pillars and although they had no children, she helped raised a niece, Minnie L. Farish. Because of practices of racial exclusion and denied membership in the Mississippi Nurses Association, five Black registered nurses in Jackson, Mississippi in 1945 had the conviction that there was need for an organized independent Black nurse's club to serve as a forum for sharing information. It was this steering committee that met and pooled their efforts and resources to aid in improving the status of Black nurses in Jackson and surrounding areas. It was at this time the Colored Women Club, later known as the Colored Registered Nurses' Club, became a reality.

Pillars was awarded by proxy the 14th and last Mary Mahoney Medal given by the National Association of Colored Nurses for distinguished service to nursing and the community at the Essex House in New York, January 26, 1951. Currently, the award is presented by the American Nurses Association to a minority nurse for distinguished service.

Pillars died June 15, 1970 at the age of 78 and is buried in Garden Memorial Park Cemetery in Jackson, Mississippi. The club changed its name to the Eliza Pillars Registered Nurses' Club in her honor.

On April 22, 1982, a charter was obtained and the Eliza Pillars Registered Nurses' Association, Inc. (EPRNA) of Jackson, Mississippi became an organization dedicated to excellence in health care. As the interest of the nurses in the state grew, the necessity too organized statewide became apparent.

In 1984, plans began, with the state divided into seven districts with the headquarters located in Jackson. In 1985, the name was changed to the Eliza Pillars Registered Nurses' State Association, Inc. (EPRNSA). Pillars was inducted posthumously into the Mississippi Nurses' Association's Hall of Fame during the observance of their Diamond Jubilee October 15, 1986. By 1989, all seven districts were organized and functioning to meet the needs of the people in their respective communities in Mississippi.

In February 1991, the Jackson district donated a portrait of Pillars to the Mississippi State Department of Health where it is proudly displayed in the main foyer. In 1995, the Eliza Pillars Registered Nurses' State Association celebrated its 50th Anniversary. The celebrations reinforced the positive self-image of Black registered nurses, developed pride in the past, hoped for the future, and a better understanding and appreciation of the struggles and contributions of Black Mississippi nurses. Today, the membership continues the work of its founders and namesake by upholding to the philosophy of providing excellent health care to the African-American communities in Mississippi and the nation. Eliza Farish Pillars' work, life, dedication, and inspiration will be remembered forever by the nurses in Mississippi.

BIBLIOGRAPHY

Carnegie, M. E. (1986). *The path we tread: Blacks in nursing: 1854–1984*. Philadelphia: Lippincott.
Carnegie, M. E. (1995). *The path we tread: Blacks in nursing: Worldwide, 1854–1994*. New York: National League for Nursing Press.
Eliza Pillars Registered Nurses' Association. (1989). Bylaws, scrapbook, and historical files. Jackson, MS.
Jackson nurse receives Mary Mahoney Medal. (1951, January). *The Mississippi RN*, 6.
Morton, M., Roberts, E. R., & Bender, K. W. (1993). *Celebrating public health nursing: Caring for Mississippi's communities with courage and compassion: 1920–*

1993 (pp. 13–14; 25). Jackson, MS: Mississippi State Department of Health.

Roberts, E. R., & Reeb, R. M. (1994). Mississippi public health nurses and midwives: A partnership that worked. *Public Health Nursing, 11*(2), 57–63.

Sewell, G. A., & Dwight, M. L. (1984). *Mississippi Black history makers.* University of Mississippi: University Press.

Underwood, F. A., & Whitfield, R. N. (1938). *Public health and medical licensure in the state of Mississippi: 1798–1937* (Vol. I, pp. 80; 91–92). Jackson, MS: Tucker Printing House.

Underwood, F. A., & Whitfield, R. N. (1950). *Public health and medical licensure in the state of Mississippi: 1938–1947* (Vol. II, pp. 103–105). Jackson, MS: Mississippi State Department of Health.

Rosie Lee Calvin

GERTRUDE PLOTZKE
1906–1997

Gertrude Plotzke set up the Chicago Board of Health Mothers' Breast Milk Station in 1938 and was the Station's first supervisor. In the course of running the Station, Plotzke devised schemes to collect, pasteurize, store, and distribute human milk to hospitals and homes where nurses and mothers fed it to sick, underweight, and, most commonly, premature infants. Public health nurses from around the country came to Chicago to observe Plotzke's facility in preparation for opening similar operations in other cities.

Plotzke was born to Joseph Plotzke, a city fireman, and Mary Kwasniak on September 7, 1906 in Hammond, Indiana. Her Catholic parents met in Chicago after emigrating from Poland. They moved to Hammond shortly after their marriage in 1898. Plotzke was the seventh of their ten children.

Plotzke began her nurses' training program at St. Margaret's Hospital in Hammond in the late 1920s. She later received her registered nurse degree from Jackson Park Hospital in Chicago. In 1937 she went to work for the Chicago Board of Health

as a public health nurse, caring for new mothers and their babies in their homes.

Plotzke opened the Chicago Board of Health Mothers' Breast Milk Station in 1938 at the behest of Chicago Commissioner of Health Herman Bundesen. Human milk stations were not new to the United States. Physicians, public health bodies, and medical charities had collected human milk for the use of sick infants whose mothers did not breastfeed them since at least 1910, when Boston-area pediatricians opened a Wet Nurse Directory. By 1929 at least 20 American cities had facilities which provided bottled human milk to babies who needed it. But the Breast Milk Station in Chicago—which became a cornerstone of the Chicago City-Wide Plan for the Care of Premature Infants inaugurated in 1935—was unique in that it focused largely (although not exclusively) on the needs of premature infants, and was launched as part of the Health Department's concerted effort to lower the infant mortality rate.

Bundesen chose to better premature infant care in the city not only because premature birth was the largest cause of infant death in Chicago in 1935, but because Chicago was already a center for the innovative care of premature babies. At the Premature Station housed at Sarah Morris Children's Hospital, Julius Hess, later dubbed the father of neonatal medicine, and Evelyn Lundeen, the station's supervising nurse, developed what became widely acknowledged as standard care for premature infants. A primary aim of that care was provision of appropriate nutrition, deemed to be human milk until an infant weighed at least 4 or 4 1/2 pounds. This decree influenced the Board of Health to revise its health code in 1931 to require hospitals to provide all hospitalized premature infants with human milk. In 1938 the Board of Health decided to make it easier for hospitals to locate human milk by supplying it free of charge through their Milk Station.

The Breast Milk Station was located on the city's south side, at Sixty-third and Cottage Grove Avenues. Designed by Plotzke, the Station consisted of a bathroom, a utility room, a scrub room, a milk-collection room where women sat together at a large table and expressed their milk, and a small pasteurizing plant where nurses pasteurized and bottled the milk and sterilized equipment.

Plotzke located potential human milk donors via public health nurses or through doctors who worked at the Board's many free maternal-care or well-baby clinics. When these nurses or doctors examined a mother who produced a lot of milk and who had a particularly healthy baby to show for it, they told her about the Breast Milk Station and asked her if she wanted to earn extra money by selling her milk. If she expressed an interest, a nurse accompanied her to the Breast Milk Station for a thorough physical. A dental examination was part of the physical—Plotzke deemed a mother's ability to consume a variety of foods essential to good milk production. Donor-mothers continued to receive free medical examinations for as long as they supplied the Station with milk—the Station's doctor took their blood pressure and cultured their throats weekly and drew their blood monthly to check for venereal disease. Donors' babies received regular physicals as well. Refusing to take a mother's milk at the expense of her baby's health, the Station doctor charted the weight of all donors' babies.

The Board of Health paid women 5 cents an ounce for their milk in 1935, 9 cents an ounce in 1944, and 13 cents an ounce by the time the station closed in the early 1960s. Mothers also earned street car tokens and a quart of cow's milk each day. Plotzke intended the cow's milk to enhance lactating

mothers' diets, so she insisted that they drink half the quart before they left the Station. Otherwise, she feared, they would take the milk home and give all of it to their children.

Because the Breast Milk Station was located in an African-American neighborhood, virtually all the station's donor-mothers were African-American. During the early years of operation, as many as 45 women arrived at the Station each morning to express their milk. Donating milk was a particularly convenient way for a mother with an infant to earn money during the Great Depression. In the Station's later years, only an average of 10 mothers donated on a daily basis. Mothers usually expressed their milk daily at the Station for 6 to 9 months after the birth of their baby, but at least one mother donated for 2 to 2 1/2 years with each of her several babies.

Donors lined up at the Station's three sinks every morning, 7 days a week, to scrub their fingernails, hands, arms, and breasts in a ritual carefully devised and taught to them by Plotzke. Plotzke's lessons in sanitation and hygiene made such an indelible impression on these women that when nurses from other locales occasionally came to observe the Station's procedures, donor-mothers complained that the nurses were not washing themselves properly and that they might contaminate the milk.

After scrubbing, mothers donned sterile white gowns, and placed masks over their mouths and bandannas over their hair. Then they placed disinfected towels under their breasts and hand expressed their milk into sterile tin cups for an hour. Plotzke and her assistant then measured each donor's milk, poured the milk into 2-, 4-, and 8-ounce bottles, and placed the bottles on ice in buckets. Each mother donated from 16 to 45 ounces of milk daily.

After mothers left, Plotzke and her assistant—scrubbed, gowned, and masked as if about to perform surgery—pasteurized the milk in a 15-gallon pasteurizer. Then they cooled their cache immediately. As orders began to arrive they filled them, labeling each bottle with the name of its ultimate destination, either a hospital or a private home. After filling orders, they sterilized all the equipment to be used the following day—the tin cups and bottles as well as the towels, gowns, and masks worn by mothers. They cleaned the pasteurizer with chlorine. They dated and froze bottles of excess milk in the Station's deep freeze, a rare and coveted piece of equipment in those days. If the day's demand exceeded the day's supply, they thawed stored milk and repasteurized it before sending it on to a hospital or private family.

Hospitals and families requesting the milk picked it up themselves; the Station had no delivery service until much later in its history. A public health nurse visited any baby receiving the milk at home to assure that the baby gained weight and received proper care. Demand for the milk waned over the years. In 1943 the Station collected 108,000 ounces of breast milk, which it distributed to more than 1,100 infants. In 1950 the Station issued 72,897 ounces of human milk to 1,098 babies. In 1951, 830 premature, underweight, and sick babies consumed 53,000 ounces of the Station's milk. In most instances, medical personnel credited the milk with saving a baby's life.

In 1948 the Board of Health promoted Plotzke to Superintendent of Nurses. Her new duties included supervising the city's well-baby clinics as well as the Mothers' Breast Milk Station. The Chicago Board of Health closed the Breast Milk Station shortly after Bundesen's death in 1960.

Plotzke retired from the Board of Health in 1969. She married Earl Rosenberger, a retired manager for Goodyear, in 1970.

After her marriage, Plotzke moved to South Holland, a suburb south of Chicago, and then to a southwestern suburb, Oak Lawn, after Rosenberger's death in 1973. She moved to the Belhaven Nursing Home in Chicago in September 1996. She died of a heart attack at St. Francis Hospital in Blue Island, Illinois on March 1, 1997. She is buried at St. Michael's Cemetery in Schererville, Indiana.

BIBLIOGRAPHY

Chicago Board of Health. (1931). Regulations for the Conduct of Maternity Hospitals, Maternity Divisions of General Hospitals, and Nurseries for the Newborn. In *Chicago Board of Health Revised Code of 1931.*

Chicago Department of Health. (1943). *Annual Report of the Department 1943.*

City of Chicago. *Employment history for Gertrude Plotzke.*

Health Department, City of Chicago. (1940). *Report of the Board of Health for the Year 1940.*

Health Department, City of Chicago. (1950). *Annual Report of the Chicago Health Department for the Year 1950.*

Health Department, City of Chicago. (1951). *Report of the Chicago Health Department for the Year 1951, including a report of "Progress on the Prevention of Needless Neonatal Deaths."*

Hess, J. H. (1951). Chicago plan for care of premature infants. *Journal of the American Medical Association, 146,* 891–893.

Lundeen, E. (1937). History of the Hortense Schoen Joseph Premature Station. *The Voice of the Clinic, 2,* 8–11.

Papers of Julius Hess. Special Collections, Regenstein Library, The University of Chicago.

Talbot, F. (1927). Directory for wetnurses. *Boston Medical and Surgical Journal, 196,* 653–654.

Wolf, J. H. (1996, December 10). Interview with Gertrude Plotzke Rosenberger, by author. Chicago, IL.

Wolf, J. H. (1997, April 28). Interview with Josephine Zuzak Sobolewski (Mothers' Breast Milk Station supervisor after Plotzke's promotion). Chicago, IL.

Wolf, J. H. (1997, December 12). Telephone interview with Sister Marien Plotzke (Plotzke's sister).

Jacqueline H. Wolf

Q

MILDRED DERICOTT RORDAME QUINN
1908–1989

Mildred D. Rordame Quinn was the second Dean of the College of Nursing, University of Utah, succeeding Hazelle Macquin in 1954. She was the first instructor appointed to the faculty of a new Department of Nursing Education in the School of Education in 1943 and quickly emerged as a key figure in creating a sound baccalaureate curriculum, in establishing affiliations with community agencies, and in elevating a rather fragile program to full college status. As Dean, she was instrumental in attracting federal funds to develop the master's degree in Nursing and in creating a unique clinical field at Shiprock, New Mexico, for nurse-midwifery and child nursing among the Navaho people. Construction of a five-story, state-of-the-art educational facility to house the College can only be attributed to her political acumen and her aggressive courage in pursuing goals of the school.

Mildred Quinn was a child of the Intermountain West. She was born in 1908, in Liberty, Idaho, across the border from Utah's Bear Lake. As an eager high school graduate, she moved to Salt Lake City and earned her diploma at the Salt Lake General Hospital School of Nursing in 1932. Later, as a young widow with a son, Quinn recognized the need for further education and studied for a year at the University of Oregon in 1942 to earn certification in Public Health Nursing. That specialization reflected her deep interest in the care of children and their families.

Mildred Dericott Rordame Quinn

Between 1943 and 1954 Quinn taught Public Health Nursing at the University of Utah, became the Director of the Basic Program, and advanced in rank to Assistant Professor. One of her major roles was as a counselor for the 200 Cadet Corps students enrolled each year under the Bolton Act of 1943.

A postwar letdown affected the College program, particularly in adjustment to loss of the Cadet students and accommodation of nurses studying under the G.I. Bill. When Dean Macquin, fearful that Quinn would resign to take a better position, advised the University President of her intention to step down as Dean and she recommended Quinn as her successor. Summoned to meet with President A. Ray Olpin, Quinn was surprised to be offered the position and accepted after a 2-week delay.

Years later Quinn recalled that she went home and prepared a "working document," outlining what she would achieve in 5 years as Dean and the resources she would require to meet those goals. The budget for the College in 1953 was an astonishing $25,000 and annual salaries of $3,000 were common. There were only five academic positions at the College, supported by "clinical supervisors" stationed at three community hospitals. Students spent long clinical hours at the hospital in a system reminiscent of the diploma schools. In 1954, a thousand clinical hours a year at the hospital were required of students, accommodating the staffing needs of the hospitals, of course. The formula of 1:5, or 1 university credit hour for 5 hours a week of clinical practice, was the standard formula (Clayton, 1983, pp. 25–128).

Quinn required that there be clarification of the status of all clinical faculty and a clear demarcation of educational goals of students vis-à-vis the economic needs of the hospitals. Credit for clinical practice was to be reduced to a 1:3 ratio. An adequate budget must be provided by the University to hire qualified faculty in the five major areas of nursing practice. NLN accreditation would be achieved in 1 year, guaranteeing a nearly impossible achievement. Remarkably enough, League accreditation was achieved in 1 year, as promised, in 1955. That means that qualified faculty were in place in all required areas. The other goals were addressed including establishment of the 1:3 ratio of credit to clinical hours.

Discussion of a medical center on campus began in the 1960s. Quinn was a member of the planning committee. At about that time, she was invited to join a national committee reviewing applications for funding of construction grants for schools of the health professions. At some point, Nursing was segregated out for special treatment, providing an apparent "window of opportunity." Quinn said later, "When I came back home I decided this is the move we ought to make. We ought to have a building." It was as simple as that (Clayton, 1983, p. 50).

Quinn talked with the faculty and gained universal support. A letter of intent was signed by President Olpin. The time crunch was on and an estimate of cost was prepared and sent to Washington just under the deadline and the letter of intent was approved.

Constructing a College of Nursing around a philosophy of nursing was unique, according to Dr. Jessie Scott, Director of the Division of Nursing, Washington, D.C. At her request Quinn developed a bulletin to assist other schools with their construction plans. The bulletin was completed in 1966 and subsequently was included with all application forms issued by the Division (Clayton, 1983, p. 55).

The construction grant was approved and actual construction began in 1966 with dedication in 1969. Cost of the building was $2,607,000. Because it was one of the first buildings to receive federal funding, many purely esthetic features were allowed, such as wood paneling and the generous use of open space.

Nurse-midwifery was developed as a component of the Maternal-Child graduate program. Students were first admitted in 1965. There was initial support from the Department of Ob-Gyn at University Hospital and the students had adequate clinical opportunities in association with medical students, interns, and residents. A change in departmental administration in 1969 led to restrictions on the nurse-midwifery students. Additional clinical facilities would have to be found.

At about the same time a crisis developed at the USPHS Hospital at Shiprock, New

Mexico, 400 miles due south of the College of Nursing in the desolate Four Corners area on the Navaho Reservation. Dr. Getz, the sole obstetrician for the 25,000 square mile area, was about to resign in frustration because he could not manage services for the huge population of the Shiprock Chapter. A nurse mentioned the new nurse-midwifery program at the University of Utah. Dr. Getz called Quinn and asked if a nurse-midwife could be recruited to assist him. Clinical placement at the Navaho Reservation suddenly was an almost viable idea. Contacts with the Indian Health Services in Washington, D.C. were encouraging. A meeting in Shiprock on April 2, 1970 led to establishment of a midwifery service, financed by the USPHS and the College. There were positions for two nurse midwives and a nurse aide. Lorraine Sevcovic, nurse midwife and a faculty member, became the Service Unit Director. Two or three graduate students would be rotated through the Service under her supervision. And they were to be ready to go into action in three months (Clayton, 1983, p. 97).

The proposal for funding the Project was written and submitted in 2 weeks. Mildred and the University Vice President for Health Affairs presented the proposal to the Navaho Health Advisory Board at Window Rock, New Mexico. The Board included one woman, Annie Waniki, who was perhaps the most powerful individual in attendance. Assured by the 5-year plan for the Project, involvement of Navaho people throughout, and no provision for anthropologists on the staff, the Board approved the program.

The Project was enormously successful and remarkably complicated. Problems with logistics were hair-raising. For example, there were no housing facilities, no rentals, and no motels in Shiprock. Students and faculty were housed in two small concrete "Indian houses." The entire Project operated out of one small office at the Hospital. Recruiting personnel was not a problem as soon as budget and space were available to assimilate them. Student Navaho health aides were recruited and their training initiated. The language problem was obvious and a continuing one, but the health aides provided key communication resources.

The Project was not allowed to build permanent structures on the Reservation, but permission was granted to place two mobile homes near the hospital to house students and staff. Quinn purchased one and Ms. Sevcovic bought the other. Grant funds were used to purchase four large mobile units to construct a highly functional, well-equipped clinic, with room for both midwifery and child services. Faculty and students at the College assisted in furnishing the clinic with donations of money, toys, and furniture.

A Navaho ceremony of dedication was held, with traditional blessings by the Navaho medicine man. Annie Waniki approved, saying, "It is good." By 1974 there were 38 employees of the Project, including a physician, and 63% of the employees were Navahos. Seven satellite clinics had been established from 30 to 90 miles distant from the Shiprock clinic. Navaho babies, children, and their mothers enjoyed better health. It was a wonderful enterprise.

The academic portrait of Mildred Quinn hangs in the administrative foyer of the College of Nursing, recognizing the grand dimensions of her contributions to the profession and to the College. Structured in a vaguely Renaissance style, it presents several symbols: the Nightingale statue as the soul of Nursing, books presenting the academic dimension of the profession, the necklace representing Quinn's beloved Native Americans, and the ring to encircle her cherished family. She died on December 18, 1989, and was buried in the Bountiful City Cemetery.

PUBLICATIONS BY MILDRED DERICOTT RORDAME QUINN

(1955). You, too, can have a new school house. *Nursing Outlook, 3,* 50–52.

[Co-Developer] (1966). *A guide for projecting space needs for schools of nursing.* Washington, DC: United States Debt of Health, Education, & Welfare.

[Associate Editor] (1978). *Family and community health: The Journal of Health Promotion and Maintenance.* Rockville, MD: Aspen Systems.

Reinhardt, A. M., & Quinn, M. D. (Eds.). (1980). *Family-centered community nursing: A sociocultural framework* (Vol. II). St. Louis: Mosby.

Taylor, C., & Quinn, M. D. (1966). *Measurement and prediction of nursing performance.* Salt Lake City, UT: University Press.

BIBLIOGRAPHY

Clayton, B. C. (1983). E. L. Cooley Oral History Project. Interview with Mildred Quinn. Tapes and transcriptions archived at Marriott Library, University of Utah, Salt Lake City, UT.

Highlights. Forty years of excellence. (1978). Salt Lake City, UT: University of Utah Press.

Bonnie Clayton

R

DOROTHY E. REILLY
1920–1996

Dorothy E. Reilly was an internationally known nurse educator and scholar who contributed to the development of nursing education in the United States and Canada through her writings and consultations. She was inducted into the Hall of Fame of the American Nurses Association in 1998.

Born on February 6, 1920, in Holyoke, Massachusetts, to James Augustus and Mary E. (Kincade) Reilly, she began her nursing education at Mt. Holyoke College in 1937, receiving her diploma 2 years later. She then matriculated at Columbia University, Department of Nursing, and graduated with a bachelor of science degree in 1942. After working as head nurse for the Institute of Ophthalmology and at Presbyterian Hospital in New York City, she held various posts as medical surgical nursing instructor, private duty nurse, and science instructor. In 1948, she enrolled in the master's program at Boston University, School of Nursing. While pursuing her degree, she held a teaching fellowship and taught a course "Principles of Teaching."

After receiving her master's degree in 1951, Reilly joined the nursing faculty of Columbia University, where her major responsibility was curriculum development and program planning for undergraduate students. During that time, she also pursued her doctorate in higher education, receiving her degree in 1967. Two years later, she moved to Wayne State University, College of Nursing, where she became full professor in 1973. In addition to her responsibilities for curriculum development and the preparation of teachers of nursing, she also directed the Office of Community Educational Services, which served as the outreach program of the College of Nursing.

Reilly was a prolific author. She completed her first book in 1955 and continued writing until her death. Two of her books won the American Journal of Nursing Book of the Year Award: *Behavioral Objectives in*

Dorothy E. Reilly

Nursing: Evaluation of Learner Attainment (in 1976) and *Clinical Teaching in Nursing Education* (in 1992). In addition to authoring numerous books and articles on nursing education, she served as consultant to schools of nursing throughout the United States, Canada, Europe, and Australia.

The recipient of many awards and honors, Reilly was especially proud of her Distinguished Alumnae Award from Columbia University-Presbyterian Hospital, the Sigma Theta Tau Award for Excellence in Nursing Education, and Mt. Holyoke College Sesquicentennial Alumnae Award. She was a member of many nursing organizations and was accepted into the Academy of Nursing in 1977.

In March 1996, 1 month prior to her death, her article "A Teacher Looks Back," was published in the *Journal of Nursing Education.* Teaching, like all helping professions, derives its art from caring, valuing, and continuing the search for self, she stated. Reflecting on her role as a teacher, she realized the importance of the continuing analysis of teaching events on her own development. The article was significant, not only for her insights, but also because it demonstrated the recovery of her ability to write again following a stroke a few years earlier.

Dorothy Reilly developed models for outreach education programs and evaluation in nursing. A major contributor to curriculum design and a master teacher, she was a mentor to many. When she retired from the nursing faculty at Wayne State University in 1987, she continued her involvement with nursing issues and with community efforts to improve health care and educational opportunities in Detroit. She died on April 7, 1996.

PUBLICATIONS BY DOROTHY E. REILLY

Books (Selected)

Nursing student responses to the clinical field. (1958). New York: Department of Nursing, Columbia University.

College graduates choose a nursing career. (1964). New York: Columbia University Press.

Behavioral objectives in nursing: Evaluation of learner attainment. (1975). New York: Appleton-Century-Crofts. (Japanese edition, 1980).

Teaching and evaluating the affective domain in nursing. (1978). New Jersey: Slack.

Behavioral objectives: Evaluation in nursing education (2nd ed.). (1980). New York: Appleton-Century-Crofts.

One approach to masters' education in nursing. (1980). American Association of College of Nursing (Series 80, No. 1, 1980).

Graduate education through outreach: A nursing case study. (1990). New York: National League for Nursing.

(With M. Oermann). *The clinical field: Its use in nursing education.* (1985). East Norwalk, CT: Appleton-Century-Crofts.

(With M. Oermann). *Behavioral objectives: Evaluation in nursing* (3rd ed.). (1990). New York: National League for Nursing.

(With M. Oermann). *Clinical teaching in nursing education.* (1992). New York: National League for Nursing.

Articles (Selected)

A teacher looks back: The route to mastery. (1996). *Journal of Nursing Education, 35,* 131–133.

Progression of clinical experience. (1958). *International Nursing Review, 5*(3), 76–77.

Why a conceptual framework? (1975). *Nursing Outlook, 23,* 566–569.

Preparation of objectives for continuing education programs. (1976). *Occupational Health Nurse, 24,* 30–33.

Research in nursing education: Yesterday, today and tomorrow. (1990). *Nursing and Health Care, 11,* 139–143.

(With A. Orb). Changing to a conceptual base curriculum. (1991). *International Nursing Review, 38,* 56–60.

BIBLIOGRAPHY

Oermann, M. Interview with Dorothy Reilly (1996). *The World: Who's Who of Women Educators,* 1979.

Who's Who in Nursing Education. Washington, DC: Society of Nursing Professionals, 1984, 1986–1987.

Marilyn Oermann

Agnes Shoemaker Reinders

AGNES SHOEMAKER REINDERS (SISTER M. THEOPHANE) 1913–1993

Agnes Reinders was a pioneer in the nurse-midwifery profession. She was committed to nurse-midwifery education and practice. During her career, she was a moving force behind several key innovations, such as the first graduate level nurse-midwifery education program, the first freestanding birthing center, the formation of the nurse-midwives' professional organization, and the publication of its journal. Later in life, she was a pioneer in establishing continuing education for nursing. These accomplishments indicate her importance: without her commitment and action, nursing and nurse-midwifery would not have become what they are today.

Agnes was born in her grandparents' farmhouse on August 27, 1913. Her early years were spent on a family farm in Owensboro, Kentucky, where she grew up in a Depression era family. As the second of nine children, she learned to be responsible and organized at an early age. Both of her parents valued education, thinking, and curiosity. In addition to chores, there were newspapers and books available to challenge their minds. She received an excellent high school education.

Reinders became a nun, joining a Roman Catholic order as a Medical Mission Sister after completing high school. She received the name Sister M. Theophane. The order was known for promoting the professional education of their members and others to provide services to as many people as possible.

In 1941, Sister Theophane graduated from a 5-year baccalaureate nursing program at Catholic University of America, Washington, DC. Her leadership abilities were readily apparent; she became head nurse of a medical-surgical unit in a local hospital for 6 months. She then became the obstetrical supervisor of a 57-bed maternity unit, including labor, delivery, postpartum, and newborn nursery. While there, she learned about the need for nurse-midwives from Mother Anna Dengel, the physician founder of the Medical Mission Sisters. Care for women had always been a primary concern for Medical Mission Sisters. Nurse-midwives were needed to provide services to essentially normal, healthy childbearing women in Santa Fe, New Mexico, so that the only obstetrician in town could attend to surgery and complex cases. Sister Theophane was asked to participate. Therefore, in 1943 she attended and graduated from the 6-month program at Lobenstine School of Nurse-Midwifery, in New York City, with a certificate in nurse-midwifery.

In 1943, Sister Theophane immediately began work as the director and founded the Catholic Maternity Institute (CMI) in Santa Fe, New Mexico. Her roles in the nurse-midwifery service included administration, fund raising, construction, budget management, and personnel development. Sister Theophane was skilled in all these areas. She was particularly known for working collaboratively. CMI was viewed as an outstanding example of success through interagency cooperation and a commitment to patient care. The certified nurse-midwives' (CNMs') practice included home births, but CMI also opened the first free-standing nurse-midwifery birth center in 1951, called La Casita.

Demonstrating her commitment to education, within 1 year of her arrival in Santa Fe, Sister Theophane began planning the curriculum for a nurse-midwifery certificate education program affiliated with Catholic University. The program opened in 1945 and was the first nurse-midwifery school with a university affiliation. Sister

Theophane then went back to Catholic University in 1946 on a leave of absence. She earned her master's degree with a major in Administration and a minor in Supervision. Upon her return to Santa Fe, she resumed her Directorship of the CMI. She expanded the educational program to offer the first master's degree program in nurse-midwifery in 1948 through its affiliation with Catholic University. She had an additional role as faculty, Assistant Professor in Maternal and Newborn Nursing.

During the next decade, her activism for the nurse-midwifery profession blossomed. In 1954, Sister Theophane began a letter-writing campaign to organize CNMs. This was a direct response to national movements in nursing that indicated that the interests of CNMs were not represented well in other nursing organizations. Formerly, they had been a recognized section within the National Organization of Public Health Nurses, but this was no longer possible when that organization was absorbed into the American Nurses Association and the National League for Nursing. Therefore, Sister Theophane surveyed CNMs about their desires for organizing. She chaired the Committee on Organization. The decision of the CNMs was to separately incorporate as an organization, the American College of Nurse-Midwifery (ACNM) in 1955. (The organization was later named the American College of Nurse-Midwives in 1969.) Sister Theophane became the first editor of the professional publication, the *Bulletin of the American College of Nurse-Midwifery* (now known as the *Journal of Nurse-Midwifery*) and served in this capacity until 1959. She also served as President-elect of the ACNM from 1955 to 1957; and, from 1957 to 1959, served as its second President. Meanwhile, she continued as Director of CMI until 1958.

Throughout these years Sister Theophane was at the forefront of national movements to address sound standards for the education of nurse-midwives. She was a part of innovative national conferences on nurse-midwifery education in 1958 and 1967 that laid the ground work for university affiliations, the core competencies of nurse-midwifery education, and accreditation of educational programs that are still a part of the profession today.

Her career track cycled back to hospital and administrative nursing. From 1958 to 1964, she served as Administrator of Holy Family Hospital in Atlanta, Georgia. Once again, the administrative role included grassroots organizing, fund-raising, and developing and managing the hospital. In this capacity, she worked to have an integrated hospital in a segregated city.

Sister Theophane took a sabbatical from 1964 to 1965, during which she left the order and resumed the use of her name, Agnes Shoemaker. From that point in her life, she returned to teaching administration. In 1965, and until her retirement in 1978, Reinders worked at Marquette University College of Nursing in Milwaukee, Wisconsin. She was a member of the graduate faculty of the Nursing Service Administration Program. She taught research and facilitated the submission of grant proposals. She also worked (unsuccessfully) to establish a nurse-midwifery educational program at Marquette University in the late 1960s and early 1970s. She then became administrator of Continuing Education in nursing from 1973 to 1978. While in Milwaukee, she met Henry Reinders at a Catholic singles group. Henry had been a widower for about 10 years and had four grown children, all daughters. They were married in 1970 at their parish, St. Anthony of Padua.

In 1978, Reinders retired from Marquette with the rank of Professor Emeritus. She remained active with the Retired Faculty Committee. She trained Eucharistic ministers at her church. She also organized volunteers for the Silk for Life project, to assist South American people to grow a cash crop to replace the cocaine producing coca trees. Mulberry bushes were planted in order to raise silkworms. The silk was sent to weavers to produce marketable items that supported the workers in this cottage industry.

In September 1993, during the last month of her life, Reinders spoke to the first class of the Marquette University College of Nursing Nurse-Midwifery Program. It was at least 20 years since she had tried to establish a program at Marquette and she was pleased it had finally occurred. She spoke to the student nurse-midwives, the CNM faculty, and invited guests with pride about the profession of nurse-midwifery and its commitment to healthy mothers and infants. She emphasized the importance of clinical competency in living out this commitment.

Reinders had a ruptured cerebral aneurysm 3 weeks later. She awoke after the aneurysm and clearly declined any surgical attempt to correct it. She died quietly on September 28, 1993, approximately 1 year after her husband. She was buried in Evansville, Indiana. A memorial fund in her name was established at Marquette University College of Nursing to provide assistance to students.

In summary, Agnes Reinders is viewed as a courageous forward-thinker. She had a long and inspiring career, serving as nurse-midwife, educator, administrator, scholar and fighter. With her vision and energy, she facilitated important innovations in nurse-midwifery and nursing. Her memory is an inspiration.

LIST OF HONORS

1978   Professional Services Award from the national University Extension Association for outstanding service in developing continuing education.

1980 Hattie Hemschemeyer award, highest honor in nurse-midwifery profession.

1984 Inducted into the Hall of Fame, Delta Gamma Chapter, Sigma Theta Tau International, Marquette University College of Nursing.

1993 Inducted as a Fellow of the American College Nurse-Midwives.

PUBLICATIONS BY AGNES SHOEMAKER REINDERS

Lancour, J., & Reinders, A. A. (1975). A pilot project in continuing education for critical care nursing. *Journal of Nursing Administration, 5*(8), 38–41.

Reinders, A. A. (1969). *Feasibility study: Graduate nurse program in maternal and newborn nursing leading to a master of science degree in nursing* (Unpublished research financed in part by the Wisconsin Division of Nurses). Milwaukee, WI: Marquette University College of Nursing.

Reinders, A. A. (1974). Nursing and some large moral issues. *Nursing Clinics of North America, 9*(3), 547–556.

Shoemaker, A. A. (1967). Curriculum trends in nurse-midwifery. In *Can maternity nursing meet today's challenge? Report of the Ross round table on maternal and child nursing* (pp. 57–65). Columbus, OH: Ross Laboratories.

Shoemaker, M. T. (1946). Is nurse-midwifery the solution? *Public Health Nursing, 38,* 644–648.

Shoemaker, M. T. (1984). *History of nurse-midwifery in the United States.* [Originally produced as a master's thesis, Washington, DC: Catholic University of America Press in 1947. Reprinted and published, New York: Garland Press.]

BIBLIOGRAPHY

American College of Nurse-Midwifery. (1958). *Education for nurse-midwifery: The report of the work conference on nurse-midwifery.* Santa Fe, NM: Author.

American College of Nurse-Midwifery. (1968). *Education for nurse-midwifery: A report of the 2nd work conference on nurse-midwifery education.* New York: Maternity Center Association.

American College of Nurse-Midwives mourns death of Agnes Reinders. (1993) *Quickening, 24*(6), 1, 28.

50th celebration reunion: Remembering Catholic Maternity Institute Santa Fe. (1994). [Unpublished booklet with video].

Paquette, M. K. (1989). Agnes Shoemaker Reinders, MSN, RN, October 11, 1984. In *Hall of Fame Delta Gamma Chapter* (pp. 8–13). Milwaukee, WI: Marquette University College of Nursing, Delta Gamma Chapter, Sigma Theta Tau International.

Stohs, N. J. (1980, June 5). Nurse-midwife not new, says pioneer in field. *Milwaukee Journal.*

Tom, S. A. (1980). Agnes Shoemaker Reinders: A biographical tribute. *Journal of Nurse-Midwifery, 25*(5), 9–12.

Varney, H. (1997). *Varney's midwifery* (3rd ed.). Sudbury, MA: Jones & Bartlett.

Leona VandeVusse
Lisa Hanson

EUNICE RIVERS
1899–1986

Eunice Rivers was a public health nurse who played a critical role in the Tuskegee Syphilis Study. Although the study remains controversial, Rivers is recognized as a superb nurse and skilled communicator.

Eunice Verdell Rivers Laurie was born in Early County, Georgia, on November 12, 1899, the oldest daughter of Albert and Henrietta Rivers. Her father was a farmer and sawmill worker. Recognizing the importance of a good education, Albert Rivers sent Eunice to a church-run boarding school in Fort Gaines, Georgia. After recovering from typhoid fever, Eunice Rivers attended a mission school in Thomasville, Georgia, until her father learned that the majority of her teachers were White. He then enrolled her in the Tuskegee Institute, an educational and vocational school for Blacks in Tuskegee, Alabama.

Eunice Rivers entered the Tuskegee Institute in 1918 and spent the first year learning handicrafts and other practical skills. At her father's suggestion, she transferred to the nursing program, despite her initial reservations about caring for ill and terminal patients. She flourished in her new environment.

After receiving her nursing degree in 1922, Rivers was hired by the state of Alabama as a member of the Macon County's Movable School. She traveled around the state and provided instruction in hygiene and nursing to rural Blacks. In an article published in 1926, Rivers described the health conditions in the rural communities and the effects of the program. Later, she worked for the Bureau of Vital Statistics assisting in the collection of accurate birth and death statistics for the state's Black population. The social service program was discontinued in 1931 due to lack of funds.

In 1932, Rivers became night-time supervisor at the John A. Andrew Memorial Hospital at Tuskegee Institute. After 8 months, she was approached by Dr. Eugene Dibble, head of Andrew Hospital and one of four Black physicians on the staff, to become a scientific assistant in the study of untreated syphilis in Macon County sponsored by the U.S. Public Health Service. Rivers expressed some reservations because she lacked research experience with syphilis, but was convinced by Dr. Dibble to accept the offer.

Rivers worked on the Tuskegee Syphilis Study until 1965, when she resigned her position with the Public Health Service. During those years, she played a critical role in maintaining contact with the 600 men enrolled in the study. She assisted the government physicians in the annual examinations, visited the men in their homes, and persuaded families to allow autopsies when one of the participants died. She also worked with public health programs in the community, including maternity and well-baby clinics. In 1958, Rivers received the Oveta Culp Hobby Award from the Department of Health, Education and Welfare, the third individual to receive the award.

After a series of critical newspaper reports about the Tuskegee Syphilis Study in 1972, the Department of Health, Education and Welfare appointed a review panel. The study was quickly discontinued and the Public Health Service was directed to provide all necessary care to participants and their families. In 1977, Rivers expressed the opinion in an oral history interview that much of the criticism of the study had been unfair and that the men selected were all in the secondary stage of syphilis and acute cases were screened out for standard treatment. In 1989, the play *Miss Evers' Boys* presented a fictionalized Nurse Rivers to the public. The Tuskegee Syphilis Study has remained controversial and, in 1997, President Clinton offered an official apology to the participants on behalf of the United States government.

Eunice Rivers married Albert Laurie, an orderly at Andrews Hospital, in 1952. She continued to live in the Tuskegee community after her retirement and died on August 28, 1986.

PUBLICATIONS BY EUNICE RIVERS

Health work with a movable school. (1926). *The Public Health Nurse, 18,* 575–577

(With Stanley Schuman, Lloyd Simpson, & Sidney Olansky). Twenty years of followup experience in a long-range medical study. *Public Health Reports, 68*(4), 391–395.

BIBLIOGRAPHY

Feldschuh, D. (1995). *Miss Evers' Boys* (Play script). New York: Dramatists Play Service.

Jones, J. H. (1993). *Bad blood: The Tuskegee syphilis experiment* (new ed.). New York: Free Press.

Laurie, E. R. (1991). Oral history interview, October 10, 1977. Black Women Oral History Project, Schlesinger Library, Radcliffe College. Available in *The Black Women's Oral History Project* (vol. 7) (pp. 231–242). Westport, CT: Meckler.

Lederer, S. E. (1997). Eunice Rivers (1899–1986). In L. N. Magner (Ed.), *Doctors, nurses, and medical practitioners. A bio-bibliographical sourcebook* (pp. 227–231). Westport, CT: Greenwood Press.

Reverby, S. M. (1993). Laurie, Eunice Rivers. In D. C. Hine (Ed.), *Black women in America: An historical encyclopedia* (pp. 699–701). Brooklyn, NY: Carlson.

Smith, S. L. (1996). Neither victim nor villain: Nurse Eunice Rivers, the Tuskegee syphilis experiment, and public health work. *Journal of Women's History, 8,* 95–113.

Lilli Sentz

GLENNA S. ROWSELL
1924–1987

Glenna S. Rowsell is remembered as one of the "mothers" of collective bargaining in Canadian nursing and one of the earliest proponents of professional responsibility clauses in nurses' contracts. Such clauses provide a route outside of formal grievance for addressing nursing concerns about work conditions that jeopardize the quality of patient care. She frequently reiterated that the hats of professionalism and unionism could both be worn on the same head. Crisscrossing the country in the late 1960s under the sponsorship of the Canadian Nurses Association (CNA), Rowsell shared her extensive knowledge of labor legislation to help nurses amend existing provincial legislation and develop new legislation permitting collective bargaining. Many nurses had their introduction to collective bargaining at Rowsell's educational workshops.

Little is known of the personal life of Glenna S. Rowsell, other than her birth in 1924 in St. John's, Newfoundland, a British protectorate before it joined Canada in 1949. Rowsell graduated in 1948 from the St. John's General Hospital (SJGH) School of Nursing and worked as a staff nurse in the hospital's operating room until February 1950. For 6 months in early 1950, she was an assistant instructor in the SJGH School of Nursing, before enrolling in the 1-year diploma program in clinical supervision offered by the University of Toronto's School of Nursing. After completing the clinical supervision program, Rowsell re-

Glenna S. Rowsell

turned as nursing arts instructor at the SJGH for 1 year, from July 1951 to August 1952, when she returned to the University of Toronto to complete a 1-year diploma program in nursing education and administration. In August 1953, Rowsell was appointed Associate Director of Nursing Education at the SJGH, a position she retained until February 1961. While in this position, Rowsell completed requirements for a degree in nursing at the University of Toronto, graduating in 1960 with a B.Sc.N. From March 1961 until June 1966, Rowsell was director of CNA's School Improvement Program, initiated to assist Canadian hospital schools of nursing to upgrade their educational programs. The School Improvement Program was one of four recommendations of the CNA's Pilot Project for the

Evaluation of Schools of Nursing in Canada, carried on from 1958 to 1959 to determine schools' readiness for a program of accreditation. Of the 25 programs examined, only five were found to be of sufficient quality to merit accreditation, if such a program existed.

Making a dramatic change in her career focus, Rowsell became in 1966 CNA's first Nursing Consultant for Social and Economic Welfare. Along with Evelyn Hood and Nora Patton in B.C., Joyce Gleason in Manitoba, and Anne Gribbon in Ontario, Rowsell was one of the "mothers" of nursing collective bargaining in Canada. Until 1969, she travelled from province to province, helping nurses' professional associations prepare the needed social and legal structures to allow them to begin collective bargaining. Since 1944, the CNA had been on record as approving collective bargaining for nurses, providing that the bargaining agent was the provincial professional association. Only the Registered Nurses Association of British Columbia (RNABC) had accepted the responsibility for collective bargaining on behalf of its members, and by 1959 achieved province-wide bargaining, whereby all eligible nurses were covered by one collective agreement. By the early 1960s, employers' pervasive refusal to use staff nurse salary schedules recommended by provincial nursing associations, coupled with a nation wave of unionization among other professional and white-collar workers, led nurses in Alberta, Manitoba, Ontario, New Brunswick, Nova Scotia, Prince Edward Island, Saskatchewan, and Newfoundland to begin unionizing. Within a few years, nursing became one of the most completely unionized occupations in Canada. From August 1969 to August 1977, Rowsell was the chief executive officer of the New Brunswick Nurses Provincial Collective Bargaining Council, forerunner of the New Brunswick Nurses's

Union. She returned to CNA in 1977 as Director of the Labour Relations Services Department, inaugurated to provide CNA members and provincial bargaining units with data collection and analysis, information distribution, educational programming, and research related to labor issues. Rowsell retired from this position in 1985 and died on November 27, 1987 after a lengthy illness.

An active participant in professional associations at the provincial, national, and international levels, Rowsell served as elected CNA member-at-large for social and economic welfare and as a member of the board of directors of the Canadian Nurses Foundation, which funded Canadian nursing research. She achieved international recognition for her work as a member of the Canadian delegation that lobbied to get the Nursing Convention passed by the United Nations' International Labour Organization, and served on the socioeconomic committee of the UN's Inter-Council of Nurses. Rowsell is remembered for her concerted efforts to improve the working conditions of staff nurses through collective bargaining for better wages, conditions of employment, and fringe benefits.

PUBLICATIONS BY GLENNA S. ROWSELL

Numerous editorials and information articles about labor relations and collective bargaining for nurses published in *The Canadian Nurse* journal and the newsletters of provincial nursing associations, especially New Brunswick.

Changing trends in labour relations: Effects on collective bargaining for nurses. (1982). *International Nursing Review, 29,* 141–145.

BIBLIOGRAPHY

Biographical File: Glenna S. Rowsell. Available from the CNA Library, 50 The Driveway, Ottawa, Ontario, K2P 1E2.

Jensen, P. M. (1992). The changing role of nurses' unions. In A. Baumgart & J. Larsen (Eds.), *Canadian nursing faces the future* (2nd ed., pp. 557–572). Toronto: Mosby Year Book.

Sharon Richardson

S

HILDA SALOMON
1895–1983

As a pioneer nurse-anesthetist, Hilda Salomon was a highly respected and widely recognized leader who contributed significantly to advancements in her field of nursing practice. Along with a group of her colleagues, she participated in the establishment of the National Association of Nurse Anesthetists in 1931, which, in 1939, became known as the American Association of Nurse Anesthetists (AANA). Ms. Salomon served a 2-year term as president of the organization from 1935 to 1937. She also was instrumental in organizing the Pennsylvania Association of Nurse Anesthetists and served as its president.

Hilda Salomon

As a leader in her professional organizations, she was a strong advocate of human rights, and her ideas were considered very radical by many of her peers. In her brief memoir, *A Half Century of Memories*, she recalled her valiant struggle in the early years of the AANA to persuade her peers that they should admit Black and male nurse anesthetists as members of the organization. In her own words, "Many harsh words were exchanged. It wasn't until 1944–47 that my original idea was accepted" (Salomon, 1981). In fact, her proposal had come under bitter attack by the members of the Board, and according to the brochure that was printed in honor of Salomon's 85th birthday, part of the opposition leveled at her at that time stemmed from the fact that she was Jewish.

Salomon was born on August 27, 1895, the daughter of Abraham and Sadie Harris, in Lynn, Massachusetts. From her youth, her life was touched by personal tragedy. One of four children, she was orphaned by the age of 10. She grew up in Lynn, MA, where she and her siblings were raised by their grandmother. In October, 1916, she was married to Leo Salomon, who died tragically in a work-related accident early in 1917. It was after this event that Salomon entered nursing school at the Union Hospital in Lynn. In her memoir Salomon wrote, "As far back as I can remember, my greatest ambition was to serve people: the sick, the poor, and the underprivileged."

She graduated from nursing school in 1920, and at the invitation of one her cousins, went to Philadelphia. There are no official documents available to corroborate exact dates, but according to one source, Salomon first went to work at a small hospital where stomach diseases were treated. At some point, she decided to enter the training program for nurse-anesthetists at Lankenau Hospital School of Anesthesia. She completed her training in the Lankenau program in 1923, and accepted a position as a nurse-anesthetist at the Jewish Hospital in Philadelphia where she was appointed Chief of the Department of Anesthesia in 1924. In her work, Salomon emphasized the importance of education by organizing monthly meetings and by inviting all the nurse anesthetists in the Philadelphia area to attend. Thus they were given the opportunity to hear key speakers and to learn about new developments in anesthesia. In 1929 Salomon launched the Jewish Hospital School of Anesthesia, which graduated 218 nurse-anesthetists during the 18 years it was in operation.

In 1948, Salomon resigned as Chief Anesthetist at the Jewish Hospital, but continued to work as a nurse and anesthetist with an otolaryngologist until 1958 when she decided to retire. Soon after, however, she registered as a volunteer at the former Jewish Hospital in Philadelphia (by then it was known as the Northern Division of the Albert Einstein Medical Center). Within a few years, she was back at work as a Resident Nurse at the high-rise apartment dwelling for the elderly located near the Einstein Medical Center. She remained professionally active in her later years. Just a few years before she died at the age of 88, she finally retired and went to live with her cousin, Bertha Vinecour, in Florida.

Salomon received many accolades and awards throughout her career from her colleagues and professional organizations. In 1969, she was feted with the Third Annual Agatha Hodgins Award for Outstanding Accomplishment by the AANA. Just a few months before she died, she was presented in August 1983 with a special "Humanitarian Award" by the AANA President at the organizations's 50th annual meeting. She was characterized as the "first lady of the Pennsylvania Association [of Nurse Anesthetists]," and her many accomplishments have been recognized by her peers. Former students and colleagues recall her as a person of great professional dignity and integrity, who radiated personal warmth and commanded everyone's respect.

PUBLICATIONS BY HILDA SALOMON

Hilda Salomon . . . A half century of memories. (1981). *A 50 Year Retrospective, American Association of Nurse Anesthetists 1931–1981.* Park Ridge, IL: American Association of Nurse Anesthetists.

BIBLIOGRAPHY

AANA pioneer Hilda Salomon dies. (1984, January). *AANA News Bulletin.*

Happy 85th birthday. (1980). [Brochure developed by members of Ms. Salomon's family on the occasion of her 85th birthday. Obtained from her cousin Bertha Vinecour presently residing in Hudson, FL.]

Benner, E. R. (1998). Personal correspondence and interviews with Ms. Salomon's cousins, Bertha Vinecour and Howard Alber. Unpublished.

Undated statement read on the occasion of the establishment of the Hilda R. Salomon Loan Fund in the Pennsylvania Association of Nurse Anesthetists.

Evelyn R. Benson

THELMA M. SCHORR
1924–

Thelma Schorr was a major figure in American nursing journalism, from 1950 when she served as assistant editor of the *American Journal of Nursing* to serving as president and publisher of the American Journal of Nursing Company, 1981–1990. She was born December 15, 1924, in New Haven, Connecticut, the daughter of Rebecca and Simon Mermelstein. Her mother, who was hospitalized many times when Thelma was a child, died when Thelma was 14. With the family heavily in debt for hospital and funeral bills, Schorr went to work at a clothing store, selling dresses. For 2 years, she went to high school from 8 a.m. to 12 noon, then worked from 1 to 9 p.m. and 9 a.m. to 9 p.m. on Saturdays.

Thelma M. Schorr

In 1942, Schorr entered Bellevue Hospital School of Nursing, New York, NY, graduating in 1945. In 1952, she received a BSN from Teachers College, Columbia University, New York City. She has been married to Norman Schorr, a public relations counselor, since 1955, and they have three daughters.

She served as charge nurse of a male medical ward at Bellevue Hospital, New York City, from the time she graduated until she was offered an editorial position at the *American Journal of Nursing* (*AJN*) in 1950. How was it that a Bellevue head nurse was offered the opportunity to join such an august organization? "In 1949," she said, "as a Bellevue head nurse, I wrote a petition to protest the 'dumping' of TB patients into open wards with no isolation equipment.

All 45 nurses working in medicine signed it. No one in hospital administration or in the office of the New York City Commissioner of Hospitals paid any attention to it, so we went directly to the newspapers. It made front page headlines, and then the hospital quickly accepted all of our recommendations. The Commissioner warned that I'd 'be a troublemaker' all my life" (Schoor & Zimmerman, 1988).

Even though Thelma was not yet a member of the American Nurses Association, the president of the New York State Nurses Association called and offered assistance. "They sent their Public Relations Committee members," Schorr said, "and they were wonderful, guiding me all the way, making sure nothing happened to me."

Because of this "notoriety," Thelma's name came to the attention of the editors of *AJN*, who wanted to do a story about the successful collective action at Bellevue. She was invited to lunch to talk about her experience. "I was offered a job the next day." she said. "But because I didn't have a baccalaureate, for the next 2 years I worked at AJN part time and attended Teachers College at Columbia until I completed my degree."

At the publishing company, then a subsidiary of the American Nurses Association, Schorr's name was officially added to the masthead in 1952. She rose from assistant editor to associate editor, then to senior editor and executive editor of the magazine. Barbara Schutt, who was editor at the time, had a heart attack in 1970. Shortly afterward, she resigned, and Schorr was appointed editor-in-chief, serving from 1971 to 1981. At that point, she was appointed president and publisher of the company— the third woman in that position since the company's inception in 1900. At that time the company included, in addition to *AJN*, *Geriatric Nursing; MCN: The American Journal of Maternal Child Nursing; Nursing Research;*

Nursing Outlook; the *International Nursing Index* ; the *AJN Career Guide*; the *AJN Nursing Boards Review*; and the Educational Services Division, which produced both print and interactive materials.

She has been the recipient of numerous awards and honors. In 1997, Schorr was honored with the Nursing Leadership Award from the Nurses Educational Funds, an organization that awards scholarships for graduate education. She was named an Honorary Fellow in 1994 of the prestigious American Academy of Nursing. In 1992, she received the first Kaplan/Landy Award as the Outstanding American Jewish Nurse from Hadassah, the Women's Zionist Organization of America.

She has been awarded three honorary doctorates: Curry College, Milton, MA, 1988; Norwich University, Northfield, VT, 1986; and the University of Pennsylvania, Philadelphia, PA, 1985. Boston University gave her its Award for Distinguished Service in Nursing in 1975 for her leadership as editor of AJN.

During her career, Schorr dedicated much of her time to speaking before nursing audiences, delivering at least 25 speeches each year at many state, national, and international nursing conferences. Her major goal, she says, was "to encourage nurses to speak up." She wrote in an editorial, "You can't be Gloria Steinem at a meeting and Phyllis Schlafly on your ward." She wanted nursing to be strong and independent, and she continually stressed the important differences between nursing and medicine.

To assist students who wanted to know more about their nursing leaders, Schorr and Anne Zimmerman organized a book of autobiographies of 49 contemporary nursing leaders. Published in 1988, the book, *Making Choices, Taking Chances: Nurse Leaders Tell Their Stories*, contains detailed biographical information on leaders such as Madeleine Leininger, Sister Callista Roy, and Ruth Watson Lubic.

Throughout her career, Schorr served as a valued board member and consultant to various nursing organizations. For almost 20 years, she served on the board of the Nurses Educational Funds. After retiring in 1990 from the American Journal of Nursing Company, she flew to Geneva, Switzerland, to work as a consultant to the International Council of Nurses (ICN). Her official "retirement" consisted of "3 days," she said. She began by preparing the proceedings of an ICN meeting on research and developing a press kit for International Nurses' Day. She subsequently produced several ICN publications on such topics as AIDS, costing out nursing services, and nursing research. At the same time, she began serving as editorial consultant to *Imprint*, the official publication of the National Student Nurses Association, an organization that she had worked with throughout her career in various advisory capacities.

Schorr was also instrumental in founding two organizations important to nursing's growth in publishing and politics. The first is INANE, the International Academy of Nursing Editors, and the second is the Washington Nurses Roundtable. INANE founding members, like Shirley Smoyak, insisted that the organization "not be serious," and "that there not be any rules, bylaws, dues, or organizational structure." The acronym INANE fit this iconoclastic approach perfectly.

The second organization she cofounded with Sheila Burke, who was on the staff of then-Senator Bob Dole, was the Washington Nurses Roundtable, a support group of nurses in high-level jobs in the federal government, in Congress, and in political positions. It began as an interview of nurses working as legislative staff aides on Capitol Hill and has developed into an important networking vehicle for nursing's Washington decision makers. The group still meets and includes nurses in key positions in the government and organizations associated with the government.

Schorr assumed a leadership position with the Community HealthCare Network (formerly the Community Family Planning Council) in 1994.

In 1997, she joined the board of the Oncology Nursing Press, the publishing arm of the Oncology Nursing Society. She focuses on editorial and publishing issues, with consulting responsibility for the *Clinical Journal of Oncology Nursing*.

In 1994, she began serving as a member of the National Advisory Board, Hadassah Nurses Councils. She edited the group's newsletter, *Nursing: The Jewish Connection*. Currently the Nurses Councils are conducting fundraising efforts to establish a clinical master's program in nursing at the Hadassah School of Nursing in Israel in conjunction with the University of Maryland. As of this writing she is working on an anthology depicting a century of American nursing as seen through the eyes of the *American Journal of Nursing*.

PUBLICATIONS BY THELMA M. SCHORR

With Zimmerman, A. (1988). *Making choices, taking chances: Nurse leaders tell their stories.* St. Louis: C. V. Mosby.

Monthly editorials as Editor-in-Chief, *American Journal of Nursing*, 1971–1981.

Sally Kilby

DORIS RUHBEL SCHWARTZ
1915–

Doris Ruhbel Schwartz was born in Brooklyn, New York on May 30, 1915, the daughter of Henry and Florence M. Schwartz. She had one brother, Donald. She received her diploma in nursing from Methodist Hospital School of Nursing in Brooklyn in 1942.

She enlisted for 4 years in the U.S. Army Nurse Corps serving on a hospital ship in the Pacific theater. After discharge with the rank of Captain, she worked as an editorial assistant for the *American Journal of Nursing* and as a public health nurse with the Visiting Nurse Association in the Red Hook section of Brooklyn while continuing her education. She was awarded a Bachelor of Science degree from New York University in 1953 and a Master of Science degree in 1958.

Doris Ruhbel Schwartz

In 1951 she joined Cornell University Medical College and Cornell University-Hospital as Clinical Associate Professor of Public Health and remained there until 1980 as professor of public health nursing, codirector of the family nurse practitioner program and, finally, major developer and codirector of one of the first geriatric nurse practitioner programs. As a faculty member, Schwartz advocated strongly for interdisciplinary approach to the needs of the elderly in the community and modeled for students a thoughtful nursing approach to each individual. She recognized and taught the need for measuring patient outcomes as a basis for planning nursing care and became an initiator of the movement to discontinue the use of restraints from the elderly in nursing homes.

Schwartz was the recipient of several fellowships during her career including a Rockefeller Fellowship to the University of Toronto in 1950–1951, and a Mary Roberts Fellowship with the American Journal of Nursing in 1955. As a Fogarty Fellow with the Fogarty International Center, National Institute of Health, (1975–1976), she spent a sabbatical year participating in community health and a geriatric assessment project in Scotland with Sir Ferguson Anderson. During the same year she was supported by a National Science Foundation Fellowship.

For her contributions as teacher, researcher, and writer, Schwartz was chosen to be a charter member of the American Academy of Nursing. In 1979 she was honored with the Pearl McIver Award for distinction in Public Health Nursing from the American Nurses Association, the American Public Health Association's Distinguished Career Award and Sigma Theta Tau's Founders Award.

Doris Schwartz published more than 65 articles, ranging from letters about her World War II experiences in the *Reader's Digest* to articles in international publications and professional journals. In addition she authored, coauthored or contributed to seven books including *The Elderly Ambulatory Patient: Nursing and Psychosocial Needs*, the first geriatric nursing study published as a book in the United States. Her writings reflected her own personal experiences and interaction with clients and revealed her dedication to supporting the personhood and individuality of each.

One of her projects while at Cornell had been compiling an oral history of the

School through interviews with former faculty, many of whom were living in retirement life care communities across the country. She observed these communities closely and subsequently testified at hearings held by the United States Senate Select Committee on Aging in May, 1983, after she had, herself, become a life care community resident. In 1979, Schwartz suffered a stroke, retired from Cornell and moved to Foulkeways, a lifetime care community operated by the Society of Friends near Philadelphia.

In spite of some residual effects of the stroke, Schwartz continued writing and reviewing publications in 1980 and gave the keynote address at the White House Mini-conference on Aging in San Diego that same year. In 1981 she became a senior fellow with a part-time appointment at the University of Pennsylvania School of Nursing, consulting with the faculty for gerontological nurse clinicians, teaching a few classes and participating in the Robert Wood Johnson "Teaching Nursing Home Program." In the same year she was elected as a senior member of the Institute of Medicine.

The book to which she contributed during her sabbatical *Geriatrics and Geriatric Nursing* was published in Great Britain in 1981. From 1981–83 she participated in the University of Pennsylvania Wharton School study of continuing care retirement communities. She maintained an active professional schedule of travel, workshop attendance and speaking, and reviewing manuscripts for the journal *Geriatric Nursing*. The Center for Nursing History at the University of Pennsylvania holds the archives of her papers.

Her autobiography, *Give Us to Go Blithely: My Fifty Years in Nursing* was published in 1991 and named Book of the Year by the *American Journal of Nursing*. In 1992 Doris Schwartz was awarded the Mentor Award by the Alpha Upsilon Chapter of Sigma Theta Tau and 1994 was one of seven nurses nationwide to be honored with the Lillian D. Wald Spirit of Nursing award on the occasion of the 100th anniversary of the visiting Nurse Association of New York.

Doris Schwartz was recognized as a "Living Legend" by the American Academy of Nursing at their November, 1997 meeting, celebrating her exceptional contributions to community health and nursing of the elderly during her career.

PUBLICATIONS BY DORIS RUHBEL SCHWARTZ (SELECTED)

Books

Anderson, W. F., Caird, F. I., Kennedy, R. D., & Schwartz, D. (1982). *Geriatrics and geriatric nursing.* New York: Arco.

Schwartz, D. (1990). *Give us to go blithely: My fifty years of nursing.* New York: Springer Publishing Company.

Schwartz, D., Henley, B., & Zeitz, L. (1964). *The elderly ambulatory patient: Nursing and psychosocial needs.* New York: Macmillan.

Strumpf, N. E., Evans, L. K., & Schwartz, D. (1991). Physical restraint of the elderly. In W. C. Chenitz, J. T. Stone, & S. A. Salisbury (Eds.), *Clinical geronto-logical nursing: A guide to advanced practice* (pp. 329–344). Philadelphia: W. B. Saunders.

Articles

Schwartz, D. (1948, March). Nursing care can be measured. *American Journal of Nursing, 48,* 149.

Schwartz, D. (1949, July). Nursing in Red Hook. *American Journal of Nursing, 49,* 7.

Schwartz, D. (1982). Catastrophic illness: How it feels. *Geriatric Nursing: American Journal of Care for the Aging, 3,* 302–306.

Schwartz, D. (1986). Letters from a life care community. *Journal of Gerontological Nursing, 12*(8), 16–21.

Schwartz, D. (1989). Shall I be a geriatric nurse? *Imprint, 36*(4), 33–34, 37.

Schwartz, D. (1990). The use of physical restraints for the elderly. *Imprint, 37*(4), 54, 56–57.

Schwartz, D. (1996). Learning is a two-way street: Reciprocity and rewards. *Geriatric Nursing, 17*(1), 22–23.

Schwartz, D. (1997). Doris Schwartz: A creative role for faculty in community health. *Geriatric Nursing, 18*(2), 83–84.

Strumpf, N. E., Evans, L. K., & Schwartz, D. (1990). Restraint-free care: from dream to reality. *Geriatric Nursing: American Journal of Care for the Aging, 11*(3), 122–124.

BIBLIOGRAPHY

Academy recognizes living legends. *Nursing Outlook, 46*(1), 39–40.

Anonymous. (1986). Doris Schwartz: Community health nurse extraordinary. *Geriatric Nursing, 7*(3), 155–156.

Doris Schwartz. *Who's who in American Nursing* (6th edition). (1996–1997). (p. 566). New Providence, NJ: Marquis.

Schwartz, D. (1986). Letters from a life care community. *Journal of Gerontological Nursing, 12*(8), 16–21.

Schwartz, D. (1996). Learning is a two-way street: Reciprocity and rewards. *Geriatric Nursing, 17*(1), 22–23.

Schwartz, D. (1997). Doris Schwartz: A creative role for faculty in community health. *Geriatric Nursing, 18*(2), 83–84.

Marian J. Brook

FLORA MADELINE SHAW
1864–1927

A teacher and leader of Canadian nurses, Shaw was internationally known as an authority on nursing education. She was highly respected for her work as President of the Canadian Nurses Association and her long involvement with the International Council of Nurses. Shaw firmly believed in the importance of adequately preparing nurses to fill the positions of administrators and teachers in nursing training schools. As first Director of the McGill School for Graduate Nurses in Montreal, her skilled guidance led the school to become a leader in this area in Canada. When she died unexpectedly at age 63, her nursing career had spanned over 30 years.

Flora Madeline Shaw was born on January 15, 1864 in Perth, Ontario. Her parents were both Scottish. Her father, Henry Dowsley Shaw, was a prosperous business mer-

Flora Madeline Shaw

chant. Her mother, Flora Madeline Matheson, was the daughter of Roderick Matheson, one of the first settlers in Ontario when he came to Perth in 1816.

Shaw received her early education in a private school in Perth. Later, she attended Mrs. Mercer's Academy in Montreal, a fashionable school for young women of middle-class families. Perhaps influenced by her aunt, Shaw embarked upon a nursing career. In 1894, she enrolled in the Montreal General Hospital Training School for Nurses. From 1896 until 1903 she was assistant superintendent at the school, except for the single year, 1899–1900, when she was superintendent of nurses in a small women's hospital in Boston, the Women's Charity Club Hospital.

In 1903, Shaw enrolled in a hospital economics course at Teachers College, Columbia University. While in New York, Shaw was matron of the nurses' home of the Presbyterian Hospital. From this experience she authored her first nursing publication on

floor plans, furnishings, and management. She was also an instructor in dietetics. In 1906 she received her diploma in Teaching in Schools of Nursing from Columbia and returned to Canada.

Shaw accepted the position of Instructor of Nurses at her alma mater, the Montreal General Hospital Training School for Nurses, from 1906 to 1909. During this time, she began her lifelong association with professional nursing organizations. In 1908, she became the first secretary-treasurer of the Canadian Nurses Association, then called the Provisional Organization of the Canadian National Association of Trained Nurses. The following year, this organization became an official member of the International Council of Nurses. With regret, she resigned her position due to illness. Shaw spent the next 6 years regaining her health in sanatoriums in Saranac Lake, New York, and Ste Agathe-des-Monts, Quebec. Her health recovered, Shaw returned to Canada in 1914 after a trip abroad to England. With the outbreak of World War I, she worked as a volunteer social worker at the Montreal branch of the Canadian Patriotic Fund.

In 1920, Shaw accepted the position of Director at the newly created McGill School for Graduate Nurses in Montreal. McGill offered certificate courses in teaching, supervision, and administration in schools of nursing, the first school in Canada to do so. Under her leadership, the school became a highly respected department of the University.

Shaw contributed mightily to professional nursing organizations and activities. Foremost a nursing advocate, she worked to secure important amendments in connection with the Registration Act for Nurses in the province of Quebec. She was a member of the National Executive Committee of the Victorian Order of Nurses and participated in both local and national boards of the Order. In frequent demand as a speaker and educator, she still found time to steadily publish in the professional nursing literature. From 1922 to 1924 Shaw served as President of the Canadian Association of Nursing Education. At the same time, she was President of the Association of Registered Nurses of the Province of Quebec (ARNPQ). In 1925 she attended the International Council of Nurses meeting in Helsingfors (Helsinki), Finland. She resigned from her position with the ARNPQ to assume the Presidency of the Canadian Nurses Association on August 27, 1926.

Exactly 1 year later, Shaw died in Liverpool, England. She was returning from the Interim Conference of the International Conference of Nurses at Geneva that she had attended as a Board member and representative of the Canadian Nurses Association. At the meeting, she had extended an invitation to hold the 1929 International Conference of Nurses in Montreal.

For 9 years before her death, Shaw had lived with her close friend, Florence Rothwell, a social worker. Shaw was an active member of the Church of St. John the Evangelist. Friends and colleagues described her as direct, unpretentious, generous, and decisive. The nurses of Canada mourned her loss at a funeral service held in Montreal in September 1927. In 1929, a book detailing the lives of nursing pioneers in Canada was dedicated to her by the History of Nursing Society at the McGill School for Graduate Nurses. In 1934, Montreal General Hospital unveiled a memorial tablet in tribute. In 1957, the Flora Madeline Shaw Chair of Nursing was established at McGill University. This endowment was the successful 30-year culmination of a memorial fund in her honor by the Alumnae Association of the McGill School for Graduate Nurses.

PUBLICATIONS BY FLORA MADELINE SHAW (SELECTED)

Nurses' homes: Their furnishings and equipment. (1906). *American Journal of Nursing, 6*, 672–676.

The visiting nurse. (1909). *Canadian Nurse, 5*, 11–20.

The training school curriculum. (1911). *Canadian Nurse, 7*, 300–304.

Nursing progress in Canada. (1924). *Canadian Nurse, 20*, 636–638.

Nursing education in Finland. (1926). *Canadian Nurse, 22*, 195–196.

Nursing education in universities in Canada. I: Canadian University Courses in administration and teaching in schools of nursing. (1927). *I.C.N., 2*, 181–186.

BIBLIOGRAPHY

Beamish, R. (1970). *Fifty years a Canadian nurse: Devotion, opportunities and duty.* New York: Vantage Press.

The Canadian Nurses' Association. (1926). *British Journal of Nursing, 74*, 278.

In memoriam: Flora Madeline Shaw, R.N. (1927). *British Journal of Nursing, 75*, 206.

McGill University, School for Graduate Nurses, History of Nursing Society. (1929). *Pioneers of nursing in Canada.* Montreal: Canadian Nurses Association.

Memorial service for Miss Shaw. (1927). *Nursing Times, 23*, 1065.

Memorial to Miss Shaw. (1928). *American Journal of Nursing, 28*, 1118.

Pennock, M. R. (1940). *Makers of nursing history: Portraits and pen sketches of one hundred and nine prominent women.* New York: Lakeside Publishing Company.

Reed, F. L. (1927). Flora Madeline Shaw: From national to international and onward. *I.C.N., 2*, 260–261.

Tunis, B. L. (1966). *In caps and gowns: The story of the School for Graduate Nurses, McGill University, 1920–1964.* Montreal: McGill University Press.

Sharon C. Murphy

MARION WINIFRED SHEAHAN
1892–1994

Marion Sheahan was a public health nurse and administrator whose distinguished career spanned more than 50 years. Through involvement in professional and health organizations at the local, state, and national levels, she creatively and relentlessly worked to shape the nursing profession's response to societal change. Her practical approach to problem-solving, together with a strong will and generous personality, enabled her to powerfully influence the nursing profession and health care policy.

Marion Winifred Sheahan

Marion Winifred Sheahan was born in New York City to James C. and Catherine Nolan Sheahan on September 5, 1892. She was the second eldest of four children. In 1901, the family moved to Albany, New York, where she resided for most of her life. On March 17, 1935, she married Frank W. Bailey. The couple had no children, and Mr. Bailey died in 1947.

Marion Sheahan attended public schools, and graduated from Albany High School. In 1913 she received her nursing diploma from St. Peter's Hospital School of Nursing in Albany. Sheahan later completed special courses at Syracuse University and Columbia University. She had an inquisitive mind and was a prolific reader, but earned no degrees beyond the diploma.

Sheahan began her public health nursing career at New York's Henry Street Settlement in 1917. During World War I she was turned down for enlistment, so she took a staff nurse position with the Albany City Health Department, and later with the Niagara County Health Department's tuberculosis unit. In 1920, she joined the staff of the New York State Department of Health. She remained there until 1948, serving as Assistant Director and later as Director of the Bureau of Public Health Nursing. During her tenure, she developed a public health nursing organization said to be the envy of and inspiration for public health workers throughout the nation. During the depression years, she was instrumental in shaping the Temporary Relief Act to include nursing care as a necessity of life, together with food, clothing, shelter and medical care. Model programs she developed under this Act provided health services through the training and employment of nurses in local agencies throughout New York state, and were soon replicated in other states.

Marion Sheahan began her involvement in several professional organizations in the 1920s including New York State Nurses Association (NYSNA), the National Organization for Public Health Nursing (NOPHN), and the American Public Health Association.

In 1940, Sheahan was a member of the Board of Directors of NYSNA, and a member of a committee established to determine the available nursing manpower in New York state in case of a national emergency. When the national nursing organizations joined together to coordinate nursing's efforts to meet both military and civilian health care needs during the escalating crisis, Sheahan served on the National Nursing Council for War Service as a representative of NOPHN. She served as chair of six different committees including the National Classification Committee, which coordinated the classification of nurses; the Army and Navy Committee, which worked toward the elimination of discrimination, and upon its recommendation, the Nursing Council developed a resolution that Black nurses be appointed to the military on the same basis as other nurses; and the National Nursing Planning Committee, which worked on plans for the post-war period, and continued its work into the post-war period. This committee's report, *A Comprehensive Program for Nation-Wide Action in the Field of Nursing*, is considered a highly significant document which led directly to the landmark work of Esther Lucille Brown. During the war years she also served as the President of the NOPHN and as a member of the U.S. government's Subcommittee on Nursing, a federal group with goals similar to the Nursing Councils.

By 1948, when Sheahan resigned from the New York State Department of Health, and following a visiting professorship at the University of California School of Public Health, she was hired to direct the National Committee for the Improvement of Nursing Services. This joint committee of the six national nursing organizations labored to improve nursing services by upgrading nursing service and nursing education, and by promoting interprofessional relationships. The committee's survey, analysis of data, and classification of schools of nursing provided background information for the development of the accreditation process. When the work of the committee was taken over by the Division of Nursing Services of the newly formed National League for Nursing in 1951, Sheahan assumed the directorship of the division. She later became the NLN's Deputy General Director, a position she held until her retirement in 1963.

In 1960, Sheahan became the first nurse to serve as president of the American Public Health Association. She had previously served as chair of the Public Health Nursing section, vice-president and member of the Executive Board, and an active member of numerous committees. In 1949 she was the first non-physician to receive APHA's Lasker Award, and in 1969 received APHA's highest honor, the Sedgwick Award. Other honors and awards she received include an honorary Doctor of Humanities degree from Adelphi University (1950), the Florence Nightingale Medal of the International Red Cross Societies (1957), an honorary Doctor of Laws degree from Case Western Reserve University (1961), the National League for Nursing Distinguished Service Award (1967), the Honorary Recognition Award from the New York State Nurses Association (1979), and the Pearl McIver Public Health Nurse Award from the American Nurses Association (1986). She was inducted into the American Academy of Nursing as an Honorary Fellow in 1986.

Throughout the 1950s and 1960s, Sheahan served on numerous national committees and advisory groups. She was the only nurse appointed to the President's Commission to Study the Health Needs of the Nation in 1952, and served as a member of the National Citizens Committee for the World Health Organization, the Surgeon General's Consultant Group on Nursing, the National Social Welfare Assembly and the New York Hospital Review and Planning Council.

Marion Sheahan died at the age of 101 on March 17, 1994 in Albany and is buried in Memorys Garden, Colonie, New York. In the first of *Nursing Outlook's* "This I Believe . . ." series in 1963 (pp. 102–103), Sheahan shared her patient-centered philosophy, based on the age-old purpose of nursing which she described as "caring for, giving comfort and ease, helping persons with health problems to become healed in body and mind or helping them to live with their infirmities with grace." She predicted an increasingly technological future, and believed that nursing must be part of societal change, yet must never lose sight of the centrality of the patient. "The task of nursing is to bring the patient back to the central position in the superstructure of our professional nursing practice. The task of nursing is to make the superstructure serve the patient—the purpose for which it was created."

PUBLICATIONS BY MARION WINIFRED SHEAHAN (SELECTED)

An experiment in double relief. (1933). *Public Health Nursing, 25,* 378–381.
Nurses and the C.W.A. (1934). *Quarterly News, 6,* 9–10.
The nurse in pneumonia control. (1936). *Public Health Nursing, 18,* 802–806.
Maternity nursing in rural areas. (1939). *Milbank Memorial Fund Quarterly, 17,* 113–127.
Public health nursing in the war. (1942). *Public Health Nursing, 34,* 371–379.
The work of the NOPHN must go on! (1946). *Public Health Nursing, 38,* 578–580, 620.
A program for the improvement of nursing services. (1950). *American Journal of Nursing, 50,* 794–795.
The president's commission on the health needs of the nation. (1952). *American Journal of Nursing, 52,* 987–988.
Needed: Reorganization for health service. (1962). *American Journal of Public Health, 62,* 393–400.
This I believe . . . . *Nursing Outlook, 11,* 102–103.

BIBLIOGRAPHY

Association news. (1960). *American Journal of Public Health, 50,* 1807–1808.
Pavri, J. (1993). The triumph of gentle determination. *Report, the Newsletter of the New York State Nurses Association, 23,* 11.
Pavri, J. (1995). In memoriam: Marion W. Sheahan. *American Journal of Public Health, 85,* 1719–1720.
Safir, G. (1977). *Contemporary leaders in American nursing: An oral history.* New York: McGraw-Hill.
Sedgwick Memorial Medal for 1969. (1970). *American Journal of Public Health, 60,* 171–175.
Papers. Foundation of the New York State Nurses Association Archives, Guilderland, New York.

Julie M. Pavri

RUBY M. SIMPSON
1888–1977

Simpson provided 25 years of nursing service to Canada. For 17 years, she was Director of Public Health Nursing in the province of Saskatchewan. A strong leader, Simpson also served as President of the Canadian Nurses Association from 1934–1938 during the difficult Depression years.

Simpson was born in Neepawa, Manitoba, Canada in 1888 where she received her early education. After receiving her teaching certificate from the Winnipeg Normal School, she taught in the Winnipeg public schools for 5 years. The teaching experience she gained during this period provided an excellent foundation for her later work.

A latecomer to nursing, Simpson graduated from the Training School of the Winnipeg General Hospital in 1919 at the age of 31. Her first position was as a public school nurse in Saskatchewan with the School Hygiene Branch of the Department of Education. In 1920 she taught school hygiene in the Saskatoon Normal School. Two years later she advanced to Director of School Hygiene for the entire province of Saskatchewan.

A proponent of continuing education, Simpson traveled to New York City in 1924 to take a summer nursing course at Columbia University. Four years later she returned to the United States on a Rockefeller Travel Fellowship for 4 months.

In 1928 the School Hygiene Branch of the Department of Education was transferred to the Provincial Department of Pub-

Ruby M. Simpson

lic Health. With the change, Simpson became the Director of Public Health Nursing in Saskatchewan, a position she retained for 17 years.

In 1929 Simpson journeyed to England, where she spent 3 months studying British public health nursing programs. Upon her return home to Regina, she went to work and in 1931 clearly outlined the public health nursing program in Saskatchewan. The program sought to include the entire community and emphasized the areas of school health, prenatal and infant welfare, and health education. A contributor to the professional nursing literature throughout her career, Simpson's publications document the steady progress made in Saskatchewan under her leadership.

Simpson also was active in professional nursing organizations. She served as President of the Saskatchewan Registered Nurses Association from 1928 to 1934. She left that position to assume the presidency of the Canadian Nurses Association for 2 terms in 1934, the first Western-born President. That same year she became an officer of the Civil Division of the Order of the British Empire, an honor conferred upon her by His Majesty King George V in recognition of her social service contributions to the province of Saskatchewan. In 1937 Simpson returned to England where she represented the nurses of Canada at the International Council of Nurses meeting held in London. In 1944 she was awarded one of the Canadian Nurses Association's highest awards, the Mary Agnes Snively Memorial Medal.

Described as liberal and progressive, Simpson was also known throughout her nursing career as an incisive, direct, and genial individual. After 25 years of public health service she retired in 1945 at age 57 to Vancouver Island, British Columbia, close to where her sister and niece resided. There she lived quietly, pursuing two life-long pleasures, gardening and reading. Following a long retirement, Simpson died on August 5, 1977 at the age of 89. A memorial service was held nearby on August 8 in the Chapel of the First United Church.

PUBLICATIONS BY RUBY M. SIMPSON (SELECTED)

School nursing organization in Saskatchewan. (1922). *Canadian Nurse, 18,* 759–761.

[Report on 1923 school health program in Saskatchewan]. (1924). *Canadian Public Health Journal, 15,* 404–408.

[Report on rural health aspects of school health program in Saskatchewan]. (1927). *ICN, 2,* 100–107.

Public health nursing in Saskatchewan. (1931). *Canadian Public Health Journal, 22,* 130–134.

[Nursing trends and goals]. (1936). *Canadian Nurse, 32,* 345–348; 393–395.

The committees of the I.C.N. (1937). *Canadian Nurse, 33,* 535–540.

Thirty years of growth. (1938). *Canadian Nurse, 34,* 411–416.

Mary Agnes Snively. (1938). *Canadian Nurse, 34,* 423–426.

Maternal welfare and the maternity grant. (1942). *Canadian Nurse, 38,* 400–404.

BIBLIOGRAPHY

The accolade. (1934). *Canadian Nurse, 30,* 53–56.

Browne, J. E. (1944). Ruby M. Simpson, O.B.E. *Canadian Nurse, 40,* 391–392.

Gibbon, J. M., & Mathewson, M. S. (1947). *Three centuries of Canadian nursing.* Toronto: Macmillan.

Interesting people [Retirement of Ruby M. Simpson]. (1945). *Canadian Nurse, 41,* 458.

The new President. (1934). *Canadian Nurse, 30,* 353.

Simpson, R. M. Papers. Helen K. Mussallem Library, Canadian Nurses Association, Ottawa, Ontario.

Sharon C. Murphy

Dorothy M. Smith

DOROTHY M. SMITH
1913–1997

Dorothy M. Smith was best known as the founding Dean of the University of Florida School of Nursing and for her belief that patient care and education should be integrated. Throughout her career she maintained a clinical practice while she was involved with nursing education, providing a model for nursing faculty to follow in order to actualize this concept.

Smith was born in Bangor, Maine in 1913, the oldest of three children. The family had limited financial resources, and coming of age during the Great Depression required her to find a way of being self-supporting. Smith chose nursing for its occupational opportunity. She began her nursing education at Quincy (Massachusetts) City Hospital. She received her diploma in 1936 and remained at Quincy City Hospital as Staff Nurse and Head nurse from 1936 through 1939. Smith enrolled in the Nursing Education program at Teachers College, Columbia University, completing her B.S. degree in 1941. She

returned to Quincy City Hospital as Science Instructor and Assistant Educational Director from 1942 to 1945 and served as Educational Director and Science Instructor from 1945–1947.

During this time she began to develop and teach an approach to patient care involving collection of data from the patient, creation of a problem list, and evaluation of the effect of nursing measures. This was contrary to the prevailing way of expecting nurses to learn by "trial and error and from experience" which she had come to consider as "wasteful" (Safier, 1977, p. 375). Thus, she accepted an offer to become Assistant Director of Nursing Education at Duke University in 1948 believing that "nurses should become educated like anybody else" (Safier, 1977, p. 373). She remained at Duke until 1951, when she became a consultant for the National League for Nursing, Division of Nursing Education for 2 years. She then became Assistant Director in Nursing at Hartford Hospital, in Connecticut for 2 years. In 1956 she was appointed Dean of the new nursing program at the University of Florida, Gainesville.

Smith saw this as an opportunity to put into practice some of the strong beliefs that had evolved from her experience: that there should be a system to patient care that could be taught to students, and that this could be accomplished best by faculty who maintained some clinical practice as well as an educational role. In order to ensure practice privileges for her faculty and that nursing students would learn in an environment that provided the kind of care they should emulate, Smith insisted on a organizational model that linked nursing education with nursing service. Thus she became both the founding Dean of the University of Florida College of Nursing and the first Chief of Nursing Practice at the Shands Teaching Hospital when it opened in 1958.

Until her retirement as Dean in 1973, Smith maintained a clinical practice in the hospital. She spoke nationally and internationally on her commitment to keeping nursing research and education closely linked to evidence-based patient care. Her writings during the 1960s discussed the formal process of data collection, problem identification, and monitoring of outcomes of interventions which she believed to be the clinical role of nurses. Throughout her career, Smith often served on various committees of several state and national nursing organizations, and served a 2-year term on the Board of the Florida Nurses' Association.

She was awarded an honorary Doctor of Science degree by the University of Rochester (NY) in 1972. In 1982 she was elected an honorary member of the American Academy of Nursing.

Following her retirement as Dean, Smith published (with Eileen Becknell) the textbook *System of nursing practice: A clinical assessment tool* in 1975.

In 1996 Dorothy Smith was honored as a "Living Legend" by the Academy and commended for her vision of nursing education and research fully integrated with patient care. Her commitment to this ideal was credited as being a major factor in the renewed commitment of nursing to clinical practice, as evidenced by the shift of master's programs from administration and teaching to advanced clinical practice and the transfer of the focus of nursing research to effectiveness and outcomes of interventions. Smith died on August 16, 1997 at Indian Harbor Beach, Florida at age 84 and was buried in Weld, Maine. She was survived by one brother and by a foster daughter.

PUBLICATIONS BY DOROTHY M. SMITH

Books

Becknell, E. P., & Smith, D. M. (1975). *System of nursing practice: A clinical assessment tool.* Philadelphia: F. A. Davis.

Articles

From student to nurse. (1963). *Nursing Outlook, 11*(10), 735–736.

Myth and method in nursing practice. (1964). *American Journal of Nursing, 64*(2), 68–72.

A clinical nursing tool. (1968). *American Journal of Nursing, 68*, 2384–2388.

Is it too late? (1971). *Nursing Clinics of North America, 6*(2), 225–230.

BIBLIOGRAPHY

Academy recognizes living legends. Dorothy M. Smith. (1996). *Nursing Outlook, 44*(6), 291–292.

Dorothy M. Smith, founding Dean of Nursing, dies. (1997, August 22). *The Friday Evening Post.*

Safier, G. (1977). Dorothy Smith: Nurse. In G. Safier (Ed.), *Contemporary American leaders in nursing: An oral history* (pp. 270–283). New York: McGraw-Hill.

Marian Brook

EDITH H. SMITH
1891–1987

Edith H. Smith was a multifaceted nurse leader, recruiter, and educator. Her career included the Navy Nurse Corps (1917–1919); the League of Red Cross Societies, Paris, France (1924–1930); Stanford Hospitals and School of Nursing, Palo Alto, CA (1933–1940), the Subcommittee on Nursing, Office of Defense, Health and Welfare, Federal Security Agency, Washington, DC (1942); the National Council for War Service (1943); the Committee on Careers in Nursing, National Nursing Council (1944–1947); and Syracuse University School of Nursing (now College of Nursing) where she was founding dean and professor (1943–1957).

Edith H. Smith

Born in Coronado, CA, in 1891, she spent her early years in Honolulu where her father was a newspaper editor. Back in California, she graduated from Lane Hospital School of Nursing at Stanford University in 1913, receiving an A.B. degree from Stanford University in 1916, with a major in English and a minor in French.

She served in the Navy (1917–1919) as part of the Stanford Medical Unit (Navy Base Hospital No. 2), in Scotland and London, and described her work as "bedside nurse, head nurse, and in emergency surgery" (Smith, 1950). She held the rank of Second Lieutenant, and in later years belonged to the Navy Nurse Reserve.

In 1924, after a short period with the YWCA in New York City, she began 5 years as an assistant and teacher in the Nursing Division of the League of Red Cross Societies, headquartered in Paris, France. During this period, she authored a monograph, *Red Cross Nursing*, published in English, French, and Spanish, and also published several articles in *The Public Health Nurse*. Her field work included observing and teaching in Austria, Italy, Hungary, and Czechoslovakia, and teaching international nursing courses at Bedford College for Women, University of London (Smith, 1950).

She returned to New York and entered Columbia University from where she received an M.A. from Teachers College in 1933. She then became Professor of Nursing and Director of the Nursing Service at Stanford University Hospitals. Her major reminiscence of this time was that the Nursing School and Nursing Service were under the Medical School at Stanford, an organizational relationship which she found difficult and, in the end, unworkable. She may well have been asked to resign in 1940.

For the next several years, Smith held a variety of positions in Washington, DC, all related to nursing and the "war effort." She served as Nursing Consultant, Health and Welfare Division, Federal Security Agency, in Washington, DC, in 1941. In 1942 she was Assistant Executive Secretary for the Subcommittee on Nursing in the Office of Defense Health and Welfare Services.

At the beginning of 1943 she took part in a 3-month "experiment" as College Recruitment Representative for the East Coast, National Nursing Council for War Service, describing her work as speaking, writing, and travel.

Her role as college recruiter brought her to New York state, where she came to the attention of the Chancellor of Syracuse University, William P. Tolley, who wanted to establish a nursing school.

In her interview with him, she insisted that she not report to the Dean of Medicine, a standard procedure for nursing schools in universities with medical schools, and when he agreed to have her report directly to him, she agreed to become the founding dean. She later wrote: "Several fundamental principles were agreed upon during our early conferences. The school, if established, should be an independent, autonomous school, having equal status with other schools in the University, with its own dean and adequate budget. It should function within the framework of the University, with freedom to develop its own objectives and program, while holding always to the true course of a university. The faculty should have full academic status. As soon as possible, the school would have its own instructors in all clinical fields and in public health, and they should be in full control of the educational program for students. The criteria for the selection of students would be high, and the students would be free to participate in all University activities; only in this way could they develop their talents to the utmost and have all possible opportunity for self-expression" (Reynolds & Harris, 1996).

Forty-three students began on June 28; another 60 came in September, and a third class was admitted in January 1944. And in July of 1943, the Cadet Nurse Corps was established, so that, suddenly, there was also a "war program" to develop and operationalize.

The School (now College) has indeed thrived. Some of Smith's major contributions during her 14-year tenure are:

- Her persistence in persuading the War Department to provide a residence and an academic building
- Establishment of the Department of Nursing Education (for R.N. students) in 1947, with main campus and outreach courses
- Approval of the baccalaureate program by the National Organization of Public Health Nursing
- Early integration of Blacks and others including six Japanese-American students recruited from internment camps
- The founding of a Master's Program in the early 1950s
- Enrollment of many international students into the Registered Nurse and Graduate Programs.

Edith Smith died on November 7, 1987, in Los Altos, California.

PUBLICATIONS BY EDITH H. SMITH

The fourth English-speaking conference on maternity and child welfare. (1926a). *The Public Health Nurse, 18*, 643–645.

The League of Red Cross Societies. (1926b). *The Public Health Nurse, 18*, 184–186.

Red Cross nursing. (1928). League of Red Cross Societies (translated into French and Spanish).

The Nursing Advisory Committee: League of Red Cross Societies. (1929a). *The Public Health Nurse,* 110–112.

Papworth Village Settlement. (1929b). *The Public Health Nurse, 21*, 365–367.

One more word about married student nurses. (1942). *American Journal of Nursing, 42*, 1149–1150.

Educators look at nursing. (1943). *American Journal of Nursing, 43*, 573–576.

Current aspects of student nurse recruitment. (1946). Paper presented at the Meeting of the American Hospital Association, Philadelphia.

BIBLIOGRAPHY

Reynolds, A. & Harris, B. L. (1984). *Dean Edith H. Smith and the early years* [Videotape]. (Available from Syracuse University College of Nursing, 426 Ostrom Ave., Syracuse, NY 13244).

Reynolds, A., & Harris, B. L. (1996). *Nursing at Syracuse University in the forties: Tradition and transition, war and peace.* (Syracuse University College of Nursing History Series, Paper #3). Syracuse, NY.

Smith, E. H. (1943). Educators look at nursing. *American Journal of Nursing, 43,* 573–576.

Smith, E. H. (1950). *Faculty questionnaire* (Office of the Vice-Chancellor, Syracuse University).

Barbara L. Harris

AGNES HANNAH VON KUROWSKY STANFIELD
1892–1984

Agnes Hannah von Kurowsky, famed for her influence on Ernest Hemingway's fiction, was a competent professional nurse from the last year of the First World War on into the Thirties. During an active nursing career of about 15 years, she worked in Europe, Haiti, and the Eastern coast of the United States. She is buried at Arlington National Cemetery because of her "exemplary dedication to the nation."

Kurowsky was born January 5, 1892, in Germantown, Pennsylvania, the daughter of Agnes Theodosia Holabird and Paul Paul Moritz Julius von Kurowsky. Her father, who died in 1910 of typhoid, was a naturalized American citizen of Polish, Russian and German ancestry. Her mother's father, Samuel B. Holabird, served as Quartermaster General of the U.S. Army during the Reconstruction period. Kurowsky spent most of her early years in Washington, D.C., though she also lived for a time in Alaska and Vancouver.

Kurowsky got her nurse's training at Bellevue in New York City. During training, she nursed psychopaths and alcoholics, as well as mothers and their new babies and patients with contagious diseases. Bellevue's praise of her personality and her administrative ability got her a job at Long Island College Hospital after her training. But Kurowsky wanted adventure and also wanted to get more involved in World War I, and applied to serve as a Red Cross Nurse. At that time nurses who worked with the military served under Red Cross auspices.

Kurowsky was sent to Italy and since she kept a diary during the whole time, we know some details of her work. She arrived in Milan June 11, 1918. By July 26 she was in residence at the American Red Cross Hospital. There she met two patients who placed her name in history: Ernest Hemingway, through his fiction, and Henry Serrano Villard, through editing and publishing her diary. In October she volunteered to go to Florence for 4 weeks to nurse typhoid patients. After another few days in Milan she was ordered to Treviso, near Padua, where she worked long hours under poor conditions. There were many deaths among the patients, but she wrote Hemingway that "I am very happy indeed, because I feel I am doing some really worth while work" (Kurowsky, 1989). In mid-January, after the war was over, she was transferred from Treviso to Torrel di Mosto to nurse orphaned children who had been injured by the explosion of leftover bombs and patients with severe cases of typhoid. By March, Kurowsky was in charge of the small hospital, and she held this position until she returned to the U.S. in July, 1919.

During the rest of her professional career, Kurosky alternated between work at home and abroad. After working at Bellevue for 6 months, once again her adventurous nature carried her abroad. She volunteered to be a Red Cross Nurse in Russia, but travel in Russia was forbidden, so she was assigned to Rumania. She nursed in Bucharest until September 1920, meanwhile learning Rumanian. After that stint, she traveled in Europe before going back to the U.S. for 4 years of private duty nursing. In the spring of 1926, she reenlisted in the Red Cross in order to work in Haiti, where the American military government needed a French speaker to work with probationary nurses. In Haiti, she was commended for setting such high standards. Her last nursing job began in 1931 when she went to work at a tuberculosis sanitarium in Otisville, New York.

To the public, the most important period of her life was the short time in 1918 that she nursed Ernest Hemingway in Milan. Though she had two engagements and two marriages, it was the brief romance with Hemingway in 1918 that put her in the history books. The 26-year-old nurse and the 19-year-old patient, both free, uninhibited spirits, spent 2 months in the Milan Hospital and then corresponded for 3 or 4 more months. The effect on Hemingway was strong and lasting. Kurowsky was Hemingway's first love, and he used her, according to most critics, as a model for the heroines in *A Farewell to Arms,* "A Very Short Story," and "The Snows of Kilimanjaro."

It was her character and personality that had such an impact on the men in her life and on her nursing career. Remembering 1918 when he arrived very ill with jaundice at the Milan Hospital, Henry Villard called her a "ministering angel . . . who combined brisk competence with exceptional charm" (Kurowsky, 1989). She was tough and efficient with a strong sense of responsibility. Yet she genuinely cared for people and was warm and generous in dealing with them. Her jaunty, impish manner and her spir-

ited, easy temperament attracted people to her.

Kurowsky's first marriage—in Haiti in 1928—to Howard Preston Garner lasted only 2 years. In 1931 she met William Stanfield, a widower with three children, and married him 4 years later. At this time she left nursing to help her husband run a resort hotel in Virginia Beach, Virginia. The marriage lasted 43 years until her death at 92. She had no children of her own. At various times in her life, scholars and family members contacted her for information about her experience with Hemingway. She died Nov. 24, 1984 at Gulfport, Virginia. Because of "her gallant and commendable services" with the American Red Cross, she is buried in the Soldiers' Home National Cemetery at Arlington, Virginia, alongside her parents and grandparents.

BIBLIOGRAPHY

Baker, C. (1969). *Ernest Hemingway: A Life Story.* New York: Scribner's.

Bullough, V., & Bullough, B. (1978). *The care of the sick: The emergence of modern medicine.* New York: Prodist.

Kert, B. (1983). *The Hemingway women.* New York: Norton.

Mellow, J. R. (1992). *Hemingway: A life without consequences.* New York: Houghton Mifflin.

Reynolds, M. S. (1976). *Hemingway's first war: The making of A Farewell to Arms.* Princeton: Princeton University Press.

von Kurowsky, A. (1989). *Hemingway in love and war: The lost diary of Agnes von Kurowsky, her letters, and correspondence of Ernest Hemingway.* (Edited with essays by Henry Serrano Villard and James Nagel). Boston: Northeastern.

Gwendolyn Whitehead Brewer

T

DOROTHY M. TALBOT
1918–

Dorothy Talbot was a pioneer in the field of public health nursing.

On August 18, 1918, she was born to Parker McComb and Mildred Wilcox McComb in Hurley, New Mexico. After graduation from high school at the age of 15, she was sent to the Texas State College for Women in Denton, Texas, now known as Texas Women's University, where she majored in chemistry and bacteriology. After 3 years of study, she left Texas Women's University to enter a baccalaureate program in nursing at the Jefferson Medical College School of Nursing in Philadelphia, PA. Three years later in 1939 (although her diploma is dated 1940), she graduated from nursing school and became an R.N.

Her first job after graduating was in the health center at Texas Women's University. Dorothy married Raymond James Talbot on August 1, 1940. They had 3 children, Raymond James Jr., Patricia, and Betty Sue. After her wedding, she left her position in Texas to join her husband who was in the Navy. In 1942, Raymond was sent overseas, so Talbot and her son lived with her parents in Louisiana. She found work and became a teacher for the Red Cross's nurses' aides training program. She also was enlisted to train cadet nurses in the armed services as well as student nurses and aides in the hospital. In 1945, she returned briefly to Texas to get her long delayed bachelor's degree.

She returned to Louisiana and worked as a public health nurse. In 1957, she decided to return to school to work on a master's degree in education. She and her 2 daughters moved to New York so that she could attend the Teachers College at Columbia University where she graduated in 1958. Her son stayed with her husband in north Louisiana.

While holding the position of director of the public health nursing program in the School of Public Health and Tropical Medicine at Tulane University, she earned a master of public health degree in 1962 and a doctorate degree in 1970.

In 1974, Talbot accepted the position of professor at the University of North Carolina at Chapel Hill. She served as chair and professor in the department of Public Health Nursing at the School of Public Health. Talbot was a nationally renowned author and speaker on public health. She was an education co-leader on a tour to the former Soviet Union and the Orient. She also worked as a private practice consultant in Chapel Hill, North Carolina.

Talbot was the first to receive the Ruth Freeman Distinguished Service Award given by her peers in the American Public Health Association. She also received the Meritorious Award from the Southern Health Association.

PUBLICATIONS BY DOROTHY M. TALBOT

Books

Professionalization among student nurses in Peru: A sociological analysis. (1970). New Orleans, LA: Tulane University.
Public health nursing: Now and as it might be. (1978). In N. L. Chaska (Ed.), *The nursing profession: A time to speak.* New York: McGraw-Hill.

Putting the health in health care. (1978). In N. L. Chaska (Ed.), *The nursing profession: Views through the mist.* New York: McGraw-Hill.

Articles

Federation of specialty nursing organizations and the American Nurses' Association: A history. (1981). *Occupational Health Nursing, 29,* 27–33.

An educational model to prepare the baccalaureate nurses for occupational health nursing. (1983). *Occupational Health Nursing, 31*(5), 20–25.

Assessing needs of the rural elderly. (1985). *Journal of Gerontological Nursing, 11*(3), 39–43.

Nurses speak out . . . what makes long term care nursing so special and rewarding? (1994). *Washington Nurse, 24,*(4), 8.

BIBLIOGRAPHY

Franz, J. (Ed.). (1989). *Who's Who in American Nursing: 1988–1989* (p. 452). Washington, DC: Society of Nursing Professionals.

Highriter, M. E. (1993). One hundred years of powerful women: A conversation with Dorothy Talbot. *Public Health Nursing, 10*(1), 3–7.

Jeanne Fielding

JOHN DEVEREAUX THOMPSON
1917–1992

John Thompson found the diagnosis related group [DRG] that changed the basis of hospital payment from one of hospital cost per patient to a flat rate based on the diagnosis and treatment groups established by physicians for patients. As a teacher of hospital administration at Yale for nearly 40 years, Thompson developed a collaborative working relationship with Robert Fetter of the Administrative Science Department, and the two introduced operations research techniques into the field of hospital management. Never without grant support, Thompson used data to optimize the size of maternity units, the size of nursing staffs in hospitals and for many other purposes. He was the first nurse since Nightingale to apply statistical sciences to the design and control of hospital operations. While Nightingale advocated examining hospital mortality by comparing death rates by the types of cases treated in hospitals, Thompson found the same concept useful in explaining and predicting hospital costs by comparing their caseloads.

As a student of history, Thompson regularly read and wrote on the history of hospitals, nursing and medicine. Together with Grace Goldin, he produced a well-known book on the social and architectural history of the hospital. He repeatedly returned to the reading room of the British Library at the British Museum, where he pored over 19th-century letters, books, and documents in an effort to understand the genesis of and then expand the work of Nightingale, his heroine. He gravitated to history later in his academic life and produced a number of papers, among them, *The Great Stench*, describing the Victorian use of the Thames as a sewer and an unfinished manuscript on Nightingale and her opponents use of statistics to determine the most salubrious location for the new St. Thomas Hospital [she lost].

Thompson was born August 6, 1917 in Franklin, Pennsylvania, and raised in Canton, Ohio. He was the second child of William McKinley Thompson, a traveling salesman, and Margaret Devereaux, who was for a time a mathematics teacher. Thompson had an older brother and a younger sister. He attended local schools in Canton and his first year at Ohio State University was cut short by illness and the poverty imposed by the Depression prevented his return to his mother's alma mater. An uncle, who was a military physician, recommended he attend nursing school, probably the only place in America at the time where one could simultaneously obtain an education, room, board and a small stipend.

He enrolled at the Mills Training School for Men Nurses at Bellevue Hospital in New

York City in 1936, completing the program in 1939. He was art director for the hardcover publication celebrating the 50th Anniversary of the Mills School of Nursing for Men. Thompson was one of a number of distinguished men of his generation who found their way to the nursing profession seeking the same economic opportunity as did the women members of the profession in the decades before and since the Depression. After a short stint in hospital practice (night shift: urology and prison psychiatry), Thompson enrolled in the Navy prior to World War II and served throughout as a pharmacist's mate in the Atlantic on a aircraft carrier. After the war he returned to New York and enrolled at City College of New York, again working at Bellevue, receiving his bachelor's degree in business with distinction in 1949.

Thompson began his long association with Yale University as a student of hospital administration after college. He completed his training there in 1951 and spent the next 5 years at Montefiore Hospital in Bronx, New York, working for Dr. Martin Cherkasky, the hospital director. Thompson hired Lydia Hall who developed the Loeb Center for Nursing and Rehabilitation which, in 1966, became the model for the Medicare extended care benefit.

Thompson was married April 19, 1952 in Staten Island, New York to Andriana Natale, M.D., a surgeon he met at Montefiore. When she completed her residency in general surgery, the young family moved to New Haven. Together they produced 7 children [Margaret, Monica, Anthony, Siobhan, Dierdre, Julie and Mary Clare], all raised in New Haven and educated at Catholic schools there.

John Thompson returned to Yale in 1956, first as assistant director, then as Professor and Director of the Program in Hospital Administration. Thompson was a colorful teacher sporting a distinctive moustache, a cigar, and in later years, a sportsman's vest which, after the DRG was adopted for use in Medicare reimbursement, he referred to as his flak jacket. He used the language of the Navy to illustrate important points, always a concern to the members of religious communities who were invariably admitted to his program.

Thompson had a grasp for numbers and their meaning and was wise enough to seek out a partner in Bob Fetter who was schooled in them. Together they used an amazing array of applied statistics for hospital operations that became more sophisticated with every new development in calculating and then computing. He could always be seen with a table of data from which he would draw a line graph visualizing relationships. Most recently he depicted the overall sickness of hospital patients after the length of stay reductions occasioned by the Medicare DRG based prospective payment system. On sabbatical in Belgium at Katholic University in Leuven, Thompson authored the *Leuven Lectures*, a review of classic and contemporary efforts to merge mathematics with hospital care. His influence there has endured and data from nurses and doctors is now used to reimburse Belgian hospitals. He inculcated his students with the need for evidence to buttress any professional argument. At the same time he never let anyone forget the patient was first and was said to have produced several generations of humane hospital managers. Thompson and Fetter received the 1991 Baxter Prize for their contributions to Health Service Research.

Thompson had a long and productive professional association with the Yale School of Nursing and the professional nursing community in New Haven. His joint appointment to the faculty there was begun with Dean Florence Wald and developed under the clinical programs of scholarship and care that flourished under the leadership of Deans Donna Diers and Judith Krauss. He served for years on the Board of Directors of the Visiting Nurses Association of New Haven and was an advisor to and member of the Board of Trustees of Connecticut Hospice, the nation's first edifice constructed for that purpose.

Thompson loved classical music, especially the opera. On his official retirement from Yale (he never stopped working there) in 1988, he was entertained by the Whiffenpoofs and his students presented him with a round trip ticket to Vienna, where he enjoyed the opera season. The Navy taught him to play cards and cribbage was a skill he taught and played with all his children during summers at Lake Winnipesaukee, New Hampshire. Thompson died in 1992 on August 13, after his 75th birthday. He is buried at St. Laurence Cemetery, just across the street from the Yale Bowl.

John Devereaux Thompson will long be remembered for his DRG work. He was, however, a unique and special teacher who helped humanize hospital administration.

PUBLICATIONS BY JOHN DEVEREAUX THOMPSON

Books

Thompson, J. D., & Goldin, G. (1975). *The hospital: A social and architectural history.* New Haven: Yale University Press.

Thompson, J. D. (1977). *Applied health services research.* Lexington, MA: D. C. Heath.

Articles (Selected)

Fetter, R. B., Thompson, J. D, & Mills, R. E. (1976). A system for Cost and Reimbursement Control in Hospitals. *Yale Journal of Biology and Medicine, 49,* 123–126.

Fetter, R. B., Shin, Y., Freeman, J., Averill, R. F., & Thompson, J. D. (1980). Case mix definition by diagnosis related group. *Medical Care, 18* (February 2).

Thompson, J. D., & Fetter, R. B. (1963). The economics of maternity services. *Yale Journal of Biology and Medicine, 36* (August 1).

Thompson, J. D. (1963). The great stench or the fools argument. *Yale Journal of Biology and Medicine, 64* (August 1).

Thompson, J. D. (1968). On reasonable costs of hospital services. *Milbank Memorial Fund quarterly, 16*(1), part 2.

Thompson, J. D. (1980). The passionate humanist: From Nightingale to the new nurse. *Nursing Outlook, 28*(5), 290–295.

Thompson, J. D. (1984). The measurement of nursing intensity. *Health Care Financing Review,* November, pp. 47–55.

Thompson, J. D., & Diers, D. (1985). DRGs and nursing intensity. *Nursing and Health Care,* October.

BIBLIOGRAPHY

Diers, D. (1986). Editor's note. *Image, 18*(2), 79.

Mills School of Nursing for Men at Bellevue Hospital. (1938). *Fifty years at the Mills School of Nursing for Men at Bellevue Hospital.* New York: Author.

Edward J. Halloran

ELNORA ELVIRA THOMSON
1878–1957

Elnora E. Thomson was a pioneer in the development of educational programs and practice initiatives in mental health and public health nursing. During her long and distinguished career, Thomson gained national and international recognition for her leadership in professional nursing organizations.

Thomson was born on November 4, 1878, in Oedo, Illinois, to John Calvin Thomson and Mary Eliza Edwards. She had an older sister, Clara. Her father was a wealthy banker and the family situation allowed Thomson to enjoy a comfortable childhood and adolescence. Thomson attended public school in Wellinton, Kansas, but most of her education was in private schools and with tutors. She planned to enter Wellesley College, but her mother's health took a turn for the worse and the family decided that it was important for Thomson to remain at home. They em-

Elnora Elvira Thomson

ployed a tutor and Thomson read the Wellesley classics curriculum before being presented to society, at the age of 18. After a "gay social year of ice skating, parties and dancing," Thomson's goals changed and she entered Presbyterian Hospital School of Nursing in Chicago. By 1909, she had completed her diploma in nursing and done postgraduate work in social work at the Postgraduate School of Civics and Philanthropy in Chicago.

Her first job was as chief nurse at the state mental hospital in Elgin, Illinois (1910). Her acquaintance with Julia Lathrop (Hull House and later chief of the United States Children's Bureau) began at this time. In 1911, Lathrop recruited Thomson to the position of executive secretary for the Illinois Society for Mental Hygiene, a position she held until 1918. During the 1917–1918 academic year she also held an appointment as director of the department of public health nursing at the Chicago School of Civics and Philanthropy. These experiences were instrumental in her developing conception of the interface between social work and public health nursing and would continue to influence her position on the practice of public health nursing and the education of its practitioners. In 1918, she accepted a 1-year appointment to the American Red Cross Tuberculosis Committee to go to Italy and establish a program in public health nursing education. The American nurses working with Thomson provided much needed care during the influenza pandemic, endearing themselves to the Italian people and increasing program support from the Italian government. Thomson returned to her position at the Chicago School of Civics and Philanthropy in August 1919.

In 1920, Thomson moved to Oregon to begin the public health nursing program at the Portland School of Social Work. She directed an early Commonwealth Fund demonstration grant in child health in Marion County, Oregon and served from 1923–1925 as the director of the Far-Western Office of the American Child Health Association in San Francisco, California. She was awarded the rank of professor in 1925 in the school of social work and expanded her administrative duties as director of health and nursing education. Her expertise as a teacher was recognized by other universities. She taught in summer sessions at the University of Chicago, University of Minnesota, and the University of California at Berkeley and Los Angeles. In 1932, when the Oregon State System of Higher Education was formed, the school of social work was closed. The importance of the nursing program as a regional resource was recognized, however, and authority for the program was transferred to the University of Oregon School of Medicine. Thomson became the first director of the department in 1933, a position she maintained until her retirement in 1944.

Thomson was much sought out by social work and state and national nursing organizations. Her longtime association with the American Nurses Association (ANA) began in 1917 in Illinois, when she was president of the state association. By 1922, she had become involved and served as a director of both the National League for Nursing Education (NLNE) and the National Organization for Public Health Nursing (NOPHN) as well as serving as first vice president of ANA. During this time she was also a member of the national committee on nursing service of the American Red Cross. From 1930–1934, a difficult time for the ANA, Thomson served as president succeeding Miss Lillian Clayton. Among the issues and accomplishments of the association in this time period were the resolution of the discussions that resulted in the resignation of Janet Geister as director of headquarters; the 1932 statement defining professional nursing and the professional nurse; the arrangement under which NLNE would function as the educational department of ANA; approval by the House of Delegates of the 8-hour work day; collaborations with the Federal Emergency Relief Administration and others on projects to reemploy nurses left unemployed by the Great Depression, and working with the National Council of Women at the 1933 Century of Progress exhibit in Chicago and National Association of Colored Graduate Nurses. Thomson went on to chair numerous committees for ANA, including the advisory committee for the American Nurses Memorial at Bordeaux, France and the program committee for the 1941 ICN International Congress. She also chaired the committee on constitution and bylaws for American Association of Colleges of Nursing and served on joint committees at the local, state, and national levels. She presented workshops and seminars throughout the country on public health nursing education.

After her retirement in 1944, Thomson joined the faculty of University of California at Berkeley. In 1954, her health began to fail when she suffered several strokes. Thomson died on April 24, 1957. A memorial service was held at the Cypress Lawn Funeral Home in San Francisco on May 8, 1957. She was cremated and her ashes placed in the Portland Crematorium, Portland Oregon.

Thomson brought to Oregon a sense of what public health nursing education and practice should be. Her astute assessment of how needs in rural Oregon differed from those she had known in urban Chicago produced a program with a distinctly Western approach. Thomson's ability to make others feel important, while getting them interested in her work, brought unusual sources of support to the department. Her leadership style was collaborative reflecting her warm and friendly nature. Her judgments were sound; she led by example influencing professional nursing at a time of great change.

PUBLICATIONS BY ELNORA ELVIRA THOMSON

Thomson, E. E. (1912). Mental hygiene in Illinois. *AJN, 12,* 287.

Thomson, E. E. (1923). To the children of Oregon. *The University of Oregon Extension Monitor: Oregon Child Welfare, 11,* 3–4.

Thomson, E. E. (1930). Ideals for service and education. *AJN, 30,* 809–812.

Thomson, E. E. (1931a). Harmon plan. *AJN, 31,* 591.

Thomson, E. E. (1931b). New year and its problems. *AJN, 31,* 75.

Thomson, E. E. (1932a). Friends of nursing: Mrs. Saidie Orr Dunbar. *AJN, 32,* 185–186.

Thomson, E. E. (1932b). International office. *AJN, 32,* 17.

Thomson, E. E. (1932c). Nursing comes of age. *AJN, 32,* 497–498.

Thomson, E. E. (1934a). Relationships. *AJN, 34,* 439–442.

Thomson, E. E. (1934b). Tomorrow's community nursing service. *AJN, 34,* 794–795.

BIBLIOGRAPHY

American Nurses Association. (1946). *The American Nurses Association 1896–1946: Tomorrows and yesterdays as told on the fiftieth anniversary of the association's founding.* New York: Author.

Flanagan, L. (1976). *One strong voice: The story of the American Nurses Association.* Kansas City, MO: The Lowell Press.

Goostray, S. (1969). *Memoirs: Half a century in nursing.* Boston, MA: Boston University Mugar Memorial Library.

Simonson, E. (1947). A great personality, Elnora Thomson. Unpublished baccalaureate thesis.

Soule, E. S. (1940). Elnora Thomson. *Biographical Sketches 1937–1940.* New York: National League for Nursing Education.

Thomson, E. (no date). Curriculum vitae and other documents. Portland, OR: Oregon Health Sciences University School of Nursing Historical files.

Barbara Conway Gaines

Helen Marguerite Tobin

HELEN MARGUERITE TOBIN
1922–

Helen Marguerite Tobin was an early leader in hospital staff development. She helped identify and expand the role of the staff development educator, and had a major influence on the growth of nursing staff development as an important component of continuing education in nursing.

Tobin was born April 10, 1922, in Three Rivers, Michigan, the youngest child of Dr. Herman and Mary Kirk Tobin. Her brothers were Wendell and Forrest, and Pauline was her older sister. Her father was a veterinarian.

She attended the Borgess Hospital School of Nursing, Kalamazoo, Michigan. After receiving her diploma in 1943, she was a staff nurse in obstetrics and in the operating room at the Three Rivers Hospital for a year.

Tobin entered the U.S. Army Nurse Corps in November 1944, serving as a staff nurse in medical units. After basic training at Camp McCoy, Wisconsin, she was stationed at Fort Custer and Percy Jones Hospital, Battle Creek, Michigan, and at Fort Riley, Kansas, before going overseas. She was then sent to Batangus, the Philippines, from April 1945 until the following February. She also served in the Army Reserve from 1949 to 1958, resigning with the rank of Captain.

Hers was a closely knit family, and her older sister Pauline was Tobin's best friend and role model. They both attended the Borgess School of Nursing and served in the Army Nurse Corps. Shortly after World War II they both enrolled in the Frances Payne Bolton School of Nursing at Western Reserve University in Cleveland, Ohio. Pauline died of cancer in 1973.

Tobin was awarded her B.S. degree in 1949, after which she was appointed to the staff of the University Hospitals of Cleveland. For the next few years she held various positions at the University Hospitals, while she completed requirements for her master's degree in nursing service administration at Western Reserve University. She received her degree in 1957.

From 1957 to 1960 she was assistant director of nursing research and development at Cleveland Metropolitan General Hospital. Here, her primary responsibilities were methods improvement and providing leadership in carrying out some nursing studies.

The next year Tobin returned to the University Hospitals of Cleveland as director of centralized staff development, a position she held until her retirement in 1985. She was named to the clinical faculty of the Frances Payne Bolton School of Nursing in 1965.

In her position she exerted strong and creative leadership, not only in her work setting, but across the country. She was convinced that an effective staff development program enhanced the quality of nursing care within the institution supporting it. She was highly regarded by her colleagues, served as a mentor to many nurses, and consulted with a number of international nurse visitors.

Tobin devoted considerable time to the ANA's Council on Continuing Education, serving on its organizing committee, its interim executive committee and on its first executive committee (1974–1976). She was a member of the committee that developed the ANA Guidelines for Staff Development and helped plan 14 workshops held throughout the country to implement the Guidelines, serving on the faculty of half of them. She was a frequent speaker on staff development at national meetings.

Tobin and three colleagues wrote the first definitive book on nursing staff development, published in 1973, and revised 6 years later. Titled *The Process of Staff Development: Components for Change*, the book was widely used.

Tobin had a broad perspective on staff development, viewing it as an integral part of continuing education. As director of a department, she encouraged independence and self-directed learning. She made learning opportunities available to the staff, and promoted their personal and professional growth.

In recognition of her contributions to nursing, Tobin received many honors and awards and at the Sixth National Conference on Continuing Education in Nursing in 1974, she was honored as one of 12 national leaders in the field. In 1977, she was elected a Fellow in the American Academy of Nursing, the first staff development director to be elected to the Academy.

The Helen Tobin Writer's Award was established in 1994 by *the Journal of Nursing Staff Development*. The award was named in her honor to commemorate her contributions to nursing staff development throughout her illustrious career.

Tobin remained in Cleveland after her retirement. She provides assistance to elderly friends, cooks at a soup kitchen for the homeless, enjoys caring for her home and flowers, and travels in the United States and Canada.

A pioneer in continuing education, Helen Tobin had a leading role in the development of hospital staff development in the United States and elsewhere.

PUBLICATIONS BY HELEN MARGUERITE TOBIN

Books

(With Yoder, P., Hull, P., & Scott, B.). (1973). *The process of staff development: Components for change.* St. Louis: CV Mosby (Revised 1979).

Articles (Selected)

(With J. S. Wengard). What makes a staff development program work? (1971). *American Journal of Nursing, 71,* 940–943.

Staff development: A vital component of continuing education. (1976). *The Journal of Continuing Education in Nursing, 7,* 33–39.

Philosophies and goals: Identification to implementation. (1977). *The Journal of Continuing Education in Nursing, 8,* 22–27.

(With J. Beeler). (1988). Roles and relationships of the staff development educator . . . A critical component of impact. *The Journal of Nursing Staff Development, 4,* 91–96.

BIBLIOGRAPHY

Cooper, S. S. Conversations with H. M. Tobin, 1974–1998.

Meet the editorial board. (1985). *The Journal of Nursing Staff Development, 1,* 7–8.

Tobin, H. M. Curriculum vita, University Hospitals of Cleveland; Frances Payne Bolton School of Nursing, Case Western Reserve University, Cleveland, Ohio.

Tobin, H. M. (1998, February 8; March 14). Letters to S. S. Cooper.

Wise, P. S. Y. (1985). Living History Series: Helen M. Tobin (interview). *The Journal of Continuing Education in Nursing, 16,* 65–69.

Signe S. Cooper

W

FLORENCE SCHORSKE WALD
1917–

Pioneer of the hospice movement in the United States, and founder of Hospice Care in America, Florence Wald envisioned the need to maximize quality of life for the terminally ill. To accomplish this, Wald turned to hospice care, a movement rooted in a philosophy that focuses on the comfort and spiritual needs of the terminally ill individual so that death can be a meaningful time for patients and their significant others. As a clinical nurse and later as dean of the Yale School of Nursing, Florence Wald saw that intensive curative treatment was being continued even though it no longer turned back the disease process and that patients and families were not involved in making decisions. Decisions were made by the doctor; nurses who wanted to answer patients' questions were discouraged and even forbidden to do so. Pharmaceutic con-

trol of pain was inadequate. Family suffering and went unattended. End of life was not acknowledged. Patients who refused continued curative treatment were discharged against advice. Wald knew that as healthcare professionals we could do better and that this stage of life could be enhanced, allowing people choice, and the opportunity to die with dignity and in relative freedom from pain.

In 1963 Wald heard a lecture given by Dr. Cicely Saunders, a physician who was in the process of opening the world's first modern hospice, Saint Christopher's, in London, England. Five years later, Wald resigned the Deanship of the Yale School of Nursing to study and bring about change in care of the terminally ill in the United States. Though it meant a deep cut in the family budget, this decision had their full support. During this period, she and her husband traveled several times to London to study Dr. Saunder's hospice. When it opened in 1967, Wald worked there a

Florence Schorske Wald

month, immersing herself in the philosophy and process of hospice care. After returning to Connecticut she and several Yale colleagues formed an interdisciplinary team of nurses, physicians, and clergy giving care to terminally ill patients and family whether in hospital, nursing home or in the patients home. Over 2 years, Wald conducted a study of 22 patients, recording their thoughts, feelings, and how the patient's families fared. In 1971, in support of his wife's findings, Henry Wald left his engineering position and returned to Columbia University to earn a degree in health facility planning. His Master's thesis became the feasibility study for a hospice in the Greater New Haven Connecticut area. In 1974, hospice services for the terminally ill at home came into being, while a building was being constructed. It opened in 1980. Wald's vision and devotion, coupled with the efforts of an interdisciplinary team and with insights from community mem-

bers who were survivors from a death in the family, demonstrated the viability of hospice care in the United States and led the way to a strong, nationwide movement that developed quickly and extensively. Today there are thousands of hospices nationwide that offer an alternative to intensive, curative, medical technology with palliative, medical, spiritual, and hands on support. Wald literally ingrained the philosophy of dying with dignity into American life. In her desire to expand the scope of hospice care, Wald found a new venue for her quiet and persistent advocacy. In 1995, she became acquainted with the National Prison Hospice Movement, founded in 1991 by Federal prison inmate Fleet Maull, in response to the increased number of prisoners nationwide, especially older inmates and those with AIDS. Currently, she serves on its advisory committee. When questioned by the authors why at this point in her life she was motivated to devote her time and energies to the inmate's cause, Wald replied, "When we were first trying to get hospice going we connected with middle class people. We overlooked those economically deprived, especially African Americans with limited education, little hope of becoming self sufficient or prosperous, and who die young. Their time in prison offers an opportunity for learning to cope with critical health problems."

In an effort to address the needs of the dying inmate, realizing they were to work with a system laden with regulations and a society unwilling to give prisoners education and training skills, Wald, along with the president of the Connecticut chapter of the National Prison Hospice Association, for 2 years investigated the needs and resources of hospice care in the Connecticut prison system. They interviewed inmates and corrections employees to assess the feasibility of a hospice program, and discuss the possibilities and obstacles in creating prison hospice care. They found that very sick inmates were maintained in the general population in an effort to prevent the isolation and depression often associated with the process of dying; that pain management was a dilemma for many, since 80 to 85% of inmates had a substance abuse history; and that the most important consideration for a dying inmate "is to have a trusted human companion with him or her until the end." Additionally, they found that a dying inmate experiences the same emotions as people who are dying outside the prison setting—regret, anger, discontent, and bitterness. They also feel the shame of dying in prison, which they view as "the ultimate failure." For security reasons, family members and friends are rarely allowed to visit a dying inmate, and compassionate leave was only available when the inmate had less than 6 months to live. The study concluded that inmates be trained as hospice volunteers to support their dying peers and/or that dying inmates receive compassionate leave with outside hospice care providers, especially if the dying prisoner is still connected with family. "It would not cost taxpayers dollars to have inmate volunteers to help terminal inmates and it would have a rehabilitative effect on the volunteers. Considering the growth of the prison population, that is a good thing."

In May of 1998, the study findings were presented at a program co-sponsored by the Open Society Institute and The Albert Schweitzer Institute for the Humanities bringing together hospice clinicians and administrators, Department of Corrections administrators, officers and caregivers. A steering committee reflecting this membership was formed. Walds' belief is that health services for all must include those in prison as well as in open society. By the program's end, Wald had ignited another movement. The work continues.

Born Florence Sophie Schorske on April 19, 1917, in New York City, Wald was the younger of two children and attended school in Scarsdale, New York. As a child, she spent a great deal of time in the hospital due to a chronic respiratory ailment. The care she received from nurses inspired her to go into the nursing profession. In pursuit of this goal, in 1938 Wald graduated from Mount Holyoke College with a bachelor of arts degree and, in 1941 received a master's degree from the Yale University School of Nursing.

Initiating her nursing career as a research technician with the Army Signal Corps in World War II, she met Henry Wald, an engineering student and a subject for the study she was conducting. Soon after, when he asked her to marry him, she declined; "I was at a time when I was lost and couldn't move forward. Being so sick as a child had been a big psychological setback and I needed to find my ethos." Next, Wald worked as a staff nurse with the New York Visiting Nurse Service. Ensuing positions included 6 years as a research assistant in the Surgical Metabolism Unit of the College of Physicians and Surgeons in New York, and 2 years as an instructor at Rutgers University School of Nursing in New Jersey. She returned to Yale in the 1950s to earn her master's degree in mental health nursing and became an instructor in the program. In 1957, she was appointed as an assistant professor in psychiatric nursing. In 1958, when she was 41 years old, Wald was appointed dean of the Yale school on nursing, a position she retained for 9 years. Henry Wald, who by this time had started an engineering firm in New York City, read of her appointment. The two rekindled their relationship and were married the following year. She credits her husband with being a constant, supportive force in her life.

From 1969 to 1970, Wald continued at Yale as a research associate, and from 1970 to 1980 served as clinical associate professor. At the same time, she was an integral part of the planning staff of Hospice, Incorporated in Branford, Connecticut, a hospice model that provides holistic and humanistic care for the dying person and requires appropriate understanding of the concepts of death and dying among nurses giving care in the hospice environment. From 1997 to the present, Wald has been the Principal Investigator of "A Feasibility Study for Care of the Terminally Ill in State prisons, National Prison Hospice Association."

Florence Wald has published widely and has been bestowed many honors including:

Distinguished Alumna Award, Yale University School of Nursing, 1976

Distinguished Woman of Connecticut Award, Governor of Connecticut, 1976

Fellow, American Academy of Nursing, 1979

First recipient, Florence S. Wald Award for Contributions to Nursing Practice, Connecticut Nurses Association, 1980

Founder's Award, National Hospice Organization, 1987

Contribution to Hospice Award, National Association of Home Care, 1990

Inducted into American Nurses Association Hall of Fame 1996

Inducted into the National Women's Hall of Fame, 1998

BIBLIOGRAPHY

Beaudoin, C. Personal Inverviews with Florence Schorske Wald.

Christina Beaudoin

MABEL A. WANDELT
1917–

Educator and researcher Mabel started her nursing career caring for tuberculosis pa-

tients. The need of such patients for protracted treatment regimens stimulated her to return to school several times for further education to assist in their care. Earning a doctorate in 1954 put her in the vanguard of educated elite nurses in this country.

Mabel Wandelt was born April 13, 1917 to Mary Lucy Dunham Wandelt and Albert Henry Wandelt in Daggett, Michigan. She was the third of five children in the family. Her siblings and their birth dates are: Russell, 1913; Lois, 1915; Elinor, 1919; and Alberta, 1925. She received her primary and secondary education in that small town and graduated from the Daggett High School in 1935 as valedictorian of her class of 13, and almost immediately entered Michael Reese Hospital School of Nursing in Chicago, graduating in 1938.

Mabel A. Wandelt

Her first nursing position was at Pinecrest Sanitarium in Powers, Michigan, a 160-bed tuberculosis hospital. The salary was $75 a month plus room and board in the nurse's residence. Working with such patients sparked an interest in tuberculosis nursing as a clinical specialty, which she retained for many years.

The treatment of tuberculosis at the time was bed rest, sometimes lasting for several years, requiring considerable encouragement from the nurses to continue their treatment. Because Wandelt was actively involved in providing such encouragement, she thought she was the first person to do what we now call patient teaching. She discovered later that a colleague thought the same thing. In 1942, after working as a staff nurse for 4 years in Michigan, Massachusetts, and New York in both tuberculosis sanitaria and general hospitals, Wandelt made the decision to return to school to pursue a baccalaureate degree in public health. She enrolled at Wayne State University in February, 1942 and graduating in June, 1944 with a Bachelor of Science in Public Health Nursing. She accepted employment as a staff nurse and field teacher with the Detroit Department of Health. In 1944, she enlisted in the Army Nurse Corps and served 15 months on active duty at Gardner General Hospital in Chicago, Illinois. After being discharged as a Second Lieutenant in June 1946, she returned to the public health nursing position she had held prior to entry into the military.

The G.I. Bill (Serviceman's Readjustment Act) enabled Wandelt to enroll at the University of Michigan's School of Public Health, where she earning a Master's of Public Health degree in 1948.

Wandelt joined the Veteran's Administration (V.A.), and was assigned to the V. A. Hospital in Kerrville, Texas. Because treatment of the tuberculosis patient had changed dramatically after the discovery of antimicrobial therapy Wandelt perceived the patient teaching aspect of nursing to be even more important than previously and felt that justified more formal education.

She returned to the University of Michigan in 1951. Her goal was to learn how to improve instructions for adult tuberculosis patients and to assist nurses to improve nursing's contributions to serving this major patient need. She found that a major in guidance and counseling best met her learning needs. Earning her Doctor of Philosophy degree in 1954 placed Wandelt among the first 60 nurses in the United States to earn such a degree.

She then became Assistant Chief of Nursing Education at the V.A. hospital in Castle Point, New York. Three years later she transferred to the V.A. Central Office in Washington, D.C. where she was a specialist in tuberculosis and public health nursing. Her work raised many questions that she believed needed to be answered through systematic investigation. During the 1950s, relatively few nurses were doing research, and the Veteran's Administration did not view it as a priority. Wandelt realized that if she wanted to pursue a research career she would have to leave the V.A. and go to an institution where research was valued.

An offer to teach at Wayne State University came at an opportune moment and Wandelt left the V.A. to join that faculty in 1958. During her 15 years at Wayne State, Wandelt authored the book *A Guide for the Beginning Researcher* and collaborated with Doris Slater to develop the Slater Scale. They obtained a Faculty Development Grant enabling them to evaluate nursing care quality using the Scale and a modified Quality Patient Care Scale (Qual Pac). Subsequently, both the Slater Scale and Qual Pacs were used frequently with considerable success.

During her 10th year at Wayne State, Wandelt wrote a grant to establish its research center. The center was one of the earliest such centers established in a nursing school. In 1973 she left Wayne State to go to the University of Delaware as Assistant Dean in Nursing.

While still at Delaware, she served as a member of the Advisory Committee to the University of Texas at Austin School of Nursing's Center for Health Care Research and Evaluation in 1975. During 1975–76 Wandelt was actively recruited for the position as Director of that Center. She accepted the position and moved to Austin in 1977.

As Director she made a concerted effort to get faculty actively engaged in research. To that end she increased the resources in the Center to aid faculty in the research process. The existing Research Committee was strengthened, research colloquia were initiated, a collection of research and evaluation literature was made available in the Center, and Research Assistants and a statistician were hired. Her efforts were rewarded with a notable increase in research activities in the School of Nursing.

A nursing shortage in Texas stimulated Wandelt to study reasons why nurses were leaving hospital nursing. She and her associates conducted a landmark study that was replicated in many cities throughout the United States. A follow-up study sponsored by the American Academy of Nursing resulted in the publication of factors that contributed to a lower turnover of nursing staffs in acute care hospitals and came to be known as the "Magnet Hospital Study." Results of the study were published in 1983, a year after Wandelt's retirement from active teaching at the University of Texas.

Following retirement Wandelt stayed active, working as a volunteer in the Southwest Center for Nursing History at the University of Texas School of Nursing in Austin, Texas. She shares her home in Austin, Texas with her sister, Lois Burgett.

PUBLICATIONS BY MABEL A. WANDELT

Books

Uninterrupted patient care and nursing requirements. (1963). Detroit: College Of Nursing, Wayne State University.

Outcomes of basic education in psychiatric nursing. (1966). Detroit: College of Nursing, Wayne State University.

Guide for the beginning researcher. (1970a). New York: Appleton-Century-Crofts.

Quality Patient Care Scale. (1970b). Detroit: College of Nursing, Wayne State University.

The Quality Patient Care Scale. (1974). New York: Appleton-Century-Crofts.

The Slater Nursing Competencies Rating Scale. (1975). New York: Appleton-Century-Crofts.

(With M. E. Duffy & S. Pollock). (1985). Profile of a top-rated School of Nursing. New York: National League for Nursing.

(With G. Hales, C. Merwin, G. Olson, P. Pierce, & R. Widdowson). (1980). Conditions associated with registered nurse employment in Texas. Austin: University of Texas at Austin School of Nursing.

(With M. L. McClure, M. A. Poulin, & M. D. Sovie). (1983). Magnet hospitals: Attraction and retention of professional nurses. Kansas City, MO: American Nurses Association.

Articles (Selected)

Planned versus incidental instruction for patients in tuberculosis therapy. (1954). Nursing Research, 3, 52–59.

How should we teach the tuberculosis patient? (1955). Nursing Outlook, 4, 444–447.

Teaching is more than telling. (1957). American Journal of Nursing, 57, 625–626

(With M. C. Phaneuf). (1972). Three instruments for measuring the quality of nursing care. Hospital Topics, 50.

(With P. Pierce). (1981). The shortage of nurses in Texas. Texas Business Review, 55, 75–77.

(With P. Pierce & R. Widdowson). (1981). Why nurses leave nursing and what can be done about it. American Journal of Nursing, 81, 72–77.

BIBLIOGRAPHY

Crowder, E. (1982). Mabel Wandelt—A Biography. In Proceedings of the Nursing Research Conference Honoring Mabel Wandelt, R.N., PH.D., F.A.A.N. Held in Austin, Texas 23–25 May, 1982 (pp. 7–12). Austin,

TX: University of Texas at Austin School of Nursing Continuing Education Program with Sigma Theta Tau Epsilon Theta Chapter.

Crowder, E. (1989, February). Personal interview with M. Wandelt.

[Mabel Wandelt]. *Who's Who in American Women.* Chicago, IL: A. N. Marquis Company 1961, 1964, 1968.

Eleanor L. M. Crowder

MARY JANE WARD
1921–

Mary Jane Morrow Ward pioneered in the research of nursing instruments. Her work in the 1970s culminated in three widely used reference books. She further spread her enthusiasm for research by providing consultation to graduate students and practicing nurses in the community. Her prolific research activities extended over two decades and included participation as a principle investigator and evaluator researcher. She provided consultation for national agencies and university schools of nursing who were beginning research projects and programs. She lectured internationally, teaching nurse administrators and faculty members research strategies. Ward authored 40 publications, an amazing feat considering that she was a grandmother before she became a professional nurse.

Mary Jane Morrow was born on July 2, 1921 in the frontier town of Salina, Oklahoma to Bert Leon Morrow and Bessie Charlsie Brown. Her father was a physician and she often accompanied him on his rounds.

At 18 years of age Morrow enrolled and attended the University of Arkansas a year before transferring to Texas State College for Women. She majored in premedical studies and spent the summers assisting her father in his medical practice.

A childhood friend, Emery Ward, received his pilot wings in 1940 and was now

Mary Jane Ward

a pilot instructor in the United States Army Air Corps. He convinced Ward that she should marry him instead of returning to college. On December 27, 1941 Miss Morrow become Mrs. Ward and their first home was in Lubbock, Texas at the new Lubbock Army Flying School. The Wards only child, Hal, was born the following year in Nashville, Tennessee.

When the war ended, Ward's husband enrolled in medical school at the University of Virginia. In 1949 while assisting a friend to enroll at the University, Ward decided to become a student herself. The following year she applied and received the Elizabeth Buford Phillips Scholarship for academic excellence and leadership potential. A third requirement stated that the candidate should be of pre-Revolutionary ancestry. However she does not recall the University investigating this stipulation. Ward graduated with a Bachelor of Science degree in education.

Ward began her teaching career in Charlottesville, Virginia where she taught elementary school children for 6 years. In 1957, the Ward family moved to Boulder, Colorado and for the next 8 years Ward was a community conscious housewife, active in the League of Women Voters and the Boulder County Medical Auxillary. Her husband Emery died in an accident in 1965, and in 1969 her son, then married with two children and a member of the United States Air Force, also died in an accident.

To resolve her grief, Ward knew she would have to keep busy and decided to become involved in a health profession. She chose nursing and entered the 2-year Graduate School of Nursing at the New York Medical College in New York, NY. She became interested in nursing research and completed her first study regarding "Environmental Color Preference of Fifty Adult Cardiac Patients in an Acute Care Setting." In 1968 Ward received a master's degree in Nursing Science. She also became the first recipient to receive the Margaret Mahoney Adams Award presented for excellence in the nursing care of children.

In the same year, Ward began her clinical work as a staff nurse and charge nurse on Orthopedic, Urology and Surgical Intensive Care Units at Colorado General Hospital. In 1971 Ward taught "Medical-Surgical Nursing: Leadership and Management" at Mercy Hospital School of Nursing in Denver, CO. After receiving a United States Public Health Service Title II Traineeship, she enrolled in the graduate program at the University of Colorado School of Nursing. Through this course of study she completed four scholarly papers before receiving her second Masters in Medical/Surgical Nursing with a focus in education.

Ward received a Special Predoctoral Nurse Research Fellowship from USPHS which allowed her to continue in doctoral studies. Her research projects included "Student Membership on Representative Institutional Committees in 40 Western Colleges and Universities." In 1975 she received a Doctor of Philosophy in Higher Education-Administration and Teaching from the University of Colorado.

That same year, Ward became co-director for a project of the Western Interstate Commission for Higher Education (WICHE) in Boulder, CO. The following year she became director of the Project and completed two research projects regarding instruments used in nurse education and clinical practice. Ward was the primary author of three reference books culminating from the WICHE projects including the two-volume book entitled *Instruments for measuring nursing practice and other health care variables.*

In August 1979, Ward received a graduate and undergraduate faculty appointment from the University of Colorado School of Nursing and in March 1981 was appointed Director of Research and remained in this position the next 4 years.

In August 1985, Ward joined the faculty of the University of Tennessee, Memphis College of Nursing offered Ward, as Professor and Associate Dean for Research.

Ward then moved on to serve as Professor and Executive Associate Dean at the Nell Hodgson Woodruff School of Nursing at Emory University. She continued her work in Atlanta, GA August 1988 through June of 1992. Ward moved to Oklahoma City in 1992 where she served as Professor and Associate Dean of Academic Programs at the College of Nursing until her retirement in June of 1994.

Her status as a sought-after presenter at professional and academic meetings kept Ward on the move throughout the United States as well as Canada and abroad.

Ward was named to the National Nursing Advisory Council, American Indian Health Services, U.S. Public Health Service, DHS.

She served from June, 1983 through December 1985. Lack of space limits listing all of Ward's honors and awards but they were numerous.

Tragic life circumstances dealt Ward a blow in the sudden loss of her husband, and later her only child. Out of adversity came her great nursing accomplishments and her inspiration to students and colleagues. She encouraged fellow nurses to write, present, and conduct research. While she admitted that writing for publication was stressful and time-consuming, Ward pointed out that writing was also growth-producing and adventurous as well as rewarding. "It is rewarding," she said, "in the sense of having shared the results of your work and efforts with colleagues, of having contributed in some small way to the nursing profession, and of having learned much about yourself in the process."

Although retired in Boulder, Colorado since 1994, Ward is still experiencing life to the fullest. She audits university courses and makes beautiful quilts. She volunteers for Habitat for Humanity, the TV Channel 9 Health Fair, and serves on the International Advisory Committee for the Boulder YMCA. She continues to review manuscripts for the Mosby Publishing Company.

PUBLICATIONS BY MARY JANE WARD (SELECTED)

Family nurse practitioners: Perceived competencies and implications for nursing education. (1982). In S. Redfern et al. (Eds.), *Issues in Nursing Research* (pp. 151–177). London: Macmillan.

Family nurse practitioners: Perceived competencies. (1979). *Nursing Research, 28*(6), 343–347.

Nursing research instruments: Some considerations and recommendations. (1986). In S. Stinson & J. Kerr (Eds.), *International Issues in Nursing Research* (pp. 41–60). London, England: Croom Helm Ltd.

Writing for publication: From one novice to others. (1980). *Nursing Research, 29*(4), 263.

(With Fetler, M. E.). (1979). *Instruments for use in nursing education.* Boulder, CO: WICHE.

(With Fetler, M. E.). (1997). Research Q & A: Guidelines for critically evaluating research reports. *Nursing Research, 28*(20), 120–126.

(With Lindemann, C. A.). (Eds.). (1979). Instruments for measuring nursing practice and other health care variables (2 vols.). Washington, DC: Government Printing Office (2nd Printing, Boulder, CO, WICHE, 1982).

(With Moran, S.). (1984). Resistance to change: Recognize, respond, overcome. *Nursing Management, 15*(1), 30–34.

(With Price, S.). (Eds.). (1990). *Readings for nurse executives.* St. Louis: Mosby.

BIBLIOGRAPHY

Robinson, T. M. (1988, February). Interview with M. J. Ward, Boulder, CO.

Thelma M. Robinson

LENA ANGEVINE WARNER
1869–1948

As an early Southern nurse, Lena Angevine Warner had a varied and influential career including contributions to nursing education, military nursing, public health nursing, and professional organization of nurses.

Warner was born on May 16 or 18, 1869, on the plantation of her grandparents near Grenada, Mississippi. She was one of five children born to Missouri Jane Mayhew and Capt. Saxton Smith Angevine. Her father, a Confederate veteran, had served as Provost Marshal at Grenada during the Civil War. He, along with another daughter and other relatives, died in the yellow fever epidemic that struck the Mississippi River valley in 1878. Lena Warner survived the disease and spent the remainder of her childhood living with her grandmother in Grenada. Her education was first by governesses. She was sent to Memphis, Tennessee, where she graduated from St. Mary's Episcopal School for Girls in 1887. There she learned of Florence Nightingale and the early nursing programs in the United States.

Lena Angevine Warner

Against the wishes of her family, Lena Angevine was the first student enrolled in the school of nursing at the Maury and Mitchell Infirmary for Women in Memphis and became the school's first graduate in 1889. Immediately after graduation she went to Chicago for postgraduate training. She returned to Memphis in October 1899 and served as surgical assistant to Dr. R.B. Maury, a pioneer gynecologist. Except for the time of her brief marriage to Charles Edwin Warner, she remained in the position with Dr. Maury. In 1896 she helped organize and was the first president of the Memphis Trained Nurses Association.

A new Memphis City Hospital opened in July 1898. Warner was involved in planning for the hospital and was named the first superintendent of nurses. In this role she also was responsible for the nursing school, which later became a part of the University of Tennessee in 1926. Warner was the sole nursing instructor and is identified as the founder of this early nursing program.

In July 1898 Warner responded to a DAR advertisement in the Sunday paper for nurses immune to yellow fever to serve in Cuba for the Spanish-American War. Delayed because of illness with typhoid fever, Warner signed as a contract nurse and sailed for Cuba on April 19, 1900. She first served as Chief Nurse in charge of the fever tents at Post Hospital, Matanzas, Cuba, and then in August 1900 she moved to Columbia Barracks near Havana. An experimental station, Camp Lazear, was established November 20, 1900, one mile from Columbia Barracks by Dr. Walter Reed for work on the cause of yellow fever. Warner was placed in charge of the camp in late December 1900 and became a member of the Walter Reed Commission. She continued in this position until March 22, 1902. During Warner's service as a contract nurse in Cuba the Army Nurse Corps (Female) was established February 2, 1901. Warner's contract was annulled, and she was appointed Chief Nurse in the Army Nurse Corps in Cuba on February 2, 1901. She was discharged from the Army in 1902. After returning to Memphis she brought three separate organizations together to form the Tennessee State Nurses Association in 1905. In the role as president of the association from 1905 to 1918, she led the fight for nursing licensure. Warner led the lobbying efforts in 1905, 1907, and 1911 when the first nurse practice act in Tennessee was passed. The act in 1911 created the State Board of Examiners of Nurses of which Warner served as the first chair. She became the first registered nurse in Tennessee. Warner was also a charter member of the National Organization for Public Health Nursing.

After her experience with the yellow fever experiments, Warner focused her professional career on community nursing.

She interested the Metropolitan Life Insurance Company in establishing visiting nurse services in Memphis and directed the visiting nurse services from December 5, 1911, until 1916.

Beginning April 1916, Warner moved to Knoxville and became a health specialist for rural work through the Tennessee Agricultural Extension Service of the University of Tennessee. Through this position, which she held until her retirement in 1946, she practiced rural public health nursing and crusaded for healthful living throughout the state. She was especially interested in the health of the mountain people. She authored several lay pamphlets and conducted courses on child welfare, adolescence, care of the sick, and "mother craft" in rural areas over the state. In the year 1927 she reported over 15,000 miles of travel by rail and 4,823 by automobile.

In addition to her direct practice, Warner served as chair of the American Red Cross Nursing Service Committee in Tennessee. She held this position from 1910 to 1922. In this position she organized at least 20 Red Cross chapters and assisted in fund drives. Through the Town and Country Nursing Service of the Red Cross, Warner influenced expansion of the first rural public health nurses in Tennessee. She was awarded the ARC Certificate of Merit with ribbons for service.

Warner's career in nursing and health care spanned 57 years and influenced many groups in addition to the profession of nursing. She retired in 1946 at the age of 77. Warner died August 19, 1948, and was buried in Elmwood Cemetery in Memphis, Tennessee.

PUBLICATIONS BY LENA ANGEVINE WARNER

Experience of an Army nurse in Cuba. (1903). *Memphis Medical Monthly, 23,* 191–196.

BIBLIOGRAPHY

Greenhill, E. (1994). Lena Angevine Warner: Pioneer public health nurse. *Public Health Nursing, 11,* 202–204.

Greenhill, E. (1993). Nursing License #000001. *Tennessee Nurse, 56,* 26–27.

Kelly, H. (1906). *Walter Reed and yellow fever.* New York: McClure, Phillips.

Lagerstrom, M., & Satterfield, L. (1960). *History of public health nursing in Tennessee, 1910–1960.* Nashville: Tennessee Nurses Association.

Sims, A. (1939). *A history of extension work in Tennessee.* Knoxville: University of Tennessee.

National Archives. Lena Warner, Military records Group 112 and Office of Surgeon General Nurses 1898–1917, folder 3678.

Wooten, N., & Williams, G. (1955). *A history of the Tennessee State Nurses Association: 1905–1955.* Nashville: Tennessee State Nurses Association.

E. Dianne Greenhill

MARY MARGARET MARVIN WAYLAND
?–1946

Mary Marvin Wayland was one of the earliest nurses to identify the need for nursing research and the relationship of research to the improvement of nursing care. Her many publications focus on the role of the head nurse in the education of students.

Wayland attended the University of Minnesota for 2 years before enrolling in its School of Nursing. A member of its first class of eight students, she was awarded her diploma in 1912.

Her early nursing experiences included a year as head nurse at Columbia Hospital, Los Angeles, another year as operating room supervisor at Seaside Hospital in Long Beach, California, followed by 4 years of private duty nursing.

In 1918 she was appointed an instructor in the Vassar Training Camp, an intensive preliminary nursing course offered on the campus of Vassar College, Poughkeepsie, New York. A wartime measure, the course

Mary Margaret Marvin Wayland

was designed so that those completing it could then enroll in a cooperating school of nursing and complete its program in 2 years.

In 1919 Wayland took postgraduate work in psychiatric nursing at Bloomingdale Hospital, White Plains, New York. That year she was awarded a B.S. degree from Teachers College, Columbia University. She later completed requirements for her M.S. degree.

She served as an instructor at the Lakeside School of Nursing in Cleveland, Ohio. From 1921 to 1925 she was an instructor, then assistant professor of biology and nursing at Simmons College, Boston.

For the next 4 years she was director of clinical teaching and supervision at Bellevue Hospital, New York. During some of this time she also taught at Teachers College, Columbia University.

During this time Wayland conducted nursing studies at Bellevue, and in May 1927, her seminal article on nursing research appeared in the *American Journal of Nursing*. She wrote that with scientific research, "the art of nursing the patient would be more nearly perfected in a shorter time than it could possibly be by slow accumulation of knowledge gained through casual experience." An article about her in the *Journal* 3 years later noted that she had more to do with stimulating nursing studies than any other one nurse in the country.

Her book *The Hospital Head Nurse: Her Function and Her Preparation*, was published in 1938 and revised in 1945. In this work, she identified the significant role of the head nurse not only in the care of patients, but also in teaching students in the clinical setting.

She married Dr. Charles Wayland in 1930, and they lived for some time in San Jose, then Sierra Madre, California. After her marriage she continued to teach part-time at various California institutions and in summer sessions at the University of Chicago and Teachers College, Columbia University.

In a 1930 biographical article in the *American Journal of Nursing*, Wayland was described as "without a doubt one of the most brilliant teachers of nursing in our country." Her enthusiasm for her profession was noteworthy and her contributions to nursing outstanding.

Mary Marvin Wayland died March 12, 1946 in Long Beach, California.

PUBLICATIONS BY MARY MARVIN WAYLAND

Books

The hospital head nurse: Her function and her preparation. (1938). New York: Macmillan. (Revised with collaborators R. L. McManus & M. Faddis, 1944).

Articles (Selected)

Methods of increasing ward teaching and improving supervision. (1926). *American Journal of Nursing, 26,* 551–556.

Research in nursing: The place of research and experimentation in improving the nursing care of the patient. (1927). *American Journal of Nursing, 27*, 331–335.

Supervision of clinical instruction. (1930). *American Journal of Nursing, 30*, 1053–1060.

Are standards of nursing care changing? (1934). *Pacific Coast Journal of Nursing, 30*, 268–271.

BIBLIOGRAPHY

Archives, University of Minnesota, Minneapolis, Minnesota.

Clappeson, G. B. (1964). *Vassar's Rainbow Division, 1918.* Lake Mills, IA: The Graphic Publishing Company.

Mary M. Marvin, RN. (1930). *American Journal of Nursing, 30*, 471–472.

Mrs. Mary Marvin Wayland. (1946). [Obituary]. *American Journal of Nursing, 46*, 356–357.

Roberts, M. M. (1954). *American nursing: History and interpretation.* New York: Macmillan.

Simmons, L. W., & Henderson, V. (1964). *Nursing research: A survey and assessment.* New York: Appleton-Century-Crofts.

Signe S. Cooper

OKEL VIOLET WELSH
1923–

After receiving her registered nurse certification from the Municipal Training School at Grady Memorial Hospital in Atlanta, Georgia in 1946, Okel Welsh began a professional nursing career that spanned almost 40 years. Described by her counterparts as a "trail-blazer" during her long tenure in Miami, Welsh's achievements as a Black nurse include a number of firsts. She was one of the first Black nurses to work at Mount Sinai Hospital on Miami Beach in 1950, preparing the "colored" ward in the newly established hospital. Welsh left Mount Sinai in 1956 to take a federal job in Bethesda, Maryland at the National Institutes of Health. When she returned to Miami in 1958, she became the first Black nurse hired by the Veterans' Administration Hospital. Her long career also in-

cluded becoming the first Black nurse to work at the Professional Nurses' Registry on Miami Beach in 1963.

Okel Violet Welsh

Okel Welsh was born in Jacksonville, Florida to Eva and John McClellan on December 21, 1923. She worked locally as a home nurse after graduating from Stanton High School in 1941. The establishment of U.S. Cadet Corps enabled her to attend the Municipal Training School at Grady Memorial Hospital in Atlanta, Georgia.

After completing her training in 1946, Welsh was offered a federal job with the Department of Agriculture. At this time the Migratory Labor Health Association supported a hospital in Belle Glade, Florida and clinic in the Everglades for migratory labor workers, cane cutters, and farm hands, who originated from the Bahamas, Jamaica, and Trinidad. Welsh worked in the hospital, nursing mostly male patients until the program was phased out in 1947.

After the Everglades experience, Welsh worked for the Florida State Board of Health at the Rapid Treatment Center in Melbourne, Florida, where she treated patients with venereal diseases. On October 1, 1947, Welsh passed the Florida Boards and one month later married Balfour Anton Welsh, the supervisor of the camps in the Everglades. In the beginning of January 1949, Welsh moved to Miami and her husband joined her soon after.

Welsh's first job in Miami was at the Christian Hospital, a facility built in 1920-21 for the Black community. It was during her 7-month employment at this small hospital that Welsh realized the value of her competency in delivering babies and starting intravenous lines. She recalled, "There were no house doctors. Women came full term and ready to deliver and it was important to know how to deliver babies." Soon after the birth of her only baby in 1949, Welsh learned of the opening of the "colored section" at Mount Sinai Hospital on Miami Beach in January 1950.

Even before Mount Sinai permitted Black physicians to join the staff in 1952, Okel Welsh and Juanita Williams from Washington, D.C. became the first two Black registered nurses to work at Mount Sinai Hospital. Williams soon resigned and Welsh was made head nurse. Unlike her White counterparts, Welsh was unable to attend university programs to keep abreast of current nursing treatments and procedures—university programs were not integrated. She notes, "I was the only Black head nurse at Mount Sinai and I was told that as soon as the law permitted an integrated program I would get credit." From Welsh's perspective and those of her counterparts, however, Mount Sinai offered better working conditions and less racism than other hospitals in the area at the time.

Welsh and her husband were divorced in June 1954. In 1956, Welsh moved to Washington, D.C. She applied to the National Institutes of Health (N.I.H.) in Bethesda, Maryland and was employed in the Department of Arthritis and Metabolic Diseases. After 2 years, Welsh wanted to return home to Miami.

Accustomed to earning a federal salary, Welsh was not prepared to return to Mount Sinai and instead she was accepted by the Veterans' Administration for employment and was instructed to obtain a physical at the VA Hospital in Washington, D.C. Welsh remembers that "during this physical, race was revealed and everything stopped; however, I was already working for the government so how could the Veterans [Administration] refuse me because I was colored when the government had already accepted me?" Indeed, they eventually offered her a comparable salary and she became the first Black nurse at the Coral Gables Veterans' Administration Hospital in 1958, Welsh set the precedent. Nine months later, another Black registered nurse became employed, followed by many others. Assigned to the cardiology and non-tubercular chest floor, Welsh nursed at the Veterans' Hospital for 4 years.

In 1962 Welsh joined the Miami Beach Nursing Service Registry, a commercial nurses' registry which arranged private duty assignments. Her nursing not only permitted her to deliver efficiency and kindness to all her patients, but also occasionally brought her in contact with colorful people like Al Capone's cohorts. One patient was so grateful to Welsh for her unsurpassed care, she wrote to the local paper, the *Miami Beach Sun.* The deserved publicity provided another opportunity for Welsh to become a first. The larger Professional Nurses Registry on Miami Beach, which had not previously employed Black nurses, asked her to join their service. While Welsh worked at this agency, she was also able to attend classes at Miami Dade Community College and at Florida International University to work towards a degree in health science. The fact that earlier educational opportunities were closed to her increased her impetus to advance her own understanding of health science.

In 1973 she decided to apply for a position in a home health care agency, Florida Home Health Care. Soon after she was appointed as a home visiting nurse at Florida Home Health Care, Welsh was promoted as a supervisor in the office. Here she had another opportunity to become a "trailblazer." She was confident she had the nursing experience to work with area doctors and coordinate excellent home service to patients. Even though she was told the job was not available to her because of her color, Welsh persisted. Thus the job as nurse coordinator, previously prohibited to a Black nurse, was offered to Welsh on a trial basis. Actually she worked so hard and became so adept at her work that the business grew and she became a valued member of the team.

Welsh's long nursing career illustrates her inherent love for her profession. In spite of the obstacles she faced as a Black nurse, she demonstrated how each milestone provided valuable experience that empowered her to move forward in her profession. Firstly, her mother's confidence in her ability to nurse provided a secure background as she sought formal training at Grady Memorial Hospital. By the time Welsh completed her training she had gained not only a solid foundation in nursing skills, but also confidence to proceed according to her own will. Empowered with this valuable sense of self and the ability to effectively communicate, she unknowingly became a "trail-blazer," setting the precedent in Miami for other Black nurses to follow her path.

BIBLIOGRAPHY

Engram, Ida. (1997, December 2). Interview with Okel Welsh.

George, P. (1984). *Visions, accomplishments and challenges: Mount Sinai Medical Center of Greater Miami, 1949–1984.* Miami Beach: Mount Sinai Medical Center.

Hine, D. C. (1989). *Black women in white racial conflict and cooperation in the medical profession.* Bloomington, IN: Indiana University Press.

Simpson, G. (1995, January). 'Reflections through a mirror darkly': The history of medical care in Miami's Black community. *Miami Medicine.*

Ardala, C. (1997, June 6; October 28). Interview with Okel Welsh.

Christine Ardala

JUDITH GAGE WHITAKER
1913–

Practitioner, administrator, and educator, Judith Gage Whitaker had a long, diverse, and productive nursing career, some 46 years in the local, state, national, and international arenas. Her extraordinary achievements as Executive Secretary of the American Nurse's Association (ANA) from 1958–1969 represented the high point of her career.

Born in Spokane, Washington, February 8, 1913, to George C. and Edna Sanderson Gage, she moved with her family to Fremont, Nebraska in 1915. She attended Fremont High School, graduating in February 1929, at the age of 16 1/2 years. Too young to enter nursing school, Whitaker worked two part-time jobs and lived at home until she was 18 when she entered a diploma program, the Nebraska Methodist Hospital School of Nursing in Omaha, on February 9, 1931, graduating 3 years later, in February 1934.

From 1934 to 1937, Whitaker served as public health nurse with the Omaha Visiting Nurse's Association. In 1937, Whitaker resigned her position with the VNA to pursue private duty nursing, practicing in the Nebraska cities of Omaha and Fremont (1937–38), McCook (1938–40), and

Fremont (1940–41). While in McCook, she married Russell Albert Whitaker (in April 1938).

When the U.S. entered World War II, Whitaker assumed the newly created position of Director of Student Recruitment for the Nebraska State Nursing Council for War Service, serving from December 17, 1942, to June 1, 1943. Traveling extensively throughout Nebraska, delivering 145 informational-recruitment talks in over 100 towns, Whitaker frequently wore her white uniform and was accompanied by student nurses from Nebraska's 13 nursing schools who shared their perspectives with the student audiences in local high schools and colleges—with successful recruitment techniques.

Upon her husband's unexpected death in June 1944, Whitaker returned to Fremont, Nebraska, where she found her true calling—nursing organizational work. Accepting the tri-partite position of Executive Secretary of the Nebraska State Nurse's Association (NSNA), Executive Secretary of District Two of the NSNA, and Registrar of District Two, Whitaker strengthened the NSNA, successfully steering its transition from wartime to peacetime status (1944–49). She improved NSNA's communications with its five districts, as well as with the ANA. Services increased, programs expanded, and overall membership increased, despite sizable increases in membership dues. NSNA membership benefitted from the establishment of the Counseling and Placement Service (1945), resumption of *The Nebraska Nurse* in June 1945 after a 2-year hiatus, the creation of the Economics Security Program (1947), and the formation of the Nebraska State Student Nurse's Association (1948), which Whitaker sponsored.

In 1949, to better prepare herself academically for future administrative roles, Whitaker entered Teachers College, Co-lumbia University, receiving a Bachelor of Science degree in June 1951. She then pioneered her own master's degree in nursing organization, taking courses that specifically dealt with the growing responsibilities in the management of nursing organization, earning a M.A. degree in June 1952. While in graduate school, she worked part-time from 1950–1952 as ANA's Assistant Executive Secretary in charge of its Public Relations Unit. After graduation, she accepted a full-time position with ANA's expanding staff, as Deputy Executive Secretary (1952–58).

As Deputy Executive Secretary, Whitaker carried out ANA headquarters' policies and procedures and coordinated the various sections of the newly restructured ANA. She initiated and directed ANA's new orientation program for state nursing association executives and new ANA staff members. Her Nebraska experience aided her in coordinating the field work for ANA staff members, conducting regional workshops, making field visits to state nursing conventions, and participating in district meetings herself.

With her experience and education, Whitaker was a logical choice to replace Ella Best as ANA's Executive Secretary in August 19958. During her tenure as ANA's Executive Secretary (1958–69), numerous issues were addressed along a broad range of economic, legislative, structural, and educational fronts. Plans were commissioned for economic and welfare concerns of ANA members in 1966. The Professional Counseling and Placement Service expanded services to ANA members. Whitaker served on the Surgeon General's Consultant Group on Nursing (1961–63) which looked into the federal government's role in assuring that the nation had an adequate supply of nurses in the future. During Whitaker's stewardship, Congress passed several measures designed to aid nursing education, most notable being the Nurse Training Act of 1964. In 1966, ANA underwent another structural reorganization designed to make it a more efficient association for its professional membership; Whitaker helped formulate the Standards of Nursing Practice (1966) and the subsequent specialization, the Divisions of Nursing Practice (1966–67), and she promoted the Academy of Nursing's foundation (1966). On the educational front, in February 1965, the ANA published its *Standards for Nursing Service* and in December issued its now famous *Position Paper* on the entry-level education necessary to practice nursing; nursing education should now take place in either a university or collegiate setting, as opposed to the diploma-hospital programs of the past. As a staff member on ANA's Education Committee (1963–65), Whitaker participated in the development of ANA's first definitive statement on nursing education, which transformed the future of nursing education. And ANA's emphasis on research was reflected by Whitaker's serving as the American Nurses Foundation's first Executive Vice President (1964–68).

In addition to her administrative duties as ANA's Executive Secretary, Whitaker participated as ANA's representative in numerous professional conferences nationally and internationally. She was ANA's liaison with other professional organizations and attended state nursing conventions each year. Consultant to the U.S. Army Nurse Corps (1958–69), and to the Nursing Advisory Committee of the Defense Department (1966–69), she was also a board member to the National Citizens Committee for the World Health Organization (1960–61, 1964–65). Whitaker attended some of the International Council of Nurses' board meetings and served on the Committee to Study Structure and Function of the International Council of Nurses (1963–65).

Whitaker resigned as ANA's Executive Secretary in September 1969, but remained active in nursing as an educator with faculty positions in Continuing Education at the University of Vermont (1970–72), at the State University of New York in Albany (1972–79), and at Russell Sage College, Troy, New York (1980).

Whitaker resigned from nursing in 1980 after 46 years as one of its prominent leaders. She lived in Walnut Creek, California, for 12 years, and since 1992, has lived in San Francisco where she enjoys opera, ballet, and travel.

PUBLICATIONS BY JUDITH GAGE WHITAKER

The nurse as a professional person. (1961a). *Nursing Outlook, 9,* 217–218.
Unrealistic economic situation turns many from nursing profession. (1961b). *Hospital Topics, 39,* 37–38.
The changing role of the professional nurse in the hospital. (1962). *American Journal of Nursing, 62,* 65–69. (This article also appeared in the February 1, 1962, issue of *Hospitals.*)
Nursing seeks roads to better service. (1963). *The Modern Hospital, 101,* 149–151.
The issue of mandatory continuing education. (1974). *Nursing Clinics of North America, 9,* 475–483.

BIBLIOGRAPHY

A new President and a new Executive Secretary (editorial). *American Journal of Nursing, 58,* 1097.
Executive Secretary's Report to the House of Delegates. ANA's Biennial Conventions (1958–1968). American Nurses' Association Library, Washington, DC.
NEF, Inc. receives $50,000 check from former NEF scholar, Judith G. Whitaker. (1995). *Nurses' Educational Funds, Inc.* (newsletter), *15,* 1.
Whitaker, J. (1949). NSNA's last 5 years a period of progress. *The Nebraska Nurse, 3,* 8–9.
Whitaker, J. (1943). Student nurse recruitment. *Nebraska Nursing News, 4,* 6.
Brueggemann, D. (July 19–20, 1993; May 22–23, 1995, San Francisco). Personal interviews with J. G. Whitaker.
Who's Who in America 1978–79 (Vol. 2, p. 3448). Chicago: Marquis.

Who's Who of American Women, 1974–75 (Vol. 8, p. 1025). Chicago: Marquis.

David W. Brueggemann

JEAN SCANTLION WILSON
?–1970

Jean Scantlion Wilson devoted her nursing career to organized efforts to improve the education and status of nurses in Canada. A superb organizer, she was the first full-time Executive Secretary of the Canadian Nurses Association. Wilson served under eight presidents from 1923 to 1943, longer than any other officer in the history of that organization. In addition, she was the editor and business manager of the journal *Canadian Nurse* from 1924 to 1932.

Born in Ontario of pioneer stock, Wilson attended high school in Shawville, Quebec. In 1906, she graduated from the Lady Stanley Institute for Trained Nurses in Ottawa that was associated with the County of Carleton General Protestant Hospital.

Wilson held nursing positions in British Columbia, Saskatchewan, Manitoba, and Quebec. Her first nursing position was as Assistant Superintendent and Chief Surgical Nurse in the Vernon Jubilee Hospital in Vernon, British Columbia from 1909 to 1911. She relocated to Saskatchewan in 1913, where she was Assistant Superintendent and Operating Room Supervisor of the Moose Jaw General Hospital. In 1915 she was promoted to Superintendent of Nurses, a position she held for 5 years. During this time Wilson became active in professional nursing associations.

Wilson was a charter member of both the Graduate Nurses Association of Moose Jaw and the Saskatchewan Registered Nurses Association. From 1917 to 1920 she served as Secretary-Treasurer and Registrar of the SRNA, engaged in working toward

Jean Scantlion Wilson

the passage of the Registered Nurses' Act. As a member of the Council of the SRNA, she served on the Executive Committee of the Canadian Nurses Association, then called the Canadian National Association of Trained Nurses.

In 1921 Wilson became Honorary Secretary-Treasurer of the Canadian National Association of Trained Nurses. That same year she enrolled in the School for Graduate Nurses of McGill University in Montreal on a scholarship awarded by the Association. In 1922, the Canadian National Association of Trained Nurses decided to open a national office and employ a full-time executive secretary. The unanimous choice to serve in that capacity and organize the national office was Wilson, who was close to obtaining her certificate in administration in schools of nursing from McGill. She was appointed the Executive Secretary-Treasurer in 1923 and relocated to Winnipeg,

Manitoba. Wilson's diverse nursing and administrative experience and her professional contributions in four provinces proved invaluable in forging strong relationships between the developing organization and provincial associations.

In 1924, the Canadian National Association of Trained Nurses changed its name to the Canadian Nurses Association. That same year, the long-standing editor of the *Canadian Nurse* journal resigned and the journal office was transferred to the national office in Winnipeg. In addition to already significant responsibilities, Wilson assumed editorship and served as the business manager for the *Canadian Nurse* for the next 8 years.

The Canadian Nurses Association relocated its office from Winnipeg to Montreal in 1932. A tribute to her organizational skills, Wilson moved the combined office of the Association and the *Canadian Nurse* without interrupting the publication of a single issue. In January 1933, the first full-time editor and business manager for the journal was hired.

An expert organizer, Wilson shared largely in the planning and management of ten biennial meetings in seven provinces. She was instrumental in arranging the highly successful meeting of the International Council of Nurses in Montreal in 1929 when that city was host to nearly 7,000 nurses of the world, representing 34 countries. In 1938, Wilson was awarded the Mary Agnes Snively Memorial Medal by the Canadian Nurses Association for her many outstanding contributions.

Wilson retired to her farm in Almonte, Ontario in 1943. Humble and modest, she was noted for her business acumen and credited with keeping the Canadian Nurses Association on solid financial footing for 20 years. She died in Almonte on April 8, 1970, about 50 miles from where she spent her childhood years.

PUBLICATIONS BY JEAN SCANTLION WILSON (SELECTED)

Keeping records in our organizations. (1924). *Canadian Nurse, 20,* 71–73.
The Canadian Nurses' Association. (1929). *American Journal of Nursing, 29,* 135–139.
(With Sister Allard). (1939). Nursing in Canada. *Nosokomeion, 10,* 37–45.

BIBLIOGRAPHY

Canadian Nurse: A birthday. (1933). *Canadian Nurse, 29,* 123–127.
Gibbon, J. M., & Mathewson, M. S. (1947). *Three centuries of Canadian nursing.* Toronto: Macmillan.
Pettigrew, L. E. (1958). Convention personalities: Jean S. Wilson. *Canadian Nurse, 54,* 332, 334.
Simpson, R. M. (1943). Jean Wilson retires. *Canadian Nurse, 39,* 655–656.
Wilson, J. S. Papers. Helen K. Mussallem Library, Canadian Nurses Association, Ottawa, Ontario.

Sharon C. Murphy

MARY OPAL BROWNE WOLANIN
1910–1997

Mary Opal Wolanin was a mentor and extraordinary role model of productive aging to numerous nurses, as well as many others. She was active and involved in research, publication, and numerous advisory activities. Until her death on May 22, 1997, she was particularly engaged in researching the perceptions of nonagenarians and formulating concepts of mental frailty.

Mary Opal Browne was born November 1, 1910 to Florence Abbott Browne and Earl E. Brown in Chrisney, Indiana. The name was originally Braun, but was changed to Brown when her father's family emigrated from Germany to the U.S. in 1848. An aunt insisted that the Brown must be spelled Browne and this was later adopted by her mother after her divorce from her husband. Mary Opal was the eldest of three girls, and after her mother remarried to Noah Borror, her mother gave birth to three more children.

Mary Opal Browne Wolanin

Wolanin attended grammar school at Chase Mound School in Kansas, built on land donated by her stepfather and located about a half-mile from the family farm in western Anderson County. She then went on to Westphalia High School in Westphalia, Kansas, and Washington University in St. Louis. Her nurses training was at Municipal General Hospital School of nursing in Kansas City, Missouri, and Cook County School of Nursing in Chicago. In later years she completed her MSN degree at the University of Arizona. She also received a Certificate in Gerontology from the University of Southern California. She began study for a doctorate at Arizona but never completed it due to the illness of her husband. She was awarded an honorary doctorate form the University of Arizona in 1986.

In 1941 Wolanin enlisted in the Army Nurse Corps Reserve as a second lieutenant and was stationed at Jefferson Barracks,

MO. On October 29, 1942, she married Lieutenant Harry J. (Tiger) Wolanin and soon after was honorably discharged from the service. Before entering the service Wolanin had been a professional boxer under the name of Tiger, and he later formally changed his named to H.J. Tiger Wolanin. After her discharge, Wolanin continued to accompany her husband on his various tours of duty, working as a civilian nurse. When her husband was stationed in Biloxi, MI, she got her first opportunity to teach as an instructor in the Cadet Nursing Program there and decided this was what she wanted to follow as a career. Following Tiger's retirement from the military, the Wolanins settled in Tucson, where Tiger became a student at the University of Arizona, and Wolanin a member of the nursing school faculty.

She was very active in a variety of Arizona nursing organizations, and often served as a legislative consultant on various issues of nursing practice. She found her niche in nursing when she became director of a program to better prepare nurses for taking care of the aging patient and her work in this area made her nationally known. After her retirement she was a keynote speaker in much demand, both nationally and internationally, on what she called her "explorations" on the issue of confusions and the elderly. She repeatedly said that she made her major professional contributions after she was 70 and retired, and it was for these efforts that she was inducted into the ANA Hall of Fame.

Her major contributions to nursing were in the areas of stroke rehabilitation, confusion, medication management, mental frailty, and phenomenology of old age.

BIBLIOGRAPHY

Wolanin, M. O., & Phillips, L. (1980). *Confusion: Prevention and care.* St. Louis: Mosby.

Ebersole, P. Personal interviews and correspondence with M. O. Wolanin. San Antonio, TX.

Borror, C., & Borror B. Biographical materials. (Brother and sister-in-law of Wolanin). Wichita, KS.

Ebersole, P. (1997). Memories of Mary Opal Wolman: Geriatric nurse, mentor, friend. *Geriatric Nursing, 18*, 232–234.

Priscilla Ebersole

Bertha Wright

BERTHA WRIGHT
1876–1971

Bertha Wright, a pioneer in public health nursing in the Far West and an activist in public health and social welfare, founded the Baby Hospital in Oakland, California in 1912, now known as Children's Hospital Oakland. She was the West Coast Lillian Wald and Jane Addams. Bertha Wright was born on June 17, 1876, in Piedmont, California, the second of three children of Horatio Nelson Wright and Francis Goodrich Wright. Piedmont, located near Oakland, and across the bay from San Francisco, was at that time mostly undeveloped country, and Bertha and her brother and sister roamed at will through wild hillsides and canyons laced with ancient oak trees until 1890, when financial reverses forced Horatio to move his family to San Francisco. Bertha was born and raised in this bold and adventurous family of eccentrics and inventors, "where money came and went, a family that never said, 'what will people think?' " (M. Collins, personal communication, April 22, 1996).

Wright graduated from Girls' High School in San Francisco, and then attended nurses training at the California Women's Hospital, graduating in the late 1890s. By 1899, she was working as a graduate nurse at the California Women's Hospital. A short time later, Wright began working at the Nurses' Potrero Settlement House in San Francisco in a neighborhood with a large population of recent immigrants from Russia. The settlement house, like much of the city of San Francisco, was destroyed in the earthquake and subsequent fire in April, 1906. Bertha Wright responded to the emergency in the city by volunteering her nursing services in the temporary "tent city" set up in Golden Gate Park.

Across the bay, Oakland and Berkeley experienced a tremendous influx of refugees made homeless by the earthquake, or the Great Fire as it was referred to by Californians. The population of Berkeley doubled from 23,000 to 46,000 in the first 3 days following the earthquake, and Oakland received similar numbers of new residents. Several community and charitable groups in Berkeley joined together as the Earthquake Relief Committee to try and tackle the situation, and in 1907 they formed the Charitable Organization Society. Bertha Wright, 30 years old, was appointed to the position of Home Secretary. The Home Secretary acted as administrator, social worker, and public health nurse; in the first 6 months at the Charity Organization Society, Wright set up office and receiving 2,274 visits by those in need, and making over 600 home visits. She encountered daily the problems and effects of unemployment and poverty; illness and disability; lack of housing and poor housing; ignorance and lack of access to education and training; lack of hygiene and resources for hygiene; young children forced to work and help support their families, and children with no families; infants who were ill, and infants who died. There was no public health or social welfare; there was only charity and Wright was its agent of organization and distribution.

Under her planning and direction, the Berkeley Day Hospital and the Berkeley Clinic were founded to provide health services to the poor, and plans were made for a dispensary and general hospital. One of her early ventures was the Berkeley Day Nursery, "a Home where mothers going out to work by the day, can leave their little ones for a sum of ten cents" (Charity Organization Society, 1907–1908, pp. 7–8). The Day Nursery, the first publicly subsidized child care in California, allowed working mothers to raise their children, rather than placing them in orphan asylums, and provided education for mothers about care for their infants and children. Like her later work at the Baby Hospital, these activities required public appeals for funds with the use of "sob stories," relied on volunteer workers, fostered cooperation with other agencies, and focused increasingly on the needs of women and children.

In 1909, social worker Mabel Weed was named Home Secretary of the Charity Organization Society, freeing Wright to become District Nurse. The district nurse was funded cooperatively by the Charity Organization Society and the Berkeley School District, which provided a horse and buggy for home visits, and Wright was now the first school nurse as the well as the first public health nurse in Alameda County.

Wright was active in nursing on many levels. She was a member of the Alameda County chapter of the California Nurses' Association, and spoke at their statewide conventions on issues of public health. She was also an educator, teaching nursing and social service students at the Baby Hospital, and beginning in 1918, she taught postgraduate nursing students in a Public Health Nursing course established at the University of California in Berkeley.

The life and work of Wright cannot be separated from the influences of the times in which she lived. The Progressive Era (1890s to 1917) was a time of radical ideas, when activists in the United States worked for laws and reforms to curb the excesses of capitalism and greed, and forged new definitions of charity and social welfare. Progressive women took on public roles, and claimed those issues of reform dealing with children and women as their special and "natural" spheres. In California, Wright was among the first generation of educated women, many of whom, like their contemporaries across the nation, never married. She and her circle of progressive feminist women friends held meetings, read, conducted studies, established local and national organizations and alliances; they created institutions and set state policy affecting women and children in welfare, health care, education, working conditions, prison and foster care.

The early years of the Baby Hospital, which Wright help found, in many ways reflected the ideology of national movements. However, the Baby Hospital was also directly influenced by unique local events and history in a California that had only recently been the nation's wild Western frontier.

During her work as district nurse, Wright saw a need for a properly equipped hospital for sick babies to be cared for by trained baby nurses. Mabel Weed, a social worker, invited a group of society and professional women to a meeting in September, 1912, to initiate plans for Wright's vision of a baby hospital. One week later, by-laws were written and a female Board of Managers elected to direct the hospital and its work. A male Board of Directors was appointed to help fund the women's work and provide a legal base, as women did not yet have full legal and civil rights. While work was being done to convert the mansion to its new role, Wright supervised the opening of the clinic in a former donkey stall; treatments were conducted in the harness room. There were clinics for sick and well babies, baby hygiene classes for mothers, and home visits by Wright. A pre-paid health plan was offered: for $1 a year children could be enrolled and receive all their care.

On September 16, 1914, the building was dedicated as the Baby Hospital, with 30 beds and a cottage for contagious cases. Society women organized an association dedicated to raising funds to pay for the care of poor children. Hospital policy stated, "No child will be refused care because its parents are unable to pay the dollar." Wright, referred to as the "mother" of the Baby Hospital, continued to direct the work of the clinics and the visiting nurses.

The Baby Hospital also offered maternity care and parenting education. The women of the Baby Hospital participated in the work of the U.S. Children's Bureau by registering births, holding "Baby Saving Fairs," including the first on the Pacific coast, gathering data and conducting studies, and in 1918, joined in the activities of the "Year of the Child."

Although often described as a "spinster," Wright had found in Weed a life partner. Working together at the Charity Organization Society, and equal partners in founding the Baby Hospital, they also shared an intimate committed relationship. They lived together for over 40 years, and adopted and raised three children, Philip, Barbara, and Jean Weed. Wright and Weed lived new definitions of family, surrounded by a circle of close-knit personal and professional friends who met regularly in the feminist library of their home. In their own time, in their social milieu, two women setting up a household together was not uncommon nor questioned. Wright was a tall and large-boned woman with a presence both commanding and caring. She was eccentric and funny with melodramatic tendencies, and was also a pragmatist. Weed, on the other hand, was a theorist with radical progressive and socialist ideals and political skills. A synergism of their individual gifts and ideas took place within the context of their relationship and their work.

In 1924, the family moved to Woodside, California and Wright, after more than 25 years in nursing, worked part-time at a local clinic while raising the children. Weed continued her career in social work as director of children's work for the State Board of Charities and Corrections, and later as assistant director of the California Department of Social Welfare. The two women cared for many foster children in their home, and Wright continued to so share her limitless love for children until long after Weed's death. Wright died on May 7, 1971 in Palo Alto. Weed and Wright are buried side by side in Alto Mesa Cemetery, Palo Alto, California.

Wright's nursing career is best remembered for her role in founding the hospital today know as Children's Hospital Oakland, but in fact, the history of the Baby Hospital continued its parallel with the Children's Bureau. By 1929, the Children's Bureau was radically changed; despite tremendous protest from powerful women and grassroots organizations, its control was taken away from women and fell under the power of male medical doctors. In 1929, the titular male board of directors of the

Baby Hospital seized power from the women administrators, eliminating the Board of Managers, and placing all control of the hospital in a new Board of Directors who immediately appointed a male majority to every hospital committee. In the style of the settlement movement and the Progressive Era, Wright worked with a dedicated cadre of women, but every step in the initial decade of the Baby Hospital was shaped by her towering presence. Her ability to assess a need, envision a plan, and carry it to meaningful completion, while uniquely infusing her creation with her sense of love, humor, dedication, practicality and a melodramatic flourish reflect why she was referred to as a legend in her own day. Wright was a nurse who "took charge" in the chaos after the Great Fire to create the necessary structure of public health, and to provide caring health services to infants and children.

BIBLIOGRAPHY

Berkeley Commission of Public Charities. (1912). *Report 1911–1912*. Bancroft Library, University of California, Berkeley, CA.

Board of Directors, Baby Hospital. (1912–1935). Meeting minutes. [Unpublished bound volume with pagination]. Children's Hospital Oakland, Oakland, CA.

Board of Managers, Baby Hospital Association. (1912–1929). Meeting minutes. Vols. 1–4. [Unpublished bound volumes with pagination]. Children's Hospital Oakland, Oakland, CA.

Charity Organization Society. (1908). *Annual Report 1907–1908*. Bancroft Library, University of California, Berkeley, CA.

Czock, M. (1938). Bertha Wright. *The Bambino, 1*(3), 1, 3.

Hunt, R. D. (Ed.). (1932). Miss Mabel Weed. *California and Californians* (Vol. 3, pp. 432–433). San Francisco: Lewis Publishing Co.

McDuffie, J. H. (1937). Letter. *The Bambino, 1*(1), p. 3.

The maternity clinic. (1915, April). *The Baby Hospital Bulletin, 1*(8), 1.

Morgan, M. (1967). *The hospital women built for children*. Oakland, CA: Children's Hospital Medical Center.

Muncy, R. (1991). *Creating female dominion in American reform 1890–1935*. New York: Oxford University Press.

Marjorie S. Hammer
D. Jeanette Nichols

Biographies in Volume 1

Elizabeth Conde Glenn
Hazel Avis Goff
Emma Goldman
Minnie Goodnow
Annie Warburton Goodrich
Stella Goostray
Sister Mary Olivia Gowan
Elinor Delight Gregg
Lystra Gretter
Carrie May Hall
Lydia Eloise Hall
Anne Lyon Hansen
Bertha Harmer
Esther Voorhees Hasson
Alma Cecilia Haupt
I. Malinde Havey
Sally Cain Hawkins
Nellie Xenia Hawkinson
Helen Scott Hay
Mary Eugenia Hibbard
Mary Agnes Hickey
Agatha Cobourg Hodgins
May Shiga Hornback
Thelma Marguerite Ingles
Anna C. Jammé
Sally Lucas Jean
Deborah MacLurg Jensen
Florence Merriam Johnson
Joanna Mabel Johnson
Julia Crystine Kasmeier
Sister Elizabeth Kenny
Alice Magaw Kessel
Dita Hopkins Kinney
Ellen Newbold LaMotte
Mathild Helen Krueger Lamping
Roose Hawthorne Lathrop
   (Mother Alphonsa)
Eleanor Lee
Mary E. Lent
Mary Ashton Rice Livermore
Laura Rebekah Logan
Clara Louise Maass
Anita Newcomb McGee
Isabel McIsaac
Pearl L. McIver
M. Helena McMillan

Mary Eliza Mahoney
Ada Mayo Stewart Markolf
Stella S. Mathews
Mary Lathrop Wright Matthews
Anna Caroline Maxwell
Darius Ogden Mills
Lucy Minnigerode
Maude Blanche Muse
Mildred Emily Newton
Clara Dutton Noyes
Marty Adelaide Nutting
Katherine M. Olmsted
Betty Ann Olsen
Geneva Estelle Massey Riddle Osborne
Sophia French Palmer
Sarah Elizabeth Parsons
Mavis Orisca Pate
Blanche Pfefferkorn
Harriet Newton Phillips
Mary Genevieve Phillips
Drusilla Rageu Poole
Amy Elizabeth Pope
Louise Matilda Powell
Sister Regina Purtell
Frances Reiter
Helena Willis Render
Linda Ann Judson Richards
Mary Roberts Rinehart
Isabel Adams Hampton Robb
Mary May Roberts
Margaret Sanger
Helen Irene Denne Schulte
Louisa Lee Schuyler
Alma Ham Scott
Emma Edmonds Seelyer
Mother Elizabeth Ann Bayley Seton
Clara S. Weeks Shaw
Nancy Cornelius Skenadore
Elizabeth Sterling Soule
Adele Grace Stahl
Mabel Keaton Staupers
Jessie Lulu Stevenson (West)
Isabel Maitland Stewart
Julia Catherine Stimson
Euphemia Jane Taylor
Frances Charlotte Thielbar

Biographies in Volume 2

Ellen Gertrude Ainsworth
Marian Alford
Lydia E. Anderson
Mother Angela (Eliza Maria Gillespie)
Edith Augusta Ariss
Lois Marintha Austin
Lucy C. Ayers
Edith Annette Aynes
Bessie Baker
Emma Maud Banfield
Mary Rose Batterham
Anna Totman Beckwith
Edna Behrens
Eleanor Robson Belmont
Jeannie Saylor Berthold
Ella Best
Josephine Beatrice Bowman
Rena E. Boyle
Annie M. Brainard
Mary Williams Brinton
Marion Turner Brockway
Brother Sebastian Brogan
Amy Frances Brown
Martha Marie Montgomery Brown
Sadie Johnson Metz Brown
Helen Edith Browne
Mother de Sales Browne (Frances Browne)
Helen Lathrop Bunge
Charlotte Burgess
Mother St. Francis Xavier (Mother Cabrini)
Lillian (Bessie) Carter
Martha Jenks Wheaton Chase

Luther P. Christman
Ellen Evalyn Church (Marshall)
Martha Jane Clement
Anna Laura Cole
Charity E. Collins
Hazel Corbin
Pearl Parvin Coulter
LeRoy N. Craig
Namahyoke Gertrude (Sockum) Curtis
Emma D. Cushman
Louise M. Darche
Sue Sophia Dauser
Mabel Davies
Mary E. P. Davis
Philip Edson Day
Agnes Gardiner Shearer Deans
Clare Dennison
Kezi Payne de Pelchin
Naomi Deutsch
Josephine Aloyse Dolan
Anita Dowling Dorr
Mary T. Dowling
Rosemary Ellis
Bertha Erdmann
Sara Matter Errickson
Maud Frances Essig
Mary Evans
Margene Olive Faddis
Katharine Ellen Fayville
Gertrude LaBrake Fife
Alice Fisher
Julia Oteson Flikke

Martha E. Rogers
Hannah Anderson (Chandler) Ropes
Martha Montague Russell
Katherine Anne Alexia Sanborn
Marjorie E. Sanderson
Levia Bissel Sanford
Emilie Gleason Sargent
Frances Schervier
Mathilda Scheuer
Rozella May Schlotfeldt
Barbara Gordon Schutt
Jessie M. Scott
Gladys Sellew
Anna Pearl Sherrick
Cora E. Simpson
Margaret Elliot Frances Sirch
Jessie C. Sleet (Scales)
Sarah E. Sly
Martha Ruth Smith
Brother Camillus Snyder
Eugenia Kennedy Spalding
Marietta Burtis Squire
Mabel Keaton Stauper
Beatrice Van Homrigh Stevenson
Anne Hervey Strong
Elizabeth Eleanor Sullivan
Irene H. Sutliffe
Ethel Swope
Susie (Baker) King Taylor

Julie Chamberlain Tebo
Elnore Elvira Thomson
Margaret Anthony Tracy
Susan Edith Tracy
Joyce E. Travelbee
Sojourner Truth
Stella Boothe Vail
Jane Van de Vrede
Phyllis Jean Verhonick
Eugenia Helma Waechter
Lena Angevin Warner
Emma Louise Warr
Ysabella Gertrude Waters
Harriet Helen Werley
Myrtle Viola Werth
Claribel Augusta Wheeler
Carolyn Ladd Widmer
Mary Bristow Willeford
Anne A. Williamson
Maud H. Mellish Wilson
Sophie Gran Jevne Winton
Annie Turner Wittenmyer
Helen Wood
Lucia E. Woodward
Jane Stuart Woolsey
Mary Lewis Wyche
Susie Yellowtail
Helen Young
Anne Larson Zimmerman